Psychoanalysis
and
Motivation

Psychoanalytic Inquiry Book Series

Psychoanalysis
and
Motivation

Joseph D. Lichtenberg

with a contribution by
June L. Hadley

THE ANALYTIC PRESS

1989   Hillsdale, NJ   Hove and London

The Analytic Press

Distributed solely by

Lawrence Erlbaum Associates, Inc., Publishers
365 Broadway
Hillsdale, New Jersey 07642

Set in Palatino type

Library of Congress Cataloging-in-Publication Data

Lichtenberg, Joseph D.

Psychoanalysis and motivation / Joseph D. Lichtenberg : with a contribution by June L. Hadley

p. cm. – (Psychoanalytic Inquiry Book series : v. 10)

Includes bibliographies and index.
ISBN 0-88163-084-5

1. Motivation (Psychology) 2. Psychoanalysis. 3. Developmen tal psychology. 4. Self psychology. I. Hadley, June L. I. Title. III. Series.

[DNLM: 1. Motivation. 2. Psychoanalytic Therapy. WI PS427F v. 10 / BF 503 L699p]
RC489.M655L53 1988 1989
153.8–dc19
DNLM/DLC
for Library of Congress

88-37025
CIP

Printed in the United States of America
1 2 3 4 5 6 7 8 9 10

Contents

Acknowledgments

My debts are many. The fundamental idea of the five motivation systems, the core matrix of this book, is mine, but, as a quick survey of the reference list will attest, the research and observations I integrate are to a great extent the work of others. Besides the brilliance of their specific research, colleagues such as Mary Ainsworth, Louis Sander, Daniel Stern, Gerald Stechler, Linda Gunsberg, Robert Emde, and Henri Parens have guided me through the intricacies of neonatal and infant experimental studies. My broader conceptual debt begins with Freud, Hartmann, Spitz, Rapaport, and teachers like Margaret Mahler and Annemarie Weil, from whom I learned to relate experience with theory. More immediately, I am deeply appreciative of those colleagues with whom I have shared the adventure of an investigation of the "self" under the inspiration of Heinz Kohut: Ernest Wolf, Michael Basch, Arnold Goldberg, Marian and Paul Tolpin, Anna and Paul Ornstein, Daphne and Robert Stolorow, Frank Lachmann, James Fosshage, Estelle and Morton Shane, Naomi and Arthur Malin, Jules Miller, Howard Bacal, Bernard Brandchaft, and Alan Kindler.

Writing a book, like raising a child, flourishes within the matrix of a supportive family. I am remarkably fortunate that my family members provided me not only with needed encouragement and the patience to abide my physical and psychological absences, but also with concrete facilitating support: my wife, Charlotte, as editor, advisor, and impeccable critic; my children, Ann Lichtenberg Shofer, as educator, increasing my knowledge of learning disabilities, Maryland Pao Holland, as physician, keeping me abreast of new knowledge in pediatrics, and Amy Lichtenberg and William Pao, for a thousand little helpful tasks performed with kindness.

I have been extremely fortunate in having a group of friends on whom to call to read a chapter critically and advise me on its logic and clarity: Lawrence Friedman, John Gedo, Warren Poland, and Rosalea Schonbar. Most of the clinical vignettes I include here are from my own clinical practice. For other, illuminating clinical examples, I am grateful to Etta Levinson, Douglas Chavis, and Anna Ornstein. June Hadley's chapter on neurobiology adds a dimension to my conception, and Andrew Schwartz has helped me to understand more of this burgeoning field of information. Likewise, Leon Wurmser, Donald Nathanson, and Virginia Demos have added to my knowledge of affects. Donald Silver and Melvin Bornstein, my co-editors of *Psychoanalytic Inquiry* for so many years, are constant sources of thoughtful suggestions, encouragement, and appreciation. Other colleagues and organizations provided opportunities for me to present my ideas in their formative stages to audiences and discussants who could point out to me contradictions that required me to think through problems. This opportunity enabled me to expand my conceptions and grow more certain of their cogency. I wish to thank Lotte Kohler, Peter Kutter and Janos Paul in Frankfurt, Victor Schirmer in Philadelphia, and the American Psychoanalytic Association and the National Council of Self Psychology.

Paul Stepansky of The Analytic Press has been understanding in his encouragement as well as a valued advisor. Eleanor Starke Kobrin's copy-editing has helped to make the text much more readable.

My final debt is to my patients, to those people whose faith in my intent to help restore their disturbed physiological regulation, impaired sense of intimacy, reduced sense of efficacy and competence pleasure, overreliance on antagonism and fear, and reduced capacity for sensual pleasure and sexual excitement permitted them to work with me over the 40 years I have spent in this field. They are, and have been, my ultimate teachers—inspiring me to try to understand the motives in the baby and developing child in all of us.

Preface

Psychoanalysis and Motivation asks a good deal of the reader. My goal is to deal with the heart of what we know about motivation and, by taking a fresh look at underlying motivational systems, to extend our understanding. To follow my presentation, the reader is asked to become familiar with new terms, selected to avoid conceptual pitfalls and metapsychological artifacts carried by more familiar designators of dual drive theory. I have chosen such terms as physiological regulation, attachment, affiliation, exploration, assertion, aversion, antagonism, withdrawal, sensual, sexual, and model scenes as broad designators, while attempting to preserve intact the evocativeness of their conventional nontechnical meanings. Naturally, I have not coined these terms or initiated their technical use. Thus I ask the reader to follow, in each chapter on the systems (chapters 3, 4, 5, 6, 7, and 8), discussions that begin with prior usages and then take up the approach I offer, the research and observations with which I support my contention and the clinical examples I provide to bear out these usages.

Every book takes shape in a historical perspective. The most immediate historical link to this volume is my 1983 evaluative review of infant research and psychoanalytical development theories. The next most influential connection is Daniel Stern's (1985) *The Interpersonal World of the Infant*. In chapter 2, I summarize Stern's main findings, which serve for me as a bridge between self psychology and the theory of motivation I present. Stern's and my own efforts to present a wide-ranging view of developmental studies are but two of a growing body of similar attempts to integrate infant research with psychoanalytic theory: *Models of the Mind* (Gedo and Goldberg, 1973). *The Psychological Birth of the Human Infant* (Mahler, Pine, and Bergman, 1975). *Psychopathology and Adaptation in Infancy and Early*

Childhood (Greenspan, 1981), *Developmental Theory and Clinical Practice* (Pine, 1985), and "Development terminable and interminable" (Emde, 1988 a and b).

Emde proposes an extensive revision of the terrain of motivation in the infant. He suggests that activity, self-regulation, social fittedness, and affective monitoring constitute the basic motivations of infancy. Emde's work, like mine, recognizes the need for a major revision in the theory of motivation of the prerepresentational self and its affective core (Emde, 1983, 1988). Emde's proposal of activity, self-regulation, social fittedness, and affective monitoring emphasizes functional capacities, whereas my motivational systems are built around basic needs. We both describe the progress from innate programs to learned patterns and have many other easily recognized correspondences. The reader eventually will have the opportunity to compare all the new readings of the experiential world of the infant. But first the reader will have to absorb my meaning, and it is for this undertaking that I wish to provide some orientation.

The first two chapters lay the groundwork for the main propositions that are to come. In these I set out my assumptions (chapter 1) and a concept of the self that provides the main overview of motivation as it develops in infancy and persists throughout life (chapter 2). The body of my proposal of five motivational systems is laid out in the succeeding six chapters. The final two chapters (9 and 10) integrate the motivational systems into clinical practice, illustrating how they orient the therapist through the creation of "model scenes." Chapter 11, contributed by Dr. June Hadley, suggests integrations between the motivational systems and current findings in neurobiology.

The reader faces two main obstacles: first, to appreciate what constitutes the separate organization of each system; and, second, to appreciate the dynamic relationship of the systems that facilitates the experience of unity and of seemingly seamless shifts in motivation. First, five distinct experiences of needs, functional programs, and affect states must be recognized as constituting separate, self-organizing, self-stabilizing systems of motivation. To help the reader delineate the organizational distinctness of each system, I include in my chapter on each system references to the relationship of that system to the others. The second obstacle, to appreciate the dynamic relationship of the systems, is more difficult and also more crucial to the application of my theory as a way to illuminate introspective and empathic understanding of experience. Organization and system connote structure to anyone familiar with psychoanalytic theorizing, and a wrenching of one's mind is required first to appreciate five organizing systems and then to shift to thinking about them as fluctuating modes of experience in which changing groupings of motives dominate conscious and unconscious thoughts, feelings, and actions. The reader may have to cope with a seeming paradox in my presentation. How can the reader reconcile a self psychology theory that has at its core a holistic view of experience with a proposal that calls vigorously for attention to distinctly different, even competitive, dominances of experience? Part of the answer lies in my conception of the self as a center for initiating, organizing, and integrating motives.

So here is what I ask the reader to do. Picture yourself as you read this—in the foreground of your experience is a desire to explore my meaning and to assert your own understanding and opinion. Your self silently organizes and integrates this motive into your past experience. But lurking around are other motives as well. You may have some associations to me—some prior attachment connections that are being enhanced. A degree of intimacy pleasure adds to the feeling of competence you are enjoying as you understand my meanings. Or you are hungry and nibbling as you read, reading remaining dominant but hand and mouth engaging in physiological regulatory motive. Or this introductory explanation proves irksome as you impatiently wish to get on with reading the text, and in your aversive reaction you withdraw your interest and wish to flip forward to chapter one.

Now, introspectively reflecting on sequences such as this, you can sense that nothing has changed and everything has changed. Nothing in the holistic unity of self-initiating, organizing, and integrating experience has changed (of course, in pathological conditions this would not be so); but the dominance in what you are motivated to do is constantly shifting either in the central dominating system or in the other systems that provide subset motives. No more of this for now. I hope you can see the obstacle—to convert an understanding about systems into a sensing of how experience works in the dynamic manner by which we follow the endless, moment-to-moment shifts in motivations expressed in wishes, thoughts, actions, and emotions in ourselves and others.

Psychoanalysis and Motivation

Introduction

RATIONALE

PSYCHOANALYTIC THEORY AT ITS CORE is a theory of structured *motivation*, not a theory of structures. My purpose in this book is to consider how to conceptualize a psychoanalytic theory of structured motivation that can explain both the observations of infants that have produced so much new information in the past decade and the clinical experience of those who treat people of all ages.

My thesis is that motivation is conceptualized best as a series of systems designed to promote the fulfillment and regulation of basic needs. I delineate five systems (Sameroff, 1983), each comprising distinct motivational and functional aspects. Each motivational system is a psychological entity (with probable neurophysiological correlates). Each is built around a fundamental need. Each is based on behaviors clearly observable, beginning in the neonatal period.

The five motivational systems are: (1) the need for psychic regulation of physiological requirements, (2) the need for attachment-affiliation, (3) the need for exploration and assertion, (4) the need to react aversively through antagonism or withdrawal, and (5) the need for sensual enjoyment and sexual excitement. During infancy, each system contributes to self-regulation in mutually regulatory interactions with caregivers. At each period of life, the fundamental needs and the wishes, desires, aims, and goals that derive from those needs in each motivational system may be rearranged in different hierarchies indicated by different conscious and unconscious preferences, choices, and proclivities. From moment to moment, the activity of any one system may be intensified to the point where it provides motivational dominance of the self. The "self" develops as an independent center for initiating, organizing, and integrating

1

motivation. The sense of self arises from experiencing that initiating, organizing, and integrating. Experiencing has an active (agent) and passive (receptor) mode.

Why do we need a new theory of motivation? Isn't the vitality of motivation guaranteed in the human by instincts or instinctual drives? I argue that motivations arise solely from *lived experience*. Based on the particular lived experience, motivations may or may not achieve optimal vitality. Whatever biophysiological urgencies and innate neurophysiological response patterns underlie psychological motivations, the vitality of the motivational experience will depend initially on the manner in which affect-laden exchanges unfold between infants and their caregivers. Later, the development of symbolic representation enhances the potential for flexible, self-created reorganization of lived experience. A psychoanalytic theory of adaptive and maladaptive motivational functioning is about lived experience throughout life. Lived experience is about how we human beings consciously and unconsciously seek to fulfill our needs and desires by searching in potential events for affects that signal for us that experiential fulfillment.

Certainly it might be argued that psychoanalysis, using a theory of instinctual drives, already has made a major contribution to the understanding of human motivation. As a result of Freud's discoveries, dreams, seemingly irrational thoughts and actions, and mental—and many physical—symptoms have all been revealed to be based on motivations: some conscious, many outside conscious awareness. Even seemingly simple conscious intentions have been found often to be compromises of complex competing motivations with past experience partially or totally controlling present choices.

These momentous contributions notwithstanding, a call for revision, I believe, comes from the continuous problem psychoanalytic theoreticians have encountered in assigning significance to motivational sources. These shifting attempts to give primacy to one or another source include: trauma opposed to instincts, sexual instincts opposed to the dominant mass of ideas, sexual instincts opposed to instincts of self-preservation, sexual instincts opposed to aggressive instincts, sexual drives and aggressive drives opposed by primary and secondary autonomous ego functions, and the pressure of drives as opposed to the primary organizing potential of object relations. That there have been so many shifts in assigning priority to one or another source of motivation suggests dissatisfaction with past and current ways of viewing and applying theory. The tension that results from this dissatisfaction is particularly noticeable in current debates between drive theorists and object relation theorists and between object relation theorists who incorporate drive theory and self theorists who do not. (See Greenberg and Mitchell, 1983, for an extensive review and critique of these controversies.)

Another call for new approaches rises from studies of development of the neonatal, infantile, and toddler periods of life. In 1983, I reviewed the extensive and largely recent findings of research on the first years of life and concluded that these findings cast considerable doubt on the motivations earlier ascribed to infants and toddlers. (Lichtenberg, 1983b). I argued that the findings of research and observation indicate that infants are not passive, unorganized, unrelating, tension-ridden creatures, as drive theory portrays them. The data from naturalistic and experimental observations reveal that infants in the first year of life evidence a high level of organization and human relatedness. I suggested that this high level of patterned activity and learning is not best explained by assuming an early capacity for intrapsychic symbolic self- and object representations. Although early experience does receive a form of encoding in memory, I presented reasons for believing that the symbolic representational capacity we regularly deal with in child and adult psychoanalysis does not develop until approximately 18 months of age. I recommended that the infant's mode of functioning prior to that time be conceptualized in terms of perceptual-affective-action patterns of increasing organization and complexity and that the toddler's mode of functioning be viewed as a continuation of these patterns augmented by a system of sign-signal communication and a sense of self as director.

Without an assumption of internal symbolic representations of self and object in the infantile period, we are forced to look for new means to understand motivation. That is, we must seek a way to conceptualize motivations that fits both the psychic life of the infant in the phase before symbolic representation and the psychic life of the older toddler, child, and adult who employs symbolic representation.

For many analytic clinicians and theoreticians, the dual drive theory, despite its seeming to "settle" the source of motivation through a reference to instinct, has proved to be a Procrustean bed that required us to crunch disparate aims into two categories. One effort to solve this problem came from ego psychologists, who assume that the ego has independent sources of energy, as well as aims. The vast literature of Hartmann (1964) and his colleagues and the further revisions in motivational theory by Rapaport (1967) have explored the basic concepts of Freud's structural hypotheses with

enormous inductive sophistication. I am taking off in a different direction and will not attempt a comparison, which would extend the
length of this work greatly.

Other theoreticians, for example G. Klein (1976), attempted large-
scale revisions conceptualizing multiple sources for motivation.
Their theories bear a clear similarity to the proposals I make here.
An important difference is that they lacked the informational base
of current infant research and observation from which I derive
much of my inspiration and documentation. Other theoreticians
single out one or another area of motivated behavior as both a dominant feature of motivation and the source from which other motivations are derived. Prominent among such attempts are those of
Bowlby (1958) to focus on attachment, Hendrick (1942) on mastery,
and White (1959) on efficacy. I shall discuss each of these under the
motivational system in which I place them. I shall present my reasons for believing that each constitutes a dominant motivation at
some moments but is not any more fundamental than other motivational sources. When one is dominant, the other systems become
more or less influential subset motivations. In many ways, Piaget's
(1936, 1937, 1952, Piaget and Inhelder, 1960) developmental hypotheses constitute a special case. They have received the most extensive
discussion by psychoanalysts (Wolff, 1960; Sandler, 1975;
Greenspan, 1979) making point-by-point comparative studies. I
place the majority of Piaget's findings in developments in the motivational system derived from the need for exploration and assertion, although a careful reading of Piaget indicates that he and his
followers touched on motivations in all the systems. Many of these I
reviewed in *Psychoanalysis and Infant Research* (1983b). A fundamental
difference between Piaget's epistomological approach and mine is
the relative significance that I place on affect as an amplifier of all
experience and as a target for motivated recruitment of functions.
Another difference is the distinction between cross-modal processing of sensory input and Piaget's theory of separate assimilation
and accommodation of each sensory mode with step-by-step integration. As Stern (1985) argues, the existence of cross-modal processing of information supports his and my own contention for an
earlier and more unified development of the sense of self.

An important impetus for my delineation of motivational systems
arises from the clinical studies of self psychology. Kohut's (1971,
1977, 1984) theory gives motivational primacy to each person's attempt to develop in accordance with his or her "design." Cohesion
of the self develops, consolidates, and is restored when supported
by an empathic ambience. In agreement with much infant research,

Kohut conceptualizes a constant interrelationship between *motive*, to achieve and restore self cohesion, and *environment*, the empathic responsiveness. Successful response to need is seen as producing an emotionally meaningful and structurally supportive selfobject experience. This is a powerful clinical theory but very sketchy in some of its essentials. What is the person's "design"? How do caregiver and infant communicate for an empathic ambience to develop? Self psychology has placed its greatest emphasis on needs that are primarily relational in nature (mirroring, alterego, and idealizing transferences). In moment-to-moment experience, what other needs (food, water, sleep, toy play, protective discipline) must be responded to empathically for cohesion to be established or restored and for a selfobject experience to occur? If in the view of self psychology, traditional analytic theory overemphasizes sexuality, and if in the view of traditional analysts self psychology ignores or underemphasizes it, what does infant observation tell us that would help us to strike a more accurate balance? I believe that the informational yield from the clinical application of self psychology, combined with the data of infant researchers and observers who utilize a multitude of theoretic frameworks, can build a motivational theory that will begin to respond to some of the questions I have posed.

Since the publication of *Psychoanalysis and Infant Research* in 1983, the papers and books presenting and summarizing new findings in research on development have been extensive in number and evocative in content. Stern's (1985) *The Interpersonal World of the Infant* deals with many of the same issues that I raised. I will draw liberally on Stern's ideas, particularly those having to do with the development of the sense of self and of vitality. In the study of motivation I present in this book, I have drawn from sources that led Stern to write:

> By presenting us with a plethora of motivational systems that operate early, appear separable, and are backed by some imperative, the infant faces us again and in a new way with longstanding arguments about the distinctions between id instincts and ego instincts. . . . Has classical libido theory, in assuming one or two basic drives that shift developmentally from one erotogenic zone to another and have a variety of vicissitudes during development, been helpful in viewing an actual infant? The consensus is no. The classical view of instinct has proven unoperationalizable and has not been of great heuristic value for the observed infant. *Also, while there is no question that we need a concept of motivation, it clearly will have to be reconceptualized in terms of many discrete, but interrelated, motivational systems* such as attachment, competence-mastery, curiosity and others. It is of no help to imagine

that all of these are derivatives of a single unitary motivational system. In fact, what is now most needed is to understand how these motivational systems emerge and interrelate and which ones have higher or lower hierarchical standing during what conditions at what ages. The pursuit of such questions will be hampered if these motivational systems are assumed a priori to be derivatives of one or two basic, less definable instincts rather than more definable separate phenomena [p. 238, italics added].

Instinct, or drive, theory conceptualizes an internally centered prime mover. It is doubtful that motivation operates in so restrictively an appetitive manner. Certainly needs do have the potential to recruit functional activity, but in the ordinary course of events motivation can be aroused from either the inside or the outside. When a slightly drowsy baby is offered a rattle, the possibility of grasping, looking, hearing, and mouthing can set into motion a powerful exploratory-assertive motivation. The potential for functioning can ignite a spark that kindles other strikingly impelling motives. In each system, affects play a major role by amplifying the experience of motivations as they unfold, providing experiential targets for motivational aims. Thus, strictly speaking, each system is not a motivational system but a motivational-functional system (G. Stechler, personal communication, 1985). Motives inevitably call forth instrumental functions guided by affects. Functional possibilities with affective amplification call forth motives; For linguistic simplicity I shall refer to *motivational systems* rather than *motivational-functional systems*.

I refer to motivation as occurring in systems in order to emphasize that we are dealing not with structures or functions but with continuously ongoing processes. Where "structure" connotes stability, "system" connotes change and plasticity. Change and plasticity seem more appropriate to describe both the alteration in state of the small infant and the shifting dominance of motives in the everyday life of the adult. Moreover, system conveys activity, such as organizing, initiating, and integrating, and thus fits well with the view (Wolff, 1966) that infants *never* exist in a phase in which they are the passive recipient of drive pressures and environmental forces.

When "structure" is replaced by the concept of systems, development . . . can be viewed as the product of a complex interactional system which is constantly changing, integrating, transforming, and moving to more complex organizational levels. In such a model no one system would be considered as superordinate; no one phase or stage is viewed as decisive and every clinical issue . . . becomes increasingly elaborated over time. The infant . . . is viewed as moving in multiple interrelated ways toward greater psychological complexity, increasingly gaining a sense of his own personal reality, "reality" being something the infant actively constructs [Tyson, 1988].

ASSUMPTIONS

My first assumption is that whatever infants do with observable consistency, they are motivated to do. Thus, infants are observed to take nourishment at regular intervals, the implication being that they are motivated to do so. Since they can be observed to use their facial expression and whole body responses to display interest at the sight of the breast or bottle and pleasure with the milk intake, it can be inferred that feeding involves perception and affect and that both perceiving stimuli and experiencing affect are functional components of a motivational system in operation. That infants cry when not fed implies that they are motivated to indicate their aversion to a dystonic state. Further, the shift from crying before feeding to interest and joy with feeding indicates that infants are motivated to make the transition from the hunger state to the feeding state and that affect amplification provides a compelling pull to their motivational trigger. That mothers adjust their feeding procedures to their infants' signals of readiness and infants alter their timing and rate of sucking in response to cues from their mothers indicates that mothers and infants are motivated to engage in self-regulations that conform to the mutually regulatory requirements of an interactional system. Even so mundane an example as the feeding experience indicates, I believe, that, from the beginning, the human being is motivated to perceive, feel, act, learn, and engage, through self-regulation, in a mutually regulatory interactional system.

My second assumption is that when related behaviors occur in larger patterns, these patterns imply significant motivational systems. For example, hunger is but one of a group of physiologically based requirements that are observable; others include the regulation of breathing, thermal range, waste elimination, total stimulus intensity, tactile and proprioceptive stimulation, equilibrium, and sleep. The infant is motivated to signal disturbances in a need-satisfaction range of each, and the mother is highly attentive so that she can respond to alterations in each. What these needs have in common is that disturbance in their regulation sets off loud affective alarms in the regulatory system of both partners (infant and caretaker). By contrast, success in their regulation constitutes a relatively noiseless substratum or foundation that facilitates optimal unfolding of the regulatory motives of the other systems.

The third assumption is that each group of patterns constituting a motivational system has an effect on motives derived from the other motivational systems. In some observable behavior, the systems are interlinked. For example, feeding not only involves regulation of a physiological need, but also is an important element in the fulfillment of attachment motives and makes a contribution to stimulating sensual desires as well. In general, success in the regulation of any motivational system contributes to success in the regulation of the other systems. With feeding this is obvious with respect to hunger regulation, attachment, and sensual pleasure. A well-fed infant is motivated to want to eat, to be active with mother, and to enjoy sucking and mucous membrane stimulation.

Again with feeding as a model, the motive to explore, if directed to the examination of the bottle or the spoon, may compete with the motive to eat. Or an exploratory motive may be incorporated into the basic pattern of eating if directed to the taste of different foods. Still another system will inevitably come into play: through the activation of their aversion system, infants can signal a mismatch between their needs and their caregiver's offerings, thus contributing to both maternal regulation and self-regulation as they apply to food and procedural preferences. Thus, if we consider one of the motivational systems as dominant in a behavior pattern, we can recognize the regulatory effect exerted by and on each of the other motivational systems. When the regulation of the physiological need of hunger is the dominant motive, success will stimulate attachment, limit aversion responses to signals, and facilitate easy transition into exploratory or sensual seeking behaviors. On the other hand, prior failures in attachment or heightened aversion activation may interfere with success in the regulation of hunger.

The fourth assumption is that within the first 18 months motives in each system undergo transformations and refinements based on the possibilities inherent at each level of neurophysiological maturation. At first, motives operate to promote the unfolding of preprogrammed responses and preferences within a narrow range of regulatory potentials—that is, they seem to be reflexlike. The preprogrammed responses promote the development of behavior that rapidly shows evidence of learned preferences and, later, evidence of anticipation, planning, and intention.

Subsequently, infants can be observed making choices between alternatives, thus demonstrating an awareness of their own subjectivity and that of people around them. In this progression of motivated behavior, what can be said about the awareness of wishes and

desires? My assumption is that, from the beginning, motivated behavior in each of the systems is experienced—that is, felt—as an
affect and registered in memory as a perceptual-affective-action
event and thus contributes to an emergent sense of self (see chapter
2). As regulation progresses, the infant becomes increasingly aware
of the aim of the regulatory effort (the thumb to be sucked, the
block to be grasped, the smiling mother to exchange smiles with).
The self is then "wanting" and acts as an agent to satisfy that want.
But the self as subjectively wanting is more difficult to specify until
planning and expecting become more refined (at roughly 8 to 15
months) and the infant regularly looks to caregivers for subjective
guidance and referencing. Intrapsychic definition of the self as a
wanter (subjective, reflexive awareness of the self wanting) probably requires symbolic representation (beginning at 18 months).
Take, for instance, Billy, a bright 24-month-old, doted-on only
child. Billy, asked by his father, dressed to go off to tennis, why he
looked so sad, replied, "Billy sad. Daddy go. Billy wants to go with
Daddy."

The fifth assumption is that the individual characteristics of self-
regulation achieved in each motivational-functional system will receive symbolic representation in primary- and secondary-process
modes. Once this occurs, motives are subject to complex defensive
permutations, but, despite these transformations, some continuities
persist.

The sixth assumption is that, although any observable behavioral
psychic phenomena may appear to be derived from motives of two
or more of the five motivational systems, often it is possible to observe that larger units of phenomena are derived predominantly
from a single system with consistency over time.

Miss D, a 29-year-old writer, was seen for a consultation for re-
ferral to continue her analysis, which had been interrupted after
four years because she found a better job in another city. She described her problem as severe anxiety and depression triggered by
her breakup with a man. Although this had occurred four years earlier and she had a current boyfriend, she still suffered from it—
blaming herself severely for the loss. Her relations with her family,
especially her mother, were extremely troubled. If she did as her
mother wished—surrendered herself to her mother's desire for
closeness—her mother was wonderful and generous. If not, her
mother was hurt and "bitchy," and Miss D felt angry, guilty, and
desolate.

Weekends were the worst times for her; during the week she became easily absorbed in her work. She was startled to realize that
even at her worst times of anxiety and depression, during which

she had been terrified that she would go crazy or commit suicide, she had not only been able to do her job but had received a promotion.

Although she fought and struggled with her mother and her boyfriends, she got along well with other people, who generally regarded her as witty and charming. She added that it might surprise her analyst, but sex was OK for her and had been from the beginning. While it was true that she had affairs to punish her boyfriend and got into peculiar situations, the sex itself was fine.

Clinical experience indicates that many generalized statements such as those offered by Miss D must be regarded with judicious skepticism. Nevertheless, summarized overviews of a person's experience often illustrate the divisions maintained between motivational systems. In the consultation, motivations from psychological need states were not mentioned. Motivations derived from the attachment affiliative system occupied the foreground of her problems. Motivations arising from the exploratory-assertive system were the source of considerable creative productivity and satisfaction. Motivations arising from the aversion-antagonism-withdrawal system were active influences in her dealing with problems of attachment and affiliation but otherwise did not appear to be a source of significant problems. Motivations derived from the sexual-sensual system, like those from the exploratory-assertive system, were reported to be a source of satisfaction.

My seventh assumption is that the five motivational systems can each be recognized at any point in the life cycle but are not in themselves the determinants of the mode of overall organization that characterizes any life epoch. Each motivational system at each period is influenced by biological-neurophysiological maturation, development, or senescence, which sets the organizational potential for the period. The organization of the neonate period lies in a continuum of sleep-awake states (non-REM sleep, REM sleep, drowsy, awake active, awake quiet, fussing, and crying). Behaviors indicative of each motivational system are recognizable if the 24-hour cycle of infant life is scanned for them, but a dominant mode of organization is change in state and its relation to the caregiver-infant mutual regulatory system. In contrast, the mode of organization in adolescence is characterized by each motivational system's coming into play with shifting intensity, often calling for realignment. Adolescents struggle to assume more personally centered preferences in physiological regulation—food fads, sleep patterns, stimulus levels. Disengagement from family attachment and shifting affiliations with other individuals, groups, and value systems restructure their relational motivations. Exploratory-assertive motives demand new pathways for mastery. Aversions become intensified, fluctuating antagonisms flare up, and moments of withdrawal become self-regulatory modes of protection against being overwhelmed by the turmoil. And sexuality as a consummate urgency can either overwhelm other motivations or be relatively easily incorporated into the adolescent's other motivations in ways that defy simple explanation.

My eighth assumption is that when any motivational system strongly dominates, the other motivational systems may appear to be subsidiary to that one system. A dynamic general systems theory of developmental systems (Sameroff, 1983) helps to explain this assumption. At any moment, the entire system—in this case the total motivation and functioning of the person—achieves a wholeness and an order. If, hypothetically, each of the five motivational systems were equally active, the wholeness of the system (cohesion of the self) would result from the integration of the five subsets. If two are predominant, wholeness and order result from their integration, the other three being quiescent or subsets. The concept of two predominant systems coincides with the dual drive theory, in which sexual and aggressive drive systems are treated as the only subsets that need to be taken into account. All motivation is then regarded as the result of the dialectic tension between the two subsets. Alternatively, motivation and function can be separated into two subsets in which function, as in the concept of the ego, is assigned motivational capacity and the outcome is the result of dialectic tension between a motivational system (id) and functional system (ego).

Only one motivational thrust is presented as dominant in the preeminence of libidinal drive in early psychoanalytic theory, of attachment in Bowlby's (1958) concept, of mastery and competence (see Broucek, 1979), and of destructiveness in death instinct theories. How can we explain the persuasive cogency of each of these theories despite the inherent contradictions each presents for others? I believe that an answer lies in the properties of systems. Each subset of sufficient scope tends to be adaptively self-organizing and self-stabilizing. In the course of self-organizing, the hierarchical level begins with its functional core (regulation of physiological requirements, or attachment needs, or exploratory assertion and needs, or the need to indicate aversion, or the need for sensual pleasure). With the core function at the top of the hierarchy, subsidiary functions are organized at lower levels (aversion as signals in each of the others, or the possibility of obtaining sensual pleasure from aversion activities such as sexualizing antagonism). Each system becomes self-stabilized with a relative degree of hierarchical spread. Therefore, at any moment it is possible to find attachment motives, for example, in each of the other motivational systems. When one motivational system dominates, the positions that the other systems occupy will be determined by historical factors and current conditions. For example, when the physiological requirement of hunger predominates, motivational guidance comes from *past* experiences of attachment relations with "feeders," explorations with taste, aversions to specific foods or settings, and sensual enjoyment from "wine, women, and song." In the *immediate* situation, this guidance is translated into action by the possibilities currently available. Predominance of the one system then achieves the wholeness and the order of the total motivation and functioning of the person, who might be described as "driven" by hunger.

My last assumption deals with the concepts of self and selfobject experience. I believe that the self as the container concept best fits this way of viewing motivation. I define the self as an independent center for initiating, organizing, and integrating. While self, person, and identity are all related terms, *self* as defined here emphasizes motivation (initiating) and its function with respect to experience (organizing and integrating). The overarching concept that conveys the mutual relationship of self-regulation and regulation between self and environment is that of a selfobject experience. This experience is a particular affective state characterized by a sense of cohesion, safety, and envigoration. My hypothesis is that for each of the five basic motivational systems at each period of life, there are specific needs and that when these needs are met, the result is a selfobject experience. When these needs are not met, the person experiences a sense of disturbed cohesion, ranging from acute alarm signaling the need for air to disquietude when a distracted friend fails to respond to one's greeting. I distinguish between needs and wishes. Need satisfaction is fundamental to the maintenance of self-cohesion and is the source of selfobject experience. Wishes are manifold conscious and unconscious motivations derived from each system, often competing with another. Wishes and needs may coincide, as they do in the wish and need of toddlers to have the caregiver put them to sleep with a reassuring kind word. Wishes and needs may not coincide, as in a toddler's wish to follow a lost ball into the street and yet need protective restraint. Traditionally, psychoanalysts have been extremely adept explorers of wishes—ferreting out secret desires in the "unconscious" as a topographic locale. The traditional emphasis on conflict and compromise in symptom formation has also placed analysts in the forefront of studying wishes derived from drives, executive functions, and morals, ethics, and ideals. Historically we have devoted less concentrated effort to the discernment of needs; thus our ability to distinguish between need and wish remains preliminary in many instances.

The Self And Other Conceptual Tools

PSYCHOANALYTIC THEORY GAINED much from Freud's attempt to reorganize the topographic model of states of consciousness into hypothetical "structures" or groupings of functions—the id, ego, and superego. I (Lichtenberg, 1983b) have pointed out the problems of using an id-ego model to explain the findings of infant research. Despite these difficulties, other interpreters of the research findings (Weil, 1970; Tyson, 1982; Dowling, 1985) choose to retain these concepts as "container" formulations into which to fit the data of infancy and thereby retain the clinical utility the tripartite model has provided.

The most salient argument mounted against ego psychology as it evolved, particularly in the United States under Hartmann, has been its experience-distant, machinelike rendering of the human dilemma (Guntrip, 1971; Greenberg and Mitchell, 1983). The proponents of the structural hypothesis cite conflict as occupying the very center of human experience and note the rich way in which Hartmann's ego psychology accounts for both conflictual and nonconflictual processing of internal and external stimuli. Since 1973 I have explored the sense of self as a means of integrating experience-near formulations, and I continue this effort in this study. My initial attempt was to provide a conceptual base to self as a concept in the experiential realm (Sandler and Jaffe, 1969) parallel to the exploration of structure (id, ego, and superego) in the nonexperiential realm of functions. Since then, the applicability of self to the task of capturing and containing human experience has been exhaustively tested by the clinical explorations of self psychology. But in its formative period, self psychology, like ego psychology, had to rely largely on astute empathic reconstructions for its view of infancy.

More recently, self psychology has become informed by observational and experimental data from the efforts of Basch (1977, 1988), Tolpin (1971, 1986), and myself (Lichtenberg, 1983, 1987) to integrate the studies of such researchers as Sander (1975, 1980, 1983a, b, 1986), Stern (1985), Stechler (1982, 1985, 1987), and Beebe (Beebe and Stern, 1977; Beebe and Lachmann, 1988a, b). These findings point the way to reformulating conceptualizations about the first few years of life held by self psychology as well as by ego psychology. Throughout the book, I shall attempt to show how a conceptualization of motivational systems can be integrated with recent reformulations of self.

Serious problems must be acknowledged at the outset. Any effort to build a psychological foundation out of experience inevitably runs into difficult questions. How well can one human being know the experience of another? To what extent does an experiential focus confine the inquirer to examining phenomenology, thereby losing Freud's hard-won success in exposing the realm of the unconscious? These problems are inevitably compounded in the study of early life, where the ordinary method by which we enter the mental state of another person through empathy encounters the opacity of the infant's strikingly different mode of mental organization. Further, we cannot use our highly trained ability to perceive and uncode conscious and unconscious aims and goals by the familiar methods of following verbal associative paths on the couch or symbolic actions through play therapy. Until the middle of their second year, children do not develop the symbolic processing required for this mode of analyzing experience. To speak of an *experiencing* self *motivated* to seek attachment or *motivated* to indicate aversion requires a number of assumptions. To conceptualize what an emerging self is experiencing as the infant seeks and finds, or does not find, an attachment calls for considerable imagination and a willingness to suspend disbelief. Stern (1985) has already taken some giant steps in this direction; these I will follow and attempt to extend.

Another problem with addressing self and motivation from an experiential focus is that I find myself frequently employing nonexperiential language. For example, I conceptualize the basic unit of observation from which I draw inferences as perceptual-affective-action patterns. A number of these have innate origins. Terms such as these have a neurobiological ring to them. I would argue that this usage is appropriate since the structure we are dealing with ultimately is the brain. But a self perceives stimuli, a self feels affects, and a self kicks, cries, sucks, and grasps. The terminology is then transitional between an experiencing we cannot be sure of and a neurobiological structure to which we try to give psychological meaning. This problem applies similarly to my suggestion of motivational systems. Each motivational system consists of an interrelated group of needs and wishes that share functional attributes and have a hierarchical arrangement along a particular line of development. Fundamentally, each motivational system has a neurobiological base assuring survival. This is the need end of the hierarchy. Next in the hierarchy are elemental, learned schemas that develop into increasingly complex programs of intentions and planning. At a still higher level are wishes in the psychoanalytic sense of symbolic representations of aims and goals, ambitions, and ideals. All three levels—need in the form of basic requirements, intentions and planning in the form of perceptual-affective-action patterns, and symbolic representations in the form of wishes—persist throughout life. We need to form attachments. To assure the continuity of the bonds of attachments that we form, we have a vast repertoire of learned schemas and intentions that we play out as preconscious automatisms (Hartmann, 1964), such as greeting and parting rituals. We give symbolic representation to a seemingly infinite variety of wishes and fantasies involving attachment that enrich our intrapsychic realm.

A final problem with using hybrid (Slap and Levine, 1978) terms that bridge the nonpsychological and psychological realms lies in my use of motive. We all agree that when we are dealing with wishes expressed in actions or in unconscious fantasies, we are dealing with motives. We can carry this concept fairly comfortably into the realm of presymbolic infancy as long as we can infer planning and intention from the behaviors under observation. My assumption that whatever an infant—even a neonate (or near-term fetus)—does consistently is motivated seems at first glance to be speculative at best. Can the innate pattern of newborns to turn their heads away from the noxious odor of ammonia (Bower, 1971) be a motive? Is it not merely a reflex? Or, even if we dignify this elementary form of behavior, is it not little different from what a paramecium can accomplish? Where in the term "an innate perceptual-affective action pattern" (the affect being indicated by a flickering facial expression of distress) is there an indication of selfness or of experience? There is little to identify self an an independent center of initiating, organizing, and integrating, even if we assume that affects, in their most primitive and fleeting forms, are experienced. This is a thin thread at best. Nonetheless, I propose that the purposefulness of this behavior lies along a seamless line with other aversive behaviors soon to arise (see chapter 7). Witness

Fraiberg's (1982) description of Greg, who at three months never looked at his mother, never smiled or vocalized at her. Greg's teenage mother alternated between depression and outbursts of rage. She avoided Greg whenever she could, afraid she would brutalize him as she herself had been brutalized. Even when he was in distress, Greg never turned to her. If his father or the clinical observers were present, Greg would make eye contact, smile, and vocalize with pleasure.

I suggest that the neonate's response to ammonia and Greg's response to his mother share the same essential purpose, and I propose that this commonality of purpose is an indicator of an aversive motivational system. I believe it is more parsimonious to speak of an aversive motive whether the phenomenon we are considering is an innate (reflexive) perceptual-affective-action pattern of averting the head, or Greg's learned pattern of never looking at his mother, or a representation that Greg may form later in which his mother is symbolized as repellent in some fashion. Thus, motive bridges activities such as innately doing, early learning and later intending, and still later symbolically representing. The concept, however, becomes more psychologically meaningful when we can speak of an experiencing self.

I have used the example of avoidance and withdrawal activity at the level of innate and early learned patterns, patterns evidencing planning and intention, and symbolically represented patterns to demonstrate the hierarchical arrangement of the aversive motivational system. Rather than using avoidance and withdrawal, I could have used an example of innate, learned, and symbolic antagonistic patterns for the aversive system. I might provide, as I shall do later in detail, other hierarchically arranged examples in the motivational systems involving physiological regulation, attachment-affiliation, exploration-assertion, and sensual-sexual stimulus seeking. Considerable support for a progressive hierarchical development comes from recent studies of brain physiology. In tomography studies (Chugani and Phelps, 1986) in infants five weeks of age and younger, glucose utilization was highest in the sensorimotor cortex, thalamus, midbrain-brainstem, and cerebellar vermis. By about three months, glucose metabolic activity had increased in the parietal, temporal, and occipital cortices, the basal ganglia, and the lateral hemispheres of the cerebellum. The increased glucose utilization during the second and third months in the basal ganglia, all cortical regions with the exception of the frontal and association cortices, and the entire cerebellum was consistent with EEG changes and with the suppression by cortical input of the startle and tonic-neck reflex. By three to four months, random limb movements began to be replaced by more coordinated movements. Between 8 and 18 months, the pattern of glucose utilization developed to the point that it resembled that of adults; prominent activity in frontal and association cortices became established. Chugani and Phelps note that this progressive increase in glucose utilization is consistent with anatomical studies showing an expansion of dendritic fields and an increase in the capillary density of the frontal cortex. They suggest that these changes coincide with finding that hypothesis development begins at eight to nine months and that alertness increases and anxiety develops during this period (Kagan, 1979).

In thinking about this type of evidence about development, we can emphasize the continuities (the progressive elements) or the transformations (the changes in organization from predominance of subcortical functioning, to the predominance of cortical, noncognitive, associational functioning). As my interest is in motives, I emphasize the continuities (progressive development) in each of the five motivational systems while recognizing transformations (the changes in organization from innate to learned, to planned intentional, to symbolically represented patterns). Stern's (1985) stages in the development of the sense of self similarly emphasize continuity while recognizing organizational changes into more complex domains of self-experience. Continuity does not imply a simple progressive pattern of increments. According to Stern, "Development occurs in leaps and bounds; qualitative shifts may be one of its most obvious features" (p. 8). The periods between two and three months, to a lesser degree between five and six months, between nine and twelve months, and around fifteen and eighteen months are times of major change. In the relatively quiescent intervals, new integrations consolidate. We cannot say with certainty what causes these marked qualitative shifts in the organizational patterns of infantile life; the maturational changes in the central nervous system noted earlier seem the most likely explanation.

Stern (1985) describes four senses of the self, each defining a domain of self-experience and social relatedness. The sense of an emergent self forms between birth to two months. The sense of a core self forms between two and six months. The sense of a subjective self forms between seven and fifteen months, and a sense of a verbal self after that. Stern notes that "once formed, each sense of self remains fully functioning and active throughout life. All continue to grow and coexist" (p. 11).

THE SENSE OF AN EMERGENT SELF

Imagining what a neonate experiences is extremely difficult. Stern (1985) offers the interesting postulate "that the infant can experience the process of emerging organization as well as the result" (p. 45). What would such an experience of process and product be like? It is unlikely that it would have a point of reference—the self as place. Stern and I both believe that the organization of body coherence is likely to occur later, and the sense of the body's acting and feeling as a unit is prerequisite for a sense of self as a reference point. What does the life of neonates consist of? During the alert wakeful state, they are engaged in learning about the relations between sensory experiences. During drowsiness and sleep, they are in a low state of sensory receptivity. During crying periods, they concentrate on responding to dystonic stimuli and are relatively unreceptive to anything but the relief of distress. The process during the alert wakeful state would be the lively unfolding of innate perceptual-affective-action patterns. Neonates have inborn perceptual preferences, and they scan the world around for evidence of these patterns in the sights, sounds, smells, tastes, and touches they are offered. Very quickly they abstract out of a preferred pattern that which is relevant to it and seek its repetition. We can assume that forming an organized schema, for example, giving order and coherence to a perception, is as powerful a motivation for the neonate as it is throughout life. My view of the experience of neonates in the awake state is they have at first a kaleidoscope of stimuli out of which they very quickly abstract and organize a perceptual set that is preferred. Within a very few days of recurrence, this perception will convey familiarity as the affective-action pattern is repeated. Stern presents a great deal of experimental evidence demonstrating that neonates experience more perceptual unity than is suggested by the separate sensory modalities schemas of Piaget. "They can perceive amodal qualities in any modality from any form of human expressive behavior, represent these qualities abstractly, and then transpose them to other modalities" (Stern, 1985, p. 51). Infants experience not sights and sounds and touches, but the more global qualities of these sensory modalities combined in the form of patterns. This is the emergent sensing of process and products in the form of *making* order of stimuli and *having* an awareness of qualities of shapes, intensities, and temporal patterns.

Haith, Hazan, and Goodman (1988), in their study of expectation and anticipation of dynamic visual events by three-and-a-half-old infants, provide an example of the emergent sensing of process. The infants were presented an alternating and an irregular series of 30 slides. The infants developed expectancies for the visual events in the alternating series and not for those presented irregularly.

> These findings indicate that 3.5-month-olds can detect regularity in a spatiotemporal series, will develop expectancies for events in the series, and will act on the basis of those expectations even when those actions have no effect on the stimulus events. We believe that infants are motivated to develop expectations for noncontrollable spatiotemporal events, because these expectations permit them to bring their visual behavior under partial control [p. 467].

The authors emphasize that the infants were motivated not to accomplish the cognitive representations of objects through match or mismatch responses, but to develop their capacity to organize a perception as dynamic events unfolded.

The striking characteristic of the life of neonates appears to be recurrent, changing states of arousal. As infants pass from drowsiness and sleep to an awake state, they may experience these changes as going from darkness to light or, more properly, to a cross-modally sensory rich state if they experience a period of alert wakefulness. In these instances, the sensory richness rapidly passes from amorphousness to some level of order. But neonates often awake to a state of crying and physiological need or move from alert wakefulness to a dystonic state. In these less harmonious instances, a dystonic state may be experienced as one of a rapidly rising stimulus overload, which, when responded to by the caretaker, leads to a rapid diminution of the dystonic affect. These marked changes in state closely approximate the traditional conception of the unpleasure-pleasure principle. Such high-tension state changes must also result in a sense of emergent self, but one quite different from that which grows out of the active creation of perceptual order. The sense of emergent self that derives from these experiences is more apt to be passive and to involve an affective sense of distress and some perceptual discontinuity moving to restoration and perceptual receptivity. Inevitably, the continuity of self-emergence passes back into the darkness of sleep. We do not know what the effect of the passage to sleep is on the emergent sense of self. Is it the same if sleep follows the alert waking state of actively creating order as it is if sleep follows an exhausted state of crying and relative perceptual discontinuity? In either case, sleep seems throughout life to be restorative to the reemergent sense of self.

The idea that the sense of an emergent self arises from the neonate's experience conforms with the definition of the self as an independent center of initiating, organizing, and integrating. The initiative is restricted to independently setting affective-action patterns into motion. The awareness of agency is limited to a sense of having set something in motion, to the organization of perceptual data, and to the automatic cross-modal integration of this data. This elemental sense of self is emergent in that being active and creating order both arise out of absent or amorphous levels of awareness. The sense of emergent self probably contains little experience of integration as states of arousal change; this function is still largely being performed through the ministrations of the caretaker. Even this limitation is not total. Neonates in mildly fussy states can relieve their own distress by activating exploratory activity, such as fixing their eyes on a mobile or working to get their fingers into their mouths.

Stern suggests that the experience not only is of the process and product of organizing but also involves a sense of social relatedness. Externally, the social relatedness is obvious, but what is the experience like to the sense of emergent self? Stern finds his answer in a particular quality of affect receptivity. He provides experimental evidence that when an infant's spontaneous activities are responded to by caregiver attunement, the infant experiences a particular type of affective response that Stern calls a vitality affect. When a baby is rocking herself, her mother may place a hand lightly on her, moving in rhythm with her. Or the mother may begin to sing a song that carries the same beat—the response being cross-modal (that is, combining auditory, tactile, proprioceptive, and equilibrium modes of response). Our appreciation of the baby's response to indications of caregiver attunement should not, in Stern's view, be restricted to observing distinct, specific, categorized affects such as joy, sadness, fear, or anger. We should be alert to such qualities of feeling as surging, fading away, fleeting, explosive, crescendo, decrescendo, bursting, and drawn out.

Stern's concept of vitality affects suggests that a common thread runs between the affect states experienced when the infant creates order in the alert wakeful state and the affect states experienced when caregiver responsiveness relieves his distress in the crying state. Stern notes that vitality affects of crescendo and decrescendo are inextricably involved with all the essential processes of life— mounting hunger and getting fed, falling asleep and emerging out of sleep, and feeling the coming and going of all categorical affects, whether barely perceptible or strong. Infants, thus, are experiencing qualities of rise and fall, burst or fade, sometimes from their own activity and sometimes from the activities of their caregivers.

How mother picks up the baby, adjusts the diapers, runs her fingers through the baby's hair, moves toward or away—all contribute to a social relatedness. This relatedness is experienced invariably as an affective exchange, sometimes as categorical affects such as joy, anger, sadness, or fear, sometimes as vitality affects accompanying the interactions, sometimes as both.[1] From the mother's facial and vocal expression and from the multitude of her different activities, the small infant can abstract general affective qualities such as liveliness, or the slowing down that occurs in depression, or the jerky tension of anger, or the soothing down of comforting, or the persistent modulating of a calm unruffledness. "In this fashion the amodal experience of vitality affects as well as the capacity for cross-modal matching of perceived forms would greatly enhance the infant's progress toward the experience of an emergent other" (Stern, 1985, p. 59).

Neonates are viewed, therefore, as abstracting global qualities of perceptual and affective experience. From their innate capacity to perceive in this way, infants are gradually and systematically able to identify invariant constellations of self and others. The coming into being of the sense of self is accompanied by the emergence of the sense of others, possessing qualities of order and a sense of learned familiarity. Stern argues persuasively for the existence of levels of creating order and learning that have global qualities and that proceed side by side with the more slowly developing assimilation and adaptation schemas of Piaget and the constructionists. Stern lays the groundwork for a sense of social relatedness involving a sense of the emergent self and a sense of the other that develop at an earlier time than the Piagetian view suggests.

---

[1]A. Schwartz and D. Nathanson (personal communications) have independently questioned Stern's proposal that vitality affects are a separate type or category of affects. Schwartz states that affects do possess a quality of velocity captured in Stern's designations of crescendo and decrescendo. I believe that this quality is extremely important for experiencing the tuning upward, or vitalizing, of feeling states and the tuning downward, or calming and soothing, of other feeling states. I will continue to use Stern's designation of vitality affects to connote this quality rather than attempting to support a proposal for a different class of affects as such. The quality of vitalization through tuning upward and soothing and restoring through tuning downward is crucial to appreciate what infants and people of all ages are seeking to feel, and that they in fact report feeling, in many experiences based on motivations in each of the systems. It is this quality which is central to the selfobject experiences that self psychology credits with being the building blocks of self-strength. It is this quality which is lost when self-cohesion undergoes fragmentation and depletion.

THE SENSE OF A CORE SELF

The sense of a core self develops between the second and seventh month of life. Stern argues that infants possess the equipment and the opportunity to experience themselves as an entity separate from others. If this is so, then the infant's experience is essentially self being with others, not self merged with, fused with, symbiotically linked with, or undifferentiated from others. How are we to know if Stern's view or the traditional view is more convincing? The infant from two to seven months cannot reveal, except through perceptual-affective-action patterns, psychological differentiation (or, for that matter, the merger or fusion that has heretofore been assumed). Reading merger fantasies backward from the fantasies of adults or from poetic allusions to oceanic states tells us about an idealized state of human relatedness, the infant's supposed Garden of Eden. Such retrogressive projection from symbolic representations is subject to as much social bias as is the child's presumed asexual life. In an effort to set aside preconceptions, Stern asks what criteria would have to be met for it to be believable that postneonatal infants experience themselves as entities separate from others, so that "being with" is not "being merged with." He reasons that if infants experience agency and volition, body coherence as locus, affective coherence as a source of awareness, and continuity of experience in the form of memory buildup, they must be considered to be capable of differentiation in any ordinary sense of that word. Of course, Stern speaks here of differentiated as opposed to undifferentiated, merged, or fused; not in the sense of later experience of subtle identifications and changes in state of the postsymbolic period.

How do infants gain a sense of body coherence and agency? They receive a constant source of information from actions they perform on themselves—proprioceptive feedback from the action and sensory feedback from the part acted on. This information differs from that received from actions performed on others, where the proprioceptive feedback is present but the sensory response is absent. And it differs from actions performed by others on infants, where the sensory response occurs, but proprioceptive feedback is lacking. Strong evidence suggests that infants track experience in ways that allow them to pick up these differences. They recognize the consequences of their actions, as evidenced by their ability at three months to distinguish whether turning their heads against a pressurized pillow is reinforced each time, each third time, or on a variable schedule (Watson, 1979). Infants produce a constant reinforcement schedule through their own actions—each time infants touch themselves, they experience both proprioceptive feedback and a sensation where touched; each time infants vocalize, they feel their chest resonating; each time they close their eyes, the world goes dark; and each time they turn their heads, the visual sights change. Do infants draw the necessary causal connection from this information to separate the world into self-caused and other-caused effects? Stern argues that they do, because by three or four months of age they can appreciate time relations, they can correlate the intensity or duration of a behavior and its effect, and they can appreciate spatial relations. Because of these capacities for discrimination, the infant can establish that one set of experiences, which we call self, is constant; while another set of experiences, those of the non-self, or the other, varies. For example, infants occupy a position from which they view and hear others moving toward them and away from them. Stern refers to an unpublished study by Walker-Andrews and Lennon (1984) in which five-month-old infants were shown two movies side by side, one of a Volkswagen approaching and one of the same car receding. The infants looked at the approaching car if at the time they heard the sound of the motor getting progressively louder, and at the receding car if the sound became softer.

Coherence of the core self, then, builds on the invariance of agency, especially volition and proprioceptive feedback. To this coherence is added a sense of self as a locus in space, as a source for temporal sequencing, and as the locus of particular rises and falls in intensity. Concurrently, the mother is experienced as a separate source of volition, of temporal sequencing (in vocal games), of intensity gradients, and of "form," especially the emotional communications of her face. Affect sharing is a part of the lived experience from the earliest days of life, when neonates imitate mother's facial expressions, especially when she exaggerates them. While imitation involves making a facial form, affect attunement involves matching qualities of intensity (its level and changes over time), timing (temporal beat, rhythm, and duration), and shape (the form abstracted and expressed in some other mode). In Stern's studies, attunements occurred at a rate of about one every minute during playful interactions. Most attunements involved intensity matching, and most occurred across sensory modes, baby's vocalization being matched by mother's facial expression, arm movement, or both. Stern's original contribution is his identification of vitality affects—the dynamic, kinetic qualities of feeling—as the main characteristic of the inner state that is being attuned to. He reasons that during an average mother-infant interaction, discrete affect displays occur only occasionally; thus affective attuning could not be continuous if it were limited to categorical affects. Stern carefully distinguishes between attunment and fusion or merger. While attunement involves a great sense of intimacy and attachment, it promotes a sense of agency, of volition, and of coherence rather than a loss of boundaries or loss of differentiation of self. In each attunement sequence, infants initiated fully half of the responses and exercised considerable control over the patterning.

Stern then asks, is the infant of two to seven months capable of remembering the experience of agency, coherence, and affect? He suggests, as I have, that a motor memory, a perceptual memory, and an affect memory occur as integrated units, each "a small but coherent chunk of lived experiences" (p. 45). Where I have described these as the memories of perceptual-affective-action patterns, he calls them representations of interactions that have been generalized. His emphasis is on the repetitive nature of the patterns that give rise to a structured memory and to the ability of the infant to abstract from a series of particular experiences the more invariant, predictable average. Stern concludes that between the second and the seventh month, "the infant gains enough experience with the separate major self-invariants [agency, coherence, and affectivity], and the integrating processes reflected in episodic memory advance far enough, that the infant will make a quantum leap and create an organizing subjective perspective that can be called a sense of a core self" (p. 99).

Just as a core self is formed by abstracting invariant experiences of self, so the sense of other people is formed by abstracting consistent experiences with them. Stern postulates that what is remembered of the lived experience is a generalized version of repeated episodes of self interacting with others. This is similar to my suggestion that infant memories are built up from repeated, pooled instances of perceptual-affective-action patterns involved in mutually regulatory interactions. Small variations in each subsequent episode lead to adjustments in the representation of the generalized interactions. When one of these representations is recorded in memory, it organizes the manner in which the subsequent episode is responded to. A sense of "being with" is evoked with the memory, since the infant's lived experience is predominantly of a shared regulatory world. In any immediate lived experience, infants can compare the mother who is interactive with them against the standards of the generalized memory of her from prior lived experiences. Nuances of differences, especially in the mother's mood, such as her being joyous or sad, pleased or angry, interested or distracted, may be quickly apprehended and may serve as a stimulus for altered motivations.

THE SENSE OF A SUBJECTIVE SELF

Stern suggests that the next quantum leap in the sense of self occurs between the seventh and ninth month: "Infants gradually come upon the momentous realization that inner subjective experiences, the subject matter of the mind, are potentially shareable with someone else" (p. 124). Infants looking at a toy will want mother to look at it too. Infants intending to get a toy will want mother to hand it to them or will be sensitive to mother's contradictory intention. Infants becoming excited look to mother to join in; infants becoming frightened look to mother for affirmation or calming. I have referred to the emergent sense of self-as-a-whole and the significance of sign-signal informational exchange. I have cited the importance of infants' beginning to perceive physical objects, themselves, and other people as distinct from action patterns in which they are enjoined. I call this development an imaging capacity and compare it to being able to stop an action sequence on a videotape and see the still-picture of a person or thing. The important factor is not the perceptual-cognitive capacity per se, but the change in how the infant experiences portions of the environment. The self, objects, and others as seen in a mirror are now sources of specific information. For example, toddlers looking at themselves in a mirror can recognize when they have a smudge on their noses or a label placed on their foreheads. The toddler, the observer-as-subjective-self, perceives the physical self as object; that is, both self and others are objectified. Self, others, and physical objects become "objects of contemplation" (Werner and Kaplan, 1963). Some of the information that the toddler seeks is about appearances, qualities, and properties (Piaget, 1937). Some information centers on guidance signals of dos and don'ts. Like Stern, I believe that the most important informational exchange lies in infants' recognition of matches and mismatches between their own affective state and that of their caregivers. Caregivers are no longer solely partners in interactions but are now referenced for clues about shared or opposing intentions and shared or disparate affective experience. This momentous shift from shared interactional experience to shared intersubjective experience occurs between the ninth and fifteenth month and precedes the phase of symbolic representation.

The new domain of intersubjective relatedness transforms the manner in which motivations unfold. Motivations about mother's staying or leaving begin early in these developments. Infants at nine to twelve months often show no response other than interest when mother leaves the room to go to another room if the departure is part of mother's regular intrahouse routine; but they may begin to cry when mother puts her coat on to go out of the house. For this to occur, the infant must have formed an organized memory and must be able to generate future representations of possible events and to communicate an aversive response to an incongruence between present events and future representations (Stern, 1985). Without words, the infant may be saying, "I know what is to come from what I remember of this pattern, and I don't like it, and I'm moved to tell you I don't like it." The infant further assumes from this set of intersubjective communications that crying will alter the affective state of mother.

While we can say that infants of 9 to 18 months share the subject matter of the mind, the minds of the sharers are quite different from each other. The mother's is one of symbolic representation. She integrates her perceptions, affects, and actions by means of cognitive processing in primary and secondary modes. She holds her baby in her fantasies and in her logical planning as well as in her arms. Nine- to 18-month-olds know intimately the message conveyed in mother's arms—whether yielding and inviting or tense and rejecting. They know mother's plans, however, only as consequences that affect them. From the contingent tracking of mother's actions interacting with their own volition, 9- to 18-month-olds can abstract the pattern of mother's behaviors and anticipate her intentions—as though one mind's agenda were meeting another's. Infants know how to read and share their mothers' affect, which "is the most pervasive and clinically germane feature of intersubjective relatedness" (Stern, 1985, p. 138). Through the transmittal of the message conveyed in mother's handling, patterns, intentions, and affects, 9- to 18-month-olds begin to construct a sense of intersubjective self that conforms in some way with mother's core fantasies (chapter 9) about them. Stern and B. Cramer are currently studying how this transmission occurs. They are videotaping mothers interacting with their infants while being interviewed about how they view their infants' development. The goal of this research is to find out how mothers induce behaviors in their children that conform with their own fantasies—for example, the undisputed desire for and conviction of success of Goethe's mother and Freud's mother for their first-born sons (Freud, 1917; Lichtenberg, 1978) or the belief of one of the mothers in Cramer's study that her son intended to hurt her. Subsequently, the induced patterns and the infant's memories of them become reorganized as symbolic representations of the child's self-system—the expansive, confident conqueror of obstacles or the destructive bad boy.

It is not, however, the broad overviews of identity information that I wish to deal with in this book. Rather, my primary subject is the microshifts between motivational systems, during development and in the clinical setting. The domains of self-experience and relatedness of the emergent self, core self, subjective self, and self employing symbolic representation are useful integrations indicative of organizational leaps. The five motivational systems are active in each domain and give the self-experience its volitional, instrumental, and affective coloration.

Motivation and volition are tricky words as they apply to a psychoanalytic discourse of infancy in particular and of the life cycle in general. Is the reference to conscious or unconscious motives? To say that it is both is to minimize the complexity of the problem. Moreover, in some sense it is not accurate, for I do not believe that prior to symbolic representation (around 18 months) can the infant be said to have an "unconscious" in the sense of conflictual fantasied contents dynamically excluded from awareness. Conflict in the presymbolic infant occurs with regularity in the lived experience. The emergent self must cope with polarities (Sander, 1983b) ranging from day–night to social versus physiological versus exploratory-assertive pulls. The core self must, increasingly, actively resolve many agendas with the caretakers. The subjective self lives in a state of seeking guidance in all situations of ambiguity while simultaneously pursuing more defined goals increasingly marked by open aversion (Spitz's head-shaking "no," 1957). A special feature of the unconscious realm as it comes into being with symbolic representation is that much of what has transpired probably becomes *recoded* in primary- and secondary-process modes—and what has been conflictual may then be coded into unconscious fantasy. Another special feature is that aspects of the early perceptual-affective patterns may not be reencoded but remain active in memory as potential affective-action autonomisms, that is, as procedural memories (chapter 3). These mnemonic residues constitute a psychic domain outside of the ordinary potential for awareness; that is, they are an unconscious organization but of a different nature from that organized by mental mechanisms of defense. In chapter 9, I present a view of the unconscious that is compatible with what we know of the infant and what we know of residues from clinical work with adults.

The Motivational System
Based on the Psychic Regulation
of Physiological Requirements

THE ORGANIZATION OF "STATES" IN INFANCY

EATING AND ELIMINATING, ACTIVITY AND PASSIVITY, quiescence and crying, wakefulness and sleep are central to the preservation of life. Consequently many psychoanalysts have attempted to use the psychic regulation of these activities and states in infancy as building blocks for their theories. Lewin's (1950) oral triad, Glover's (1943) ego nucleus, and Freud's (1915) ego instincts of self-preservation are examples. Other psychoanalysts (e.g., Guntrip, 1971) have been critical of the biological basis of concepts built around physiological needs. All psychoanalysts, from Freud on, have clearly demarcated a *psychological* level of representation of these bodily happenings and their regulation. In referring to a motivational system based on the psychic regulation of physiological requirements, I too demarcate a psychological level of conception. Contemporary infant research supports the developmental significance of these basic physiological underpinnings but casts their psychic organization in a different guise. This view emphasizes the regularities of organization of infant "states" over the 24-hour cycle.

Previous conceptions of the neonate period portrayed the baby as living in an autistic shell protected by a stimulus barrier. In this narcissistic stage, hunger or some other physiological need would increase in intensity, break through the "purified pleasure" of the neonate's nirvana, and lead to crying and the stirring up of aggressive urgencies. The infant's psyche was presumed to function at an extremely low level of awareness, which was broken into only by such primitive urgencies as hunger and the need for aggressive dis-

31

charge. The external world came into existence only to curtail the disturbances until a later period, when the hungry child "discovered" the object that he (or she) "recognized" as the source of the satisfaction of need. Source and infant were perceived as existing within an oceanic merged or fused duality. Gradually need, and delay in its satisfaction, cause further discrimination of an external object toward whom the child establishes an anaclitic or symbiotic relationship.

Twenty-four-hour observation of infants offers a view that contrasts with those conceptions (Sander, 1975, 1980) and contributes to a different theory of motivation. From the first day of life in a rooming-in situation, or shortly thereafter in lying-in arrangements, caregiver and newborn function as a unit. The infant moves progressively through states of sleep, alert awareness, quiescent awareness, drowsiness, fussiness, and crying. The caregiver intuitively responds to the changing states, observing the presence of hunger; elimination and the need for diaper changing; the response to eye contact, tactile stimulation, being spoken to and cooed to; and the response to being rocked or left alone. The combination of the infant's preprogrammed, state-organizing functioning and the caregiver's organizing responses creates a mutual regulating system of sensitivity previously unrecognized. On one hand, a well-organized newborn can pull an inexperienced mother toward the caregiving the infant needs. On the other hand, extremely subtle alterations in timing can move the infant toward longer daytime wakefulness and longer nighttime periods—within the first weeks. Sander's studies (1975, 1980) have demonstrated how finely tuned these organizing coordinations are for different caregivers with the same infants.

The picture that emerges from this subtle interregulating system of baby and mother in the first weeks and months is one of a relative unity of experience. In this relatively smooth unity, the passages from state to state have a consistency, a rhythm, that begins life with a smoothness not evident when therapists reconstruct infancy from the standpoint of the origins of symptoms or of personality disturbances. When the fit between infant and caregiver is good, changes of state and the internal and external regulations that bring them about proceed in a seamless manner. Affects are associated with each state, some positive, such as interest and enjoyment; some negative, such as anger, crying, and distress. When mutual regulation is successful, and state moves smoothly to state and day follow day without disturbance, both partners experience a positive overall affective coloration.

I believe that the infant's first and prototypic selfobject experience derives from this positive affective coloration in which are embedded small moments of discomfort and their relief, pleasures of active attachment, and so on. Many efforts have been made in psychoanalysis to capture the essence of this experience—Freud's (1930) oceanic feeling, Sandler's (1960) affect of safety, Erikson's (1959) basic trust. This paradigmatic experience often has been related to feeding, and later many so-called oral fantasies select sucking, eating, and hunger satiation to give symbolic representation to this positive state. I believe, however, that it is the fluid passing of days in the relative harmony of an ideal vacation or sea voyage that best resonates with the earliest selfobject experience.

Disruptions in the overall or background unity inevitably occur. These disruptions bring into the foreground intensified motivations derived from physiological requirements (as well as from attachment needs, exploratory urges, aversion reactions, and the urge for sensual enjoyment). Hunger patterns undergo a shift, bowel products become looser or some constipation and gas buildup occurs, a head cold leads to labored breathing, a diaper rash increases skin sensitivity topically, or the daytime sleep period shifts and fussiness increases. When we focus exclusively on the frequent foreground events, they give a picture of turbulence or, as psychoanalytic theory has viewed it, of untamed drive urgency. Indeed, some infant-caregiver pairs are unable to create a working fit. In these unfortunate instances, both foreground and background experiences reveal persistent patterns of disorganization and disruption. But in other than these infants-at-risk, the ordinary state of infancy is one in which physiological requirements and their satisfaction become organized within a context of a background unity of an ordered experience. Then physiological needs flow in and out of focus in the foreground along with needs from the other motivational systems.

HUNGER-SATIATION AS A
PSYCHOLOGICAL MOTIVATION

Hunger, elimination, and sleep must each become relatively defined motivational experiences. How does this come about? One answer that psychoanalytic theory has provided is that by virtue of the drivelike urgency of its biological pressure, each need achieves a level of intensity of internal perception that parallels the intensity of an external perception. The experienced intensity of external perceptions has been regarded as giving "reality" to the external world as compared with the world of daydreams and fantasies. This hypothesis raises many questions (see Lichtenberg, 1978a), but the principal problem is that it does not answer the question, what makes the intensity itself an experience (not merely a brain register)? The experience of intensity derives from affects that amplify all perceptual-action patterns. Thus, the internal perception of hunger is amplified by the affect of distress (fussiness to crying; if not relieved amplified further, to anger), and the internal perception of feeding is amplified by enjoyment (a rapid diminution of neural firing). The whole hunger sequence—signaled by affect and relieved by prompt caregiving responsiveness and the efficient giving and taking of milk or food—is further amplified by the pleasure resulting both from competence and from attachment joy. The hunger-feeding event, embedded in the alert wakefulness state and more generally embedded in the total need–caregiving cycle of changing states, becomes registered in both episodic and procedural memory. Like other physiological requirement patterns that require the participation of the caregiver, hunger–feeding builds strong memory traces because its biological rhythmicity demands consistent repetition, preventing memory extinction. Further, this redundancy is not a "flat" repetition that would lead to habituation. Rather, an interest-arousing range of variety is guaranteed by the pressure of maturational changes and the sensitivity of caregivers both to respond to the infant's call for variability and to introduce subtle alterations themselves.

The biological factor of repeated need plus the redundancy of caregiver response gives "intensity" to hunger as a lifelong motivation. But successful mutual regulation contributes more than intensity, more than strong affective tones, to the perceptual-action pattern of hunger–feeding. Successful mutual infant-caregiver regulation creates a *definition of hunger* as a motive—a definition we commonly refer to as "reality." The infant alone is privy to the information of his physiological requirement, the caregiver provides a confirmation or disconfirmation. Correct confirmation—The baby is hungry. I'll feed her—defines for the mother the infant's state. It labels and matches the specific need. Even more important, it begins the infant's process of self-organization with the inner perception of hunger recognized and responded to by the mother. On one hand, this confirmation contributes to the infant's trustful reliance on the mutual caregiver-self regulatory system—a gain in attachment. On the other hand, the confirmation contributes to self-differentiation through the recognition of a hunger-feeding sequence, the cues to which are internally perceived information that adds to the definition of a "true" self, in Winnicott's (1960) term. My point is that the reality of a self-state such as hunger-satiation (or any other physiological need) derives from a combination of an internal perception and a confirmation of an external empathic recognition and response. The result is a combination of a positively toned attachment and the differentiation of the self as a source of an internally recognized motivation. With the older infant, motivation can be appreciated when we are certain that behavior patterns are planned and intentional. But how can we conceptualize motivation in the developing neonate? Sander (1983) offers a thought-provoking explanation. He states that since the maintenance of continuity is one task of self-regulation, the individual can be viewed as setting up an ecological niche in which he re-creates conditions that enable him to experience familiar states by which he recognizes himself.

To summarize: A physiological requirement of the infant is met by an appropriate need-satisfying response by the caregiver. This event is recorded in the infant's memory as a procedural experience and as one of a series of related events in a chain of episodes. The caregiver's correct empathic recognition of the infant's internally perceived information about the need-state gives confirmation to a sense of body-centered reality—a contribution to the development of the "true" self. The internally required repetition of the physiological need and its satisfaction (its biological rhythmicity) ensures its recurrence, establishing a sense of familiarity of state. The sense of familiarity and of being able to re-create continuity becomes a positively toned affective state that aids in defining and differentiating the self. Each facet of the fulfillment of these motives adds not only to the self-organization and to the fit between infant and caregiver within the mutual regulatory system, but also to a quality of affective substrata called by Kohut (1971) a selfobject experience.

A feature of the traditional psychoanalytic theory of motivation is its reduction of contextual complexity. By its emphasis on intrapsychic developments, environmental factors are reduced to composite concepts such as external reality, the average expectable environment, or the facilitative environment. In contrast, I view infant research within several contexts. The broadest is the interactional matrix of infant and caregiver over the 24-hour period covering the functioning of all the motivational systems. If we narrow the focus to those interactions involving primarily the fulfillment of physiological requirements, we are describing a considerable number of diverse phenomena. If we focus only on hunger–feeding, we must

retain an interactional perspective to achieve an intrapsychic understanding.

As with all mammals, feeding in the human neonate starts with
sucking, an activity that performs two major functions: obtaining
nutrients and fluids and deriving comfort and calming from maternal contact and from the act itself. Sucking is thus a highly organized, innately programmed activity but one that is remarkably
flexible. Rats, which normally are born blind, are totally dependent
on olfactory clues (from saliva) to activate suckling, whereas farm
animals born sighted and mobile are less dependent on smell. Under the most natural conditions of home delivery and breast feeding, human infants will spend three to five minutes licking their
mother's breast before beginning to suckle. Even when they are
given a bottle, their first spontaneous activity is to lick (Blass and
Teicher, 1980). Both breast- and bottle-fed babies can be activated to
lick by touching their cheeks or lips. Human infants do discriminate
on the basis of olfaction. Six-day-old breast-fed infants prefer a
soiled rather than fresh breast pad, and eight-day-old infants prefer
their own mother's pad to that of another woman (MacFarlane,
1975). Interfering with the smell, for example, with eau de cologne,
led infants to reject mother's breast (Peto, 1936).

The flexibility of the human infants' innate program for sucking
was demonstrated by an experiment of Sameroff (1984). Sameroff
intended to demonstrate learning under different reinforcement
contingencies. In one situation, the infants had to squeeze a nipple
with their lips and tongue at various pressure levels in order to receive milk; in another situation, they had to create various levels of
negative pressure in their mouths by enlarging the oral cavity. The
majority of the infants did not require reinforcement training to accomplish the task but quickly moved from their initial sucking behavior to the required pressure threshold and then maintained it.
Sucking, Sameroff concludes, is a highly organized response system
already at birth. This supports my contention that the emergent self
of the neonate has available to it a motivational system, that the
infant is not totally unformed and helpless, impelled by blind
drives.

Sucking and feeding are coordinated flexibly and vigorously with
the positive experience innately programmed for survival. Sucking
itself is a potent organizer of neonate activity. On the basis of evidence that fetuses not only suck their thumbs and fingers, but do so
frequently, newborns who remained restless after feeding were provided with two minutes of nonnutritive sucking on a pacifier. Their

activity level decreased during sucking and increased again when the pacifier was withdrawn. One group of restless infants was allowed to suck freely prior to their first feeding. Often they sucked for as long as an hour. With nonnutritive sucking opportunities, neonates' respiration became deep and even, the arousal level improved either toward deep sleep or alert responsiveness, neuromuscular coordination improved, and these babies seemed to nurse well at the breast. Even weak, immature infants sucked nonnutritively when the opportunity was provided and seemed to derive benefit from this innately programmed activity.

Nutritive and nonnutritive sucking in the neonate regulates activity by contributing to the formation of a positive, shared interaction that is flexibly, innately programmed and subject to rapid experiences of learning. Often, feeding terminates in sleep, and sucking is reactivated on awakening in children under 12 weeks of age. This finding coincides with the traditional psychoanalytic tension-reduction, or Nirvana, theory of pleasure. But even in the neonate, this is far from an invariant finding. And even when sleep follows some feedings, observation over the 24-hour cycle discloses periods of fussiness, quiescent wakefulness, and nonnutrient alert wakefulness. In children older than 12 weeks, feeding is not usually terminated by sleep. Infants play with the nipple or bottle and hold it in different positions. The nipple no longer dominates the child's attention, and nonnutritive sucking is redirected. As the stomach fills, attention is directed elsewhere, and pauses for play activities increase (Blass and Teicher, 1980).

How can we conceptualize these findings? The most obvious phenomenological answer is that a hunger-satiety cycle is established. I believe this answer is essentially a biological statement. For a psychological statement, I suggest that a pattern of psychic regulation is established in relation to a regularly recurring altered physiological state. My emphasis is on psychological, not physiological, regulation. The psychological regulation derives from the lived experience. When infant and caregiver are well matched, the lived experience will be good to optimal physiological regulation. This will be the result of a good to optimal adjustment of the hunger–satiety cycle and a good to optimal sense of what Spitz (1962) calls the indispensable element of "reciprocity: The circular exchange of affectively charged actions between mother and child" (p. 291). Spitz illustrates reciprocity in the behavioral interplay of the feeding situation as a mother puts the nipple of the bottle into the mouth of her seven-month-old son: "He reciprocates by putting his fingers into her mouth; she answers by moving her lips on his fingers, where-upon he twiddles his fingers, and she responds with a smile; all the while he stares at her face with rapt attention" (p. 291).

Spitz's observation moves away from the traditional emphasis on feeding as a stimulant of oral drive: "That it stimulates the primal cavity, the oral region, is only part of its significance." Speaking of breast feeding in words that apply to the lived experience of competent bottle feeding, Spitz states that "the importance of breast feeding in establishing object relations does not lie in the fact that it assuages hunger and thirst. . . . I consider the widely different, but simultaneous sensory percepts during breast feeding part of a total experience of consistent multiform contact with the mother's body" (p. 296).

From a traditional view of oral drive satisfaction, with relief of hunger leading to libidinal discharge, or even of oral stimulation triggering the libidinal cathexis of the mouth, Spitz's emphasis thus shifts to the total experience of feeding as a spur to establishing object relations. This dramatic change in perspective was largely in response to data coming from two sources: Harlow's (1960) experiments with surrogate-raised baby rhesus monkeys and Spitz's (1962) discovery of the hospitalism syndrome of infants raised in a foundling home. In these instances, the monkey and human infants were fed a nutritious diet; their failure to thrive clearly appeared to stem from a source outside the assuagement of hunger and thirst. Like Spitz, I believe the overwhelming evidence points to a failure in object relations (what I would call a major disturbance in the attachment motivational system), but that especially in the institutionally raised human infants, the regulation of the physiological need for relief of hunger must have also failed. How could the caregivers who fed these infants sterilely, in ritual fashion, have established with them the reciprocity of holding, sucking rhythms and rates, specific diet needs, schedules related to demand, and the overall contact necessary to effect a good regulation? For some caregivers and some babies this may have occurred, and these infants may have been the ones who survived with the least failure to thrive. Spitz argues that a mothering activity does not become effective for the human child as an isolated action-interaction sequence but "as an action sequence embedded in the whole variegated pattern of the individual mother-child relations" (p. 294). He adds, "How little we still know of the interdependence of the various systems, somatic and otherwise!"

My position is that without neglecting the search for interdependence, we should approach the regulation of physiological needs and the development of attachment as separate motivational systems. All the physiological needs (hunger, thirst, elimination, tactile stimulation, equilibrium, thermal control, and sleep) have in common a specific, rather quick-acting signal system conveying information of need and consummation to the caregiver and a feedback system conveying the same information to the emergent self. I consider the needs for attachment activities to be equally profound, but the feedback from failure to meet an attachment requirement at any given moment seems less clearly defined to both caregiver and infant than is, say, unmet hunger. Developing babies will have as their lived experience the regulation they get of hunger, but they have an internal marker that will indicate whether or not this is right for them. I offer as a hypothesis—which I cannot prove—that some problems of trust in the regulatory efforts of others may derive from this internally recognized failure.

The distinction I make between nutrition and regulation of attachment may seem artificial because behaviors that contribute to both motivations coexist in the lived experience of infant feeding. Nutrition becomes a specific issue in a number of abnormal states such as milk intolerance, coeliac syndrome, esophogeal atresia, and famine. Many attachment behaviors, especially the repeated cycles of mother-infant "social" communicating occur at times of alert wakefulness, when hunger or other physiological needs are quiescent. Normally, however, feeding is an attachment event of great significance, and infants who, for whatever reason, cannot take nutrients comfortably prejudice the sociability of their mother's receptiveness and, as a consequence, the normality of their attachment. Alternatively, mothers whose pattern of feeding is markedly aberrant prejudice the motives that evolve in the attachment system. Nonetheless, in these cases the disregulation of physiological needs and of attachment will follow separate although related paths.

CASE ILLUSTRATION OF THE PSYCHOLOGICAL REGULATION OF PHYSIOLOGICAL REQUIREMENTS AS A SEPARATE MOTIVATIONAL SYSTEM

To illustrate the concept that psychological regulation of physiological need constitutes a separate motivational system, I will use a beautifully documented case illustration studied and described by Kris (1962) and Provence (1983). The essence of the case is that Anne Adams, a healthy, appealing newborn, began, during her first year of life, to suffer some of the same physical retardation and developmental arrests that were found in the foundling-home babies, although Anne was raised in a stable home by a seemingly devoted mother and an adoring father. Mrs. Adams's words at Anne's birth, although not in themselves highly unusual, in retrospect loom prophetic of her belief that Anne was aggressive and destructive to her. Having suffered a small perineal tear, she complained that the baby had torn her apart. Cramer's (personal communication) studies have demonstrated that a mother's fantasy of her infant's destructiveness can have a profound effect on attachment, tilting the lived experience toward severely aversive patterns. This happened with Anne. But a mother's viewing her infant as destructive does not by itself preclude successful regulation of physiological needs; it certainly does not lead inevitably to a major disturbance in nutritional state such as Anne developed. Therefore, I shall consider Anne's feeding experience as a separate entity, teasing out of the Kris and Provence reports that aspect of the caregiving and Anne's response to it.

When Anne was a newborn, the pressure of physiological needs appeared to be moderate; Anne could easily wait for feeding and was promptly comforted by holding. Mrs. Adams had expressed a wish to breast-feed, but by the third day it was apparent that this involved "too great a conflict for her, and she gratefully accepted the pediatrician's suggestion that she shift to bottle feeding" (Provence, 1983, p. 235). She explained that she was afraid her large breasts would smother the baby. In time it became clear that Mrs. Adams "was unable to make any feeding fully satisfying and pleasant for Anne. She could not mobilize herself to feed the baby at the first signs of hunger and gave the bottle only after Anne's crying was prolonged and intense" (p. 238). The delay was often as long as a half hour.

Mrs. Adams held Anne at a distance across her lap, minimizing body and social contact while giving her a bottle. From Anne's earliest infancy, when not observed by the pediatrician, Mrs. Adams read during the feeding, unable to muster interest in the baby or in the possibilities of cuddling. While Mrs. Adams's method of feeding at a distance looked uncomfortable to the observer, Mrs. Adams did not appear to be bothered by it. She seemed not to notice that Anne's legs were left dangling or stiffly stretched without touching her mother's body.

From the beginning, Mrs. Adams expressed resentment at night feedings. She stated at four weeks that although Anne took only 20 to 30 minutes for a daytime feeding, she wanted to spend an hour and a half at night taking the bottle. Mrs. Adams's solution was twofold. She avoided as much as possible picking Anne up from the crib, not to "spoil" her. She put Anne to sleep in the prone position so that Anne would suck her thumb and thus sleep through the night without being fed. Anne's response at two and a half months was to cry lustily when hungry, but at three months, she was sucking her thumb for as long as half an hour in the early morning, apparently contented. This observation "suggests that the hunger, that is, the physiological need, was present, but the baby had made some kind of adaptation to the mother's habitual lack of promptness in feeding her since when she saw the bottle she would, as Mrs. Adams said, 'suddenly become voracious' and take it hungrily" (Provence, 1983, p. 237). At four and a half months, Anne, who had previously sucked her thumb selectively and with apparent pleasure and relief of tension, was now sucking her whole fist instead. It seems that Anne's crying was making Mrs. Adams "feel wild inside" and was serving as a stimulus for increasingly intense spankings rather than tenderness. At this time, Mrs. Adams expressed dissatisfaction about the "unnecessary frequency of feeding and asked permission to give more solids to lengthen the interval between feedings" (Provence, 1983, p. 241). At six months, Anne was taking long daytime naps in addition to sleeping 12 hours at night. She was still amiable and responsive to the pediatrician and her mother, but during the next eight weeks she suffered a rapid decline. By the time she was eight months old her misery and depression were prominent. She had screaming spells of ten or more minutes and by the end of the first year, her apathy and depression were increasingly replaced by overt rage. When Anne was almost a year old, Mrs. Adams expressed concern about the baby's diminished appetite. "At the same time a feeding was observed in which Mrs. Adams was unable, for inner reasons, to permit the child to have more milk when she obviously wanted it" (Kris, 1962, p. 192). This was one of many instances in which Mrs. Adams insisted on rationing quantities of food unrelated to Anne's needs of the moment. Some feedings at this time involved tigerlike exchanges of glares, and Anne's crying often grew into tantrumlike violence.

Anne's birth weight was five and a half lbs., placing her in the 25th percentile of normal infant girls. At three months she had dropped to the 10th percentile. "She still maintained an adequate nutritional status at six months. Then the weight curve dropped below the 3d percentile. At this point, she looked very thin" (Kris, 1962, p. 211), limp, unmuscular, sad, and lacking in vitality. The lowest point was at nine months. She passed the 3d percentile at one year, dropped again between 12 and 15 months, reached the third percentile again at 15 months. Then her weight began to rise again to around the 10th percentile, and at three years her general appearance and demeanor were relatively normal.

Among the many questions Kris and Provence raise and the many interesting hypotheses they advance, I shall discuss three from the standpoint of the five motivational systems: 1. How is Anne's response to her mother's feeding to be understood? 2. How is Mrs. Adams's approach to Anne to be understood? and 3. How do different aspects of Anne's deprivation relate to each other?

How is Anne's response to her mother's feeding to be understood? Kris and Provence both note that Anne's signaling of hunger quickly became erratic. At times she held back without apparent distress, at times she voraciously took the bottle when offered, at times she sucked her thumb to last through the delay, at times she cried uncontrollably, and at times she lapsed into prolonged sleep. Anne's erratic signals clearly were contingent on Mrs. Adams's erratic feeding procedure of delay, withholding, refusal at night, and spanking. Everything about Mrs. Adams told Anne "keep your distance", and Anne tried within limits to comply. Kris and Provence note that in her early diminished crying and appealing for contact, Anne resembled deprived, institutionalized infants who were not responded to when a need for feeding or contact was felt and expressed. Provence (1983) posits two interpretations of the significance of Anne's diminished signaling of hunger: (1) As a result of some satisfying feeding experiences Anne may have replaced the bottle with the thumb, possibly having hallucinatory gratification for a time; (2) "Thumb sucking may have been an autoerotic activity *without* the hallucinatory gratification and pleasure normally derived from the ministrations of the mother that lead to more energies cathecting the outside" (pp. 237–238). Both Kris and Provence argue against the hallucinatory hypothesis—when thumb sucking, Anne did not seem clinically to be anticipating a gratifying experience. "We assume that when the actual satisfaction originally was regularly 'too low' the imprint of the memory image related to satiation would not be of the kind to serve as an adequate supplement to the actual experience" (Kris, 1962, p. 209).

My explanation for Anne's diminished signaling of hunger, her prolonged waiting and thumb sucking sometimes and her vigorous crying at other times, is that Anne had developed a tilt toward precocious self-regulation at the expense of optimal mutual regulation of hunger. I do not believe in any case that infants hallucinate breasts or bottles or nipples—these are the products of symbolic representation, a development of the second year. But I do agree with Kris that memory images of recurrent satisfying feeding experiences are an adequate supplement to smooth out and stabilize moments of minor dissatisfaction in subsequent actual experiences. Forming, storing, linking, generalizing, and recovering such memories are essential functional capacities available to the emergent self. I do not believe that overcoming a primary autoerotic tendency is the prime requisite for cathecting the outside and the developing of object relations. Optimal mutual regulation of hunger satiation is in itself a significant form of object relation; attachment responses, another significant form of object relation, exist outside of feeding or other physiological need satisfactions. Both were disturbed in Anne, but as separate developmental occurrences. Anne was not sucking her thumb because she could not relate to her mother or others—she did relate to her mother, the pediatrician, the other observers, her father, and her aunt and uncle. She was not turning inward to autoeroticism, surrendering attachment capacity. She sucked her thumb because that was the form of feeding behavior she had under her control when she needed to deal with hunger. To the degree to which she could successfully self-soothe through thumb sucking, she could improve her chances to handle hunger, form attachments, explore and be curious, and experience a modicum of sensual enjoyment despite some persistent gnawing in her stomach. What was sacrificed by her diminished signaling, or prolonged crying, or prolonged sleep was primarily any sense in her emergent self of trust or confidence in mutual regulation of a primary physiological need. What was sacrificed by the mother's failure in her part of the regulation was more than the shared pleasure in feeding, cuddling, and closeness. It was the sense of efficacy and competence as a caregiver. Mrs. Adams's depression reflected this loss as, trapped in her own unconscious disturbance, she systematically kept Anne at the edge of starvation.

How is Mrs. Adams's approach to Anne to be understood? Kris (1962) states that "she is driven to repeat what she views as her own experience, thus illustrating one of the ways in which the cycle of generations affects the parent-child relationship" (p. 189). Kris notes that without being aware of it, Mrs. Adams experienced Anne as a rival, a competitor for attention, and an intruder in her life. She was bitterly disappointed that Anne was a girl, as her parents had been with her. She wished "for a male child with whom to identify—the wish for the penis" (Kris, 1962, p. 194). A second unconscious theme "presumably more deeply buried, concerns the reproachfully harbored longing for a true mother, the wish to be and not to have the infant" (p. 194). Kris relates this wish to Mrs. Adams's own dietary struggles. Her weight fluctuated markedly with her mood swings. Whenever she was depressed, she turned to sweets, which she associated to the candy and cakes her father had brought her. Kris states that when we identify Mrs. Adams's longing for a true mother and for the penis, we have named "only deeply rooted impulses active in every woman. . . . and have not reached anything which seems specific" (p. 194). Kris then attempts a more detailed reconstruction of unconscious fantasies. He offers an ingenious solution to why Mrs. Adams fed Anne as she did. He notes that not only was the feeding relation characterized by deficits, but there was a "provocative element in it, an attempt to heighten the child's tension" (p. 195). This heightened tension manifested in Anne's crying, and Mrs. Adams's feeling wild inside was the prodromal for the spankings. Kris suggests that this permitted Mrs. Adams the enactment of a fantasy containing "a struggle between a little girl and her father, a 'battle of wills' in which the girl is beaten by the father" (p. 195). Kris adds that the child in the fantasy stands for "a female phallus and it is the phallus which is being beaten" (p. 204n). Thus, Mrs. Adams's feeding Anne at a physical distance can be interpreted as the influence of the superego, a protective shielding of Anne from damage by the mother's aggressive impulses.

In Kris's explanation, the specificity of the pattern of delayed and inadequate feeding provides provocation for Anne to cry and for Mrs. Adams to feel wild, lose control, and hit Anne—thereby unconsciously expressing her pleasure-giving beating fantasy. Alternatively, keeping physical distance in feeding, along with reduced cuddling and contact, is a defense against the sadistic urges felt toward the penisless girl baby and rival. I find this explanation unsatisfying because a mother who unconsciously may want to justify spanking her baby for crying hardly needs to starve her to produce the occasion for an abusive reaction. I take more literally and simply Kris's suggestion that "Mrs. Adams is driven to repeat what she views as her own experience" (p. 189). I suggest that Mrs. Adams unconsciously followed the feeding pattern with which she herself had been fed: an initial attempt at breast feeding followed by bottle feeding and other handling at a physical distance with delay, crying, attempts at compliant adaptation, and overall an inadequate nutritional status—all in an atmosphere of antagonism, abrupt handling, yelling, and mutual withdrawal, and depression. Obviously, I can offer no direct proof for my contention that Mrs. Adams was "simply" reenacting the pathological form of regulation of nutritional needs that she had received. The case record itself is inconclusive. Mrs. Adams's mother (Anne's grandmother) "led an unhappy and frustrated life. . . . she was idle and dissatisfied. Housework was done by servants, and care of the child was entrusted to various hands, e.g., even to the maternal grandmother. She breast-fed the baby, but obviously did not know how to bring up a daughter" (Kris, 1962, p. 187). I have reported case examples of my own and of others that illustrate the specific repetition of residues of perceptual-affective-action patterns of a pathological nature carried forward into adult life (Lichtenberg, 1983, pp. 200–203; Anthi, 1983). For example, Monica, a child with esophageal-atresia, was perforce fed "at a distance" through a tube into her stomach (Engel, 1979). As an adult, to the surprise of the observers, Monica, feeding her baby orally, maintained the *same* distance. I have observed a distancing feeding pattern similar to Anne's, but without the nutritional deficiency (Lichtenberg, 1978a, 1983b).

Studies of memory, especially the differentiation of two information storage systems, one "procedural" and one "declarative" (Squire, 1986) provide empirical support for my speculation. "Declarative memory includes the facts, episodes, lists, and routines of everyday life. That is, it can be declared, brought to mind verbally as a proposition or nonverbally as an image. It includes both episodic memory (specific time-and-place events) and semantic memory (facts and general information gathered in the course of specific experiences)" (Squire, 1986, p. 1614). Procedural memory is not directly accessible to consciousness. It is accessible only through performance, when one engages in the skills or operations in which the knowledge is embedded. Procedural learning is regarded as phylogenetically old, having developed as a collection of encapsulated, special-purpose abilities. The capacity for declarative knowledge, on the other hand, is phylogenetically recent, utilizing the highest cortical centers. Thus, in the infant, procedural learning and its long-term memory storage can be seen as deriving from innate, preprogrammed perceptual-affective-action patterns using the available brain centers, whereas declarative learning and its long-term memory storage require brain centers that mature later. Thus, as an infant, Mrs. Adams would have been able to form a long-term memory of the feeding procedures used by her mother and the surrogate feeders, her grandmother and the servants. Once she was cued to perform the same functions, she did so "unconsciously," as did Monica, who as a child had been fed through a tube and who later fed her baby at a similar distance. There is an immediately perceptible problem with this explanation: Mrs. Adams is not remembering and reenacting her own procedure as the baby sucking, but the procedure of the caregiver feeding her. The memory of the procedure must have been encoded in its regulatory form—the mutual interaction of the partners—and furthermore the memory must be capable of immediate reversal of functional roles. This proposition that roles are reversible possibly echoes Freud's dialectic conception of the "partial instincts" of sadism and masochism, of voyeurism and exhibitionism. I cannot present any evidence from memory studies that demonstrates that the fluidity of procedural roles is inherently present in long-term stored memories.

A second problem lies in the claim of the specificity of the procedural repetition, even if we accept that reversal of roles is a property inherent in the memory. While specificity of repetition might allow us to explain cases like Anne's and Monica's, what about the many cases in which the feeding procedure differs in any number of ways from that which the mother received as a child? Here I draw on the familiar psychoanalytic proposition that trauma organizes (Schur, 1966) or fixates and is the source of the repetition compulsion. Alternatively, success in the regulatory response to physiological and other needs leads to a much more flexible generalized encoding of lived experience. Kris (1962) notes that the effect of comfort is to produce memories of food satisfaction that will substitute "for the missing elements in actual satisfaction in any concrete situation" (p. 209). When a concrete feeding situation falls somewhat short of a regulatory success, it can be generalized into the group of remembered experiences of satisfaction so that what is learned is an expectation of another positive regulatory exchange. "Perception and memory interact to produce an anticipation of the future when the child learns to wait for its feeding and registers in the mother's preparation the cues for the forthcoming satisfaction" (p. 210). The child's confidence in the expected result leads to greater flexibility in response—the ability to wait a little longer or to change a response and try a new food offering. The memory of these repetitions, with small adjustments, will be abstracted and averaged into what Stern (1985) calls "Representations of Interactions that have been Generalized (RIGs)" (p. 97).

To make his point, Stern, like Kris, compares the effect of regulatory successes with the effect of a regulatory failure in feeding, the infant's nose becoming occluded by the breast. He notes Gunther's (1961) report that one episode of breast-occlusion appeared to influence the newborn's behavior for several subsequent feedings. Stern (1985) postulates that if breast-occlusion episodes recur again and again, the specific episodes will be generalized into "a structure about the likely course of events, based on average experiences" (p. 97). The infant will come to expect a disregulation in feeding. If, on the other hand, the breast-occlusion experience is a one-time or rare occurrence and breast or bottle feedings generally go well, the single episode will not become a normal, expected part of daily living. Depending on the intensity of the experience and on some degree of periodic recurrence, the episode may cease to be an active or even retrievable memory, or it may become organized into an episodic memory that stands in contrast to the general scheme of expectations. Memory, in comparison to the structuralized set of generalized expectations, "is failure-driven in that the specific episode is only relevant and memorable as a piece of lived experience to the extent that it violates the expectations of the generalized episode" (Stern, 1985, p. 96). For Anne, the generalized episode was one of overlong delay in feeding with no coordination between amount of food offered and nutritional need. When, later, the semi-starvation was reversed, what would remain? Or, if the way Anne was dealt with by Mrs. Adams represented the way Mrs. Adams had been handled as an infant, what remained of her infant experience? Kris (1962), answering for Mrs. Adams, states that she had a deeply buried, reproachful longing for a true mother. I would add that she had a generalized memory structure (nonepisodic) of a persistently unsatisfying feeding procedure. Later she might have formed a different, more ideal image of the way she as a mother would want to feed and nurture her children. But, unfortunately, the procedural memory would remain inflexibly resistant to later intentions to feed and relate in a positive, loving manner. Flexibility and blending of one procedural inclination with new opportunities is far greater between organized experiences of a similar positive affective nature than between opposites.

What led to Anne's recovery is not clear. Kris states that the relationship between mother and child began to improve as soon as Mrs. Adams could institute a teacher-pupil exchange with Anne. The two could now function as companions, and Mrs. Adams could feel relieved of the sense of responsibility for a physiologically needy infant. I place more weight on two procedural changes that are noted in the record. When Anne was nine months of age, Mrs. Adams, following the pediatrician's advice, began to eat while feeding Anne "and as a result seemed able to make the meal more

pleasant for Anne" (Provence, 1983, p. 245). Satisfying herself may
have provided a procedural model for Mrs. Adams to satisfy Anne
better.[1] When Anne was a year old, she was more actively moving
about and exploring her environment. "The crying at night had
stopped, but she was continuing to wake several times. She would
search for and find her bottle in the crib and go back to sleep with it
and her bunny" (Provence, 1983, p. 249). Now, in a sense, both
"infants" were able to take feeding into their own hands, Mrs. Adams by feeding herself along with Anne and Anne with her own
self-soothing bottle and bunny. I postulate that, as the second year
progressed, Anne could do more self-feeding with both bottle and
solids. She could self-regulate better than Mrs. Adams could respond; thus, Anne's sense of self would be one in which only self-
regulation could be relied on, mutual regulation of physiological
need being largely tainted with deprivation and antagonism.

Kris (1962) adds in a footnote an observation that I believe provides crucial evidence for my thesis that a procedural memory repetition was being reenacted. Three years after her birth, Anne had
become a friendly and mostly smiling child with a small, graceful
body and a satisfactory physical status. Mrs. Adams, now having
had extensive beneficial contact with the concerned staff of the Yale
Child Study Center, finally had the son she desired. Kris states:

> Observers in the well-baby clinic noted that the mother overlooked
> the growing restlessness of the infant boy, and when the pediatrician
> brought it to her attention, the mother offered the baby a pacifier,
> pensively adding that she would not have done this with Anne.
> When the pediatrician suggested that she feed the baby, she put him
> across her knee and once more there was minimal contact between
> her own and the child's body. As the child fed, the mother continued
> to talk to the pediatrician [p. 799n].

---

[1]I treated an extremely depressed and agitated, insecure young woman who con-
fessed that she was battering her recently adopted infant son. The uncontrolled slap-
ping occurred when the feeding infant would spit up any milk. It was clear that my
patient experienced this as his rejection of her good offering, but it was not clear
why this provoked her to uncontrollable rage. She mentioned casually something
about her diet. When I showed interest, she reluctantly revealed that her physician
husband had placed her on a strict diet, removing all of the foods she enjoyed,
threatening to withhold sex and love unless she complied absolutely. With my help,
she recognized that in her food-needy state, she could not bear to see good food
"rejected" and that she had displaced her rage from her husband to the baby. While
terrified of her husband, she decided that defying him was the lesser of the two
evils. She instituted a procedural change in which she herself ate one of her favorite
snacks just before or during the feeding, and the battering stopped.

How do different aspects of Anne's deprivation relate to each other? The record of regulation of other physiological needs is sparse. Mrs. Adams is reported to have been tolerant of Anne's rocking. During the first year, messiness was borne by Mrs. Adams with suppressed anger. During the second year, Mrs. Adams instituted bowel training, and she and Anne became locked in a battle characterized by Anne's wild, tigerlike looks. Mrs. Adams during the second year offered Anne the bottle as a calming substitute but during the third year instituted weaning, with more battles as Anne clung to the bottle. Thus, in the area of regulation of physiological needs, aversion responses continued to dominate all or most of the interactions with a deficit in tactile pleasurable stimulation.

Anne's attachment experiences provided few opportunities for intimacy pleasure. From birth on, the observers regarded Anne as an infant with a high potential for human relatedness. An important marker for the progress of attachment is the regulation of communicative exchanges, and Anne was progressively "starved" here also. Held at a distance, with minimal eye contact, body contact, and verbal interchanges, Anne became by 15 weeks a visual searcher screening for adult contact. Whereas at nine weeks her socially linked cooing and babbling had been advanced, thereafter this critical marker began a steadily progressive decline. Although maturation continued with a normal progression of vowel sounds and changes in tonal range of the voice, vocalization was sparse due to its minimal use in social interchange. By the 34th week, vocalization was her lowest performance, seven weeks below her age. At this time Anne gave a positive social response to the examiner's approach but a negative reaction to Mrs. Adams. While physically capable of hand-to-hand approximation, she did not play pat-a-cake when offered by the examiner. In fact, the nature of the attachment was not a positive, playful, social exchange with well-regulated turn taking at initiation but was the meeting of antagonists, mutually frustrated and depressed. On the positive side, some contacts with her father, which, unfortunately, were limited, were more receptive and joyous.

Development of the exploratory-assertive motivational system was also impaired. While her alertness as an infant was normal to high, by three and a half months she "was not utilizing fully the motor abilities available to her through maturation; she was not as active in reaching out and in changing position as she could have been given her level of maturation. There was also a relatively low investment of interest in toys" (Provence, 1983, p. 239). At six months, although she could reach out and grasp toys, she showed

little interest in doing so. To the sound of a bell and other potentially interesting noises, she responded by closing her eyes. When
held in a standing position at six to eight months, Anne would not
extend her legs to support her weight. Kris (1962) relates these findings to inadequate tension discharge, and Provence (1983) sees
them as outgrowths of the libidinal attachment deficits affecting ego
development. I see them as a primary regulatory failure on the part
of Mrs. Adams to provide Anne with the stimulation of reciprocal
play with toys and then to foster Anne's play while noninteractive
but close at hand. This is not play to attach or to discharge tension:
this is play to explore and discover contingencies and practice competence and gain a specific pleasure from it. Mrs. Adams treated
Anne's legs dangling off the edge of her lap while she was feeding
her as inconsequential—not as an organ of motility Anne would
need to move actively and engage the world and explore it. The
availability of play material could carry Anne but so far on her own.
At 34 weeks, she was able to match two cubes, holding one in each
hand and approximating them in the midline. "She would retrieve
a toy she had dropped within reach but would not change position
to get it if the toy was out of reach, nor could she solve the problem
of uncovering it if it were hidden within reach" (Kris, 1962, p. 201–2).
I consider Anne's lowered motivation for exploration and assertion
to reflect lowered interest on her part and lowered affirmative responses from Mrs. Adams. She could obtain some degree of competence pleasure, and this carried her forward in her exploration; but
she received few or no activating, encouraging, or approving responses. The lack of positive attachment thus took its toll. In the
later period, when Mrs. Adams assumed the role of teacher with
Anne, this area of learning was encouraged and Anne's delayed
motivation quickly picked up. Another factor that limited
exploratory-assertive motivation was the state of aversion. A striking finding in children who had a manic-depressive parent (Gaensbauer et al., 1984) is that as aversive tendencies increase, exploratory
play decreases. We might say that the subtle interplays of
antagonism-withdrawal, of frustrating and being frustrated, become
the consuming "game," and toy interest loses out.

Unlike the lack of nurturance to stimulate Anne's sense of regulation in the motivational systems of physiological needs, of attachment, and of exploration and assertion, the stimulus to activate
motives in the system of aversive responses was abundant. Despite
the provocation of delayed, inadequate, and malattuned feeding
from birth on, Anne resisted being dominated by aversive counter-

responses. In the early weeks, she could easily wait for feeding and could be soothed by holding. She could use nonnutritive sucking to achieve delay. When the pediatrician noted this, Mrs. Adams answered that she was not impressed. Finally Anne began increasingly to withdraw into sleep or to cry persistently. Mrs. Adams would try to wait for the crying to stop; she said that it was like the crying of a cat. The crying drove her wild inside, and she began spanking the infant. Anne's crying spells increased after two months, and their rising intensity after three months was apparent. By six to nine months both Mrs. Adams and Anne had withdrawn into lonely, depressive states. When Anne was nine months old, Mrs. Adams "described in a diary she had been asked to keep that the child cried to exhaustion, was inconsolable until she fell asleep, and though she cried in a similar fashion before, she had never cried to such a degree" (Kris, 1962, p. 212). Kris notes that observers of an episode of Anne's crying had felt as though they were witnessing a tragic experience of "a child that could not be reached or comforted, but was left to her own uncontrollable despair" (p. 212).

Mired in the generalized aversive state of irritable withdrawal, Anne's specific aversive reactions were blunted. "She did not use her ability to creep to move away from something she did not like. In such situations she could only cry in a distressed way" (Provence, 1983, p. 246).

Toward the end of the first year, Anne's apathetic aversive state altered. Her cry became more angry—her mother called it screeching. Anne actively fought her mother with rage, alternating with moments of appearing sweet and docile. This freeing up of Anne's aversive antagonism appeared to be the result of changes in the family. They were on vacation, Mr. Adams was more available, supportive relatives visited, and the depressed mood of both mother and child lifted. Mrs. Adams saw Anne's open opposition as well as her compliance as making her less of "a negative thing" and more of a person. As I see it, aversion, which had been an intractable affective-action state, now served more of a signal communicative function that both Anne and Mrs. Adams could recognize. Rather than being locked into the earlier established pattern of withdrawal, Anne shifted to overtly antagonistic aversive responses that permitted action. Some of the action centered on controversy, but some of it was manifest in exploratory-assertive motives. She could now physically move away from her mother to investigate her surrounding world.

During her 13-month examination, Anne gave aversive signals of anxiety at the approach of the pediatrician. When she heard the sound of a normal pitch and loudness of conversation, she tensed her body. By heeding these signals, the pediatrician, who approached Anne slowly and silently, was able to roll a ball back and forth several times with her. "At this her face lighted up; she smiled broadly, turned toward her mother, and clutched her briefly. She then turned back to the ball, and the game continued for several minutes. She looked very happy, smiled, and laughed, and for the first time gave the impression of having made a positive human contact" (Provence, 1983, p. 212). Anne's perceptual-affective-action patterns now showed more flexible shifts between motivational systems. Aversive responses, whether withdrawal or antagonism, appeared more flexible, more a matter of intention and choice. When heeded as a signal, the need to respond aversively could be replaced as a dominant motivation by attachment interests and by exploratory-assertive interests. Anne now was rapidly adding more functional tools in the form of "spectacular and encouraging gains" (Provence, 1983, p. 251) in language development and in motor activities. All this was exceedingly important preparation for the effect of the maturational upsurge of aggressive urgency at 18 months. Anne was able to be open in her expression of anger and hostility in her interchanges with her mother and with other children. She also used her transitional object—a bunny—as a target for her aversive responses, ferociously biting its ears.

Provence notes that even as Anne improved, coping efforts were still poorly developed, as was mastery motivation (competence) in White's (1959) sense. With this background in the presymbolic period, Anne's subjective self-experience become one in which ordinary coping in the motivational systems of physiological need regulation and attachment, and ordinary competence in the motivational system of exploration and assertion, were overshadowed by aversive motivations. In the second half of the second year, the aversive motivations received symbolic representation with full verbal coding. This raised the level at which controversy could be transacted, a level Mrs. Adams found easier to deal with.

When a child with Anne's favorable innate temperament receives adequate empathic responsiveness from her mother, aversion is apt to be primarily a signal for regulating other motives and a resource for effective enforcement of self claims. Due to the extent of the empathic failures, aversive reactiveness probably became for Anne the dominant motive for interacting with the world. As Kris (1962) states:

Even Anne the four-year-old, and her mother are interlocked in a pe-
culiarly poignant battle of wills—complicated by the fact that the fantasy of the mother has molded the child, and that the child repeats in
her relation to the mother some of the experiences which the mother
inflicted upon her much earlier [pp. 195–196].

Anne's case tells us little that we can use to sense the state of
motives for sensual enjoyment and sexual excitement as they became organized in her emergent, core, and subjective selves. The
initial neonatal observations that she sucked with interest and pleasure and was easily comforted indicated an innate responsiveness
to sensual enjoyment: She used sucking and rocking to achieve
some adaptation to her delayed feeding. Even this turned to an
aversion-dominated activity after the spankings and loud scoldings
became prominent. Anne now shifted from sucking her thumb with
pleasure to sucking her whole fist with desperation. Anne's pleasure in sexual contact may have been kept alive by her contacts with
her adoring father. Gender designation seems to have been well established and rivalry a bitter early struggle. Mrs. Adams's problems
with Anne's developing sexuality are noted in her anxious denial of
her daughter's masturbatory activity in Anne's third year.

Before concluding the discussion of the regulation of feeding
needs, I shall briefly consider the declining significance attributed
to weaning in the literature of psychoanalysis. Echoing the point of
view of some of the earlier analytic literature, Sarlin (1970) states:

For the infant, the weaning experience presents the primary *psychological* crisis of separation; and the emotional climate in which it takes
place may determine the intensity of separation anxiety, the ultimate
success or failure of individuation, and the development of autonomy
upon which genital primacy and the establishment of a mature sexual
identity ultimately depend [p. 289].

While many analysts would not give weaning as much weight
as Sarlin, it was regarded as more significant when the focus was
on the ending of an oral phase and the beginning of an anal phase
and when sadism was regarded as a derivative of the later stage of
the oral phase (and teething). Possibly weaning has received less
attention because one group of analysts, following object relations
theory in general and Mahlerian theory in particular, stress
separation-individuation as the principal determinant of the preoedipal period, while another group of analysts follow Arlow and
Brenner's (1964) emphasis on oedipal reorganization of whatever

vestiges of earlier phases persist. I would call attention to another factor—weaning as a specific procedure in recent times has lost the precision of its former definition. When the breast was withheld from an exclusively breast-fed infant, weaning was clear cut. In the feeding procedures of today, where exclusive breast feeding is rare and multiple approaches with bottle and with tentative early exper- imental use of semisolids are common, temporary feeding successes and failures become more the focus. With such practices, weaning becomes more a matter of definition. Is weaning a change in food container (giving up the breast or bottle for the spoon, cup, or fin- gers)? Is weaning abandoning nutritive and nonnutritive sucking on a nipple? What place does the use of a pacifier or finger sucking have?

Kris (1962) writes that in Anne's case, not being weaned, defined as having her bottle available in her second year, lessened Anne's distress and aversive tendencies, while Mrs. Adams's attempts to make Anne give up her bottle during the third year accentuated their battling.

Roiphe and Roiphe (1985) call attention to the common finding that many babies at ten or eleven months show a temporarily de- creased interest in the bottle and are often willing to switch to a cup because of the enhanced self-feeding (assertiveness) this enables. They note that many babies of this age treat such a change as more loss than gain, and they recommend that the effort to "wean" be post- poned until probably the end of the second year. They claim that "the baby who has weaned early will have to turn to symbolic play and symbolic objects to resolve some of the tension that would other- wise be drained off in the sucking of the bottle" (p. 71). They acknowl- edge that the boost into symbolic thinking and pretend play presumed to result from early weaning is difficult to prove except im- pressionistically; but even if it were established as a statistical fact, its consequences for the regulation of motivation remain unclear.

Ainsworth (1967), viewing weaning cross-culturally, states that to understand its effect, the context in which weaning takes place must be considered. She notes that breast feeding, as it was prac- ticed in Western countries before 1900 and continued to be practiced in places like Uganda, created a very different experience from that of infant and mother in contemporary Western countries. Thus, weaning from the breast had an impact it has lost in our culture. Ainsworth believes that of critical significance to the baby in his feeding experience is his own *active* behavior toward the mother, strengthened by her response. If whenever the neonate actively searches for the nipple "he is pretty consistently given the breast, he in a true sense is permitted to take the initiative and gain control over feeding" (p. 413). If breast feeding is maintained, infants will fumble in their mother's clothing and succeed in managing the breast themselves. Once mobile, the infants will crawl to the mother and scramble onto her lap when hungry. "The argument here is that attachment does not grow through receiving but through actively reaching out and attaching oneself" (p. 413).

Babies who do not have this demand-instigated, self-organized experience with their mother's breast and body must form their primary attachment to mother differently. Schedule-fed babies do not self-initiate their feedings, and bottle-fed babies do not enforce "the most consistent, the most multiform contact with the mother's body" (Spitz, 1962, p. 196) through breast feeding. Babies fed in these ways, which now predominate in the Western countries, do not form their primary attachment through active self-regulation of feeding and of breast-body contact; thus, they will show far less disruption of the mother-infant relationship as a result of weaning. With schedule-fed and bottle-fed babies, any effect of weaning is apt to be relatively restricted to its impact on the regulation of physiological need. Attachment disruption is related more to failures of social contact, attunement, and communication. To find the traumas of weaning that were described by analytic pioneers, it is necessary to find infants fed today more or less as those were. Is the changed pattern of feeding and weaning a gain or a loss? For the regulation of the physiological need for nutrients I doubt that it is decisive one way or the other. The development of a full range of sensory modalities associated with warmth in attachment and a maximally expansive sensual experience may indeed be diminished. This loss may lead to a tilt away from seeking sensual enjoyment and sexual excitement as a dominant motive in itself to the greater search for warmth and mirroring to support the fragile sense of attachment that troubles narcissistically inclined persons.

Information from many sources confirms the significance of the regulation of physiological requirements of a mutually satisfying feeding experience. The regulation of other physiological needs, such as elimination, tactile and proprioceptive stimulation, sleep, equilibrium, and thermal control, seems equally compelling, but confirming information is more fragmentary. I cited the case of Anne because details of the feeding procedures that contributed to the dysregulation were available and could be appraised against a background of a more normative experience.

THE NEED TO REGULATE ELIMINATION

In respect to elimination, we are on less firm ground. Case material often states that toilet training went well or was prolonged or that-the child was resistant, but seldom do we have detailed descriptions of the procedures and patterns of that training. Nor has a consistent attempt been made to relate the procedures used to their meaning for the parent, as Kris (1962) and Provence (1983) did for Mrs. Adams's feeding of Anne. Moreover, what is the normative experience against which to weigh the impact of a particular regulatory effort? Roiphe and Roiphe (1985) state that toilet training is usually instituted between 14 months and three years—quite a range in itself. When we look at other cultures, we find, for example, that in Uganda mothers expect their infants to stop soiling the bed by *seven months*. Ainsworth (1967) observed Ugandan babies before control was acquired, and found that the age range at which bed-soiling ceased was from five to eleven months. Of 28 babies studied, only three had failed to control bed-soiling by nine months. "In none of these [failure] cases did the mother pay adequate attention to the baby's signals. In each case of the establishment of early control, the baby either evacuated very regularly and predictably so that he could always be 'caught' or he began to give signals of his intentions which the mother heeded" (p. 82). Training was accomplished by moving the baby outside immediately after he woke from sleep, immediately after feeding, and sometimes during feeding if the mother read a signal of impending defecation. The baby was "held down" in a squatting position, his feet on the ground, with the mother's arm across his back, supporting it. The position is regarded both as physically facilitating elimination and as building up an association between being held in this way and actively excreting. After the baby succeeded in not soiling the bed, Ugandan mothers set three other sequential expectations—not soiling in the house, not wetting the bed, and not wetting in the house. All of these landmark accomplishments were based largely on maternal response to the infants' signaling to be removed. The babies were seldom diapered, and when "catching" failed, the mother's attitude "seemed, without exception, tolerant and accepting. A few could verbalize that it was in a child's nature to function in this way, and that it took a long time before he was old enough to learn control" (p. 81). If the baby urinated or excreted while being held, the mother exclaimed and quickly held the baby away from her. Once the initial reaction was over, she cleaned up and dealt with the baby without scolding or fuss. Most of the children did not wet the bed by 19 months; most did not achieve wetting outside the house by 21 months.

Ainsworth concludes:

> It is clear from the foregoing account that Uganda training in elimination control is at least as effective as the training methods used in our culture. It rests for its effectiveness not so much upon a schedule of holding down but upon the child's own indications of need. Before he can actually signal his needs the mother gears her practices to what she has observed of the child's rhythms, and holds him down at times when he is most likely to defecate or urinate. Soon he is able to signal his needs with special sounds that she recognizes even before he can verbalize. The extent to which control is something accepted by the child rather than imposed upon him is shown by his tendency to take the initiative himself in finding the appropriate place to excrete waste when he is old enough to get there under his own steam [p. 83].

Because all of this depends on the caregiver's presence and responsiveness, this type of regulation is vulnerable to inconsistent or inattentive mothering, diarrhea, or other illness in the child. It may be vulnerable also to disturbance in regulation at the transition between highly attentive caretaking and more independent activity, especially if necessitated by the birth of another child.

Ainsworth offers this provocative suggestion:

> It may well be that the task of learning first of all that the bed is a place *not* to be wet or soiled is an easier one than learning that elimination can take place only in one place—on a potty or toilet. Having grasped this notion it is perhaps easier to take the next step of delaying until the proper place is reached than it would be to learn that all at once without intermediate objectives [p. 84].

Parents in Western countries who report training infants under one year have depended on similar tracking either of a regular pattern of elimination that the infant adopts spontaneously or following feeding (the gastrocolic reflex). A derisive query occasioned by this approach is: Who is being trained, the baby or the mother? Ainsworth's observations point to the conclusion that not only is the mother trained to catch the baby at the right time, but the infant is also being trained to develop a heightened awareness of body indicators of bowel and urinary urges. The combination of self-awareness of bodily indicators and coordination between mother and infant provides the foundation for successful regulation. If training occurs before 15 months, the infant's intention, planning, and expectation are engaged at the level of an affective-action pattern coordinated through sign-signal communication or social referencing. In the older toddler stage, intention, planning, and expectation are engaged at the level of symbolic representation in primary and secondary process.

The double encoding in primary- and secondary-process modes constitutes both an advantage and a problem for the training of the two- or three-year-old. Because of the availability of secondary-process thinking, the toddler can be reasoned with, the process and purpose explained, fears verbalized, controversies negotiated in words, and praise for accomplishment shared with other family members. Toddlers who can recognize and verbalize their internal body signals of impending elimination can actively enter into a spirit of cooperation, controlling, and relaxing their sphincters and musculature in accordance with an agreed upon mutual plan.

In contrast to the benefits of secondary-process, sequential-logical reasoning for urinary and fecal regulation, primary-process thinking through analogy and metaphor creates problems. Whatever two- or three-year-olds are preoccupied with can find an analogy in their bodily activity. The analytic literature is replete with the metaphoric linking of feces and being flushed away with death and burial; of feces retained, with pregnancy; of urinary flow, with sexual excitement; of sphincter retention, with stubbornness; of feeling like a "shit" or being "pissed" away, with a sense of worthlessness; of being given a present, or money, or feces, with being valued; and a multitude of other connections. Each may convert any trip to the bathroom into an experience that has a meaning quite outside the regulatory intent of a training parent. For the infant trained at younger than a year, this problem does not enter into the regulatory effort since the impact is that of the lived experience alone. If a pleased mother praises rather than scolds, shames, or punishes, the regulatory successes of their joint effort will simply be encoded as indicators of competence pleasure, failures becoming flexible aversive signals. The issue will not end here, of course, since the child trained at a year old will later code the experiences of elimination in both symbolic modes and will face the same problems inherent in primary-process thinking at the later time. Toddlers who are trained after symbolic representation is accomplished, or whose prior training is being reconsolidated, inevitably must cope with concerns outside the regulation of elimination itself. Concurrently, toddlers will be reconciling controversies in attachment and sorting out the mysteries of birth and death and manifold danger situations.

Are problems arising from opposing agendas in toilet training the source of inescapable disregulation of elimination needs? Are these problems, plus other controversies and exploratory challenges, the inevitable source of broadly based conflicts? Traditional analytic theory has supposed so. Certainly it seemed well documented in many case reports of anal-phase trauma. Recently, however, references to toilet training and to anal-phase disturbances have diminished, often to be replaced by reference to the vicissitudes of separation-individuation crises. I do not believe that this is simply a result of a shift in focus. I have reviewed my own analytic material, plus the material of colleagues, and conclude that the data on which the earlier claims of anal-phase traumatic conflict were based no longer appear in the free associations of current analytic cases in the form and frequency I found in my early cases. I attribute this to a change in toilet-training methods, the markedly reduced use of irritant cathartics and enemas. I suggest that misapplied efforts to regulate elimination by irritant substances, forced entries, and authoritarian dictates created lived experiences that stimulated associative allusions to explosive destructiveness, avalanches of water and filth, anal rape, and the necessity for self-protection from constipation. The experiential actuality of what has been called the anal phase will be quite different for infants trained with only the occasional use of mild stool softeners, no regular use of enemas, and no enema tube, with its frightening nozzle bag hanging threateningly in most bathrooms. The experience of the child being trained with only the tension of exhortation and mild frustration, mixed with patience and praise, does not lead to the earlier reported traumatic outcomes or persisting conflicts.

The connection between regulatory failures and the method of training can be illuminated by a case study that provides information about the procedures used and the affective state of attachment of the partners. Harley (1971) reports the analysis of another Anne, a child of five years who had a dog phobia and a tendency to retain feces when under stress. When Anne was not quite two, her sister was born and her fear of dogs began. Around this time, she was suddenly weaned from the bottle, and toilet training was instituted. Anne responded to the training effort with fierce resistance.

She was abruptly trained immediately following two events: an enema which the father administered while the mother held her forcibly on the bathroom floor; and a bowel movement which she finally produced later that same day after the mother had forced her to remain on the toilet seat for almost two hours. This forced movement re-

sulted in an anal fissure. Anne's fear of dogs now increased significantly, and for several weeks she was also afraid a zebra in the toilet
might bite her. A few weeks after her fourth birthday, her dog fear
assumed the proportions of a phobia [p. 36].

At a point in her analysis when "experiences related to her sister's
birth and the forced enema were being relived and interpreted in
the transference, Anne developed a fear of my toilet flush (and
none other) lest my dog be in the toilet bowl and bite her." (p. 36).

Another case is from a reconstruction made during the analysis
of an adult (Lichtenberg, 1983c). The patient, Mrs. S, began an hour
in the tenth month of her analysis by telling me about a dream she
had had in which she decided to use her basement for a child's
playroom. Her associations led me to ask if the dream might refer to
thoughts of touching or playing around her "basement" or bottom.
She recalled material she had previously related, that in college her
principal means of stimulating herself had been by wiping around
her anus. She had developed a perianal itch and had scratched herself until she bled. She added in passing that her mother had frequently given her enemas. She then began a familiar pattern of
talking very rapidly and excitedly. Her thoughts became loosely
connected images of people merged indistinctly, and the thread of
what she said became difficult or impossible to follow. I found myself experiencing a mild feeling of "here-we-go-again" puzzlement
because I was unable adequately to understand the meaning and
source of Mrs. S's state of excitement. I was concerned that my interventions were contributing to her overexcited states, but I knew
that not addressing her material would not be helpful. If I seemed
to her not to be responding, her rate of speech would slow down.
She complained of being unable to think. She felt tired, fogged out,
without vitality. By my suggestion about anal play I had offered
what I hoped would be a general orienting interpretation of her
dream about the child's playroom in the basement. She provided
confirmatory information pointing to perianal masturbation, added
mention of her mother's giving her enemas, and then, predictably,
began to become overexcited.

Puzzled once more, I reflexively said to myself, "Oh shit!" Then
I heard what I had said to myself and in a rapid-fire way associated:
shit-enemas-barrage of words-looser and looser content. With these
associations as a springboard, I postulated that she was trying
to express to me that the enemas and the attendant interaction
with her mother had played a significant organizing influence in
her childhood. I suggested to her that in some way she might be

reexperiencing, through her excited barrage of words, something akin to the buildup and explosion of tension and contents during an enema. She responded to this suggestion seriously and without additional excitement. She described how her mother had asked her daily if she had had a bowel movement. If she said yes, nothing would happen. But if she said no or hesitated, she would get an enema. Mother gave herself an enema daily. The hour ended with the sharing of this information.

With the patient's initiative and cooperation, the theme of the enema experiences occupied the center of the analysis for the next ten weeks. On the basis of her current reactions, I offered interpretive and reconstructive suggestions about what the enema experience had been like. She described memories of trying to hold back the contents of her bowel but finally exploding forth. She was afraid to displease her mother but would become overly excited. To avoid an enema, she would lie to her mother about having had a bowel movement. From this description of the struggle in the bathroom, I suggested to her that the angry feelings I was experiencing as exploding forth toward me through her barrage of words were what she had felt toward her mother for giving her the enemas. For the first time since my initial interpretation of the significance of her enema experience, she interrupted our joint effort to reconstruct their memory and meaning. She took up the idea of anger and again became overexcited, emitting a rush of increasingly disconnected associations about being angry.

I again was bewildered. My attention momentarily turned inward. Through introspection, I recognized that I felt mildly irritated, and I conjectured that I had interpreted her experience not from her state of mind but from my own. I had based my assessment of the importance of her anger over the enemas on the irritation *I* had felt as the target of her verbal overload. I had rationalized this inaccurate construction by assuming her reaction to be the angry struggle children commonly wage over having their bodies invaded (an issue that was to come up later). I recalled that she had told me she was asked about her bowel movements each day and concluded that obviously it was she who controlled the frequency of the enemas. I then conjectured that her reactivated, fragmented and overexcited state might be a response to my failure to continue to understand her inner feelings and thoughts after so promising a beginning.

I asked Mrs. S if her excited talking might have been stimulated by her feeling that I had failed to understand her true feelings about the enemas when I emphasized her anger. She did not respond

directly, but then calmly said that she remembered having wel-
comed the enemas. She had regarded them as indicating that her
mother cared about her enough to do something active. I was now
able to help her reconstruct a view of her family life considerably
different from the one she had previously presented. Before, she
had portrayed her father as her lover, who had courted her with
such gallantries as "You name it, honey, and I'll get it for you. Anything, anything at all." Now she said that these promises were generally hollow, like some of her insights and her "agreements" with
my suggestions. As she did with me, her father would get instantly
excited about any suggestion she made, but he did not follow
through in a practical way. Most important, he failed to help her
curb outbursts of outrageous behavior with effective discipline. I interpreted to her that the significance of the enemas was that their
administration meant to her that, unlike her father, her mother had
tried to impose order. Mother's method—the enemas—was indeed
faulty, but it was "real" in comparison with her father's. Bit by bit,
we reconstructed a set of feelings the enemas gave her. They made
her feel all cleaned out, her anger washed away, her wildness
dampened down, and her guilt reduced by the fantasy that she was
being punished for her misdeeds. But, most of all, that mother gave
them to her made her feel important, that she really mattered to
someone.

Mrs. S was trying to tell me that she felt her mother was making
a bona fide attempt to regulate her by the same means she herself
had learned and used for herself. She wanted me to appreciate the
regulatory motive she attributed to her mother before she could allow herself to recognize more fully the problems this form of regulation posed for her. Further exploration of the disregulatory effect
of the enemas, which had continued during her early school years,
followed my calling to her attention an overpayment in her check.
From the way she dealt with my noting the overpayment, I suggested that her overpayment might be an unconscious attempt to
get me involved in checking on the quantity of her bowel movements. The next hour she said that she had been drinking brandy
when paying her bills. After a while she noticed that she felt both
sick to her stomach and sexually aroused. She took a shower and
was afraid someone like her mother would come in and find her
sexually aroused. I suggested that in her verbal barrages she had
exposed to me her state of uncontrolled excitement. If I took it as
productive analytic work, I would in effect be reliving with her the
myth she and her mother had created that overstimulation by enema was healthful. Alternatively, if I did not collude with her in

that way and recognized the experience as problematic for her, she could separate herself from her attachment to her mother and join me in considering the meaning of the reenactment. She described how she had wanted mother to know about her state of sexual excitement, but was afraid that if she did tell her, her mother would take it away. I felt that now I could reconstruct the negative oedipal meaning of her enema experience. I suggested that she had come to enjoy the sensations and the intimacy of the enemas. Consequently her bowel and anal region, as well as the sensation of painful tension, had become sexualized, and she had developed a sensual orientation toward her mother.

In Mrs. S we see a person who as a child was subjected to a faulty regulatory procedure. This affected her adult life in the form of continuing difficulty in bowel regulation. It also impaired her ability to regulate her own daughter's elimination, the daughter having entered analysis shortly after the analytic work just described because of bed wetting. Because of these experiences, Mrs. S frequently feared that attachment opportunities would become overwhelmingly intrusive. Assertive and exploratory motives were often dominated by an overintensity that marred her performance and lessened her sense of competence. Aversive reactions took the form of barrages of disconnected words or of withdrawal and withholding. But their main effect was to add to the overstimulation of sensual enjoyment and sexual excitement that had their origins in experiences of direct sensual and sexual overexcitement by her seductive father. Put another way, the problem in the physiological regulation of elimination spread to all the other motivational systems, the regulation of which became very tenuous, and a separate but related problem in the sexual motives spread as well to the other motivational systems. Mrs. S thus frequently experienced motives she could only poorly regulate and that often seemed sexualized inappropriately.

THE NEED TO REGULATE TACTILE AND PROPRIOCEPTIVE STIMULATION

Since tactile and proprioceptive stimulation is not primary to erotogenic zone theory, it has, with few exceptions (Mittelmann, 1960; Kestenberg, 1965), received less attention than have hunger and elimination. Do small infants use touch as an independent source of information? Are objects grasped only so that they can be looked at, or mouthed, or rattled for sound? In an experiment reported by

Streri and Pecheaux (1986), 32 infants between four and six months were handed small plywood shapes, which they were prevented from seeing by an attached bib. The infants were found to handle and explore the objects intentionally until habituation (loss of interest) occurred. They slid their fingers over the surface, pressed over the edges, opened and closed their hands without dropping the plywood shapes, and attempted to pass the shapes from one hand to the other. Moreover, they could effectively discriminate between the forms. The information obtained from touch was processed approximately three times more slowly than information obtained visually. Manual exploration is essentially sequential, whereas visual perception is more holistic.

Shevrin and Tousseing (1965) have reviewed the literature on the need for tactile, proprioceptive, and kinesthetic stimulation. With support from infant neurological studies suggesting "that tactile experiences during the earliest months would be particularly salient" (Bronson, 1963, p. 58), Shevrin and Tousseing claim a centrality for "tactile conflicts," which I think might more readily be assumed for those hairy primates that attach literally by grasping (Kaufman, 1976) rather than by receptors of sight and sound. Whether central or not, the need for optimal tactile and proprioceptive stimulation is well supported; the evidence comes less from normal infants, for whom these functions simply fold into an ordinary fit with the caregiving environment than from pathological circumstances. These fall into two groups; in one, ordinary babies are subjected to extraordinary understimulation or overstimulation; in the other, the disturbance results from atypical sensitivities.

Institutionalized children observed by Provence and Lipton (1962) exemplify understimulated infants. When held, these infants reacted abnormally by the second month of life. Instead of molding into the holder's arms, they felt like sawdust dolls, stiff and wooden. By five to six months of age, most by eight months, institutionalized infants engaged in rocking without observable emotional involvement or excitement. In the institution, they slept for longer periods with fewer awakenings than babies raised in families. When the babies were moved to foster homes, the excessive sleep lasted for several weeks before a reduction in total hours of sleep accompanied an overall improvement in alert responsiveness. Shevrin and Tousseing (1965) account for these changes by theorizing a heightened threshold for tactile stimuli:

> When tactile gratification is insufficient in the first weeks and months of life, the craving created by this deficit will become more insistent.

When the insistence of the craving reaches some critical point, the receptor threshold for the craving will be raised to a high enough level to protect against receptor overloading and central disruption. Once this point is reached, a seemingly anomalous situation is created; its clinical manifestation is a condition in which any amount of tactile gratification is reacted to as if it were a danger [p. 327].

The danger the infant guards against is the triggering of so insistent a craving by *any* gratification that all actions and feelings would be dominated by tactile need, "thus making it almost impossible for other needs and adaptive requirements to be met" (p. 313). Shevrin and Tousseing cite limp hypotonic responses of some infants when held as well as the stiff, wooden, unpliable responses of the institutionalized infants. They see rocking without pleasure and the excessive sleep as a consequence of the raised threshold. Shevrin and Tousseing note that "it is more difficult for us to account for the readiness with which institutionalized infants give up their rocking on the approach of an adult. We would have predicted that they would be particularly unresponsive upon being approached" (p. 332). They suggest that possibly there is a difference between environmental deficits in congenitally normal infants and infants who manifest stimulus-processing disorders from the first days of life. Provence and Lipton (1962) suggest that these infants responded like sawdust dolls because they lacked the opportunity for experiences in mutual adaptation with a mother and had thus failed to learn an interactive molding to being held. The proprioceptive response of molding is, in my terms, a particular perceptual-affective-action pattern, innately programmed, and "designed" to unfold in a particular interactive matrix. When the matrix is deficient, mutual regulation does not occur. The perceptual-affective-action pattern loses its integrity, as it did when Anne Adams's legs were left dangling off her mother's lap. Once the opportunity occurs, the infant can set the pattern into motion and after a delay may restore a completely functional capacity.

Are the sawdust doll response, or hypotonia, the rocking, and the excess sleeping due to an elevated threshold that blocks out stimulation in order to protect against a craving so dominant as to exclude all other motivations? I suggest a simpler explanation. First, the lack of tone and molding capacity results from the caregiver's failure to provide an opportunity to exercise an innate functional capacity. Soon after the opportunity is provided, normal functioning is generally restored. Second, rocking is the result of a self-regulatory effort where mutual regulation is deficient. The rocking is not a self-initiated activity patterned from a mutual activity, such as cradling or rocking in the mother's arms or being rocked in the crib by the mother, and so lacks the pleasurable quality of those social experiences. Nor is the rocking a pattern whose aim is the practice of a skill being perfected toward competence with interest as an affect. It is simply the infant's effort to pursue a regulatory need in the best form he can self-originate. Third, increased sleeping, while it may represent a threshold phenomena neurophysiologically, is an early manifestation of aversion through withdrawal. This type of withdrawal into sleep was also shown by Anne Adams, who was deprived of both feeding and tactile and proprioceptive stimulation. Withdrawal from tactile contact and excessive sleeping is also described by Yarrow (1963) in two cases, one where a child was left untended by a foster mother who favored a more lively foster child and another where a child was transferred at eight months from an actively affectionate foster mother to a rejecting adoptive mother. That these are expressions of the aversive motivational system is attested to by the responsiveness these children were capable of when adequate tactile and proprioceptive stimulation was made available. In the foster home, with stimuli of intensity sufficient to activate or reactivate the motivation to seek and respond to tactile and proprioception need satisfaction, a normal sleep pattern was restored.

The significance of activating a tactile-proprioceptive functional capacity can be recognized from Bower's (1976) observation of the timing of walking. If properly supported, a newborn will march along a flat surface. This ability normally disappears at about eight weeks, but the exercise of this innate, programmed perceptual-affective-action pattern is recorded as a procedural memory. "It has been shown . . . that if an infant practices walking at the very early phase, the experience will accelerate the appearance of walking later" (p. 39). Of course, the early experience is not crucial for learning; walking as a self-activated pattern will occur with or without the earlier procedural "priming." But the importance of mutually regulatory activation of tactile and proprioceptive functions can be appreciated when the sawdust-doll feel of the institutionalized infants and Anne Adams's loosely dangling legs and later delayed walking are contrasted with the responses of infants whose parents proudly have them "walk" while they hold them, enjoying what their babies can do.

During ordinary experiences of caregiving infants with normal innate responsiveness are not apt to experience tactile and proprioceptive overstimulation except momentarily. Repeated excessive tickling, skin rubbing, harsh handling, and spanking are the exceptions. But for infants born with hypersensitivities, overstimulation is a serious problem, making regulation in this motivational system especially difficult. Examples are infants with the sensory integrative disorder referred to as tactile defensiveness. These infants evidence the paradoxical response of being painfully supersensitive to light touch but able to accept in a normal way deep firm pressure or proprioceptive activity. They react with aversive withdrawal to light touch, stroking, having air blown onto their exposed skin, and the skin touch of many different materials. They often try to wriggle out of the arms of anyone attempting to hold or soothe them.

The effects of this innate oversensitivity to tactile stimulation can be appreciated in the following observation of six-year old Jimbo. His teacher sat behind his desk and as she attempted to point to something, her hand rubbed lightly against his skin. Jimbo screamed, "You're hurting me! You know it? I don't want you to sit there! Sit here! [next to him]" (A. Lichtenberg, 1982). If the teacher tried to approach him, Jimbo would object vehemently; but if she sat quite still, he would cuddle up to her, holding on to her arm. When she initiated a firm touch such as a hearty pat on the back or a good handshake, he would react with less immediate aversion and then seem to experience the contact in a normal manner. The near presence, or even out-of-immediate-sight presence, of a person constituted a threat of being touched, so that Jimbo would yell at his mother five steps behind him on a staircase, "Stop pushing me," or scream at the teacher who was sitting too close for too long, "You're choking me." Jimbo would experimentally touch some substances—wooden cubes or woolen sweaters—very briefly, as though craving the sensation, but he could not persist in ordinary play with blocks. He would totally avoid other substances, like finger paint, glue, and paste. No matter how warm the weather, he was comfortable only when most of his skin surface was covered. After periods of treatment specifically designed to expose them to contacts, children like Jimbo may go through episodes of intensely seeking tactile experiences and human contacts as if they were making up for a deficit (Ayres, 1979; A. Lichtenberg, 1982).

CHAPTER 4

The Attachment-Affiliation Motivational System: Part 1

STATEMENT OF THE PROBLEM

WHEN ATTACHMENT IS CONCEIVED OF as a particular form of *behavior*, the criteria used to establish its existence are that the infant differentiates the object of attachment from other objects and that the infant displays characteristic affective responses to the presence and absence of the object. These criteria lend themselves to relatively easily testable hypotheses, and Bowlby's followers (Ainsworth, Sroufe, Main, and others) have conclusively demonstrated differentiation from the mother and specific affective responses to her presence and absence by one year of age.

When attachment is conceived of as an innately unfolding experience of human *relatedness*, criteria that would establish its existence are more difficult to satisfy. At an age when answers are difficult or impossible to obtain, how does the infant experience the "mother of attachment"? What is this experience like, first for the neonate, then the premobile young infant, the mobile older infant, and the toddler? If we use a concept of self for the inner experiencer, what evidence is there of "selfness"? Is attachment a uniform experience of relatedness or one that has different forms and gradients? Is attachment formed uniquely with one person—the mother or other primary caregiver alone—or additionally with father, siblings, and others?

When attachment is conceived of as a *motivational system*, additional criteria must be met. The motivations involved in attachment must be distinguished from the motivations involved in other systems. In the presence or absence of the mother, when is the infant not motivated to attach? Put another way, can we distinguish motives to engage the mother in attachment activities from motives to

disengage from attachment activities to pursue nonattachment activities? Attachment motives must be conceptualized as they persist
(have continuity) and as they alter in different stages of development. Furthermore, since I speak of an attachment-
affiliation-motivational system, the relationship of affiliative motives
to attachment motives must be clarified.

HISTORICAL COMMENTARY

In the late 1950s and early 1960s, Bowlby's (1958) provocative statement that he considered it a mistake to "give pre-eminence to sucking and feeding" (p. 366) over such attachment behaviors as
seeking, following, and clinging stirred a heated debate (A. Freud,
1960; Schur, 1960; Spitz, 1960). Some of the debate moved off the
essential claim about the significance of attachment behaviors onto
questions about definitions of primary drives or onto Bowlby's collateral claims about early bereavement, grief, and mourning. The
central issue was, and remains, Bowlby's (1960) claim that the
child's tie to mother "is best conceived as the outcome of a number
of instinctual response systems, mostly nonoral in character, which
are a part of the inherited behavior repertoire of man; when they
are activated and the mother figure is available, attachment behavior results" (p. 9). To distinguish my view from Bowlby's, and to
remove myself from the either/or nature of the early debates, I
would paraphrase Bowlby's claim: one of a number of important aspects of the child's tie to his mother and to others as well is best
conceived as the outcome of patterns that make up an innate, preprogrammed motivational system. These patterns and those of the
other motivational systems are a part of the inherited behavior repertoire of human beings; when the patterns expressive of this motivational system are activated by the infant and their interdigitating
counterparts in the mother are activated, attachment as a mutually
regulatory experience results. My shift is from oral or nonoral pre-
eminence to that of five motivational systems; from the infant as
activator and the mother as available to the interactional (feedback)
activator-responder interplay of both; from instinctual behavior to
mutual regulation; from attachment as behavior to attachment as an
experience of intimacy pleasure.

Current infant observation makes Bowlby's (1958) suggestion that
the infant has a few instinctual patterns of behavior that serve the
biological function of binding child and mother to each other seem
an unlikely source of vigorous debate. When it was put forth, the

whole issue of attachment became embroiled in the raging controversies between sexual drive theorists and object relations theorists. Bowlby specified five patterns: crying and smiling, which evoke maternal responses; and sucking, following, and clinging, through which the infant actively seeks and sustains contact and proximity. No one questioned that babies exhibit these behaviors within a few months of birth, but what was their aim? Was it to ensure libidinal gratification and thereby diminish tension according to the pleasure principle, or was it to ensure survival through attachment as such, with its increase in stimuli and tension in violation of the pleasure principle? In theory building today, some of the heat has gone out of these arguments, largely because of the relatively lower value placed by many analysts on the economic point of view as it applies to libido as a specific form of energy.

The view I am putting forth here is that there is a false dichotomy inherent in the argument about whether the infant, in crying, smiling, sucking, following, and clinging, is motivated by the need for a gratification that would lower tension, such as feeding, or a motivation that would raise tension, such as the attachment behaviors of reciprocal smiling or touching. Both are motivations a baby may have serially or more or less simultaneously. Which motivational system is dominant cannot be determined by the behavior alone. A baby's following her mother with her eyes or crawling toward her could indicate a hungry baby's search for the bottle, a contact-craving baby's search for the mother of attachment, or an exploratory baby's interest in mother's dangling earrings. As observers, we attempt to decide by the context and trial-and-error responses, but the real answer can come only from sensing the inner world of the infant and what he or she is experiencing. For psychoanalytic theory, the careful observations of behaviors that contribute to the infant's special relationship to caretakers provide the starting point to ask the difficult questions about how this builds coherence in the inner world. Ainsworth (1967) offers this formulation:

> Attachment is manifested through these patterns of behavior but the patterns do not themselves constitute the attachment. Attachment is internal. We can conceive of attachment as somehow being built into the nervous system, in the course of and as a result of the infant's experience of his transactions with his mother and with other people. This internalized something that we call attachment has aspects of feelings, memories, wishes, expectancies, and intentions, all of which constitute an inner program acquired through experience and somehow built into a flexible yet retentive inner mechanism . . . which serves as a kind of filter for the reception and interpretation of inter-

personal experience and as a kind of template shaping the nature of outwardly observable response [pp. 429–430].

Ainsworth's restatement of Bowlby is an important advance. She shifts the definition of attachment from *behavior* to an "internalized something" that "has aspects of feeling, memories, wishes, expectancies and intentions." In traditional psychoanalytic theory, such an internalized something would be called a psychic structure having aspects of id and ego. In my usage, Ainsworth is defining a motivational *system*. This system builds complexity, beginning with the innate perceptual-affective-action patterns described by Bowlby. These patterns initiate a call for responsiveness, which I term needs. A receptivity to her infant's call, as well as a desire to help her baby initiate the call, is a wish of the mother, derived from her attachment motivational system. Thus, the caregiver's readiness to respond is, I believe, equally a part of attachment. In my definition, attachment is not what a caregiver does to, or for, or with a baby or what an infant does to, or for, or with a caregiver. Rather, it is a mutual interregulation resulting from the activation of the relevant motivations and functions of both. Each contributes the shaping, tone, and intensity that characterize the pairing of infant and mother and infant and father. Memories of prior interactions build response foundations for expectancies and repetitions within a fluid system of modifications based on variations that can be integrated. With these definitional descriptions, we remain at the level of "mechanics." What remains is the still more difficult question, what is the experience that characterizes the unfolding of attachment? This, I believe, is the core question that underlies the extensive exploration of the data from infant observation to be found in Stern's (1985) *The Interpersonal World of the Infant*. Stern phrases it differently: "I will attempt to draw inferences about the infant's subjective social experience from this new data base" (p. 5). Social experience, even in infancy, is far broader than attachment; but since attachment, or, as Stern puts it, the "quality of relatedness" (p. 186), is so central to the infant's social life, the main theme of Stern's book is the experience of the unfolding of this motivational system. Stern asks, "Where can we start inventing infants' subjective experience of their own social life?" and gives an answer that correlates with mine: "I plan to start by placing the sense of self at the very center of the inquiry" (p. 5).

In fact, the senses of self of two (or more) persons occupy the center of the inquiry. One, the infant's sense of self, which is emerging, consolidating a core, and becoming subjectivity aware, interacts with the other, the caregiver's sense of self, which is stable and employs conscious and unconscious symbolic representation (and unconscious procedural memory). A logical way to address the interaction of the forming self of the infant and the formed self of the caregiver is to follow the central thread of relatedness, as Stern has done. Others have singled out such dimensions as communication, informational exchange, and learning, which Stern uses to develop his conception. I shall begin with these.

COMMUNICATION AS ATTACHMENT

Bowlby singles out crying and smiling to evoke maternal responses, and sucking, following, and clinging to actively seek proximal contact. Here attachment takes on its literal meaning, to attach. But the broader meaning, stated by Ainsworth (1967) as an inner program acquired through experience, invites consideration of nonproximal attachment by visual and auditory informational exchange. Papousek, Suomi, and Rahn (1986) turn the issue around, putting communication first:

> Human communication is based on an innate integrative and communicative preadaptedness, including learning, categorization, imitation, and overt expressions of two fundamental regulatory alternatives, the one being interpretable as approach and assimilation, often perceived as pleasure, and the other related to avoidance, rejection, and displeasure [p. 3].

How adapted are infant and caregiver to preverbal communication? Infants read to from Dr. Seuss books while in utero evidence recognition of the sound pattern after birth (De Casper and Fifer, 1980). What this means is that, by birth, infants can process phonological contrasts. Eimas et al. (1971) summarizes a considerable body of experiments conducted by himself and a group of other researchers. The point of departure of these studies is not attachment or even communication per se, but rather the question of why it is that the human child masters language without the formal training needed to learn reading or arithmetic. The infant must have an innate capacity to process the basic elements of speech, such as prevoiced and delayed voice onset time; positions of stops in articulation; categories of vowels, liquids, and glides; and pitch contours.

In one of the experiments reported by Eimas and colleagues, infants from one to four months old were tested by measuring their sucking rates or their heart rates. When exposed to a sound such as "bah," they responded first with interest, evidenced by an increase in sucking or heart rate. When the sound was repeated, interest waned and the activity rate diminished. Then another sound, "pah," was introduced. It evoked a sudden rise in sucking or heart rate. How did the infants distinguish between these different sounds? Where they sensitive to the gradations of change from "bah" or "pah," as they might be in visually discerning the gradations of change from blue to yellow? Apparently not, for the response of the infants exposed to synthetic sounds that produced gradients was abrupt, not gradual. Clearly, in the innate process, each sound was heard as a separate category, just as primary colors are perceived as separate categories. Thus, perceptual categories—not continuous gradations in the acoustic properties of the speech signal—shape the perception of speech. Like adults, infants respond categorically both to acoustic cues that differentiate the place of articulation of a consonant and to other cues that signal the distinctions between nasal and stop consonants, such as those between "mah" and "bah," and between stop consonants and semivowels, such as the initial sound of "wah." In a different experimental design (Kuhl et al., cited in Eimas, 1985), the attention of six-month-old infants was held by a toy while a vowel sound /a/ (as in pop) was repeated over a loudspeaker. When the vowel /i/ (as in peep) interrupted the sequence, the infant turned away from the toy and toward the loudspeaker. The infant was rewarded by the sight of an illuminated mechanical stuffed rabbit on top of the loudspeaker. When acoustically less distinct vowels were used, the infants could still detect the differences, although less reliably.

How sensitive to the functions of communication and attachment are these innate processing skills? In another of the experiments reported by Eimas et al. (1971), six-month-olds who could detect vowel changes readily were confronted with arbitrarily chosen variants never found in human speech. They could neither differentiate automatically nor be trained to do so in spite of rewarding. They responded only when the background and contrasting sequences represented categories of sound that are components of ordinary human vocal exchanges. This finding adds weight to the evidence that the inborn mechanisms are specialized for human speech perception. These findings also make a strong case for an innate foundation for a perceptual side of communication that operates at or before birth and facilitates the swift acquisition of language. What evidence is there for attachment to the specific linguistic environment of the infant's family? Are babies who will later speak English born with the ability to discriminate the sounds of English, but not the sounds of Hindi or Kikuyu that their adult counterparts normally do not master? When tested, these infants proved to have the same ability to process categorically distinctions important in other languages. This was true of infants the world over. But while the distinctions were readily recognized at six to eight months by infants from an English-speaking background, at 12 months, the infants could not detect the same contrasts that adults fail to master. In other words, infants in the second half of the first year are so sensitive to the nuances of the language spoken to them by people to whom they are attached that their perceptual acuity patterns are already set to reflect that attachment. The capacity itself is not lost; given the right opportunities, adults can be retrained to perceive the nonnative distinctions. For example, after considerable experience with spoken English, native speakers of Japanese can distinguish *r* and *l* categorically almost as accurately as native English speakers can. The central determinant of this discriminatory acuity is not the lack of opportunity to function and a resulting loss of ability; it is, I suggest, primarily an affinity for one's family's speech, perceived with categorical discrimination even before birth. When this discrimination becomes highly selective, by the age of one year, the infant responds to speech that qualifies as the "mother tongue." Moreover, powerful as innate categorical perceptual capacity is, this ability could not account for the perception of all the possibilities within a given language without the focus provided by a search for meaning. The multitude of vowel categories of different languages points to the necessity for experience with speech in a meaningful context to augment innate detectors.

Although infants are born with an hitherto unexpected capacity for speech perception, they have for some time only a limited capacity for vocalization and must rely for the first two months principally on crying. Crying is more than a vocalization; it involves also an appearance of helplessness. The combination is a powerful elicitor of parental response (Ainsworth and Bell, 1969; Emde, 1981a). Crying thus has the advantage of providing a strong alerting signal, not easily ignored. But it has several disadvantages as a form of communication. First, it sends a relatively indiscrete message. Although Wolff (1969) claims there is a discernible difference between a hunger cry and a pain cry, there is no general agreement that a clear difference exists. Most observations of maternal responses indicate that caregivers depend on the context in which the crying occurs, as recognized from past experience, to be able to discern the nature of the infant's distress. Second, crying produces a state in which receptiveness to information is minimal compared with that in alert wakefulness or alert inactivity or even drowsiness. Third, crying may sometimes have a negative effect on the caregiver, arousing aversive responses rather than a concerned search for the cause of the distress. One study of child abuse (Bell, 1975) indicates that a child in a large family may, by shrill crying, provoke battering. Prechtl (1963) found that persistent crying with rapid and unpredictable state changes elicited rejecting and overanxious attitudes from seven of eight mothers at the end of the first year. Alternatively, when crying summons prompt, distress-relieving responses, the fit between mother and infant leads, in later infancy, to less frequent resort to crying as a signal of distress and more frequent use of other means of communication (Ainsworth and Bell, 1969). The infant does not treat the prompt responsiveness as a "reward" for crying—which would lead to more crying, as might be predicted by stimulus-response theory—but as a communicative success, creating confidence in communicative attempts.

With the exception of the cry, the newborn cannot control breathing sufficiently to prolong expiration for modulating vocal sounds. As control of subglottal air pressure improves during the first eight to ten weeks of life, the duration of occasional vowellike vocal utterances increases, and gliding intonation contours appear in pitch with increasing frequency. The fundamental voicing acquires the traits of a musical instrument. These melodic intonations both give pleasure to caregivers and allow them to differentiate changes in internal states (Papousek et al, 1986). When the infant is between two and three months old, modulations in the fundamental vowellike voicing alone enable a "conversational" interchange between caregiver and infant, from which the caregiver can understand much about what the infant likes and dislikes. The production of elementary consonantlike sounds between three and six months does not change the basic pleasure sound of melodic cooing. It adds variety to the sounds infants themselves practice or play with during monologues. In the dialogues with the caregiver, the infant's vocalizations become increasingly intentional contributions to their exchanges. After seven months, the intentional quality is more demonstrable, in that vocal runs are often of shorter duration with rapid transition from signals of pleasure to signals of aversion.

In the first year, the infant is thus innately programmed to provide signals through vocalizations that increasingly resemble speech. In this way, infant vocalizations serve as communications that further attachment. However, much of the infant's vocalization expresses exploratory-assertive motives. The infant practices and plays with sound, exploring vocal and "musical" possibilities, exclusive of future linguistic meaning as vocal symbols. This activity remains in memory as a procedure that is practiced and learned. Vocal practicing helps the infant to learn through self-initiated efforts. The memory of making melodic intonations remains a part of every human's procedural repertoire, a way of vocalizing that emphasizes the speech contours we refer to as "baby talk." Starting at around two or three years of age, boys and girls will spontaneously and automatically talk baby talk when speaking to young infants.

Infants, then, are born equipped to respond to human speech elements in their phonetic categories and to be increasingly varied vocalizers. They are thereby adapted to play their part in a communicative dialogue with their caregivers. What does the caregiver contribute to the communicative exchange? Papousek and Papousek (1986) report a surprisingly large proportion of relevant, unintentional, intuitive components on the parental side of these interchanges. One intuitive behavior caregivers invariably employ is engaging the infant in eye contact. This action—holding the infant in the midline 9 to 12 inches in front of the parent's face or gazing down at a feeding infant—sets up an intimacy pleasurable to both participants. In addition, eye contact draws the infant's attention to the caregiver's face, especially to the complex display of movements in the perioral and periorbital areas. Infants are visually engaged by both vocal and nonvocal communicative signals and affect displays, which they often imitate. Parents intuitively accompany recognition of the infant's return eye focus with a greeting response, "Hi ya!" in a high pitched voice. By two months, infants can count on this greeting and can themselves "reward" the parent with a smile. The greeting is but one of many means parents have to provide young infants with a large number of episodes, often 20 per minute, during parent-infant interactions, when the parents make themselves contingent, easily predictable, and manipulatable by the infant (Papousek and Papousek, 1977). The parents may have one set of routines and verbal pattern for feeding, another for bathing, and another for diaper changing. The evening feeding may be a more leisurely social time, day feedings more businesslike. Awakening may be slow and gentle or lively and cheery. A parent's homecoming time may develop its own ritual of kissing, arousal, or tossing about. With each, the infant signals, "I like it, do it again", or "Not today, I'm too fussy", or "It's too fast, I'm startled", or "I'm tiring, let's stop." The content of the caregiver's prattle may reflect this mutual regulatory exchange. Parents may ask questions and answer them: "Is baby hungry? I should say so!" Instead of using the speech form of adult questions and answers, parents may use speech to get attention: "Is baby hungry"; to praise: "What a good girl"; to soothe: "Oh tut, tut, tut, that's all right honey"; to share a problem: "Aw, oh"; to lullaby: "Sweetheart, sweetheart, close your little eyes." It is not the lexical but the prosodic message that plays the dominant role and represents the first prototypical speech offering to presyllabic infants (Papousek et al., 1985). Parents the world over follow the same essential pattern in talking to infants, a pattern as tuned to the infant's receptive capacities as any design could make it. These speech registers are characterized by syntactic simplicity, segmentation, a slow tempo, a limited repertoire of highly repetitive, expressive melodic patterns enhanced by pitch variations using endings with an overall rise (Stern, MacKain, and Spieker, 1982).

In studies of parental use of baby talk, three features stand out. First, parents are unaware of many of their communicative behaviors in spite of the obvious relevance of these behaviors to the developing social communication. Second, parents unknowingly include in their intuitively developed repertoires many potentially didactic interventions, so that learning is a continuous process in the parent-infant exchanges. Third, when, by experimental design, parents alter their intuitive behaviors, changing the contingency and predictability of the patterns, infants become upset and display aversive responses (Papousek and Papousek, 1977).

I believe the evidence to be convincing that communication is a major regulatory feature of the parent-infant social exchange. What evidence indicates that it is also an integral contributor to attachment? As I stated earlier, within 10 days breast-fed infants develop a smell recognition and preference for their mother's used breast pad (MacFarlane, 1975). At this same time, they turn their heads preferentially to their mother's voice rather than to their father's or that of another woman (Brazelton, 1980).

> The contrast of the infant's behavior and attention span when he was interacting with his mother, rather than an inanimate object, was striking as early as four weeks of age. . . . You could indeed tell from looking at a toe or a finger whether the infant was in an interaction with an object or a parent—and by four weeks of age, even which parent it was" [Brazelton and Als, 1979, pp. 357–359].

Thus, very young infants react with differential, preferential, and discriminatory recognition to their mothers. But are the infants reacting to mother's smell or physiognomy or vocal pattern as disco-ordinate experiences? In an experiment reported by Beebe and Stern (1977), mothers approached their six-week-old infants, who were lying quietly, and placed their face in the babies' visual field. The infants responded with mounting excitement all over their bodies. If mother, following instructions, held her face expressionless and was silent, the infant at first increased responsive feedback gestures and vocalizing. When mother failed to respond, the infant's efforts became more frenetic and disorganized, until finally the baby lapsed into a pained immobility. The infants clearly expected a coordination between the visual and the auditory stimuli presented normally by their mothers.

An experiment by Kuhl and Meltzoff (1982) describes the richness of the coordinate response to vision and speech of 18–20-week-old infants. Thirty-two infants were shown two juxtaposed filmed images of a woman's face articulating, in synchrony, two different vowel sounds, a sequence of ten /a/ vowels (as in pop) and ten /i/ vowels (as in peep). When the sound track presented one or the other vowel sounds, 73.6% of the infants detected the correspondence between the aurally and visually perceived speech information; they looked longer at the face that matched the sound. The experimenters then set out to determine what auditory information the infants used to detect the correspondence between a sound and its facial articulation. Instead of the vowels being presented with consonants (pop and peep), the vowels alone were presented as computer-generated sounds. Now only 54.6% of the infants could match the face to the sound. A vowel accompanied by a consonant, as it would be in normal speech, was the principal information that the infants detected. A further observation added another dimension. Ten infants who heard the vowels presented as they would be in normal speech produced vowel sounds that resembled the adult female's. As in conversational games with their parents, the infants were taking turns, alternating their imitations with the speech of the woman on the film.

We can draw several conclusions from these experimental findings. First, young infants are predisposed to recognize information picked up by different modalities, vision and hearing, and to integrate this information. Thus, sound is more than sound; it is related to articulation as it is produced normally in the form of ordinary human speech. Second, the intermodal equivalences of a speech sound and the visually perceived articulation of that sound are commonly augmented and integrated with imitated motor and vocally emitted copies formed in a conversational, take-turns fashion.

Meltzoff and Moore (1977) have demonstrated that the facial movements component of this imitation, with or without the vowel
sound, can be imitated by infants of one month. Third, we can
speculate that infants are experiencing their mothers not as bits and
pieces of stimuli—a sound plus a sight that they have to put together laboriously (the part object theory)—but as an integrated
whole. The nature of this integrated whole is interactional; that is,
mother the speaker (her articulating face, her vocalizations, her
movements, her affect) is a perceptual-affective-action pattern coordinated with a perceptual-affective action pattern of the infant's.
What Kuhl and Meltzoff's (1982) experiment using filmed images
does not demonstrate is that the prototypic capacity the face reveals
will, in the naturalistic setting, be experienced with its particulars—
mother's own facial and vocal qualities, her affect and timing, the
special vitality of her "Hi yah." It is this special quality into which
her son or daughter becomes swept up.

"Being swept up" indicates, I believe, a powerful motive to engage in communicative exchange, to explore the specifics of attachment, and to learn the nature of the interregulation of an emergent
self and an empathic engaging caregiver. Using the language of systems theory, Brazelton (1980) states that as a young infant becomes

> able to organize preprogrammed and learned responses in order to
> reach out for and respond appropriately to an external stimulus or
> toward a whole adult behavioral set, he gets energized in such a pow-
> erful way that one can easily see the base for his entrainment. The
> matching of his responses to those in the external world must feel so
> rewarding that he quickly becomes available to entrain with them,
> and he becomes energized to work toward inner controls and toward
> states of attention which maintain his availability to those external
> sequences. In this way, "entrainment" becomes a larger feedback sys-
> tem which adds a regulating and encompassing dimension to the two
> feedback systems of internalized control and of externalized stimulus-
> response. Hence, entrainment becomes an envelope within which he
> can test out and learn about both of his feed-back systems [p. 224].

Brazelton's statement describes the infant's motivation, his being
"energized in such a powerful way," to match his responses to
those in the external world and to test out and learn about the experience of his emerging capacities and the mother with whom he
is interacting. Put in much simpler terms, a particular mother's
style captivates her infant, who senses her not only as an audience
but as a full participant in the "play." But we know that not every
performance has an equally captivating effect on an audience, at-

taching the responder with equal intensity. Infants whose mothers speak to them in tender and modulated styles will respond with greater vocalizations of their own, whereas when depressed mothers employ an affectively impoverished style, infants are less responsive.

I agree with Papousek et al. (1986a) that to interpret attachment, we must consider not only social learning but intrinsic releasers and reinforcers of integrative processes, emotional expressions, and social communication. To communicate is both a motive and a functional capacity of great power in the formation of attachment in the preverbal period of infancy as well as later. But being in active communication is only one facet of the motive for attachment, as can be seen more clearly as we consider Stern's (1985) concepts of different forms of relatedness.

FORMS OF RELATEDNESS AND ATTACHMENT

Is a Lengthy Period of Differentiation of Self a Developmental Necessity?

While the evidence that attachment *behavior* unfolds from the earliest days of life now appears to be incontrovertible, the implications for attachment as an experience of neonates and maturing infants remains a subject of lively debate. In this debate, Stern (1985) has taken a radical position, which has called into serious question the stance of many psychoanalytic theoreticians that there is a lack of differentiation between self and object. In these theories it was a seldom questioned assumption that infants experience themselves as without boundaries or any means to appreciate distinctions between themselves and their surroundings or between one aspect of their surroundings and another. A major task characteristic of infancy was thus to differentiate self from other and mother from all animate and inanimate others. This assumption was based on three supports: First, the functional equipment of the infant, even the primary autonomous ego functions of perception, memory, and motor control recognized by Hartmann (1964), did not seem remotely sufficient to permit the discrimination between self representation and object representations until the end of the first year. Second, difficulties forming or maintaining boundaries between self-representations and the representations of others were ubiquitous in all psychoses, borderline and narcissistic disorders, and at some moments in the transferences of even the most classical psychoneurotics. Third, merger fantasies, often associated with feeding and with sleep (Lewin's, 1950, oral triad), are universal in myth, literature, the visual arts, and dance and are easily evoked when one watches mothers with small babies.

A challenge to the assumption of a long period of slowly worked out differentiation was mounted by adherents of Klein and Fairbairn, who assumed that object seeking was necessary for the infant's survival against the destructive potential of the death instinct or internally destructive drive energies. In their theories, boundaries having very fluid demarcations exist from the beginning, and interchanges of primitive drive derivatives, by way of projection and introjection, characterize the infant's relatedness with a part-object breast. Non-Kleinian analysts met this challenge with a combination of rebuttal and absorption. A central point in the rebuttal was that the timetable of presumed happenings in the neonate and young infant hypothesized from reconstructions was not supported by empirical evidence. Thus, non-Kleinian analysts have argued that the Kleinian timetable is a less likely fit with existing knowledge of infant behavior than is the more prolonged developmental stage hypothesis of traditional analytic theory. Further, non-Kleinian analysts could buttress their timetable with observations of Spitz (1959), A. Freud (1965), Provence and Lipton (1962), Pavenstedt (1956), and others.

However, with an altered timetable, the idea that the infant relates first to part objects and later to whole objects in itself was completely compatible with the concept of stages of differentiation of the object (Lichtenberg, 1979). Furthermore, those aspects of Kleinian theory that would give greater weight to aggression, balancing it more evenly with libido in a dual drive theory, could be appropriated from the Kleinian canon and incorporated into modifications of ego psychology. For Jacobson (1964), this led to an emphasis on fusion and defusion and an extremely complex relationship between self- and object representations in which introjection was an early means of transforming relatedness into internal structure. For Kernberg (1975, 1976) and Mahler (1968), the path from Klein led to an emphasis on splitting as the normal means of experiencing early relatedness (Lichtenberg and Slap, 1973). The emphasis they placed on splitting gave rise to a different version of the problem of differentiation. Infants needed first to organize their experience along hedonic lines—all good and pleasurable versus all bad and painful—and then relate self and object in each pairing to self and object in the other. This required, in Mahler's (1968, 1975) view, a long process of three years before object (and self-) constancy. Any challenge to the preexisting assumption of differentiation as a basic task of infancy that arose from Klein was blunted by differing hypotheses about what needed to be differentiated and how differentiation was to come about. For Kernberg (1975, 1976), differentiation followed the path from destructive aggressiveness based on oral greed and envy, through splitting, to more ego-integrating mechanisms of repression. For Mahler, differentiation followed the path from autism, and all attention turned inward in coenesthetic experience to symbiotic relatedness through splitting and the process of separation-individuation to object constancy. Further support for construing differentiation as a step-by-step task came from the observations of Piaget (1936, 1937) and his concepts of the construction of the nature of space and of objects. While taking a totally differing stance about drives and the significance of relatedness and of affects, Piagetian and psychoanalytic theories have many correspondences in their respective accounts of stages or phases of development (Greenspan, 1979).

In opposition to the timetables and formulations of both Kleinians and non-Kleinians, Stern (1985) mounts his argument that data about infants, most of which were collected subsequent to the work of the theoreticians mentioned,[1] points to radically different conclusions. Stern asserts that by approaching the question of differentiation without preconception, psychoanalysts can find support for the contention that a differentiated self forms early in life without going through phases of fusion or symbiotic merger. Collaterally, Stern asks, if a differentiated core self develops directly, are others (non-self) perceived as also differentiated? From the point of view of my thesis about motivational systems, these are crucial issues. If attachment is a motive linked to innate functional capacities and responded to by a corresponding attachment-motivational thrust from caregivers, but the infant does not differentiate self from caregiver, then would not attachment alone be the sole motive of neonates and developing infants? How could we conceptualize other motivations unless infants differentiate a "self" out of the merged interactional matrix? For example, how could we construe a separate motivational system involving exploration and assertion or a system involving psychic regulation of physiological requirements without implying some differentiation of self and, particularly, of others? For my thesis of separate motivational systems to be correct, an

---

[1] In the instance of Mahler, the timing of the data collections overlaps considerably. The issue is not that there are not new data, but that the Mahlerian playroom observations were made on infants older than six months.

emergent self must be able to experience differentially one moment dominated by the need for attachment with affects of pleasure-in-intimacy and another moment dominated by the need to explore and to act assertively with affects of interest and pleasure in competence. Similarly, an emergent self must be able to experience differentially the human responsiveness of attachment provided by a caregiver and the human or inanimate object available for exploratory investigation.

THE SENSE OF A DIFFERENTIATED CORE SELF

Stern (1985) argues that if the evidence of observation and research indicates that the infant can experience agency, coherence, affects, and continuity, the development of an organized sense of a core self can be assumed. Stern reasons that the ordinary events in the life of the developing infant must guarantee consistent opportunities for the repeated experience of agency, coherence, affects, and continuity. From their experiences in social interactions, infants can draw inferences about themselves. From their experiences in nonsocial activities, infants can draw different inferences about themselves. Each set of inferences adds to the sense of self.

For a sense of self-agency to form, infants must experience a sense of volition behind their motor acts. The sense of volition could not develop if infants' motor activities were random "discharge" movements, if infants were not aware that their actions were occurring, or if infants lacked the potential for awareness of the consequences of their actions. Observations of neonates indicate that little truly random activity occurs. Within a few days of birth, the apparently random movements of the hands in front of the eyes lead to visual tracking and, often by ten days, enough control to bring the thumb or other fingers into the mouth (Murphy, 1973). By four months, infants preshape their fingers and hands to fit the size of an object they are reaching to grasp (Bower et al., 1970). Tracking with eyes and turned head, putting fingers in the mouth, and grasping objects are consistently repeated motor acts performed by infants with or without the presence of caregivers. Repeated with equal consistency are motor acts that make up the social interactions. In fact, as Stern documents, how caregivers conduct themselves in social interactions guarantees both high levels of engagement and repetition for their infants. Caregivers move into their babies' focal gaze range, speak baby talk with exaggerated pitch contours, and exhibit exaggerated facial displays. Each adult is apt to use a characteristic theme and variation format, repeating the same words several times, with only minor variations in language, cadence, or emphasis. Body touching games (I'm going to get you; this little piggy; hide and seek) all have a basic format and an infinity of minor variations. It is evident from observing these exchanges that the adult is discovering and regulating the level of alertness and excitability the baby responds to with interest and pleasure. Less immediately evident, but clearly recognizable from split-screen video, is the active regulation infants exercise by averting their gaze and head to discontinue when overstimulated or by facial and body cues to activate repetitions. "When one watches infants play their role in these mutual regulations, it is difficult not to conclude that they sense the presence of a separate other and sense their capacity to alter the behavior of the other as well as their own experience" (Stern, 1985, p. 75).

If we accept the evidence that infants exercise organized, seemingly volitional motor acts when alone or when in social interaction, we can ask by what mechanisms infants are aware of their own activities and distinguish between those occurring in different situations. As I described in chapter 3, proprioceptive and tactile sensations are consistent sources of feedback information not only when infants are moving their bodies, but also when they are at rest, maintaining an antigravity position (Papousek and Papousek, 1979). Infants can simultaneously experience tactile and proprioceptive sensations in two body parts, as when moving the thumb into the mouth. When grasped by their mothers, infants experience sensations only at the site of the grasp, with tactile sensation predominating over the passive proprioceptive. When infants reach for an external object, the sensation is of the movement and the tactile experience of touching or grasping. These sensory experiences alone would be a shaky reed on which to hang a belief in the development of self-agency were it not that infants are remarkably skilled trackers of contingencies (chapter 6). By the age of three months, infants can distinguish between situations in which each turn of the head is rewarded, or when every third turn is rewarded, or when the reward is more variable. Thus, when their interest is aroused, each act infants perform contains a sequence of initiation → awareness of movement → awareness of the effect that results. Bringing the thumb to the mouth is a self-initiated action experienced proprioceptively as arm and thumb move and tactilely and proprioceptively as the mouth is entered and sucking begins, and then experienced as pleasurable in effect. Once mastered, it has 100% predictability. If the mother tickles the infant's tummy, no volition or initial proprioception is involved, only the effect. If the mother holds the baby's wrists and plays pat-a-cake before the baby knows the game, the infant experiences proprioception but not volition. "It is in this way that the infant is in a position to identify those invariants that specify a core self, core other, and the various amalgams of these invariants that specify self-with-other" (Stern, 1985, p. 80).

Again, accepting that awareness of volition, proprioception, and contingent effect secure for the three- to six-month-old a sense of agency, does that agency have a locus? How does the self become experienced as a single, coherent, bounded physical entity? How is the infant able to experience others as coherent entities distinct from the self? The clearest situation occurs when the infant is in a relatively static position and is responding to mother at some distance in the same room. The infant perceives mother moving against a background as a coherent entity, each part of her body and her voice forming a single unit occupying a single locus in space. The appreciation of time adds an additional identifying feature to the coherence of self and other. Separate parts of the body must move "together synchronously to a split second, in the sense that starts, stops, and changes in direction or speed in one muscle group will occur synchronously with starts, stops, and changes in other muscle groups" (Stern, 1985, p. 83). You can't "pat your head, rub your belly, and count all at the same time" (p. 84). Infants' voices heard in their own ears and resonating in their chest, eye scanning, touch, and proprioceptive sensations share a common temporal structure, whereas the sounds, sight and movements of others have a different temporal structure. For coherence of others to be appreciated, the infant must be able to distinguish some features from others. Mother must be the same person whether she is wearing different clothes or whether she is smiling, surprised, or angry. Infants are helped in this recognition by their cross-modal perceptual ability—mother still smells and sounds and moves the same, so the disparity of the visual cue is more easily disregarded. By using information from one orientation of presentation or from one sensory mode, infants can keep track of the identity of an object despite changes in size or distance or position. Fagan (1976, 1977) found that five- to seven-month-old infants exposed to a full-face or a three-quarter view could recognize a profile never seen before. And recall that when five-month-old infants were shown a movie of a car approaching and another of a car receding, they would look at the car whose movement matched the sound becoming louder or softer (Walker-Andrews and Lennon, 1984).

Along with the perceptual-action patterns that give coherence to the emerging sense of self, consistency of affective experience provides repeated invariant augmentation to each experience. Inherent affect patterns of joy, interest, surprise, distress, and anger appear at birth or within a few months. Each categorical affect is rich in potential for heightening awareness of self. In addition to the qualities of feeling that we ordinarily identify as a particular emotion, each affect experience consists of specific patterns of proprioceptive and tactile feedback from the facial skin and musculature, alterations in respiration and blood-flow rate, vocal accompaniments, and patterns of arousal and activation integrated with the affect (Tomkins, 1962, 1963; Ekman, Levenson, and Friesen, 1983). Attraction is integrated with interest and joy; withdrawal or antagonism is integrated with distress and anger. Infants thus have information about their affective state that is consistently localized within the self regardless of the manifold sources of stimuli that might trigger the affect.

Nachman and Stern (1984) tested their hypothesis that infants recall affects they have experienced previously. Seven-month-old boys and girls were exposed to hand-puppets. One group witnessed a rousing game of peek-a-boo with the puppets and smiled in response. The other group witnessed a neutral, unarousing facsimile of the game. A week later, when observing the same puppets, the smilers looked preferentially to the smile-evoking puppets and smiled again, even though now the puppets were *stationary*. The infants who had been exposed to the neutral scene did not smile and looked away from the puppet seen earlier and looked toward a novel one. The experiment demonstrated that affective experience is remembered and recall can be recued by a cognitive experience. The experiment suggests that self-experience gains in coherence when opportunities to repeat an affect are presented.

As Stern (1985) notes, all the reported experiences of perception, motor activity, and affects would not build coherence of a sense of self if infants were unable to tie them together, to build a self-history through memory. Perceptual memory is active at birth. Recall that babies who had been read to from Dr. Seuss books while in utero indicated familiarity when the passages were presented after birth (De Casper and Fifer, 1980). Memory of motor plans has also been demonstrated experimentally (Rovee-Collier et al., 1980). Three-month old infants were placed in a crib with a mobile that moved by a string attached to their feet. They quickly mastered the technique to activate the mobile and evidenced pleasure. As many as eight days later, infants brought back to the same crib with the same mobile would begin to kick at a high rate even though there was no string and no movement of the mobile. The memory that triggered this action plan could be extended for several weeks beyond the eight-day extinction period if the infants were shown the moving mobile before the experiment was repeated.

What is the nature of early memory (say of the three- to six-month-old infant) that would support the idea of a core sense of a differentiated self living in an experiential world with others clearly perceived as separate? Stern (1985) has two original answers to this question. First, memories are of episodes of lived experience that have been averaged and represented preverbally in what he calls Representations of Interactions that have been Generalized (RIGs). Second, when a similar specific episode cues the memory of an interaction with another who has performed a self-regulating function, the activated memory will include an "evoked companion." "The evoked companion is an experience of being with, or in the presence of, a self-regulating other, which may occur in or out of awareness. The companion is evoked from the RIG not as the recall of an actual past happening, but as an active exemplar of such happenings" (p. 112).

Stern supports his suggestion that lived experiences give rise to generalized memory representations of groups of related episodes by experiments that demonstrate that infants can abstract and average information from perceptual stimuli. In one experiment, reported by Strauss (1979), ten-month-old infants were shown a series of schematic face drawings with differences in some detail in each. Then, when tested to detect the presence or absence of novelty, the infants chose a drawing they had not seen, but one that averaged all the facial feature sizes and placements. Further support comes from the logic of the proposal. Infants are constantly behaving as though they were reacting to each event or episode of lived experience by matching it against previous experiences. If a match is identical, there may be the initial pleasure of recognition but rapid diminution of interest. If there is a small variation, interest and attention are more apt to be maintained. What is the infant matching the current experience against? It seems more logical and parsimonious for the infant to be matching the experience of her mother presenting her with her favorite rattle against not the last similar episode or every previous episode, but a generalized representation of the whole series.

Stern's concept of generalized representations of lived interactions is a reasonable working supposition. It fits well with the core sense of a coherent self that functions with a sense of agency in interaction with the animate and inanimate environment. I earlier referred to Stern's position as radical because he totally rejects even moments of loss of this sense of self, even in those interactions most characteristic of the intimacy of attachment. The qualities of that intimacy find a place in his theory in the shadow cast by the evoked companion over all experiences, those of being alone as well as those of being with. I agree that the shadow of the primary figures of attachment carry across the totality of the infant's experience, what Winnicott (1963) called the environment mother (Lichtenberg, 1979), but I am not convinced that the evoked companion idea is necessary or optimal.

Let me reexamine the evidence. I noted that the optimal situation for infants to build a working model of the invariants of themselves and of others occurs when they see and hear from some distance. As Stern (1985) notes, "At the close range of face-to-face interactions, the mother's mouth, face, and voice obey the invariant of common locus of origin, but her hands may be holding or tickling the baby" (p. 82). What belongs to whom in that situation is obviously made more difficult for the infant to discern. Add to this the possible difficulties of discernment in the rapid-fire interchanges and switchings of starter and responder roles in close-up baby talk conversations. Further, when the mother "is quite close, the infant observes that parts of her are moving relatively faster than others. This generally means that parts of her become the background . . . for other parts of her" (p. 83). And while synchrony is not absolute between, say, mother's and infant's movements or mother's speech and infant's movements, the joy in the closeness in tempo might override the infant's capacity to detect very small differences in temporal structure. Stern's point that affects are powerful sources of invariant experiences whose locus in the infant's body is relatively easily placed is for me a telling one, but it, too, cuts both ways. In the intimacy of attachment exchanges, mothers faces are often exaggeratedly expressive, and infants have an innate response pattern of imitating affective expressions. Hence, the sense of sharing of affect in many situations may override the sense of agency that arises from initiating smiling or crying.

My examination of all the evidence leads me to conclude along with Stern that self-with-other is the dominant experience of the infant by the end of the first half year of life. However, unlike Stern, I give more significance to the variance in the differentiation present in the experience of self-with-other when attachment motivation is ascendant. If, along with Stern, we accept that the evidence of innate and learned perceptual cognitive development casts serious doubt on those radical theories which hold that differentiation and boundaries are only laboriously formed over an extended period, we still might consider that Stern's equally radical position overstates the case by proposing more *fixity* in differentiation than the same evidence supports.

Possibly some of our difficulties arise from the term differentiation; it has such cognitive connotations, whereas we are trying to deal with the infant's experience. Very shortly after birth, infants "differentiate;" that is, they show a preference for their mother's soiled breast pad over that of another woman, their mother's voice over their father's, their mother's voice coordinated with her face over a discoordination or breach in expectancy. What does this differentiation mean experientially? Clearly, it means that infants experience an order in their world that with persistent reconfirmation, provides the interest and pleasure of matching expectancies with innate and learned preferences. It probably means, as Stern believes, that in the search for preferred matchings, some sense of *otherness* has a solid hold on perception. Also in the neonate period, the specific ministrations of the caregiver affect the regulation of crying, feeding, and sleep patterns (Sander, 1975) so that otherness and a sense of regulation are deeply entwined. As the infant's sense of self-agency and coherence grows, sensing the self with one or another particular other seems to be a natural occurrence. The problem is how to conceptualize this natural developmental occurrence without either adultomorphizing or reverting to a tabula rasa.

I have tried to imagine infant experience by emphasizing first an action-affect-dominated, kaleidoscopic world of brief, differentiated perceptions coming in bursts. During alert activity states, infants viewing at a distance can easily extend the bursts of differentiated perceptions with increased discernment of foreground and background points of reference. Memory encodings of these extended bursts of more integrated perceptions of self-with-other remain dominated by action and affect—more as if one were living in a motion picture world than in a still photo world. As the distance between self and other diminishes, distinctions blur as single objects such as the eyes stand out or, if even closer, merge into one, Cyclopean eye. But I believe that even in optimal conditions for perception, when neither affect dominance nor closeness of object occurs, infants experience their world more as we do in dreams. In a dream as dreamed, not as told, segments of quite integrated perceptual units float with some breach of the unities of frames of reference of time, place, or person. That is, in the imagery itself, some degree of differentiation of frame or object, of person or place, co-exists with some detachment from full coherence unless fitted in by the secondary revision of words. The analogy to dream imagery misleads us if we fail to make the crucial distinction that dreams are the product of symbolic representation, a development of the second half of the second year. The analogy holds only for certain formal elements of dream imagery whereby some degree of differentiation is always present and some degree of differentiation is always absent.

To recapitulate: Stern (1985) states,

> All the events that regulate the feelings of attachment, physical proximity, and security are mutually created experiences. Cuddling or molding to a warm contoured body and being cuddled; looking into another's eyes and being looked at; holding on to another and being held . . . can never occur unless elicited or maintained by the action or presence of the other. They cannot exist as a part of known self-experience without an other [p. 102].

According to Stern, the predominant experience is to be with a state-regulating other rather than to merge. No one really knows what the experience is like for the infant. Pine (1981, 1986) vigorously defends the concept of merger. Brody (1982) suggests that the positive moments to which Pine (1981) refers be described as short affective states of mutually blissful closeness between mother and infant. My conjecture is that during the moments when attachment motivation and behavior are dominant, the infant never loses the sense of a being-with, but the experience has distinctively loose boundaries. The perceptual aspects during physical closeness—visual, tactile, and olfactory—create fuzziness in the infant's focus. My view is similar in some respects to Pine's. Pine acknowledges the compelling argument that the infant's perceptual and memory functioning is incompatible with "the idea that an infant is unaware of the mother-infant boundary and experiences itself as merged with or undifferentiated from the mother" (1986, p. 564). Pine distinguishes moments in which higher cognitive functioning leads to articulated awareness of boundaries from moments such as "when the infant, in the mother's arms, having sucked vigorously at breast or bottle, progressively calms and falls 'into' sleep as his body tonus relaxes and he 'melts' into the mother's body" (p. 566). I agree with Pine that these are meaningful moments and that the special quality of the experience is not fully captured by Stern's suggestion that they are felt as changes in state. I also agree with Pine that these experiences probably reverberate with adolescent and adult experiences of loss of boundary and merger, but I believe the later experiences to be most commonly metaphors for what the self experiences about the self. In the adult, the experiencing, or subjective, self remains intact as a point of reference for the merging self, and an external "other" remains intact as a point of reference for whom or what the self is merging into.

My clinical experience suggests that even autistic children or delusional or withdrawn schizophrenic patients are acutely aware of the differentiation of self and other. They can maintain themselves with far greater intactness when exploratory-assertive motivation is dominant. Rather than experiencing themselves as undifferentiated or merged, they are exquisitively aware and wary of the other, often resisting with every fiber of their being the lure of attachment motivation because intimacy and even the slightest sense of closeness and boundary looseness is functionally and emotionally disorganizing. These illnesses are not exemplars of autistic or symbiotic stages or phases unmastered; they are, in my opinion, primary pathological states whose relationship to normal infant experience has been assumed without a shred of solid evidence. I therefore see no reason to retain for infancy names having pathologic connotations, such as autistic or symbiotic phase, and thereby maintain spurious associative connections to pathological conditions, as Pine and others recommend. Likewise, I am not persuaded by Pine that analytic theory should single out as affectively central in the infant's day those moments when boundaries may be looser. I am arguing that attachment motivation clearly is very important and the special affective experience of intimacy triggered by it is of lifelong significance, an argument that parallels Pine's although derived from a different theoretical perspective. However, I suggest that centrality is less useful as a claim for any experience or motivational system than is the moment-to-moment shift from one to another and the contribution each makes to the complexity of human experience.

THE SUBJECTIVE EXPERIENCE OF SELF AND OTHER

> The next quantum leap in the sense of self occurs when the infant discovers that he or she has a mind and that other people have minds as well. Between the seventh and ninth months of life, infants gradually come upon the momentous realization that inner subjective experiences, the "subject matter" of the mind, are potentially sharable with someone else [Stern, 1985, p. 124].

The quantum leap is from an experiential world lived and encoded as interactions to one lived and encoded as intersubjective. I (Lichtenberg, 1983b) have suggested that instrumental in the transition from a kaleidoscopic interactive experience to an intersubjective experience is a markedly different mode of perceiving by the infant; I have designated this mode as an imaging capacity. The imaging capacity refers to the cognitive change through which infants achieve a focused awareness of an object contained in a perceptual-affective-action pattern. Through the imaging capacity, infants are able to define, focus on, and examine a component of an action pattern, such as the expression on a face as compared with experiencing the face only as a feature in the action pattern of a conversational game, or to a ball itself rather than the ball as part of a rolling-back-and-forth game. The imaging capacity is similar to what occurs when one sees a moving train as a fused blur and then singles out a particular car and sees it relatively distinctly as the diner.

I was drawn to this formulation by the observation of infants seeing themselves in a mirror (Brooks and Lewis, 1976; Lewis and Brooks-Gunn, 1979; Modarresi and Kenny, 1977). At first the infants show a delight similar to that which they show in response to any other visual display they are interested in. At a certain age, say 9 to 12 months, the response changes. They become more sober and pensive; the image in the mirror becomes an object of contemplation (Werner and Kaplan, 1963). I suggest that this change represents a kind of deconstructing of the previous action mode whereby one object, the image in the mirror, becomes singular as the infant displays more interest in its properties—as if one stopped a taped TV show to look more closely at an actor one was interested in. The contemplative mirror activity coincides with the time when infants treat all objects—toys and people—with increased interest in their properties, their front and back, the sounds they can make, their textures, and the like.

I am somewhat displeased with my choice of term because imaging has so restrictively a visual connotation—forming a discrete visual image, as in a still photograph where previously there was a motion picture. The mirror experiments on which I based by formulation, of course, involve visual perceptions. But the evidence from other experiments suggests that, even when one sensory mode is dominant, full perceptual registery is intermodal. In that case, the imaging capacity allows infants to achieve a more discrete awareness of the intermodal properties of an object.

I have followed the line of reasoning that their own selves become objects whose properties infants contemplate in a more discrete fashion through the imaging capacity. This interest applies not only to their own appearance, as demonstrated by the mirror experiments, but also to other properties of self as well. Infants seem to take into account more properties of toys in their play, indicating a greater ability to plan at a higher level of intentionality. With more awareness of themselves and of others, infants enter a new stage, which is characterized by what I call sign-signal informational exchanges (Lichtenberg, 1983b) Thus, toward the end of the first year, infants become more refined signalers of their wants and intentions and, of equal importance, more focused and perceptive readers of the signals conveyed by their caregivers. Mothers continue as essential regulators, but the mode of regulation becomes increasingly guidance through informational exchange. Here I have emphasized the "traffic signal" function of looks and words that say stop or go, safe or dangerous, nice or naughty.

Stern's (1985) depiction of the subjective self and mine of the infant after the maturation of the imaging capacity are essentially similar, with Stern's terminology having the advantage of being more experiential. Stern asks, what is so reinforcing about "intersubjectivity?" and answers, "achieving security needs or attachment goals" and "inclusion in the human group as a member with potentially sharable subjective experiences" (p. 136).

The Attachment–Affiliation Motivational System: Part 2

SUBJECTIVE EXPERIENCES CENTRAL TO THE ATTACHMENT MOTIVATIONAL SYSTEM

THE SUBJECTIVE EXPERIENCES CENTRAL TO the attachment motivational system can be demonstrated by four observations of infants at about one year in attunement activities, departure-reunion experiments, strange situation experiments, and play with "transitional" objects.

Attunement

Observations of attunement activities indicate that infants by one year experience attachment as a being-with that involves information about the affective state of one another. Each recognizes that the other has an affect state to which the other responds. Attunement is not empathy; that is, it is not yet information about the total inner state of mind and the general context to which that state of mind is related (Basch, 1983). The adult in the attunement pair is capable of both the emotional resonance and cognitive processing characteristic of empathy, the infant is capable only of experiencing the emotional resonance. Stern (1985) discovered that when infants at 9 to 12 months expressed affects as part of action sequences, such as exuberantly shaking a rattle, crawling across the floor, pushing a block back and forth, mothers made some response in the form of a body movement, vocalization, or facial expression that matched their infants in rhythm, intensity, and duration. During play interactions, attunements occurred every 65 seconds. This activity on the mother's part is intuitive. Until shown the examples on videotapes, mothers were largely unaware of their attunement responses. Stern asks, does this sharing or communion between mother and infant have an impact on the infant? In comparison with mothers' activities that sped up, slowed down, or interrupted the infants, where an alteration in infant response could be observed, attunement responses appeared to have no demonstrable impact on the infants. The babies continued to shake their rattles, or crawl, or push their blocks. Stern had the mothers intentionally go out of phase in their response, at one time jiggling more slowly, at another more rapidly. Both times, the infants noticed the discrepancy and stopped. When the mothers resumed jiggling the infants in a match with the infants' level of joyful excitement, the infants continued their activity undisturbed. The implication for attachment motivation is that in ordinary, playful infant-caregiver interactions, a baseline of frequent "unnoticed" intuitive attunements conveys the information to infants that their internal feeling states are shared and responded to by the person or persons closest to them.

Departure-Reunion

Observations in departure-reunion experiments (Ainsworth, 1979; Sroufe, 1979) indicate that breaches in attachment in the form of departure scenes have become patterned subjective experiences by the age of one year. The infants behave in accordance with their expectancies of their caregivers' intentions, based on prior experiences of breaches. The nature of the attachment and the stress situation of its breach at times of departure have become crystallized into characteristic emotional responses to these breaches. In these experiments, one-year-olds were made comfortable in the play setting and then their mothers were instructed to leave the room for brief intervals three times. Most infants could tolerate the first departure without alarm. By the second or third departure, the infants would react in three characteristic patterns. Sixty-five percent of the infants reacted to mother's leaving by crying and to her return by seeking closeness and resisting being put down before being soothed. Once soothed, they would return to play. Observers of the mothers of these children described them as consistent and sensitive in their behavior toward their babies.

Twenty to twenty-five percent of the children showed no distress at the time of separation and avoided mother on her return. When observed at home, these infants became demonstrably anxious at indications of mother's departure. In the experimental situation, where the anxious fussy response did not occur, these infants di-

verted their attention from the perception of mother's leaving or returning by hyperattentiveness to some object in the playroom. The
mothers of these infants were observed to be manifestly angry with
their children and insensitive to their signals. These mothers were
generally emotionally unexpressive and unable to establish physical
contact in a manner that was not jarring, inconsistent, or overstimulating.

The remaining 10% of the infants were acutely distressed on departure and during the separation. On reunion, they reacted to
mother with strong ambitendent behavior. They demanded to be
picked up, but once picked up would push off angrily and continue
to protest whether being put down or being held. Observers of the
mothers of this group described them as inconsistent in their responses. At times, the mothers would ignore the children's spontaneous signals for contact; at other times, they would initiate
contact, but without regard for the children's indications.

The implications of these experimental findings for an
attachment-affiliation motivational system are many. The most significant is that infants have joined their mothers in the *subjective*
awareness that behaviors are based on *intentions*, each triggering affective responses. From the first days of their babies' life, mothers
attribute intentions to them—"She's telling me she's hungry." The
keen observational powers of infants are aimed at contingency
tracking guided by affective response. For example, to kick a crib
mobile sets it in motion, creating a visual display that triggers interest, or to smile and reach out gets mother to smile and pick me up
and add to the enjoyment. After the changes at nine to twelve
months, infants react as if they recognize that mother has an intention she is signaling. For example, prior to this change, infants observing mother pointing her finger fix their attention on the finger
as having an action pattern of its own. Then they follow the line of
gaze indicated by the finger (Murphy and Messer, 1977). Following
the gaze line to the target may be a simple result of the imaging
capacity by which infants learn that the property of the pointing
finger is to direct attention, just as somewhat later the property of a
mirror is recognized to be to give information about the self. However, infants display another facet with the pointing finger: after
reaching the target, they check back with mother to see from her
face that they have arrived at the target she intended. It is as if the
infants are testing to see if the intentional directing of their gaze
matches mother's intention to indicate a visual target.

Returning to the departure-reunion experiment (Ainsworth, 1979;
Sroufe, 1979), we can see that before they are a year old, infants

become keen trackers of mother's intentions as signaled by her actions and affects. Under ordinary circumstances in the home, one
set of looks, acts, and affects means that mother intends to go into
the other room for a moment and return; another means that she is
planning to depart and take the child with her; another, that she is
leaving the child with the sitter; another, that she will be in the
room reading her book but receptive to refueling looks and touches;
and another, that she will be in the room reading her book but will
react resentfully to interruptions. In the experimental situation, the
infants revealed the nature of their reaction to departure and reunion and, as the experimenters hoped, the nature of their attachment as an affect-laden experience. By now each infant had formed
a subjective awareness of the mutual intentions and feelings involved. One group indicated they were unhappy at being left and
wanted contact and comfort before they could be restored to play.
They also indicated that they could read their mothers as receptive
to their appeal and intentionally active and patient in soothing
them. One group indicated they intended to avoid contact and, instead, fixed on exploration elsewhere to eliminate anxiety and distress. They indicated that they had come to read their mothers as
unreceptive or unreliable or antagonistic and rejecting in response
to their appeal. The ambitendent group indicated that they intended to seek contact, having experienced it as soothing sometimes. At the same time, they indicated that they had found contact
sufficiently unreliable or painful to lead them to reject mother by
pushing off. They had come to expect of their mothers an exchange
that mixed soothing with irritability and either inconsistency or a
well-established pull-tug of alternative agendas.

The departure-reunion experimental situations are typical of
thousands of separation-loss experiences of every kind. The central
determinant in the outcome of these situations is affect. For the optimally attached group, the pattern is comfort with → distress with
separation → relief of distress, being soothed and comfort restored.
For the ambitendently attached group, the pattern is comfort with
→ distress with separation → partial relief, partial rise in irritability
with some distress persisting. For the avoidant group, the pattern is
comfort with → anxiety or anxiety avoided by rigid adherence to an
exploratory motivation → avoidance of contact, which is reacted to
as increasing rather than decreasing distress. These patterns—comfort → distress → relief; comfort → distress → partial relief, partial
irritability and residual distress; or comfort → distress → increased
distress—have their origins in every caregiver-infant interaction
from birth on. Toward the end of the first year of life, infants expe-

rience their part in these patterns as intentions. They seek comfort or protest a failure to receive it. They communicate their intentions in motor actions, prelinguistic vocalizations, and feeling states. These are experienced as part of a feedback loop, the other part of which is mother's intentional acts, linguistic utterances, and emotions. The attachment-affiliation motivational system of the individual child now bears the stamp of the predominant affective exchanges between the particular caregiver and the child. As indicated in the case examples in chapter 3, the pattern with one caregiver (the mother) may be of an anxious-avoidant type, while with another (the father or a nurse) it may be of the more secure and comforting type. By one year, the pattern of each infant is relatively stable. The attachment-affiliation motivational system may be built around interest, affection, and joy, with distress experienced as a signal that, as a rule, is followed by relief. Or the system may be built around interest, affection, and joy, with strong admixtures of easily triggered aversive motives of antagonism and withdrawal. Or it may be organized so cojointly with the aversive motivational system that the central affects of attachment are anger, resentment, hyperalertness, and avoidance.

"Strange Situation"

"Strange situation" experiments underline another aspect of attachment motivation—the need and desire for guidance to relieve the distress of uncertainty (Emde, 1987). These experiments reveal that by one year infants look to the affective expression of the mother's face for signs that signal a safe course of action. In one experiment (Sorce et al. 1985) children were placed on a table that gave an optical illusion of a drop in depth in the middle (a visual cliff). The mother was placed at the far end of the table, with an attractive toy near her. The children started out eagerly for the end of the table with mother and the toy. When they reached the middle of the table and observed the illusory decline, however, they stopped and looked at mother's face. If mother, following instructions, smiled, they would proceed, after trying to solve the problem. Some children backed over the imagined crevice line as though backing down steps; others proceeded cautiously forward. If mother, again following instructions, gave a look of anxiety and alarm, the children did not proceed. They stopped, looked troubled, and cried.

In a second experiment (Emde, 1981b; Klinnert et al., 1983), the infant is playing with toys while the mother sits in a chair nearby. A beeping, flashing robot enters the room. The startled infant instantly looks to mother's face for a reassuring smile or fear-inducing wariness. Even when reassured, the infant may look back and forth between bewitching robot and mother until fully captivated with the robot (an exploratory motivation). Stern (1985) states, "Infants would not check with the mother in this fashion unless they attributed to her the capacity to have and to signal an affect that has relevance to their own actual or potential feeling state" (p. 132). The experimenters call these experiences, in which the parent's affects serve as a guide to the infant's affects, social referencing (Emde et al., 1978; Emde, 181a, b; Klinnert et al., 1983). I regard these experiences as important developments of the attachment motivational system.

I believe that searching the affective state of the other person in situations of ambiguity plays a significant role in attachment motivation throughout life and therefore appears as a silent or overt factor in every transference during therapy. The need and desire for guidance by means of affectively referenced signals is both a motive that contributes to forming attachments and one that arises inevitably in every already formed attachment.

Transitional Objects

Spontaneous play with transitional objects, usually blankets, bottles, or soft toys by infants toward the end of the first year has intrigued psychoanalytic theorists since Winnicott's (1953) first evocative descriptions. Most commonly the blanket, bottle or stuffed toy is rubbed against the body, frequently the nose and mouth, or is cuddled and hugged. This may happen at times of distress, such as after a fall or a scolding, but most often is at a moment of actual separation, such as when mother is going out, or particularly in the moments of drifting off to sleep. The peculiarities of the phenomenon are first that while many infants are extremely reliant on their transitional object, others develop no such reliance. Second, while most infants use tactile sensations as the main sensory mode, others blend it with smell, or sound, such as that of a favorite music box. (Puppies often respond similarly to the ticking of a clock wrapped in a sock.) What is similar in all these observations is the affective state—one of calming and soothing. Previously, the affective state of soothing and calming was the result of regulatory efforts by the mother of attachment. What is new is that infants using the transitional object are able to soothe themselves. It seems logical that the transitional object is connected with the memory of the mother, functioning as a stand-in for her. Winnicott viewed the infant as creating a symbol—a combination of the needs of the true self, expressed in spontaneous gesture, and the mother's appropriate ministrations. Concrete experience is transformed into illusion, and in that illusionary space the infant creates the symbol and appreciates the existence of the object.

At issue in Winnicott's (1953) formulation is the meaning of a symbol. Is the appreciation of the object created in this way? Stern (1985) argues that infants do create the object just as they create—that is, cause to emerge—the self. But he suggests another route to the creation of the self. Each representation of an interaction that has been generalized (RIG) involves an encounter with someone who has changed the infant's self-experience. When the memory of the representation is activated, the infant encounters

an *evoked companion*. The evoked companion is an experience of being with, or in the presence of, a self-regulating other. . . . The companion is evoked from the RIG not as the recall of an actual past happening, but as an active exemplar of such happenings. . . . The evoked companion can be called into active memory during episodes when the infant is alone but when historically similar episodes involved the presence of a self-regulating other. For instance, if a six-month-old, when alone, encounters a rattle and manages to grasp it and shake it enough so that it makes a sound, the initial pleasure may quickly become extreme delight and exuberance, expressed in smiling, vocalizing, and general body wriggling. The extreme delight and exuberance is not only the result of successful mastery, which may account for the initial pleasure, but also the historical result of similar past moments in the presence of a delight- and exuberance-enhancing (regulating) other [pp. 112–113].

Stern's suggestion is appealing. It explains how the mother, involved in the unfolding of attachment motivation, casts a shadow over all the activities of the infant—an idea similar in some respects to Winnicott's (1963) conception of an environment mother. Nonetheless, I find it troubling. It seems to me that it is only after infants have begun to contemplate the properties of objects that they are likely to abstract "a particular instance of one who accompanies" (Stern, 1985, p. 113) from the representation of the generalized interaction as a whole. I am arguing that until what I call the imaging capacity begins and contemplation and subjectivity follow, it is not reasonable to assume the stamp of personalness (an evoked companion) as an abstracted component of a memory. As evidence for his position, Stern proposes that the six-month-old's initial pleasure derived from the motivation system of exploration and assertion becomes heightened to delight and exuberance because of its augmentation by the memory of attachment experiences with the evoked companion. This notion can be neither proven nor disproven. Mastery pleasure could heighten to delight and exuberance with or without an evoked companion, since the original pleasure affect can trigger further affective heightening as the combination of smile, sound, and wriggling alone can produce a crescendo of the experience (Tomkins, 1962, 1963).

In contrast to the example of the six-month-old, which I find equivocal, our understanding of transitional object play as evocation of the soothing and calming mother seems to me to be a more convincing example of an evoked companion, that is, the experience of being with a self-regulating other. That it occurs *after* nine to twelve months suggests that some maturation, such as the imaging capacity, is needed. I agree with Stern's assertion that the younger infant is able to encode into memory representations of regulatory interactions. However, I believe the formation of the self-regulating other as a "symbol" occurs later. Like Winnicott, I prefer to think of symbolic as involving illusion and subjectivity, so that the self-regulatory other, or the mother of attachment, can be a step (or two) removed from actual experience, stored in memory and reevoked. While Stern is correct that the innate capacity for abstracting removes the representations of what is stored in memory a step from the lived experience, I believe that illusion requires a second step (the imaging capacity) and that before taking this second step, infants cannot experience transitional phenomena. Even at one year, in the midst of transitional object play, what is reevoked is predominantly an affective state, and the beloved companion to that state may be experienced with a degree of fuzziness about it. The key to understanding transitional object play is that the sense of self-experiencing attachment has developed to the point where infants have subjectively recognized a preferred affective state. This affective state is closely related to that of sensual enjoyment, as I describe in chapter 8. This preferred state is based on the soothing, calming qualities of certain attachment interactions. By one year, most infants have discovered a reliable means to evoke the affects themselves. The current affective state is magnified by prior similar experiences reevoked from memory. I believe that the central function of the transitional object is not only to arouse sensual enjoyment but to provide a compelling cue to memory. Some infants can evoke the affective state and reevoke the memory without this cueing. These are the infants who do not transfer attachment behavior to a cuddly. For those infants who use the cuddly for their cue, "outgrowing" would mean transferring their reliance onto evocation of the affective state and the evoked companion by symbolic representation. By the dual coding of experience in the modes of primary and secondary process, conscious and unconscious representations and fantasies can be manipulated (interchanged) intrapsychically. Even then, the affective impact of fantasies can be augmented by cueing memory from the touch or sight or sound of a transitional object like a memento, and so, for many children, attachment to a transitional object may continue into latency and later. But in the infant of one year, the symbol is only a small step removed from actual experience. The evoked memories that are cued are much closer to lived experience than the complex alterations that result from the later processing by symbolic representation.

To return to my main point: four observations of year-old infants demonstrate subjective experiences central to the attachment motivational system. Attunement activities reveal an intuitive intersubjective substratum of being with the affective state of one another that goes on largely unobserved but not unappreciated by mother and infant. Attunement is like the heart beat of a loving attachment experience. Without the heart beat, there is no life, but it functions best when it draws no attention to itself through an arhythmia or missed beat. While attunement experiences have a quietness about them, departure-reunion experiences are "noisy," high-tension interactions calling into play major patterns by which attachment is regulated. Attunement observations tell us that when mother and infant are motivated adequately to form an attachment, the mother will intuitively provide opportunities for affective states of mutual comfort. But attachment, of necessity, brings many moments of distress in being with and many other moments when the attachment bond is temporarily broken. By one year, the history of the handling of these moments of distress is written in the pattern that has evolved. What can be read in this pattern is not its cause but the result of different possible origins. Attachments in which a history of success in relieving distress has resulted in infants' eagerly seeking reunion and restoration after soothing may derive largely from the infants' original calmness and easy soothability or from mother's great skill with a difficult neonate.

If the neonate is too difficult to regulate for the particular mother, or the mother too inexperienced, anxious, or irritable, the outcome will be twofold. First, assuming that a consistent caregiving effort is made, an attachment will form. Second, the nature of the attachment and of the motivations related to it will have an affective coloring and patterns of aversive behavior that operate in a feedback fashion. The shadow that the nature of the early attachment casts over future relations is that, when in distress, the person will have an expectation of relief, irritable pulling and tugging, or avoidance and withdrawal. These early patterns will be encoded as affect-laden interactions, recoverable as procedural memories. Subsequently, the sense of intentions by both the self and the other becomes encoded in memory as an intersubjective sense of caring mixed with varying proportions of irritability and residual or even heightened distress.

Attunement depicts being together in a caring affective state; departure-reunion depicts being apart and coming together in a state of distress. Both emphasize intuitive activities on the part of the mother to make attachment work. Strange situation experiments and observations of transitional object play emphasize intuitive activities on the part of the infant to utilize the attachment. Seeking guidance by exploring the affective cues of the mother becomes a component motive of the attachment motivational system. The guidance studied in the one-year-olds centers on signals of safety and directions for exploration, but uncertainty transcends these easily studied situations. The uncertainty that involves the value of the self in the eyes of the other has been widely appreciated under the rubric of mirroring (Bornstein and Silver, 1985b) but has yet to receive extensive experimental study of infants. With their transitional object play, infants indicate their capacity to regulate their own distress. Self-evocation of the soothing and calming of being with becomes another component motive of the attachment system. It is to use attachments to become self-dependent. To be self-dependent is not to be independent, without reliance on the attachment. Rather, to be self-dependent is to be able to rely on the self to evoke the other in a period of absence, to bridge the gap until reunion or restoration of the attachment.

In a way, we may have come full circle. The intuitive attunement responses of mothers provides the comfort and encouragement of being together and thereby establishes being-with as a desired affective state. The success or partial failure of mothers to relieve distress and restore a desired affective state through soothing is subjectively identified by the children. Subsequently, the infants are motivated to find a means to evoke the desired affective state themselves. Thus, an aspect of attachment motivation becomes to provide for oneself what one derives from the attachment experience in the absence of the possibility of being together (Tolpin, 1971). By one year, the attachment motivational system includes states of mother-infant attunement, states of distress and attempts at relief, states of seeking guidance to relieve the distress of uncertainty, and states of relieving distress in the absence of the distress-relieving mother.

FATHER-INFANT ATTACHMENT

In the original studies of attachment and in psychoanalytic theories of the development of object relationships, little or no mention is made of fathers. The neonate is met in birth by a hormonally primed mother's basic maternal preoccupation (Winnicott, 1956). What comparable state of preparedness for parenting can be claimed for the neonate's father? Greenberg and Morris (1974) studied 30 fathers of first-born normal children and found a surprising involvement, which they called *engrossment*. The bond they observed consisted of a strong attraction to the newborn. Fathers focused their attention on their newborn infants, whom they perceived as attractive, beautiful, and perfect. They wished to touch and hold the baby and experienced doing so as very pleasurable. Following the birth, they felt elated, and upon seeing their baby for the first time, they experienced an increased sense of self-esteem. The normal motor activity and behavior of the newborn enhanced the father's engrossment. Greenberg and Morris found that fathers who were engrossed early on with their newborn were likely to continue to be involved with the developing child. Other studies indicate that fathers and mothers of middle- and lower-class families are equally active and sensitive to newborn cues during the postpartum period (Parke and Sawin, 1977, 1979).

Yogman (1982) examined play sequences of fathers and mothers with three-month-old infants. Fathers and mothers showed comparable ability to interest and communicate with their infants. Father and infant spent more than 90% of the interaction in positive phases of playing, talking, and getting rested and prepared to play and talk again. Thus fathers were equally able to establish joint regulation and reciprocity in pleasurable states of intimacy—the hallmark of attachment motivation. It is therefore not surprising that children at seven to eight months and at 12 to 13 months evidenced clear indications of attachment not only to their mothers but also to their fathers. Eleven-month-old infants in situations of ambiguity used their fathers and mothers for social referencing to an equal extent (Dickstein and Parke, 1988). Both parents were preferred to a friendly female stranger (Lamb, 1976, 1977). When tested to determine whom they would approach more enthusiastically for sociability, that is, to communicate and play with, the infants often preferred father to mother, a positive preference we would not expect from the heavy emphasis on mother-infant interaction in the first year.

What accounts for this unexpected positive orientation of infants for fathers as partners in sociability and play? Fathers play with their babies in a more physically stimulating manner. Their play is more unpredictable and idiosyncratic, while mothers are more conventional in their choice of games. Mothers hold their babies more for caregiving and protective restraint, while fathers pick up babies more to play with them or because the infants indicate they want to be held. In Yogman's (1982) experiment, both parents established joint regulation and reciprocity of interaction, but there were differences in the phasic nature. With their mothers, the infants were more likely to pass smoothly from talk to rest, prepare to talk, and back to talk. With the fathers, there was a more accentuated shift from peaks of maximal attention to valleys of minimal attention. Visual games with the infant were the common choice of the mother, while fathers chose tactile games involving limb movements. The mothers also played frequent limb-movement games, but they were of a more conventional motor rhythm, such as pat-a-cake, peek-a-boo, or waving, whereas the fathers during the limb-movement games attempted to arouse their infants. Thus, mothers try games that are more smoothly and repetitively rhythmical; fathers initiate games that are more physical, varied, and arousing. Infants of both sexes like the games that both father and mother play with them, and many infants of both sexes particularly like those that father is more likely to initiate.

Is it because he is a novel stimulus that a father who is away from home all day will be responded to on his return with a more excited response than will be a mother who comes in and out all during the day will receive? Yogman (1982) reports that primary-caretaker fathers bathe, diaper, and feed with the same vigorous exciting quality typical of fathers in general. "One infant's response to his father's vigorous rubdown after the bath was to chortle, cycle his legs, and engage the father in a limb-movement game" (p. 115). The evidence is that infants' response to their fathers is not based primarily on novelty but on the character of their interactions, which is established on the parents' gender-based differences. As Brazelton and Als (1979) observe, mothers will approach their babies to help collect or contain them. They will smoothly reach around the baby's body to provide support, or they will make eye or voice contact to engage the baby's attention and regulate the stimulation level.

Fathers commonly approach their babies in ways that heighten stimulation. They may engage in games of poking or playful grabbing. Their talk to the baby may be rhythmic, but the pace is usually faster and more staccato, with the voice louder. In diapering, mothers will gently lift the baby's buttocks, slide the diaper in, and smooth the baby over as the process is completed. Fathers commonly pick the baby up by the legs, shove the diaper under, and let the baby plop down onto the table. By three weeks, a baby talked to from behind by the mother will show a smooth, controlled response. When the father's voice is heard, the baby will respond with jerky excitement. Each parent thus becomes a partner in a feedback loop patterned according to expected mutual responses.

What significance do the findings about fathers have for infant development in general and attachment motivation in particular? Since mothers and infants are more likely to engage in smoothly modulated, soothing games, especially verbal, infants when stressed prefer their mothers. Thus mother remains for normal infants the one to seek for relief from distress. Even when fathers are actively involved with their babies, most commonly mothers continue to treat primary caregiving as their responsibility.

Nonetheless, fathers contribute significantly to the infants' experience of pleasure in intimacy and thereby widen the range of infants' motivation for attachment. Attachment is not to mother in the first year or so of life and then gradually to fathers, but, with ordinarily available fathers by the second half of the first year, infants can and do turn to their fathers as alternative sources of security in attachment (Dickstein and Parke, 1988). Furthermore, they derive a different but no less meaningful experience of intimacy—one more exciting, sociable and playful. Of course, mothers also provide exciting play opportunities and fathers soothing opportunities; the distinction noted in the research observations denotes the most common or predictable exchanges. The significance of the experience of intimacy with father is suggested by clinical observations of father hunger (Herzog, 1980) of toddlers whose fathers left the home and of disturbances that follow paternal disapproval (Solnit, 1972) in girls.

Beyond attachment, it is difficult to specify the father's contribution to early development for the ordinary baby. None of the effects of fathering is easily distinguished experimentally from those obtainable from mothering alone. In situations in which father-baby involvement has been more extensive then usual, the effects of the additional contribution of fathers can be delineated. In these instances, the babies are more receptive to strangers and show less protest to separation (Kotelchuck, 1975), indicating greater openness to a wider range of potential intimacy and to exploratory assertive pleasure. Lamb and Oppenheim (1989) summarize studies that show with remarkable consistency that children with actively involved fathers demonstrate increased cognitive competence, increased empathy, less sex-stereotyped beliefs, and more internally organized control. Lamb and Oppenheim suggest, as would I, that the diversity of stimulation of the different maternal and paternal styles may be a specific factor in the promoting cognitive competence. However, they also suggest that the whole group of positive effects may have less to do with the quantity of paternal involvement than with the total family context in which the parents have worked out with each other an arrangement of satisfying flexibility and sharing.

Home observations with infants aged five months (Pederson, Anderson, and Cain, 1977) indicate that a father's behavior with his infant is closely related to the quality of his relationship with his wife and that marital conflict is associated with less competent maternal feeding and an increase in irritable exchanges. Dickstein and Parke (1988) observed that where marital conflict was prominent, social referencing of father was reduced. Atkins (1982) describes an example of a sensitive mother who

> generously fertilized the field between father and son through facilitating the child's other-directness, both to herself and, noncompetitively, to her husband. . . . Don is a wide-eyed, active little boy just past his first half year. . . . During this observation, mother was verbally playing with her son. . . . While she was talking, Don would stare at his mother's face with eyes and mouth agape. During each pause, he would burst into a smile, then seemingly delighted, simultaneously squeal and kick.

> When father entered the room, mother maintaining eye contact with Don, cooed, "There's your daddy," in the same warm even pitch. Don squealed right back at mother. She then turned him toward father at the instant that father approached. Don's eyes and father's eyes met. Father cackled, Don smiled wide and squealed and kicked. Meanwhile, mother now silent, gently continued to move Don's body toward the father [p. 146].

The findings I have described were based on observations of normal or even optimal babies and families. Other interesting findings about the role of the father derive from studies of high-risk infants (Field, 1979, 1981). Fathers' face-to-face interactions with their four-month-old infants who were preterm neonates suffering from respiratory distress syndrome were compared with mothers' interactions with the same infants. Babies with respiratory distress syndrome show less attentiveness, less frequent positive facial and vocal expressions, and more inclination to avert their gaze and experience negative affects. Parents have to provide more stimulation to elicit an attentive response but then must modulate their stimulation so as not to overwhelm the poorer processing of the infants. The fathers were aware of the babies' limitations but did not appear as disturbed by them as were the mothers. The fathers of these high-risk infants behaved toward them exactly as fathers of normal babies behave toward their more alert, responsive infants. Positive affect, smiling, and laughing occurred more frequently with the fathers than with the mothers of the high-risk infants. "Father may require less reinforcement or responsibility for the games they play, and view their role more as entertainer of the very young infant and less as conversation partner" (Field, 1981, p. 255). Thus, when we regard the situation with Annie Adams (chapter 3), in which the mother-infant relationship was extremely disturbed, we must be prepared to credit early positive attachment experiences of mutually delightful play with her father as a possible important source of Anne's resources for recovery.

To summarize the findings: Fathers are capable of responding to the birth of their child with an "engrossment" that parallels the mother's "preoccupation." Fathers actively involve themselves in play with their infant and can do so with equal sensitivity to the modulation needed to capture and hold the interest of an infant. Thus, it is not surprising, although generally not recognized, that infants demonstrated clearcut attachment reactions to their fathers. What is surprising, and even less recognized, is the observational finding of the high rate of frequency with which infants indicate preference for their fathers when opportunities arise for sociability and play. Infants retain a preference for their mothers when they are stressed, and mothers generally feel a sense of responsibility for nurturant and protective caregiving. Fathers see themselves primarily as playing with their infants, and they play differently from mothers—more vigorous, hands-on, physical games, more varied and idiosyncratic in pattern. Fathers thus contribute to their infants' diversity of experience, preparing the infant for the more varied stimulation of the crawling, walking toddler. Intimacy, then, lies both in the pleasure of smoothly modulated exchanges (primarily mother) and in the excitement of horseplay games (primarily father). The infant-father interaction actively blends attachment pleasure with pleasure in exploration and assertion. Children with actively involved fathers demonstrate increased cognitive competence and greater centering of control. Moreover, in situations with high-risk infants, fathers play actively while mothers may be easily discouraged by their infants' poorly modulated responsiveness. Fathers may contribute significantly to the development of these infants. Since the fathers are undeterred in their good-natured play, their activity with their infants may promote badly needed positive experiences of intimacy pleasure as well as skills for enjoying exploratory and assertive play.

These findings call for a revision of exclusively mother-centered portrayals of attachment motivation. These studies indicate that the attachment motivational system of the infant in the first year will become activated toward both the mother and father when each is available frequently enough to trigger affects of pleasure in individual and joint intimacy. Pleasure-in-intimacy with each parent is differently toned. By virtue of the nature of the ordinary patterns of parent-infant interaction and the ordinary assumption of responsibility by mothers; infants are apt to associate soothing, distress relieving, and security enhancing with attachment to mothers and playful stimulus arousal and hands-on rough-housing with attachment to fathers. Construing attachment motivation from early life on as an open, flexible system helps us to understand how healthy, normal babies can extract from all their experiences—those with parents and those with pets, siblings, and other familiar people—experiences of pleasure-in-intimacy that sustain an optimistic core to their developing personality. Alternatively, postulating that an open, flexible potential remains present in the attachment motivational system of many infants who are at-risk either because of developmental disturbances or unfacilitating experiences with one or the other parent, we can understand how the other parent (or regular baby sitter) can provide positive experiences that place in memory an affective state of intimacy pleasure to be sought when opportunities arise. The development of some degree of positive attachment motivation by infants raised in extreme adversity, such as concentration camps or situations of marked neglect, points to a view of the attachment motivational system as more open and flexible than would be suggested by theories of exclusively symbiotic attachment to a mother caregiver.

Further confirmation of the flexibility of the attachment motivational system comes from Pruett's (1983) study of nine infants raised in a stable, two-parent family in which the father was the primary caregiver. These nine fathers turned out to be extremely sensitive and competent caregivers, able to establish a good rhythmic synchrony with their infants, whether boy or girl. The infants were found to be vigorous, competent, thriving, and especially comfortable with and interested in stimulation from the external environment. Pruett asks, do these infants thrive because of "an usually rich fertile mosaic between primary and secondary love objects?" (p. 275). Is there a greater than suspected functional capacity, "a kind of integrating mechanism which permits a successful mosaicism?" (p. 275). That is, when both father and mother make themselves available to their infant in a family that works well together, regardless of who is primary caregiver, is the infant able to extract and benefit from more complexity in attachment experiences of intimacy and in potentialities for exploration and assertion than we have previously recognized? Has both the motivational and functional side of attachment been dealt with reductionistically in our mother-centered portrayals of merger and symbiotic unity?

PROSOCIAL BEHAVIORS AND THE DEVELOPMENT OF ALTRUISM

Research on prosocial behaviors provides an approach to tracking the developments in the attachment motivational system from interaction to intersubjectivity to symbolic representation.

> Bobby, at 82 weeks: As I [mother] was vacuuming I began to feel a little faint and sick to my stomach. I turned off the vacuum and went into the bathroom kind of coughing and gagging a little. Bobby followed me to the bathroom door, and the whole time that I was in there he was pounding on the bathroom door saying, "OK Mommie, OK Mommie?" And I finally came out and picked him up and he looked at me with a very concerned, worried look in his eyes, and I said, "Mommie OK." Then he put his head on my shoulder and began to love me [Zahn-Waxler and Radke-Yarrow, 1982, p. 116].

This sample observation by Bobby's mother was obtained from Zahn-Waxler and Radke-Yarrow's research project studying 24 white, middle-class children in three groups beginning at 10, 15, and 20 months of age. Each child was studied for nine months. Their mothers were taught a prescribed format for observing and reporting both spontaneous and simulated incidents of distress. The results were cross-checked by investigators visiting the home. "The distress of another person is a remarkably compelling stimulus for children in the first years of life: Distress elicits some form of response on between 80–90% of all occasions in which it occurs" (p. 118). Commonly the infant's reaction is no more than a sustained orientation to the stimulus with varying degrees of affective involvement. The changes that occur by ten months (imaging capacity, social referencing) suggest that infants will begin to display exploratory interest in the distressed other and gradually will gain some subjective sense of the other's state. The researchers found that in 28% of natural distress incidents, children between the 38th and 61st week (10–15 months) reacted with self-distress. Moreover, the infants made a prosocial intervention in 11% of those incidents. If the distress was simulated rather than occurring naturally, the response was quite different: the infants showed less emotional distress, more positive affect, more inclination to seek their caregiver, and fewer prosocial interventions.

The number of prosocial interventions increased somewhat during the infants' age 10 to 18 months, but the dramatic shift occurred at about 18 to 20 months, when the toddlers responded with prosocial interventions about one third of the time. Simultaneously, their own distress decreased. There were no sex differences in the responses. How might this substantial increase in frequency of prosocial interventions at 18 months be explained? I suggest that with the advent of symbolic representation toddlers have the possibility of putting themselves intrapsychically into the state of mind of the victim of the distress. Now added to the subjective awareness of distress is the possibility of a trial identification with the victim and the activation of the other role in the distress experience—that of comforter or protector. This pairing, one in distress, one providing comfort and protection, is an interplay as integral to attachment as communication, attunement, intimacy, and guidance. Once they can be represented symbolically in primary- and secondary-process modes, victim-rescuer behaviors can be played out in alternate roles, enacted in actuality, dreamt and fantasized about.

Parens (1979) illustrated a clear example of prosocial behavior. Jane was a little girl who evidenced a capacity to let go of competed-over toys

not in defeat but in a rather positive tone, seemingly altruistically. One month later Jane (1–5–2) and Candy (1–3–10) seemed to be having difficulty together. On this day they were on the point of struggling for a toy, Candy threateningly following Jane. In an effort to master this encounter Jane avoided Candy and did not respond with an affect to match Candy's. Of much importance, at one point a while later when Candy was crying because her mother had set limits on her going into the hall, Jane went to Candy, put her arm around Candy's shoulder, and comforted her for about three seconds" [p. 239].

Zahn-Waxler and Radke-Yarrow (1982) provide examples of prosocial behavior after 18 months that illuminate the complexity of symbolic play behavior, which sometimes alternated between prosocial and antagonistic behavior: "101 weeks—Subject hurts father: Hugs and kisses father, then slaps him in the face" (p. 123). Sometimes the altruism was aggressively protective: "79 weeks—Children fighting: 'No, no' and subject stands between them as one goes to hit another; put pennies (that they have been fighting over) in the corner, said 'Mommy,' and brought her over to show her the fighting" (p. 123). Sometimes the infants would offer their bottle or teddy bear, or pat and kiss an injured part. There was a considerable range in the children's abilities to make accurate inferences about the distress. The children would bring a toy to a tired mother, soothe a mother whose eyes were tearing from peeling an onion, pat their own leg instead of the injured mother's, or "heal" a dog that had just been combed by trying to patch the hair back on.

At times, the children were very sensitive to being the cause of the distress themselves; at other times they were oblivious to the effect of their hurtful actions. Likewise, the children might assume unwarranted responsibility. The children's expressions of self-distress were greater for those hurts they regarded as having been inflicted by themselves—here the altruism seemed mixed with reparation. At all the ages tested, the children could be quite conscious of and deliberate about the pain and distress they had inflicted. The older children in the study, those 28 to 33 months, showed a marked increase in aggressive response to those they had injured, a development, I believe, that signified a more consolidated sadistic intent.

Another study of children 1-½–2-½ years old clearly indicated that how children cope with emotional distress in others is significantly related to their mothers' interventions.

> The prototype of the mother whose child is reparative and altruistic is one whose communications when her child transgresses are of high intensity and clarity both cognitively and affectively. . . . This mother brings the emotional stimulus events into focus. "Look what you did!" "Don't you see you hurt Amy—don't ever pull hair." She gives evidence of emotional investment in high expectations regarding the young child's behavior. "A very disturbing thing happened today, Judy bit me. . . . I expected a hug or statement that Jerry was sorry."

Her demands are powerfully asserted in a close, one-to-one relationship in the disciplinary encounter. This is also the mother who models altruism in the caregiving of her child. . . . The effective induction is not calmly dispensed reasoning, carefully designed to enlighten the child; it is emotionally imposed, sometimes harshly and often forcefully. These techniques exist side by side with empathic caregiving. Mother's nurturance may be an important condition for the effectiveness of the induction and power [Zahn-Waxler, Radke-Yarrow, and King, 1979, p. 327].

The emotion that accompanies the child's prosocial acts may represent empathic arousal and altruism, or fearfulness, or self-incriminating feelings and reparative shame or guilt. The researchers conclude that the mother's empathic caregiving and the child's concerned emotion in altruistic acts may reflect a process of developing empathic sensitivity. Altruistic responses occurred approximately twice as frequently in children whose mothers were rated high in empathic caregiving than in children whose mothers were rated low. At the same time,

the mother's strong controlling techniques in disciplinary encounters may leave the child with anxious concern about the self. Making the child feel responsible for the grief of others may result in his continuing to feel responsible for the grief of others in other situations. The young child is especially vulnerable to guilt induction since he may be less able to distinguish clearly his causal role from the bystander role [p. 329].

These studies of prosocial behaviors provide a model for understanding the workings of the attachment motivational system. At a specific time in development, a pattern of response to a particular stimulus emerges. The pattern may involve social and communicative exchanges, affect attunement, subjective awareness of self and other, guidance seeking, or comfort seeking or giving. Each of these patterns triggers an affect of a pleasurable nature. The enjoyment of intimacy and the relief of distress augments and amplifies the attachment exchanges. Attachment experiences become desirable, meaningful, and rewarding for the infant. The person who is the object of the particular pattern of attachment behavior is primed to respond in some characteristic manner. The person may be wholeheartedly welcoming and sharing in the positive affect or ambivalently responsive or even rejecting. Within a relatively brief time, the combination of the child's innately prepared pattern and the response the child receives will shape the individual characteristics of the attachment relatedness, and especially its affective tonality.

To apply this model to prosocial behavior: Prosocial behavior was found in virtually all the children studied, with considerable similarity in response repertoires. The initial modes of response were remarkable similar in form in all the children. The initial findings occurred within a narrow time frame shortly after the first year of life, attesting to altruism's universality and probably biological maturational source. Clear, forceful, empathic parental responses enhance the child's feelings of goodness associated with altruism and making reparations. Parents may model the behavior and intuitively treat each experience as an occasion for learning. The pairing of parent and child may richly encourage the child's capacity for empathic compassion, or it may stimulate anxious, shameful, or guilty concern, or antagonism toward a victim. Clear, consistent individual differences in prosocial responses emerge in the child's affects, behaviors, and motives by the second half of the second year.

Psychoanalysis has tended to place altruistic motives as occurring well after the first year and as being conflict-derived reaction formations. I think the evidence points otherwise. Altruistic motives appear to be a universal, biologically based maturation concurrent with year-old children's intersubjective awareness of their own feelings and the feelings of others. Altruism provides infants with a mode of sharing the intimacy of soothing and relief—the same good feeling they have enjoyed as a result of their caregiver's empathy. It provides them with the pleasure of shared intimacy that comes with making reparations and repairing a brief breach in affectionate attachment. This whole experience is accentuated by the developmental leap to symbolic representation. But with this rise in cognitive potentiality comes to means to disguise aversive motives by employing words devoid of feelings, by repressing an affective predisposition (anger) and heightening its opposite (soothing affection). Thus, by the end of the second year, each act of prosocial behavior would need analysis to determine the system that dominates its constituent motives. By the middle of the third year, an upsurge of hurtful intent toward a victim assumes proportions strongly suggestive of organized sadistic motivation. Parental influence has by now become a strong influence. Parental interventions may be effective in limiting attacks on a victim, and the parent may be a model for empathic compassion; or by being too weak and lax, or too rigid and hurting, the parent may become a model of indifference or sadism.

It is beyond the scope of this book to go further into those developments of the attachment motivational system. Psychoanalytic observation has studied extensively the experiences of oedipal children and the subsequent developments of attachment through the life cycle. In chapters 9 and 10, I describe the importance of experiences of affirmation, likemindedness, and shared idealization (Kohut, 1971, 1977, 1984) for attachment. Attachment motives also center on experiences with advisors, advocates, sponsors, and mentors, as well as with lovers and rivals. The basic model for all attachment experiences is as follows: a pattern of response emerges at a particular time. In its initial emergence it is relatively universal within a predictable, relatively narrow time frame. The pattern forms around a pleasurable affect that augments and amplifies an experience of intimacy. Whoever is the object of the particular pattern of attachment (the oedipal parent, the latency group, the adolescent best friend or lover, the idealized teacher) is primed to respond in some characteristic manner. Within a relatively brief time, the combination of the pairing will shape the characteristics of the attachment relatedness, particularly its affective tonality.

THE AFFILIATIVE MOTIVATIONAL SYSTEM

The affiliative motivational system is far more difficult to delineate psychoanalytically than is the attachment motivational system from which it takes its roots. My main assertion is that at a fork in development, a person not only continues to be strongly motivated to adhere to old attachments and to form new ones, but also begins to be motivated to develop affiliations with groups with a shared relational bond, goal, belief, or ideal. The evidence I can present for an affiliative motivational system lacks the precision of the innate, preprogrammed pattern for attachment. Nonetheless, I believe there may be an innate, preprogrammed pattern to affiliate that begins with a young child's regarding his or her parents and siblings not only as individuals but as a unit—the family. This proposal requires experimental and observational verification. If it is true, it means that the small child can gain pleasure in intimacy and the sense of belonging not only from the ministrations of each caregiver, but also from the family group. Thus, children with disturbed individual relations may have another source for deriving support. The earliest behavior that unequivocally fits the description for the affiliative motive occurs during latency in team-play groups. Pursuit of a shared goal—to win the game—requires an awareness of rules and the desire to share intimacy pleasure with a transient number of individuals whose personal characteristics are less significant than being on the blue team to outrace the green is.

The psychoanalytic studies that bear on affiliation generally approach it from its negative or pathological aspect, whereas I regard the motivation for affiliation to be as integral to development and as universal in its occurrence as that of attachment. I believe that a latent value judgment in favor of individuality has led to a negative twist that psychoanalytic theorists have given to belonging. Freud (1921) tells us that in groups individuals surrender their values and ethics to a leader and march to the destructive drum beat of a Savonarola, Napoleon, or Hitler. The desire to affiliate, to enjoy intimacy within a group, invariably leads to a pairing in which the chosen or preferred group (even the transient, teacher-selected group of the blue team) is endowed by its members with positive values. We are the better team, the fastest runners, the ones who try hardest even if we lose. Inevitably, this means that to the "blues" the green team is the less able, the slower, the ones who don't try as hard. Psychoanalysts beginning with Freud have stressed the prejudicial and potentially harmful nature of the devaluation of the greens by the blues, the negative affiliated by the positive affiliated. Freud (1918) stated:

It is precisely the minor differences in people who are otherwise alike that form the basis of feelings of strangeness and hostility between them. It would be tempting to pursue this idea and to derive from this "narcissism of minor differences" the hostility which in every human relation we see fighting successfully against feelings of fellowship [p. 199].

Later, Freud (1930) used the concept of the narcissism of minor differences to describe man's reluctance to give up the satisfaction of an inclination to aggression:

It is always possible to bind together a considerable number of people in love, so long as there are other people left over to receive the manifestations of their aggressiveness . . . it is precisely communities with adjoining territories and related to each other in other ways as well, who are engaged in constant feuds and in ridiculing each other. . . . I gave this phenomenon the name of "the narcissism of minor differences,". . . . We can now see that it is a convenient and relatively harmless satisfaction of the inclination to aggression, by means of which cohesion between the members of the community is made easier [p. 114].

If we accept Freud's reasoning, affiliation as a motive belongs in the chapter on aversion; that is, it is a manifestation of aggression—

sometimes harmlessly binding communities by displacing aggression onto others. As I will indicate, most other analysts have followed Freud in this view or a variant of it. And, indeed, the negatively affiliated other—the Hun, the Frog, the Spick, the Wop, the Jap, the Kike—may be hated, shunned, or killed with righteous indignation. Affiliation, all agree, involves differential bonding, to use Pinderhughes's (1986) phrase. The negatively bonded may be treated as friendly rival or unfriendly rival, as respected antagonist or despised antagonist, as constructive critic or the source of unforgivable narcissistic injury. The ascending order of aversiveness with which negatively affiliated others are experienced means that signals of aversion—look, the other team is approaching our goal—can progress to angry mobilization of our powers to the point of persistent grudge holding and narcissistic rage. My argument is that while affiliation has an aversive side and the affiliation may become organized as antagonism (as in war) or withdrawal (as in dehumanizing ostracism), aversion need not be the basic motivation for affiliation. We would not say that because the attachment between a mother and her child may be organized aversively, the basic motivation for the attachment is aversive or a defense against aversion. The motivation for attachment involves the experience of pleasure in intimacy, a pleasure that grows with learning the rules of developing and preserving that intimacy through a variety of means of communication and modes of being-with. The motivation for affiliation is, I believe, precisely the same. The experience of pleasure in intimacy that begins with mother, father, or both at some point has as its corollary a pleasure in intimacy with the family. Modes of communication with and about family, especially defined in the presence of nonfamily, provide for the prelatency child the basis of a positive sense of intimacy in the group as compared with the individual. The difference between attachment and affiliation is in the composition of the unit—not in the affective experience sought. And the affective experience sought is the positive sense of sharing and gaining and growing.

A patient was describing his memory of the Passover Seder services of his youth. Year after year, his family and aunts and uncles and cousins would get together at the grandparents' house. He remembered these occasions as cherished moments. He looked forward with trepidation and pride to the time when he, as the youngest able to read, could take a prescribed part in the service. He experienced the whole proceeding with warmth and mastery as he gradually understood the meaning of the rituals. His therapist, remembering that the patient had many bitter feelings toward his grandfather, reminded him of these conflicting problems. The patient acknowledged that, indeed, his grandfather had conducted the Seder in dictatorial fashion, insisting on a strict adherence to ritual; and, furthermore, the patient had been distressed that his grandmother often seemed exhausted by her weeks of preparation. The patient then returned to his earlier nostalgic reminiscence, and the therapist wondered why the patient did not recognize the contradiction between his positive feelings about the Seder and his anger toward his grandfather and concern for his beloved grandmother. The patient neither saw paradox nor denied conflict, and, in my opinion, none need be presumed from this vignette. From the standpoint of attachment as a motivation, the patient was ambivalent about his grandparents, but from the standpoint of affiliation as a motivation, the patient was equivocally and unconflictedly positive in his experience of the expansiveness and building of a cohesive self that he had experienced as part of the family and religious group.

The Passover service is an interesting example of the duality of affiliation. It depicts the escape of the Jewish people from bondage in Egypt under the Pharaohs. The Lord supports the righteous chosen people and sends plagues to afflict and punish the wrongdoers. Participants in the service may therefore, receive, a bonus in the pleasure of aggression that Freud noted, but they do not ordinarily affiliate for that form of pleasure. The headlines of history tell us of the havoc wrought by affiliate groups on the nonaffiliate, but this is a disintegration of intimacy into aversiveness, not its purpose. In *The Stones of Florence*, Mary McCarthy (1963) writes

> Savonarola's puritan mobs were not always bent on arson and image-breaking; sometimes they were carried away by joy. After one of the Frate's sermons, the crowds would pour out into the squares yelling "Viva Cristo!" and singing hymns. In the squares, they would join hands to make a circle and dance, a citizen alternating with a friar [p. 167].

An observation may help to distinguish between an attachment-motivated event and an affiliation-motivated event, and to convey the basis for an affiliative motivation. In the morning, Bobby and Sally's father was following up on the swimming lessons his seven- and eight-year-old children had taken. Both could swim, and he was urging them to tread water for several minutes. He had made the pool activity as much fun as he could, and the children seemed pleased and at ease. Before long, they pleaded with their father that they were tired and wanted to stop practicing treading water. Their father convinced them to try a little longer and then let them stop. In the late afternoon, a ten-year-old playmate got Bobby and Sally and several other of their regular friends to play a game of water tag. In the game, the children circle one child, who has to touch one of the others. The children in the circle tread water until the tagger comes after them and then they swim away. Bobby and Sally, caught in the excitement of the game, continued to tread water far longer than they had earlier, when urged by their father, even though each was eager to please him and outdo the other. In the group, the general mood state was excitement and the pleasure of being part of the "gang." Roles shifted from chaser to chased, from being all alone to being one of the circle. Observation of the children revealed that skill and luck and trying hard were all applauded. Bobby and Sally exchanged looks and remarks that revealed a special code of understanding, sometimes teasing, sometimes sympathetic. The ten-year-old friend was clearly the leader, and the others looked to him to settle the recurrent disputes about whether a tag had been made, whether the rules were being followed. Praise from him or tagging him brought a special glow, a bit of awe. Thus, within a rapidly shifting scene, Bobby and Sally could experience positive and negative mirroring, a twinship, or alter ego, experience, and a sense of idealization of the group leader. These are the same experiences present in attachment, but within this group activity they proceeded with such rapidity that belonging became defined as giving and receiving a highly sustaining form of approving acceptance. Because of the sustaining sense of belonging, moments of disapproval, teasing, even fleeting ostracizing could be tolerated. Moreover, the didactic gain sought under favorable conditions with their father was accomplished without protest or "tiredness," the children having to be ordered out of the pool to get ready for dinner.

Affiliation in the sense that I am using the concept is both similar to and different from Pinderhughes's (1986) formulation. Pinderhughes refers to physiological patterns that mediate approach → affiliative → affectionate behavior. However, he postulates a drive to dichotomize so that all patterns form in antithetical pairs, programming dichotomy into the evolving mental apparatus. He cites stranger anxiety and affiliative idealizing of one parent while aggressively competing with the other as evidence for avoidance-differentiative-aggressive bonding from "cradle to grave." Pinderhughes believes that through affiliative and differentiated bonding we can have one object for each side of ourselves and thereby preserve constancy. Volkan (1985a, 1986), in his concept of the need for targets of externalization suggests a similar use for denigrating others. His reasoning is that we innately split all experience into good and bad; we are programmed to dichotomize others into friend and foe and are as bound to our enemies as we are to our friends. We are therefore forced into false idealizing or denigrating projections, creating a universal "normal" functional state of paranoia (Meissner, 1978). The manner in which the "enemy" is formed is a valuable addition to psychoanalytic thinking (Volkan, 1985b). I believe, however, that the universal need to show preferences in each motivational system has been mistakenly generalized into a drive to dichotomize. Further distinction between attachment and affiliation as motives is being lost in these worthy efforts to relate psychoanalytic theory to large group behavior and the horrors of persecution and war.

Obviously, there are numerous examples in which aversion is not restricted to a signal function. But we should not confuse the failure to sustain a positive, growth-producing motivation with an intrinsic need for "paranoia." Within the limitations of this study of motivation, I can touch only briefly on the functions served by affiliation with groups. Cole (1986) used an experimental disappointing situation to illustrate how the group, and being in a public setting, regulate affective expression. Children aged three to nine attempted to control the display of their disappointment by substituting displays of positive emotions (girls more so than boys). The older children were able to refer spontaneously to their use of expressive control, indicating that they were fully aware of rules about the settings in which disappointment may be indicated openly. Preschoolers, even though probably unaware of the social rules in a formal scene, nonetheless internalized what was expected of them in public when they were disappointed. For example, young children excluded from a group activity may already have learned to mask their personal disappointment. In contrast, the same children will reveal openly negative displays to their parents when disappointed by them. If the disappointment affects the whole peer group, however, such as at the end of recess, an open display of negative emotion is permitted and supported by the affiliation with others. The group-sanctioned expression of disappointment at having to return to class permits the child to signal aversion to authority in a form that does not destabilize the larger affiliative motivation in the school as a place of learning.

Schachter (1959) adds considerable detail to our understanding "of the circumstances that drive men . . . to seek one another out"

(p. 1) and the purposes that affiliation serves. Schachter does not distinguish systematically between needs for attachment and affiliation as I do. Nevertheless, the studies about which he reported and those he himself conducted fit in for the most part with the need for intimacy in groups rather than single intimate pairings. Schachter, citing Festinger, Pepitone and Newcomb (1952), notes two classes of need that group membership satisfies: first, the need for approval, status, and help that require singling the individual out; and, second, the need to engage in activities such as riotous entertainment and aggressive actions, which are prevented by inner restraints and require deindividuation into personal anonymity.

Festinger (1954) describes the drive for self-evaluation as

a force acting on persons to belong to groups, to associate with others. And the subjective feelings of correctness in one's opinions and the subjective evaluation of adequacy of one's performance on important abilities are some of the satisfactions that persons attain in the course of these associations with people [p. 135–136].

Schachter (1959) follows Festinger's claim that the need for social evaluation is one main source pressing the individual toward group membership, anxiety reduction being the other. Schachter asks, what does anxiety press the individual to do as far as group membership is concerned, and who is most susceptible to the pressure to affiliate because of anxiety? From his experimental studies Schachter concludes that "under conditions of anxiety the affiliative tendency is highly directional. . . . Misery doesn't love any kind of company; it loves only miserable company. Whatever the needs aroused by the manipulation of anxiety, . . . their satisfaction demands the presence of others in a similar situation" (p. 24). The urge for affiliation in situations of anxiety and ambiguity persists whether or not verbal communication is possible. Schachter found that the ordinal position in the family played a large role in the tendency to affiliate. In high-anxiety conditions, first-born and only children strongly preferred being with others, while later-born children did not. Moreover, first-born and only children were more anxiety prone and pain avoidant. Schachter suggests that the reason is that first-born children receive inconsistent training. The inconsistency is characterized by their being allowed to make noise and show aggression against other children and by their being disciplined with restrictions on physical mobility and frequent physical punishments. He speculated that the mix of attention and love with frustration of infantile dependency needs rendered the first-born forever more reliant on others for approval, support, help, and reference. The combination of more anxiety and more dependence pressed the first-born and the only child into a greater need for affiliation.

Schachter (1959) notes that most prior work established the need for affiliative groups to gain help in evaluating opinions and abilities. His contribution was to demonstrate that when emotion-producing situations are ambiguous or uninterpretable in terms of past experience, pressures arise to establish a social reality. This tendency to seek evaluation from groups in novel emotion-producing situations "help[s] us understand phenomena of emotional contagion such as panic and riots" (p. 128). Schachter tested subjects in states of induced boredom who could hear but not see one another. The subjects were instructed that they absolutely must not talk. As long as the groups were made up of strangers, compliance was total. When the groups were composed of acquaintances, they did not "talk" but groaned, sighed, and made other affective noises. The effect was that the emotional state of this group became more homogeneous, since the members evaluated their own feelings by reference to the cues they received from other group members. Schachter thus took a large step in delineating the need for affiliation in groups by going beyond the need for anxiety reduction and for the evaluation of opinions and abilities to the use of the group for evaluating emotions whenever a state of ambiguity and uncertainty exists.

In summary: I suggest that a basic need for affiliation exists as a normal adaptive motivation, the central goal of which is to experience pleasure in intimacy. The motivation for affiliation probably begins earlier but is recognizable for the other child. Affiliative motives develop imperceptibly as a variant of attachment motives. Thus, in naturalistic settings, distinguishing between attachment and affiliative needs may be difficult. Children give early recognition to their concept of the family as a unit, often insisting when photographs are taken that pets and dolls be included. I have sketched in broad outline some facets of an affiliation motivational system. At times attachment experiences with individuals and affiliative experience with groups serve similar functions. Reduction of anxiety and distress, as well as receiving an evaluation of abilities and opinions, occurs as part of both attachment and affiliation experiences. The significance of affiliation is that it provides another resource for the individual to be calmed and to be affirmed and confirmed in his self-worth.

Group experience also provides another and different opportunity for the regulation of affect. Here lies affiliative motivation's highest adaptive purpose, and its most dangerous. On one hand, affiliation to groups permits access to the sharing of feelings that the individual may be hesitant to express. This is put to valuable use in therapy groups and such organizations as Alcoholics Anonymous. On the other hand, affiliation with groups built around dissent, hatred, and disaffection promotes the consolidation of aversive motives, the deindividuation of the members, and the surrender of judgment common in riots and destructive bands. The strength of the tendency toward affiliation can be best exemplified by the shocking fact that more people have died for affiliative motives than for any other. Dominance of affiliative and aversive motivation under the aegis of idealization constitutes mankind's most lethal combination. In these instances, the pleasure of intimacy in groups of like-minded others is achieved at a terrible cost.

The Exploratory–Assertive Motivational System

EXPLORATION AND ASSERTION: A SEPARATE SYSTEM?

B ROUCEK (1979) DESCRIBES THE SIGNIFICANCE for psychoanalytic theory of findings that infants actively (assertively) respond to problem-solving experimental situations. In these experiments, the infants quickly recognized the potentials in the situation for their assertive response. Acting on this recognition, they explored the possibilities for establishing an efficient contingent relationship between their activity and an occurrence in the environment. They could be induced into the activity to receive a reward in the form of a preferred stimulus, but they sustained the activity to obtain the affective amplification of pleasure that derived from their efficiency or competence.

Broucek cites the Papousek's (1975) classic experiment in which four-month-old infants were exposed to five seconds of bursts of multicolored light. They oriented themselves toward the stimulus with interest, and then, typical of responses to unvaried stimuli, their orientation diminished after repetition. The experiment was arranged so that when the infants in the course of their movements rotated their head 30 degrees to a predetermined side three times successively within a time interval, the light display was switched on. As soon as the infants turned on the light presentation by their own head movements, their behavior changed dramatically. Their orientation reactions increased in intensity, and they continuously made all kinds of movements to try to switch on the visual stimulation again. To this point, the experiment might have been simply a proof of classic conditioning of a stimulus-reward response. But the Papouseks then made a significant observation. They found that the infants, after a few successes, would leave their heads turned 90 degrees even though the lights were to be seen in the midline. Furthermore, the infants did not seem to be watching. Nonetheless, they continued to turn on the display and responded to their success with smiles and happy bubbling.

Broucek (1979) goes on the cite Bower's work

> with a blind infant who at eight weeks of age did not smile at all. The baby had been blind from birth and so, of course, had been deprived of the visual stimuli that normally elicit smiling. However, when he was given an auditory mobile and contingent control over it, so that by kicking his legs he could produce a change of sound, he began to smile and coo. The smiles were vigorous and forceful. Normally at this age we cannot elicit smiling with sounds at all, particularly mechanical sounds of the sort we used in this experiment. Nonetheless, as soon as the baby had contingent control over this event in his external world, he began to smile. The stimulus objects in this case were small bells. Prior to the experiment the sound of these bells had not made the baby smile, and bells alone never produced a smile. Only when he was exercising control over the bells did we see smiling at this early age [p. 312].

What was the source of the pleasure? Broucek believed that the source of pleasure lay not in problem solving alone—for example, the discovery of a contingency between two external events—but in the pleasure derived from the infant's awareness that he himself had produced the result. A sense of efficacy and pleasure is experienced when the infant recognizes "a contingent relationship between one's own initially spontaneous behavior and an event in the external world and the subsequent ability to produce at will the external event through repetition of the antecedent act" (Broucek, 1979, p. 312). The infant in these experiments was motivated not by exploration alone (that is, by the discovery of the connection between two external events) nor by assertion (that is, random or reflexive movements), but by a combination of the two. Problem solving by exploration and assertion together triggers the pleasure that comes from a sense of efficacy and competence. Later in life, the integration of assertion and exploration becomes less apparent. When a lawyer vigorously states his arguments, assertion is obvious and exploration less apparent. When the lawyer is involved in a search for useful precedents, which may take place only in his mind, exploration is dominant and assertion less obvious.

Broucek concludes that awareness of being the cause, along with sense of efficacy and the pleasure associated with it, is the foundation of self-feeling. I, however, have identified the sense of achieving physiological regulation due to a satisfactory match between caregiver ministrations and the infant's awareness of need as one element of self-feeling. The sense of achieving intimacy in attachment and later in affiliation is yet another element in self-feeling. I shall add as further elements of self-feeling the sense of being able to indicate an aversive response (chapter 7) and the sense of achieving sensual enjoyment and sexual excitement (chapter 8). I agree with Broucek that exploratory and assertive motivations, and the feelings of efficacy and competence pleasure that amplify it, are indeed significant, often underappreciated elements of self-feeling.

There is a logic to Broucek's opinion that the pleasure of efficacy and competence is the foundation of self-feeling. In each motivational system, exploration and assertion are components of each activity cited—whether active or passive in orientation—and success in any motivational endeavor will be augmented by efficacy pleasure. I described in chapter 3 the problem solving involved in Sameroff's (1984) example of infants who had to alter their sucking method to obtain nutrients. Each time a baby makes a parent smile or respond in a social exchange, the baby has been successfully assertive and is likely to experience a self-feeling of competence in achieving intimacy. Prevailing over an enemy and success in seduction carry the same potential for competence pleasure. On the other hand, exploration and assertion in pursuit of the pleasure of efficacy and competence constitute a separate motivational system. To resolve this apparent paradox, we must restate the properties of systems. Exploration and assertion are a subset of the person's motivation and functioning as a whole. In that sense, exploration and assertion can be thought of as component properties of any motivational system that is dominant at a particular time. However, to support my claim of a separate system, I must demonstrate that exploration and assertion are a motivational subset of sufficient scope and separate experiential delineation to be adaptively self-organizing and self-stabilizing.

The ability to track contingency, which is an innately programmed core of this system, exists before birth. The exploration interest and assertive capacities of the fetus and newborn were demonstrated by the experiment referred to earlier (DeCasper and Fifer, 1980) in which babies who had been read to from "The Cat in the Hat" by their pregnant mothers during the six and a half weeks before birth, sucked to hear their mother's voice reading that, and not another, book. But the capacity demonstrated in this experiment is closely tied to the development of the attachment motivational system and therefore is not clear support for a separate exploratory-

assertion system. Tuber et al. (1980) tested premature twins, one hy-
drencephalic and one normal, with a sound followed at a regular
interval by a light. When the light stimulus was omitted, both infants demonstrated by changes in their heart rates a clear orienting
response, indicating that the premature human infant forms associations and tracks and reacts to contingency and its violation relatively independent of the cerebral hemispheres. This experiment
demonstrates exploration and assertion in the form of associative
learning and orientation exclusive of any link to attachment. It is
thus similar to the Papousek's (1975) experiment in which infants
turned their heads to trigger visual displays. The difference is that
their tests demonstrated the affective augmentation of competence
pleasure, whereas the experiments with the premature twins did
not. But most important to my thesis is that exploration and assertion beginning with the innate core demonstrated in the twins, develops within a few months into a distinct niche in the infant's life.

Sander (1983a) specified the niche in the infant's life in which exploration and assertion can become self-organized as an "open
space" in the coordination of caregiving behavior and infant state.
He studied the state changes in infants from birth on and noted
that where caregiving and infant response was successful, infants
during their awake state had moments of being in relative equilibrium. At those times, neither physiological nor attachment needs
were ascendant; the infant was fed, dry, and comfortable, and not
ready to go to sleep. This made possible a span of time in which the
caregiver and infant could experience a relative disengagement.
Mothers placed infants where the infants could entertain themselves, and see and hear the mothers as they continue about their
duties.

> This provides a condition allowing for options in the infant's exercise
> of an individually idiosyncratic and selective violational initiative . . .
> The infant can begin to organize his world actively with a freedom of
> option that can reflect small idiosyncracies of his experience, his in-
> terests, and his preferences giving a particular pattern to the organi-
> zation of his attention and the organization of his action in relation to
> it [pp. 97–98].

Let us take the common experience of infants focusing their gaze
on a mobile. The organization of their attention (exploration) and
the organization of their action in relation to it (assertion) by following with their eyes and tensing their musculature constitutes an activity that occurs when the infants' attention focus is not preempted

by either attachment or physiological regulation needs or the need to react aversively. Nor are their mothers preempting their potential interest, pressing attachment-centered activities on them. In such open space moments, what Winnicott (1958) called the capacity to be alone in the presence of the other, infants can discover their own personal life rather than "a fake life built on reactions to external stimuli" (p. 34). In these moments of disengagement, "the conditions are optimal for infants to differentiate effects contingent on their own initiative. The experience of contingent effects has a profound impact on the alerting and focusing of infant attention" (Sander, 1983, pp. 98–99). Sander attributed the profound and highly personal impact of these developments to the richness of individual selectivity or option that occurs. By virtue of the self-organization of what I call the exploratory-assertive motivational system, the infants are able to initiate new behavioral organizations that have "the qualities of 'real' and of 'own' " (p. 99). The affective marker for this experience lies in competence and efficacy pleasure. Expressed in the language of later life, this might be: I can recognize it, I can match it, I make it go on or off, or I have discovered it and I have altered it, and so on, exploration being closer to the "Aha!" of insight and assertion being closer to power and mastery.

To recapitulate: The Papousek's (1975) experiment indicates that infants at four months are motivated to explore stimuli that have no direct immediate connection with caregivers and to act assertively to be the cause of an effect on the nonhuman environment. When they experience themselves as being the initiators of a predictable effect, this experience triggers an affect of pleasure. Sander's (1983a) observations place such experiences in a specific ecological niche in the very young infant's life disengaged from attachment or physiological need regulation or aversive reaction or sensual enjoyment. Functioning of the exploratory-assertive system triggers affects experienced by the developing core self as a sense of realness and ownness—the effectiveness of independent initiating along individualistic lines. Following this line of thought, we are able to disentangle exploratory-assertive motivation from other motivations and to recognize specific moments in which it is not only independent but dominant.

Let us consider another experiment (Fox and McDaniel, 1982). Adults are keen perceivers of biological motion. When a small number of lights are placed on the limbs and joints of moving humans or animals, adults in a darkened room can quickly recognize walking, running, dancing, even gender. Assuming this to be an intrinsic discriminatory capacity, the experimenters tested infants to see if they would indicate a preference for displays of moving dots showing biological motion over those of moving dots differently organized. At two months, the infants showed no preference, but at four to six months they demonstrated a clear preference for the biological motion pattern. Once this capacity is present, the four to six month old infant is able to experience the competence pleasure of exploring a stimulus and asserting a preference. The infant does not cause the occurrence of the display but is nonetheless the initiator of the seeking and the indication of preference—a lower level source of competence pleasure but quite possibly an adequate source nonetheless. Now let us suppose that the infant at eight months in an "open-spaced" moment, one disengaged from attachment activity, observes an unfamiliar person walking at a distance. If the infant shows interest, is it because of the potential link to attachment, or is it for the satisfaction of an exploratory-assertive motive? If we knew that the infant was craving intimacy at that moment, the answer would be that the visual interest was serving an attachment motive. But if intimacy craving were not dominant, the person walking would function like a mobile—to present the infant with an opportunity for initiating a pattern matching of his or her own preference. In the chapter on attachment, I repeatedly emphasized the significance of the adult's consistency and predictability in social exchanges for the development of intimacy pleasure. Now, to balance that account, it should be stated that in some social play the dominant motive for the infant may be contingency detection and being the initiator of the result. During these moments, competence pleasure overweighs intimacy pleasure. When this happens "The Game is not important to the infant because people play it but rather people become important to the infant because they play The Game" (Watson, 1972, p. 338).

HISTORICAL PERSPECTIVE

Before the experimental evidence from in utero and infancy that we can draw on now, many attempts were made to place exploration and assertion in psychoanalytic theory. When drive theory occupied the central focus, exploration was seen simply as curiosity—a manifestation of libidinal drive—and assertion was seen as the instinct to mastery—manifested in cruelty and sadism (Freud, 1905, 1913). In *Beyond the Pleasures Principle* Freud (1920) offered a number of cogent observations of children and added meanings to the concept of an instinct for mastery: "In their play children repeat everything that has made a great impression on them in real life, and . . . in doing so they abreact the strength of the impression and . . . make themselves master of the situation" (p. 17). The instinct for mastery and the compulsion to repeat may be either pleasurable or unpleasurable. Freud observed that children cannot

> have their *pleasurable* experiences repeated often enough, and they are inexorable in their insistence that the repetition shall be an identical one. . . . Children will never tire of asking an adult to repeat a game that he has shown them or played with them, till he is too exhausted to go on. And if a child has been told a nice story, he will insist on hearing it over and over again correcting any alteration. If the impression is unpleasurable the compulsion to repeat has an additional reason that they can master a powerful impression far more thoroughly by being active than they could by merely experiencing it passively [p. 35].

Beyond these generalizations, Freud provided a detailed observation of his grandson. The little boy of one and a half, "greatly attached to his mother" (p. 14), invented a game of throwing small objects out of sight and then hunting for them while giving "vent to a loud, long-drawn-out 'o-o-o-o' accompanied by an expression of interest and satisfaction" (p. 14). O-o-o-o stood for *fort*, "gone" in German.

> I eventually realized that it was a game and that the only use he made of any of his toys was to play "gone" with them. One day I made an observation which confirmed my view. The child had a wooden reel with a piece of string tied round it. It never occurred to him to pull it along the floor behind him, for instance, and play at its being a carriage. What he did was to hold the reel by the string and very skillfully throw it over the edge of his curtained cot, so that it disappeared into it, at the same time uttering his expressive "o-o-o-o." He then pulled the reel out of the cot again by the string and hailed its reappearance with a joyful "da" ["*there*"]. This, then, was the complete game—disappearance and return [p. 15].

Freud's purpose in citing this example was to demonstrate that the repetition of unpleasurable experience in itself did not violate (lie beyond) the pleasure principle. He used the instinct for mastery as a convenient way to indicate the powerful force present in the repetition. The threat lay in not being able to master the distress of the mother's departure, and the solution was to turn passive into active and even resentfully to throw the offending mother away.

The concept of exploration and assertion as a goal in itself lies outside the purview of Freud's considerations.

Two analytic efforts to deal directly with exploration and assertion as goals occurred in the 1940s. Hendrick (1942, 1943) took the position that there is an inborn drive to do and to learn how to do. For Hendrick, the instinct to master had the broad implication of a need to control the environment through a progressively adaptive control of action itself. In a view similar to mine, Hendrick (1943) stated that the inborn drive to do and learn how to do involves the pleasure derived from the successful carrying out of a function: "Primary pleasure is sought by efficient use of the central nervous system for the performance of well-integrated ego functions which enable the individual to control or alter his environment" (p. 311).

Hendrick's view received little acceptance. The prevailing trend went in the direction of ego psychology, in which mastery of the environment was assigned to the ego as one of its functions. Under Hartmann's leadership, the same observational findings available to Hendrick provided for most psychoanalysts in the United States a way to view the ego as having an independent source of energy and initiative, not as the passive rider on its id-horse. While the ego psychological resolution of the problem posed by the child's problem solving through exploration and assertion was to assign these functions to the ego and retain a dual-drive theory, Hartmann et al (1946) recognized the child's *compelling* need to act adaptively.

> The child does not only experience deprivation when one of his demands is denied—the demand for food, care of attention—but also when the adult interferes with one of his spontaneous activities, whether they serve the gratification of a drive or the solution of a problem. In the child's life, various types of activities tend to be not as sharply delimited from each other as they normally are with the adult. All action is closer to instinctual drives [p. 41].

Hartmann's (1933) study of the pressure to bring a problem-solving task to completion, the Zeigarnik effect, was an early effort to explain similar phenomena.

The landmark effort to establish a theoretical-observational base for an exploratory-assertive motivational system was White's (1959) *Motivation Reconsidered: The Concept of Competence.* Using infant observations as his basis, White stated, "The urge toward competence is inferred specifically from behavior that shows a lasting focalization and that has the characteristics of exploration and experimentation" (p. 323). White reviewed both the traditional psychoanalytic theory of motivation by instinctual drive and Hendrick's (1942, 1943) call for an instinct of mastery. He concluded that competence, the capacity to interact effectively with the environment, cannot be motivated wholly "from sources of energy currently conceptualized as drives or instincts" (p. 297). Likewise, animal psychologists have been drawn to the conclusion that activity, exploration, and manipulation "might have to be assigned the status of independent motives" (p. 298). White cited Butler's (1953) experiment in which monkeys learned a discrimination problem when the only reward was the opening of a window that permitted them to observe the comings and goings of people in the laboratory. The discriminations thus formed were resistant to extinction. White carefully reviewed and refuted arguments that would conflate the motivation for competence in exploration, activity, and manipulation with behaviors based on fear, thirst, hunger, sex, and drive reduction. "Fear shows itself in either freezing or avoidance, whereas exploration is clearly an instance of approach"(p. 300). "In hunger and thirst, tissue deficits, humoral factors and consummatory responses retain an important position. The mature sex drive depends heavily on hormonal levels and is sharply oriented toward consummation. Tendencies like exploration do not share these characteristics" (p. 305). "The earlier identification of reinforcement with drive reduction has been directly attacked in a series of experiments designed to show that learning takes place when drive reduction is ruled out." (p. 304).

Reviewing the psychoanalytic literature, White cited Mittelmann's (1954) paper on motility. Mittelmann described the tremendous effort made by the child to learn to walk and to walk well and the joyous laughter that is triggered by success. Alternatively, clumsiness in motor or manipulative accomplishments may lead to self-hatred and dependence. Erikson (1959) broadened the same theme from motility to autonomy in general in the second year, and to a sense of industry during the school years, when children address themselves to motor, manual, and intellectual achievements. Erikson related the sense of industry to a need to be able to make things and make them well, even perfectly.

Drawing on general psychology, White (1959) delineated the particular conditions under which the motivation for competence flourishes. In contrast to the high pressure that arises from need or anxiety "under which we are unlikely to achieve an objective grasp of the environment, low need pressure is requisite if we are to perceive objects as they are, in their constant character apart from hopes and fears" (p. 315). In low-need pressure situations, novelty is a governing factor.

Interest seems to require elements of unfamiliarity: of something still to be found out and of learning still to be done. . . . Small discrepancies produce pleasant affect and a tendency to approach. Large one's produce unpleasantness and a tendency toward avoidance. The child at play . . . needs frequent novelty in the stimulus field in order to keep up his interest [p. 314].

White drew on Piaget's (1912) studies of the growth of intelligence to illustrate highly motivated exploratory and assertive behaviors. White noted that when pressure from hunger, sleep, or erotic needs, or from distress and fears, is absent, activities performed by infants give evidence of "sensing, perceiving, attending, learning, recognizing, probably recalling, and perhaps thinking in a rudimentary way" (p. 320), accompanied by smiles, gurgles, and laughter.

With this background, White developed a theory that in important aspects foreshadowed my own. He asked, When hunger, thirst, sex, fear and distress are not exerting pressure, what goal are infants motivated toward? White suggested that the activities of infants during these low-pressure intervals might have four aims: to appease a stimulus hunger, to reach a pleasurable level of neuromuscular exercise through activity, to achieve knowledge that will provide a more differentiated cognitive map of the environment and thus satisfy an exploratory tendency, and to achieve mastery, power, and control (self-assertion) based on influencing the environment through their activity. White dismissed as useless any effort to assign priority to one of the four. Learning to interact effectively with the environment, White called *competence*. "Activities in the ultimate service of competence must therefore be conceived to be motivated in their own right. It is proposed to designate this motivation by the term effectance, and to characterize the experience produced as a feeling of efficacy" (p. 329). White regarded effectance motivation as aiming

for the feeling of efficacy, not for the vitally important learnings that come as its consequence. . . . Effectance motivation may lead to continuing exploratory interest or active adventures when in fact there is no longer any gain in actual competence or any need for it in terms of survival. . . . Of course, the motives of later childhood and of adult life are no longer simple. . . . they can acquire loadings of anxiety, defense, and compensation, they can become fused with unconscious fantasies of a sexual, aggressive, or omnipotent character, and they can gain force because of their service in producing realistic results in the way of income and career [p. 323].

White reserved for his final main point the need to distinguish effectance motivation from those motivational sources that had traditionally been cited and to place it in its evolutionary ecological niche. Unlike the "strong" motivations of sex, hunger, and fear, the moderate persistent effectance motivation is more conducive to an exploratory and experimental attitude and, thus, to more competence interactions in general.

> Considering the slow rate of learning in infancy and the vast amount that has to be learned before there can be an effective level of interaction with surroundings, young . . . children would simply not learn enough unless they worked pretty steadily at the task between episodes of homeostatic crisis. . . . Man's huge cortical association areas might have been a suicidal piece of specialization if they had come without a steady persistent inclination toward interacting with the environment [pp. 329–330].

Thus, White's paper went a long way to establish competence as a motive or, as I would prefer, the need for exploration and assertion as a distinct motivational system. White was neither naive nor reductionistic in his proposal: "It is not my intention to cast effectance in the star part in adult motivation. The acquisition of motives is a complicated affair in which simple and sovereign theories grow daily more obsolete" (p. 323). White thereby left the way open for the urge toward competence in interacting with the environment and the feeling of efficacy to be one of an unspecified group of other motivations. And he left open the manner in which these motives integrate or compete with other motives. I find the delineation he made of effectance motivation to be essentially consonant with my conception of the need for exploration and assertion. What differences do we have? A minor difference is that he was unaware of the innate potentials of neonates for giving order and coherence to the stimuli around them, especially their capacities for cross-modal perceptual integration. As a result, relying solely on Piaget's observations, he overstressed the laboriousness of infant learning.

A more serious difference lies in his relative neglect of the human interrelational factor in motivation in general and its influence on exploration and assertion in particular. While he cited hunger, thirst, sex, and fear as competing sources of motivation, he neglected attachment either as a separate motivational system as I construe it or as a factor influencing the exploratory-assertive motivational system as I also construe it. To summarize: White presented a brilliant argument for the reconsideration of motivation in the light of the evidence for motives aimed at competent interaction with and exploration of the environment and an affective response of a feeling of efficacy. He did not construe exploratory-assertive aims and the feeling of efficacy as a motivational system, one of a group of motivational systems, each capable of dominance in an ever-shifting set up hierarchical arrangements.

WHAT CONSTITUTES COMPETENCE?

If the infant is motivated toward exploration and assertion and a pleasurable affective response that is triggered by a sense of efficacy and competence, what is the source of the infant's sense of competence? In the experiment where four-month-old infants moved their heads to turn on a light display (Papousek and Papousek, 1975), the sense of competence arose from successful contingent tracking that led to a self-learned capacity to initiate (be the cause of) activation of a preferred stimulus.

Sander (1986) suggested an earlier and more generalized source for a sense of efficacy. As a result of healthy infant-caregiver regulatory interactions, infants' initial inner experiences consolidate around the experience of their own recurrent states. Once infants' states (alert wakefulness, quiet wakefulness, crying, fussiness, REM, and non-REM sleep) become coherent and recurrent, a state itself and particularly its desired affective component becomes the aim and criterion for goal-organized intentional patterns. A sense of competence then results from the infants' being able to reproduce the experience of a desired state. Innate and quickly learned patterns of response to preferred stimuli trigger affects of interest and surprise. Novelty and detection of contingent effects prolong states of attentive arousal. As the state of aroused attentive alertness consolidates, infants can be inferred to experience, along with interest and surprise, a quality of "aliveness" quite different from their affective experience during states of physiological need, crying, fussiness, sleepiness or sleep. Looked at in this way, the exploratory and assertive activity of infants would not be to seek stimuli as such, but to experience the particular affective sense of aliveness of the aroused exploratory state. Competence would then be a measure of infants' ability to organize and regulate their activity to produce a new version of the desired state.

Let me restate this complicated idea more simply. A state becomes desired when there is an affectively pleasing reward. In the course of effective caregiver-infant interactions, recurrent states of hunger passing to satiety, attachment activities leading to the intimacy pleasure, and exploration and assertion leading to the pleasure of preferred stimuli give each experience a status of its own. Once this status-of-its-own obtains definitional recognition (memory), the infant will work to repeat it to reinstate the desired experience. Success then is twofold: having the desired "reward" (hunger satiety, intimacy, the preferred stimulus of the lights) and having the sense of success at having produced the desired state. This concept presumes that infants have a complex capacity for matching. One matching capacity permits infants to recognize that the external stimulus of the flashing light coincides with an internal criterion for a preferred stimulus. An additional matching capacity employs feedback information and contingency tracking for recognizing that the light display has been activated as a consequence of the infant's own activity. But Sander (1986) proposes another matching capacity, by which infants compare an experiential state they are in with an experiential state that past experience has marked as desired. Recognizing their ability to create the match successfully conveys a sense of competence and pleasure. This conception establishes three sources of motivation—the pleasure to be derived from a preferred stimulus, the pleasure to be derived from being the source of a desired activity, and the pleasure to be derived from being the source of re-creating a previously experienced desired affective experiential state.

This concept helps to solve a riddle of infant behavior. On the basis of stimulus-response conditioning therapy, it can be expected that caregivers who respond rapidly to an infant's cry are providing a reward that reinforces the infant's inclination to cry whenever in distress. On the basis of this assumption, mothers have been advised to let babies cry to prevent "spoiling" them and making cry babies of them. However, observation has proven the opposite to be true. One-year-old babies whose mothers have been responsive to their cries and effective in providing relief throughout the first year are far less inclined to cry (Ainsworth, 1979). Using Sander's (1986) theory, we would explain the babies' reduced crying as their having identified the state of relief and restoration of alertness that follows distress to be a highly desired affective experiential state. The babies then become motivated to work to reproduce that state. They learn to use their pacifier or bottle or blanket for self-soothing or to become preoccupied with exploratory-assertive play with a toy for self-arousal of interest. Providing their own relief from distress, that is, recreating the desired state, brings with it the pleasure of relief, augmented by an inner sense of competence.

Sander cited social exchanges as evidence that a desired state becomes a goal for organizing behavior. He noted the manner in which caregiver and the four- to six-months old infant interact to maximize the resonance of their mutual exuberance. Likewise we can infer the infants' search for an inner experience of delight and joy in social exchanges from the collapse and dejection they evidence as they abandon their efforts after repeated attempts to activate un-responsive mothers. Again we face the dilemma posed by Broucek (1979): if competence is to be found in the activation of any desired state and desired states exist in all motivational systems, is the sense of competence a basis for self-formation in general? Again, the answer must be yes, just as aversion in signal form is a factor in other motivational systems (or physiological regulation or some sensual seeking), competence pleasure is an organizing factor in physiological regulation, attachment activities, aversion responses, and sensual and sexual seeking. In these other systems, the sense of competence plays a part in their organization and augments the pleasure in each, but I believe that efficacy pleasure as such is *central* only to the exploratory-assertion system.

To support my contention, we must examine the mode of functioning of exploratory-assertive motivation. Let us return to the Papousek's (1975) experiment. The four-month-old infants are in the "open space" of disengagement from attachment needs, physiological regulatory needs, aversion reaction, or sensual need. They move their heads in the unplanned mode of changing position or following fleeting visual scans. The light display goes on. Their interest is raised as they watch the display, which then turns off. After several unplanned movements set off the display, they form the hypothesis that their movement is the cause of the activation of the display. The head movements become purposefully directed. The display is triggered. The interest shifts from the display to setting off the activator.

The original matching was between an inborn preference for a certain type of visual stimulus and its occurrence. This match triggered the pleasure of interest and surprise. If the stimulus was presented repeatedly without variation, the infants would rapidly lose interest (habituate). This matching would be similar to the mother's face appearing in the gaze range, although habituation would be less rapid because mother's more varying expressions and facial movements introduce interest-catching novelty. The second matching was between a self-initiated action and an external effect. This match triggered the pleasure of competence pleasure. This matching also would be similar of the infant's smile were responded to by the mother's smile and a social exchange began. The match, too, would trigger pleasure in competence, augmenting the pleasure in intimacy. The infant's interest would be maintained by the novelty the mother and infant would build by their theme and variations pattern. In the situation with the light display, interest was maintained, but the interest-activating light display and the activating mechanism remained the same. The infants, in pursuit of discovering the match between movements and activator, could track the contingency without any distraction of their attentional focus. The optional response took place relatively slowly so that learning occurred by small increments with error signals to indicate mismatch and a call for refinement. The arousal state was thus focused primarily on the tracing (exploring) of the match between the activity (assertion) and the eventual effect. When they could track themselves with proprioceptive informational feedback while simultaneously tracking the effect (the activation of the display), the infants were optimally positioned to appreciate that they were an activating cause. This relatively clear focus of agency made the sense of competence particularly direct and identifiable. The search for effectiveness and the sense of making that goal one's own became the active force guiding the motivational thrust.

In comparison, in social exchanges, infants are tracking a rapidly changing sequence. The feedback from mother's responsible face and voice occupy the center of the infants' attention. Feedback from their own tracking, matching of expectancy, and awareness of their casual role, while present to correct minor errors, is apt to be secondary and less distinct. Thus, in the social exchange, an innate preference for the human face and voice has led to attachment experience and intimacy pleasure. The infant's goal becomes to recreate the state of attachment and intimacy pleasure. Mother's response and the mutual state of exuberance mark the success of the motivational effort. An inferred inner experience of competence derived from being able to advance the state of intimacy exuberance augments the pleasure.

The experimenters with the light display took advantage of the innate preference for the visual stimulus to facilitate the creation of a state in which the infant had the greatest possible *distinct awareness* of having a self-initiated casual role. Tracking the contingency between self-activated movements and its effect, and repeating the sequence successfully, established the state of effectiveness and pleasure. An inferred inner experience of competence in being the cause of the effective action augmented the pleasure of that effectiveness.

To conclude: competence may be defined as the capacity to recreate any desired state. Competence pleasure is inferred to be an intrinsic experience of success in each motivational system. In the exploratory-assertive motivational system, competence pleasure is both an inferred intrinsic experience of success and an explicit demonstrable response—the infants' smiling and happy bubbling with each repetition of setting off the light display by their head turning. The explicit competence pleasure is triggered by the more direct experiencing of agency possible during exploration and assertion.

WHAT IS COMPETENCE?—
THE CAREGIVERS' CONTRIBUTION

In the open-space experience of play with inanimate objects, infants have the opportunity to self-define competence and to trigger a pleasurable affect as they recognize success in pattern matching and causing a desired effect. But much of infants' alert attentive periods are spent in interactions with their caregivers. In these interactions, the criteria on which infants can base a sense of competence must be more complex, heavily influenced by caregiver goals and interests. This was implied when the Papouseks (1986) stated that parental tendencies to teach their infants intuitively and parental pleasure from infants' success in naturalistic learning indicates that parents are intrinsically motivated to share experience and knowledge. I maintain that an important part of the knowledge parents intuitively impart to their children is the context of an exploration and assertion in which they want their baby to experience competence.

Analysis of intuitive parental behaviors indicate that parents want their infants to develop competence in communicating. They carefully play with them in the "work" of exchanges of looks, gestures, affects, and sounds cast in the conversational mode. They wish their infants to be contingent trackers, especially of the caregiving activities. When feeding with a spoon, a mother will react with delight as her infant opens his or her mouth in anticipation. The mother will augment this desired competence by opening her own mouth to teach by modeling. Caregivers wish their babies to develop interest and competence in handling an array of toys—some to capture visual activity (a mobile), some auditory (a rattle), some tactile soft (a cuddly doll or blanket), some tactile firm and manipulatable (a ball or block). The Papouseks (1986, 1986) studied the interactional context in which mothers are most apt to employ melodic contours in their speech, that is, to use patterns of speech most likely to capture and hold their infant's attention. They report that of all contexts of mother-infant interactions, melodic contours were most frequently employed in association with maternal didactic intentions that mothers frequently express in the lexical content of their baby talk. "Come on sweetheart, talk to Mommy. There. Say it again, again, say it again," or "Open your mouth, here comes the spoon, open the tunnel, the train is coming," or "Roll the ball to Mommy. Here it comes back to you," or "Look, here's teddy. You know teddy. Look how he smiles when he sees teddy." All of this, of course, before the words have direct instructional meaning but only give expression to the parental intent.

My point is that competence and its attendant pleasure become defined for neonates and growing infants both during direct caregiver infant interaction and during play activities disengaged from that interaction. When successful, infants' innate programs for tracking contingency, discerning regularities, matching patterns, and triggering pleasure provide a definition of competence as an experience. The parents' (probably equally intrinsic) motivation to share experience and knowledge defines for their infant the contexts in which they are interested in having the infant develop and enjoy competence. These will differ for each parent, father preferring and encouraging one set of competencies, mother another. They do so intuitively, making it easier for infants to track the contingencies in their behaviors. Just as in the experimental situation infants learned that by turning their heads they could turn lights on, they also learn that by smiling they can evoke a return smile, by reaching they can have a rattle handed to them. Parents intuitively allow themselves to be manipulated so that infants can express individual rhythms of activity and learn that their parents attune to their rhythms and regulate back—a mutual experience of defining and developing competence. And parents behave predictably, so their infants can learn to form expectancies and successfully match those expectancies, giving them the competence pleasure of recognition.

Bornstein (1985) summarized much of the experimental findings on how infant and mother jointly contribute to the child's development of cognitive competence. In one study, eight girls and six boys were seen with their mothers at four months after birth and, later, one and four years of age. Findings at four months had definitive predictive power for the information-processing capacity of the infants and the mothers' didactic activity. The infants were shown the same visual display several times, and the diminution in their interest was measured. The decrease in attention was believed to reflect the successful acquisition of stimulus information based on the encoding of the image in short-term memory and the ability to compare a subsequent stimulus with the remembered one. The infants were also observed for half-hour periods in naturalistic interactions with their mothers. Observers recorded when mothers didactically encouraged their infants' attention to properties, objects, and events in the environment, for example, handing the baby a toy, pointing to a picture, or naming an object. Bornstein found that infants who processed information more efficiently at four months tended to possess larger expressive vocabularies at one year and to score higher on the Wechsler Preschool and Primary Scale of Intelligence (WPPSI). Bornstein also found that a high rating for a mother as one who encouraged her infant's attention to properties, objects, and events was of nearly equivalent and independent predictive power for a high score on the standardized intelligence test at four years. Together, information processing and maternal didactic encouragement appear to constitute the major direct casual influences for cognitive achievement.

Bornstein cited other findings that help to refine the mothers' contribution to defining and encouraging competence for their children. Mothers varied from one another in their approach but were apt to be relatively consistent in their style. Some mothers stimulated their infants often, and some mothers responded more efficiently and more sensitively; but whatever style she followed the mother's approach was reasonably consistent. A study of ten twin pairs of children demonstrated the impact of the practical limitation of the mothers' attentive capacities. At their children's age four months and again at a year, mothers of twins were found to stimulate each of their infants at less than half the rate that mothers of single children in the original study had stimulated theirs. At one year, the twins possessed less than half the vocabulary and at four years scored lower on the intelligence tests. Bornstein stated, "Amidst the plethora of biological and experiential factors that eventuate in this disadvantage [on psychometric tests], these data suggest that twins' relative deprivation in maternal didactics may play a contributory role" (p. 7471).

Bornstein reflected on a different naturalistic "experiment," with otherwise disadvantaged infants who were adopted into advantaged families before their six-month birthday. These infants scored higher on tests of intelligence and achieved better in school than did children adopted after infancy. According to Bornstein, the positive influence of caretaker didactic encouragement helps to explain the correlation between early adoption, high adoptive maternal intelligence, and the achievement of adopted children.

A study of 23 mothers and their 13-month-old toddlers was made to refine categories of maternal didactics. When the mothers encouraged the toddlers to notice a *new* property, object, or event, as opposed to elaborating on what the toddler was attending, this didactic approach correlated with the children's developing verbal comprehension.

Bornstein offered as one of his main conclusions that not only is cognitive competence the result of the infant's information-processing capabilities and of maternal encouragement, but infant and mother mutually influence one another. He reported a significant concurrent association between infant habituation and maternal encouraging attention at four months, and a strong indication that infant attentional style of four months influences the maternal didactic approach observed at one year.

Bornstein offered an observation that I believe is of great significance when we consider competence in the older child, that is, in the child who possesses full symbolic representation in primary and secondary modes of organization. He stated:

> The kinds of intelligence assessed here as outcomes are admittedly circumscribed, but they are of recognized cultural value for their associations with literacy, communication, academic achievement, and social attunement. By contrast neither infant nor maternal variables predicted children's discrimination learning at four years, although WPPSI scores and discrimination-learning rate in childhood intercorrelated. Habituation and maternal didactics in infancy seem therefore to link to verbal intelligence in particular, rather than to predict children's general problem-solving abilities [p. 7472].

Problem solving, as I discuss when I consider symbolic play, is the result of success at the coordination of the two modes of symbolic representation. Language acquisition and other cognitive capacities measured on the Wechsler are tools of that process and should not be confused with the process itself. I understand Bornstein to mean that infants who process information well at four months pull their mothers into encouraging them to note more and more properties, objects, and events; and that mothers who give encouragement also stimulate more active interest and provide more opportunity to practice processing. Moreover, the cogwheel effect at four months carries over to later development. Infants who process poorly at four months, or whose mothers fail to encourage them at that age, will at 12 months be at a disadvantage for an expansion of learning; their mothers will still be encouraging attention only to what the children are able to deal with. Conversely, one-year-olds who, because of high information-processing ability and maternal encouragement, are prepared for a change in maternal didactic style will receive encouragement from their mothers to broaden the focus of their attention. All of this builds verbal comprehension and the acquisition of vocabulary. However, as Bornstein implied, when *problem solving* is introduced into our consideration, competence broadens from significant, stable aspects of cognition to an expanded motivational system in which exploration and assertion lead to the pleasure of efficacy in problem solving. The complexities of problem solving at four years of age can be accomplished only through primary- and secondary-process modes of symbolic representation. The cognitive skills of discrimination-learning are tools of that process. The recognition of the quantum leap of symbolic representation during the latter half of the second year represents a principal contribution of psychoanalysis to an understanding of learning (see Noy, 1979, and Lichtenberg, 1983b, chapter 10).

THE ORIGINS OF PLAY

We have in this volume already discussed play at length. Infants and mothers engage in conversational games, with each initiating and regulating the rate, rhythm, flow, and duration of the "runs." Fathers engage with infants in more active, less smoothly rhythmic, more idiosyncratic play. For the older child, the affiliative experience in groups can transform an activity, say learning to tread water, from the tedium of work to the fun of the pool game of Marco Polo. In addition, infants' play activities with their bodies, bottles, toys, and other objects within their perceptual sphere have been described as occurring during moments of disengagement from attachment motivation. At the same time, while not fully accepting Stern's (1985) concept of an evoked companion, I have agreed that in moments of disengagement an affective state of pleasure in intimacy likely carries over. Infants play during these moments of being "alone" retains the sense that they are in the presence of the other, of being in a holding environment, of being figuratively or, commonly, actually on a parent's lap (Call, 1968).

In respect to the motivations of exploration and assertion, play has been regarded as particular activities of infants, spontaneous or shared, that evidence direction, selectivity, and some degree of persistence. In these minievents, infants seek stimulation and contact with the environment. They welcome raised but moderate tension, interest, joy, even excitement. Novelty and variety are one source of prolonging the play episode. Another source is that infant's awareness of being the cause of a desired alteration in the environment. All these properties of exploratory and assertive motivation and functioning are in the service of learning to interact competently with the environment. In that sense, play is serious business, but the affect triggered by it is a positively toned feeling of efficacy.

All play, then, involves the exploratory-assertive motivational system. But not all exploration and assertion is play. In later infancy, exploratory-assertive experiences take on the quality of seriousness rather than playfulness. For the older child, learning may be experientially either play or work. How are we to understand the difference? I submit that by play we refer to exploratory-assertive interactions with the environment that trigger, for infants, both the pleasure of a feeling of efficacy and the pleasure of a feeling of intimacy. The combined effect of pleasure from a sense of both efficacy and intimacy gives play its special quality of vitality and becomes, then, an affective state that infants are highly motivated to recreate. Work is an exploratory-assertive activity in which the dominant affect is restricted to efficacy and competence. When children go to school, they recognize that they are leaving the setting of their attachments. The transition to school for work and play may fail because aversiveness to the demands of the strange situation may set in before an attachment to a mentor can be established. In play, intimacy pleasure with leader and peers coincides with the exploratory-assertive search for competence pleasure. In work, the exploratory-assertive search for efficacy and competence pleasure must be the sustaining motivational basis. Thus work must be commensurate with the child's ability to accomplish competently within an appropriate period of time, or aversive frustration or boredom will supervene.

In the course of ordinary interactions with their parents and with their inanimate environment, infants are guaranteed opportunities for both efficacy and intimacy pleasure. I will examine efficacy pleasure first. Since the innate need for exploration and assertion aims for the feeling of efficacy, not for the important learnings that accrue from their exercise, infants will experience efficacy whenever they make eye contact, follow a mobile, touch a blanket, mouth a finger, intentionally kick the rib, strike a rattle, and so on. Piagetians (Piaget, 1936, 1937, 1945; Decarie, 1962) have mapped the detailed passage through successive sensorimotor stages. Their findings reveal how the innate potentiality, based on the maturation of the central nervous system, for increasingly complex interactions with the environment affect the direction, selectivity, and persistence of infants' exploration and assertion. In each operational stage, competence becomes redefined by the optimal potential for problem solving allowed by the possible range of accommodations and assimilations of that stage. At one stage, neither success nor failure in the search for an object removed from view can be experienced, because the conceptual construct of "missing" does not yet exist. Pleasure in efficacy can be experienced only with objects in the immediate perceptual field.

Infants' play with a mirror furnishes an example (see Lichtenberg, 1983b, chapter 7). Between nine and twelve months of age, infants will laugh, coo and jiggle their bodies with excitement when exposed to a mirror. Each movement the infants make instantly influences the percept. The infants are the activators, like the infants who turned on the light display by turning their heads. But infants between 13 and 15 months react quite differently to the mirror. When confronted with their mirror images, these toddlers grow sober, pensive, and less active. It is noteworthy that this is the point in development at which mothers encourage their children to notice a *new* property, object, or event (Bornstein, 1985). What is the source of the change from joy to pensiveness? I suggest that the toddlers have entered a different stage of exploratory-assertive potential. They have mastered one problem: being the cause of a change in their environment. This "solved" problem has been replaced by a new and unsolved one. They are now experiencing the mirror as a source of discrete information, a sign sending signals they must learn to decipher. The new question about the mirror and about the environment in general is, what are the more complex particular properties of specific objects? With the mirror, the problem is what information is conveyed by the reflection in it? With other objects, the question may be, what are the front and back, the texture and weight? For humans, with the advent of awareness of emotional intersubjectivity the challenge becomes to discern what their facial expressional and vocal communications convey as guidance signals. The image in the mirror and many other aspects of the environment become objects of contemplation (Werner and Kaplan, 1963). Gradually toddlers recognize that the image in the mirror is a reflection of themselves and conveys information about their appearance, for example, whether they have a smudge on the face (Brooks and Lewis, 1974; Lewis and Brooks-Gunn, 1979) or a label on their forehead (Modarressi, 1980). I suggest that the affect of contemplation reflects a prolongation of the stage of interest in which "practicing" (Mahler, Pine, and Bergman, 1975) or working toward competence in problem solving becomes dominant. The joy of efficacy is not as rapidly obtained as it was in earlier infancy, when rattling the rattle or watching the mobile or causing the display in the mirror to change solved the problem set by the sensorimotor schema.

The source of motivation in infancy—to experience a sense of efficacy rather than the learning that comes as a consequence—is different in the toddler period. For the older child, the learning itself, in the sense of resolving more complex problems, becomes a more important aspect of the task. This change is encouraged by parental emphasis on a widening exploration of novel features in the environment.

How developing infants confront numbers, then number learning, and eventually number problem solving provides an example of changing levels of organization of the exploratory-assertive motivational system. One group of sixteen and another of eight infants, six to eight months of age, were tested in an original and replicating experiment (Starkey et al., 1983). The infants viewed two photographic displays presented side by side. One display contained two items (a memo pad and a comb, or a ribbon and a pipe), the other three items (a pillow, an orange, and a vase, or a candle, a brief case, and a pink cap). While the infants watched, they heard either two or three drumbeats. A majority of infants attended longer to the display in which the number of items corresponded with the number of drumbeats. The experimenters wanted to rule out a temporal correspondence rather than a numerical one. On the basis of time alone the infants might match the visual display that took longer to see with the auditory stimulus that took longer to hear. The three-beat sequence was speeded up to be completed in the same time span as the two-beat sequence. Again, the infants attended longer to the visual display that corresponded with the number of drumbeats.

Another group of experimenters (Starkey and Cooper, 1980) approached the origins of learning to count by testing 72 normal, full-term infants whose ages ranged from 16 to 30 weeks, with a mean age of 22 weeks. The authors had previously established that two-year-olds use a rapid perceptual process (called subitizing) to distinguish among arrays of fewer than four items (adult subitizing range is one to four items). The infants were shown an array of 2, 3, 4 or 6 dots until they became habituated. They were then shown an array containing a different number of dots, and their responses were observed. Dishabituation (heightened attention) occurred when the number of items was small ($2 \rightarrow 3$ and $3 \rightarrow 2$) but not when it was larger ($4 \rightarrow 5$ and $6 \rightarrow 4$). This finding indicates that at five months of age infants can perceptually process small number units, that is, like two-year-olds and adults, five-month-old infants "know" (register discriminately) when two or three dots are being shown them. They do not recognize the change in numbers when four and then six dots are shown them.

These experiments indicate that small infants are capable of discriminating, representing, and remembering particular small numbers of items. It is reasonable to assume that infants are repeatedly practicing their number discrimination when confronted by arrays of 1, 2, or 3 items in the visual, auditory, and probably tactile spheres. In the course of exercising this rapid perceptual processing, the infants are in all likelihood experiencing feelings of efficacy as they create order in their perceptual sphere. In addition, the capacity for number discrimination and the feeling of efficacy may be enhanced by some of the didactic games parents intuitively play. The "this-little-piggy" game counts toes—combining auditory, visual and tactile sensations. "One-two, button your shoe, three-four, open the door" combines auditory pairs, number naming, and often the command for infants to open their mouth on a timed beat. "One for the money, two for the show, three to get ready, and four to go" is still another counting, rhythmical, command game. All of these combine efficacy pleasure with intimacy pleasure in exercising an exploratory-assertive motivation. They provide a background of preparedness for the subsequent games of verbal counting and the higher level discrimination that is necessary for discerning whether two items are one and one or whether they are two (an apple and an orange or two pieces of fruit, a Mommy and a Daddy, or parents). Thus innate perceptual processing of small number groups relatively automatically phases into practicing more competent utilization of this exploratory tool. In turn, practicing and the feeling of efficacy that can be triggered after only a short interval are combined in infant counting games. These traditional caretaker-infant games utilize the child's perceptual capacity and add to efficacy pleasure the pleasure of intimacy. It is tempting to hypothesize that these games, passed on from one generation to another were initially intuitive responses by perceptive parents to capacities of their infants that they could not have identified directly.

Gradually, the limits of perceptual processing are stretched beyond the processing potential of small number units, and a new level of learning is introduced. At each new level, efficacy pleasure is not obtainable as rapidly as before, and, consequently, more serious contemplative affects are apt to occur. Number learning may then be experienced as play on some occasions—such as when the game atmosphere of children's educational TV is successful or in games that involve counting, such as jacks and jump rope. At the same time, as parents and school require more didactic learn-your-numbers exercises, the intimacy pleasure of individual or affiliative group games fades and the efficacy pleasure often becomes attentuated by extension of the problem-solving tension over time.

Let us now focus more directly on the experience of *intimacy pleasure* as it affects the play of infants and toddlers. I have suggested that in the ordinary disengagement from interactions with parents, the pleasure of intimacy carries over and adds a vitalization to infants' exploratory assertive activities. Infants in their playpens, jumpseats, feeding chairs, or cribs may be happily watching, grasping, banging, kicking, feeling, hearing, mouthing whatever is available as mother passes in and out of view and hearing as she goes about her routine. This optimal state of empathic facilitation cannot always be sustained. Caregivers may not be able to maintain or to convey the kind of preoccupation with their baby that enables intimacy pleasure to carry over. The most obvious reason is the physical absence of the mother. But mothers may be physically present and emotionally absent. Both physical and emotional absence result in an affective change in the infants' play.

Mahler, Pine, and Bergman (1975) described the intensity with which infants from 10 to 18 months of age explore and play. They noted that this exuberant assertiveness is enhanced by the confidence the mother exudes when she feels the child is able to function more autonomously. If aware that their mother was absent, infants became low keyed, their gestural and performance motility slowed down, their interest in their surroundings diminished, and they appeared preoccupied, pensive, and somber. Mahler and her coauthors attributed the affective change to an effort to retain an ideal state of self during the absence. They observed that the infants lost their emotional balance and burst into tears when comfort was offered by an interim caregiver but were restored from their toned-down state to their prior state after reunion with mother. The ideal state of self that preceded the absence, in the authors' view, was based on the symbiotic relatedness of the mother-infant pair and the low-keyedness on "a dawning awareness that the symbiotic mothering half of the self was missed" (p. 75).

I explain this experience in different words but with much overlap in concept. Infants of this age have expectancies of their mother's presence and of her emotional support in the form of sign-signal informational exchanges. When the expectation is breached, they may attempt to carry on by a focused concentration on

exploratory-assertive play. But the play will lack the carryover of intimacy pleasure. When confronted by other caregivers offering comfort, the infants are forced to activate patterns based on attachment
needs. The expectancies in the attachment motivational system are
not being met, and the infants must struggle with the novel but
undesirable situation. The result of the stimulation of attachment
motivation by the interim caregiver is an upset in their emotional
balance. Reunion with mother first triggers protest crying and then
calls forth familiar attachment exchanges matching prior expectancies and restoring the infant's sense of self-cohesion. Intimacy pleasure is reactivated and play is resumed with its restored vitalizing
mix of efficacy and intimacy pleasure.

Studies of children one of whose parents had a manic-depressive
illness disclosed problems in the interplay of the attachment,
exploratory-assertive, and aversive motivational systems (Gaensbauer, et al., 1984). Seven male children, four of whose mothers and
three of whose fathers suffered from a bipolar illness, were studied
at 12, 15, and 18 months of age. These seven boys and seven boys
with normal parents, forming a control group, were exposed to an
experiential situation designed to study attachment behavior and
emotional expression. The experiment began with a period of free
play and the infant's mother present. In the second episode, the
infant was approached first by a stranger and then by his mother.
An episode of developmental testing incorporating mild frustration
followed. Then, while the stranger and infant were engaged in interactive play, the mother departed, returning in three minutes. After the reunion with mother, the stranger left, and in one minute
the mother followed. The infant was alone for a minute before the
stranger and then the mother returned, and the reunions were observed. The children with the manic-depressive parent tended to
form insecure attachments; six of the seven were classified as
avoidant of their mothers at 18 months of age. Unlike normal children, by 18 months of age three of these children were more negative to their mothers than to strangers.

The pattern to which I want to draw particular attention is their
responses to free play and to the testing experience. At 12 months,
during free play these children showed significant levels of fear, a
reaction seldom observed in the control group. At 18 months, the
toddlers with a manic-depressive parent, during the free play period, derived less pleasure from the play and showed less interest
in the toys available. Instead they were more inclined toward anger.
During the testing period, they reacted to the mild frustrations
built into the problem-solving challenge with a marked increase in

distress and anger and with a corresponding diminution of pleasure and toy interest. It is noteworthy that in the separation phase following the testing, these children held their interest on the toys and ignored their mothers. In contrast, the children with normal parents shifted attention to their returning mothers. Only after the emotions of the reunion had subsided did the children renew their interest in the pleasure of exploring and actively playing with toys.

What do these findings mean? What happened to disturb the attachment experiences of the children with a manic-depressive parent and diminish the possibility for intimacy pleasure, and to interfere markedly with their pleasure in efficacy during exploration and assertion? Gaensbauer and his colleagues (1984) stated that, over and above any genetic predispositions to emotional disturbances, these children experienced disturbed caretaking environments. A major finding was that, throughout the family, translating and communicating feelings was unwelcome. Instead, support for denial of feelings was continuous, creating a pool of rage and grief that never disappeared. Davenport et al. (1945) report, "Appropriate expressions of need or anger and fear of loss of control are experienced as leading to an interruption of dependent gratifications" (p. 231). Adding to the denial and suppression of affective communication, many exchanges are inconsistent as parental moods shift from affection to helplessness, unavailability, or irritability and abusive rage.

It is clear, then, that the intimacy pleasure component of play would be disturbed profoundly by the time these infants reached 18 months. But is exploratory and assertive motivation directly affected? From the study of the parents, it is apparent that they established a situation of contradictory expectancies that profoundly skewed the development of the children's exploratory-assertive motivational system. On one hand, the mothers were highly ambitious for their sons and placed great emphasis on the child's performing in front of others. The parents themselves used work as a stabilizing factor and maintained a high work ethic. On the other hand, they provided the children with few opportunities to achieve these goals or actively inhibited them. The mothers' interactions with their children in play situations were disorganized, unhappy, tense, inconsistent, and ineffective. They blocked their infants' explorations, kept them away from children or families who had different values or ideas. Rationalizing their child rearing as protective, they discouraged their children's openness to experience. In these circumstances, play loses its pleasurable aspects of both efficacy and intimacy. Play is experienced as a demand for the child to demonstrate how well he can perform. All play becomes a "testing situation" lined with pitfalls. This was best exemplified in the 18-month-olds by their anger and distress during the testing situation, with its designed mild frustration. Failure became a disaster for these children. The fear of failure inhibits risk taking and deprives the child of the pleasures of discovery. Nonetheless, an investment in toys is compulsively retained as a less risky diversion from attachment disappointments, as evidenced in the separation phase of the experimental situation.

In summary, when threatened with loss of a sense of self-cohesion (as they, unfortunately, frequently are), children of manic-depressive parents are inclined to activate their exploratory-assertive motivational system. Their ambitious parents encourage their display of skills. By focusing on the nonhuman environment, these infants protectively displace their interest from the fragmenting potential of attachment experiences. However, the normal functioning of exploration and assertion is impaired. Exploration is narrowed; assertion becomes blunted. Further, assertion in these children, as well as in infants who suffer emotional and physical abuse, is extremely vulnerable to dominance by aversive responses of antagonism and withdrawal (see chapter 7). Intimacy pleasure is an inconsistent component of exploratory-assertive play, and efficacy pleasure is commonly lost in the disastrous effects of even minor failures. Early in the lives of these children, play takes on the dreary but driven defensive quality of compulsive work.

SYMBOLIC PLAY

Since each motivational system is present at birth and persists as an organizing force throughout life, it is easy to stress continuities in development. Exploration and assertion are ever-present dominant or subset motives, and efficacy pleasure is a persistent aim of the self. Thus, it is important to reemphasize, development in each motivational system occurs in spurts, and possibly the most significant spurt is made during the second half of the second year, when toddlers become able to use symbolic modes of organization to represent their experience. With this maturational advance, children make a quantum leap in their ability to integrate inner experience with the challenges of their environment. This enhanced capacity contributes to the cohesiveness of the sense of self.

Symbolic representation provides the creative flexibility in exploration and assertion that distinguishes the human self from the "self" of the most advanced member of the animal world. The acquisition of language as a means to communicate is so striking in children of 16 to 20 months that it has obscured the fact, recognized by Piaget and Inhelder (1962) and Werner and Kaplan (1963), that language is a manifestation, a tool, of a general symbolizing function. The change that comes with the advent of symbolic representation can be observed in the play of children beginning about 18 months. The qualities of their play help us to recognize the expansion of the children's capacities. This is so with or without language.

Furthermore, while Piaget and Werner and Kaplan have led the way in tracing the development of symbolic representation and relating it to earlier cognitive developments, psychoanalysis has made its own unique contribution. On the basis of Freud's (1900) conception of primary and secondary process, psychoanalysts have proposed that symbolic play and language usage involve the parallel interlocking development of two general modes of organization. One organization is built principally around sensory impressions (sights, sounds, tactile sensations, tastes). The other organization is built around the rules of combining and sequencing that characterize syntax, word order, and distancing between signified and signifier. Both the primary- and the secondary-process organization may use words, and both may use imagery in the contents that they form (Holt, 1967; McKinnon, 1979; Noy, 1979; Lichtenberg, 1983b). As McKinnon (1979) pointed out, the psychoanalytic formulation receives substantial support from neurophysiological studies of right and left hemispheric functioning.

Nicolich (1977) stated that the level of symbolic maturity

depends on a) the source of the scheme, that is, whether it is derived from the child's own activity or from the observed activity of others; b) whether there is evidence of pretending; c) the actors and objects; d) the number of schemes and e) whether any of the play acts were planned in advance [p. 91].

Consider the following vignette:

Anna, at 23 months, got her two favorite dolls and dropped one on the floor as she put the other in her own table seat and pretended to feed her with a spoon that was available. She looked at the doll on the floor and appeared indecisive and thoughtful. She picked the doll up and carried it and a tongue depressor to serve as spoon to her mother and said, "Suz eat." Mother play-fed the doll called Susan, and Anna happily hummed wordlessly as she returned to feeding the first doll.

In this example, the source of the scheme resided in Anna, who was quite resourceful in initiating play activities. Elements based on imitation and identification were incorporated in the play, but the schema was not primarily dependent on these. Anna was not bound to the concrete reality of doll or food but could pretend to be feeding and, moreover, could imagine the tongue depressor to be a spoon. She expanded the game from one feeder to two, seeming altruistically so as not to play favorites. Although the initial feeding followed a familiar pattern, leaving uncertain its planning in the conceptual sense, involving mother and Suz clearly evidence a planned coherence in the assignment of roles. In the initial feeding, Anna assigned herself the role of mother, and in the second feeding Suz was baby Anna, not to be left out or put aside. Self thus was a flexible psychic entity in the play (as is mother) but was a solidly cohesive entity in the sense of initiator and planner. Put another way, a cohesive self was now able to explore and assert plans in accordance with the pressures and potentialities of properties in the environment (a spoon is to feed) and with the pressure and potentialities of a subjective awareness of the psychological state of one's own and that of others (the altruistic self and the unhappiness of the one left out).

Symbolic play is a universal attribute in development during the toddler period. Nicolich (1977) studied five little girls of 14 to 19 months for a period of six to ten months. Between 19 and 26 months of age, each child evidenced symbolic play characterized by pr .ding and planning. Three of the girls evidenced symbolic play at about 21 months, one several months earlier, another five months later. At first, only a very few of the children's play episodes were of the fully planned, pretending type. Most episodes remained realistic and relatively uncomplex. Two of the girls pretended proportionately more than the others. "Both had mothers who apparently enjoyed their pretend games and set few limits on maternal participation" (p. 98).

In a study of symbolic play, Slade (1986) observed five two-year-old boys in a toddler group over a ten-month period. Slade reported that in the beginning of the third year most play remained dictated by the action properties of objects or toys. However, by the middle of the third year, ideas began to provide the structure for most of the boys' play. Substitutions, a tongue depressor for a spoon, a block for a cookie, became common. Near their third birthday, the children began to exhibit more novel and inventive transformations. Slade cited the example of a boy who, when asked to provide a doctor's light, held up a toy percolator, pointed to the perculator bulb at the "patient," and exclaimed "Here's a light." Over the course of the ten months of observation, the children's involvement in role-playing games doubled. As they neared their third birthday, their favorite play activity involved role enactments in games of fireman or cowboy. They began with a great interest in props such as hats and using their voices and sound effects to represent actions. The role enactments culminated in the emergence of minidramas of firemen actually putting out fires. Slade noted that the capacity for symbolic play in itself reflects the maturation of cognitive development, but the duration, coherence, and internal consistency of play episodes reflect the psychodynamics of the individual child. Slade described observations of three boys that demonstrated the different qualities of their symbolic play and the functions it served for each.

First was cheerful, even-tempered Andy, the youngest child in the sample. He and his mother "were a beautifully attuned pair" (p. 548). Andy's play revealed quite directly his prime motive to be exploratory and assertive. He eagerly approached new toys, activities, and people, seeking the spur of imagination, efficacy, and intimacy from toys, family members, and teachers. Slade described a charming episode when, at 31 months, Andy began playing delightedly with symbols in the form of metaphors.

> Andy is playing with the other children, making cookies out of Play-Doh. He gets up and goes over to the oven and says, "I made a pizza..ta-da!!" He says to the teacher, "I'm going to give you a cookie. I'm going to make a good one! I try to make a crocodile." He then gets reinvolved in the cookie play and decides to take some to his grandmother in the next room. He goes to his grandmother, holds out the Play-Doh to her, and says, "That's a Mama crocodile." There is then more back-and-forth movement between play and parents' room; Andy is back with his grandmother and says, "It's a Dookie one, and a Grandma one, and a Grandpa Pete! ! ! . . . I'm squeezing it . . . I'm squeezing it!" He heads back into the playroom and announces that the Play-Doh is a hamburger, then shows it to his grandmother. She suggests they need a roll, and he says, "Oooh . . . rare . . . That's not rare . . . It's good . . . Now what's the matter with it? . . . Now I'm going to turn it into catsup . . . Eat the hot dog . . . Do you want one" [pp. 552–553].

Andy's play allowed him to explore his maturational capacities, to communicate with, involve, and share with others.

Unlike Andy's play, Carey's markedly imaginative play had an anxious, frantic quality. Although he was boisterous and always on the move, playfully wreaking havoc in the classroom, he was very shy and easily frightened by strangers. In contrast to Andy's well-organized and lengthy play bouts, Carey's play was brief, disorganized, fragmented, and diffuse. Both of Carey's parents were artists who actively encouraged fantasy, with little regard for the overexcitement the play produced. Carey was often fearful when separated from his mother, forming only a play comradeship with Andy and a clinging dependent attachment to the teacher.

Carey's father has just returned from a professional meeting, and he tells Carey he had seen Darth Vader and Casper the Ghost there. [Carey's father had attended a gathering where, in fact, actors had been dressed in costumes for promotional purposes.] Carey and his father are stringing together small wooden blocks of assorted sizes and shapes. Carey touches his father with two of the blocks he is holding, as if they are antennae or a stethoscope. When his father asks him what they are, Carey says "crates," then holds them to his father's eyes. His father pretends they are horns and says he is a cow with horns. Carey replies, "No, a sheep," then takes two round and flat blocks and asks, "Are these ears?" His father says yes; Carey says, "Mighty Mouse." His father then quickly sketches a mouse and places the blocks on the drawing as if they are ears. "Hey, Mighty Mouse!" says Carey. He pounds two blocks on the table, puts them in a cup, and hands the cup to his father to drink from. His father asks Carey, "Who drinks wood?" to which Carey responds, "The Rascal Pink King Wood Eater" and smiles [pp. 553–554].

Slade regarded Carey's symbolic play as less motivated by exploration and assertion and more a means to restore closeness to his parents. She noted that he rarely played on his own, often using fantasy play to lure adults into playing with him. Slade saw Carey as exemplifying many unresolved problems of separation-individuation: fuzziness about boundaries, confusion about the distinction between real and pretend, and anxiety over physical separation from his mother. Carey used symbolic play "to gratify his parent's narcissistic needs that he be clever and creative" (p. 558).

Slade's analysis of Carey's play strikes me as completely plausible, but the data leave open another possibility. Carey may indeed have been clever and creative, but not primarily to gratify his parent's narcissistic needs. Instead, he may have been gratifying his own compelling need to explore and assert in the idiosyncratic mode of a gifted child. In children 24 to 36 months of age, it is difficult, if not impossible, to distinguish the truly creative ones from those children whose pressured, hyperexcited overstimulated behavior lies in the realm of pathology. However, many creative people demonstrate throughout their lives the very characteristics Slade noted in Carey—slippery boundaries, looseness in distinguishing reality from pretending, and comfort primarily in the presence of others whose own idiosyncratic, creative minds provide emphatic attunement. Both of Carey's parents were artists, and father and son played off each other's imagination in a remarkably gifted way. For some creative children, exploration and assertion are compellingly tilted toward the primary process mode of perceptual-affective-cognitive organization. The tilt toward this mode often results in adaptational problems for both the children and others in their environment but eventually facilitates the exercise of their special talents. (See Lichtenberg [1983b, pp. 139–140] for a discussion of Virginia Woolf's description of six-year-old James in *To the Lighthouse.*)

In Slade's third example, the pathological elements in little Erik's play left no doubt. Erik was isolated, detached, and profoundly unconnected even to his parents. His movements were stiff, and his affect ranged from a detached monotone to overexcitement. Erik's mother was extremely fragmented and anxious, and little affection or cueing or even eye contact passed between her and her son. Erik's symbolic play lagged at least six months behind that of Andy and Carey, and he spent far less time in symbolic play.

> Erik is building a structure with wooden blocks. He grabs large blocks, puts them down, and says, "Fell crush . . . crash . . . fell crush." He feels the blocks, runs one inside a block shelf, knocking others down. He brings a large block over to his building, beginning to seem frantic and overexcited. He pushes it through the block structures, saying repeatedly, "Going under." He is smiling to himself. He ignores the teacher, and when Carey leans in to look, Erik screams, "No, no don't go like this! Don't crush my thing!" Upset, he pulls out the block Carey has put in. He piles the blocks in front of the structure, making an enclosure. "No, closed, I said close the door," he says. He continues to close it up, and says he will put a house on top. He now makes noises, running blocks aimlessly across the top. Very excited, he stares at the blocks, brings his head right up against the structure, and smiles strangely [p. 555].

Slade noted that this example illustrated how Erik tended to create a private reality while playing. As she conceptualized it, Erik's attempt at assertion through role-playing games floundered on his confusion about his self-boundaries, and his exploration of make believe led him into great confusion about destruction's befalling him or others. While it may have been true, as Slade stated, that "the human qualities of symbolic play were missing for Erik" (p. 559), symbolic play, in my opinion, did allow Erik to define more of his relatedness to others than he could have were his plastic representational ability not available to him.

Slade seems to regard Erik's symbolic play as a source of pathology for him. For other children, she stated, "because symbolization was so clearly a sign of emerging separateness and autonomy, they viewed it as threatening and unacceptable, and avoided it outside the context of the mother-child dyad" (p. 557). I do not find it reasonable that symbolic representation or symbolic play is a source of pathology, a cause of the loss of self-cohesion, overstimulation, or isolation. Children attaining the level of symbolic organization acquire a momentous skill to use for working at solving problems. The ability may indeed be insufficient for the particular attempt, as it was with Erik, but to think of it as the cause of Erik's building an isolated, private world is to regard a bandaid as the cause of the failure to heal an overly large cut. Erik's lived experience left him with a self woefully vulnerable to a loss of cohesion. Without therapeutic intervention, Erik's current actual situation provided no support for problem solving to be effective in the attachment areas monitored by Slade. But symbolic representation is available for problem solving in all the motivational systems. A full evaluation of the effectiveness of symbolic play requires a broader theoretical base then one narrowly focused on the attachment motivational system.

Let me frame the issue I am addressing in a different way. Psychoanalytic theory asserts that symbolic representation in its many forms, whether play, dreams, symptoms, or character traits, is used in the effort to resolve unconscious conflicts by way of compromise formations. This is a problem-solving model, but one applied to, and essentially limited to, tensions at least partially outside the awareness of the person, and most commonly those involving human relationships. I am claiming that the exploratory-assertive motivational system is employed by children and adults alike to solve problems in adaptation whether the source of tension is conscious or not, interpersonal or not. Infant researchers have taken up this question from different viewpoints.

Wolf and Gardner (1979), for example, described two contrasting styles of early symbolic play that they called patterners and dramatists. Their descriptions of these two styles is strikingly analogous to what I have referred to as children whose play is organized primarily by secondary process—that is, patterners (see description of David in Lichtenberg, 1983b, pp. 139–140) and children whose play is organized primarily by primary process, that is, dramatists (see description of James in Lichtenberg, 1983b, pp. 139–140).

In the first example, 18-month-old A. is offered a collection of small toy replicas. She first selects the teapot and plays with the lid, fitting it on and taking it off repeatedly. She pours its imaginary contents into a cup and takes a sip. Then she makes a line of plates and cups, putting a spoon in each cup. She then takes the teapot out of the line and, pushing it along, taps each of the items in the line with it in turn. J., offered the same small toys, also selects the teapot. She, however, goes to her own toy box and picks out a baby doll. She then begins an elaborate game, shifting back and forth between feeding the doll, putting her to sleep, feeding herself, and then feeding the doll again.

Wolf and Gardner (1979) stated that to the extent that symbolic play is viewed as the redramatization of emotionally significant events, J.'s play with her doll would fit easily into the psychoanalytic definition. A.'s behavior, in contrast seemed to lack symbolic referencing. However, the authors noted that it is just as symbolic, since A. was attempting to master an equally important but different aspect of representational process. Rather than restaging the attachment and physiological regulatory relationships of meal and sleep time, "A. may be recreating the spatial structures—the orders and pairings that are, for her the salient aspects of dinner" (p. 131). This is not a replay of a familiar routine to master the attachment motivations; it is a reconstruction to solve issues of what the authors call "mapping relations." "What changes toward the end of the second year, yielding patterners their own characteristic form of symbolic play, is the transaction from simply noticing attributes to operating on them for representational purposes" (p. 131).

At 26 months, A. is given a set of blocks and invited to tell a story with them. She comments, "Make house" and builds an arch. First she places a conical block on top of the arch and then places it in the space under the arch. "She again changes her mind and builds a tower of blocks, using the cone, beside the arch. She knocks it over all at once with a laugh but then quickly rebuilds the arch. When she again places the conical block atop it she comments, 'hat' " (p. 132). At this age, J.'s play continues to be dominated by dramatizing such events as eating, sleeping, and being hurt in a fall, then soothed and comforted. A.'s problem solving remains focused on exploring physical attributes and properties. Her assertiveness is most directed to creating a pleasing visual-spatial structure.

To return to the main point: A.'s exploration and assertion center on problem solving in the arena of the exploratory-assertive motivational system, whereas J.'s exploration and assertion center on problem solving in the arena of the attachment motivational system. As far as one can tell, each selected on the basis of innate preferential patterns. Erik's preferences for selecting problems in the exploratory-assertive system and avoiding those of attachment were self-protective against insurmountable difficulties. But symbolic representation allowed Erik to work on the problems to which he must *restrict* himself; A. and J. selected the problems to which their innate preferences *led* them.

Another experiment supporting my thesis that symbolic play is performed for the purpose of problem solving was done by Fein and Apfel (1979), who studied 19 boys and 19 girls between 12 and 30 months of age. The 38 children were examined at 12, 18, 24 and 30 months. Each time, they were presented with a set of realistic toys and objects. Two findings stood out. First, although all of the children were or had been bottle fed, if they engaged in pretend feeding play at 12 months of age, they chose a cup, spoon, or even a pot as the vehicle far more often than a bottle. Fein and Apfel note that it seemed strange that the children should pointedly ignore their most familiar eating tool:

> Let's suppose that children represent in pretend play life's challenges, not life's commonplaces. At 12 months, bottles are old hat; they are things to be used when you are hungry. They are well-mastered utensils which hold little interest beyond their practical purpose. Cups and spoons, however, have been used but not mastered [p. 97].

The pot is an entirely new vehicle for feeding, although one that can be relatively easily generalized to be a container. This study suggests that the 12-month-olds selected a problem to work on that lay midway between the too well understood (nothing to explore) and the too unfamiliar to be worked with (no potential for assertion and the pleasure of efficacy and competence).

The second finding was that a major reorganization of tool and recipient combinations occurred between 12 and 18 months. By 18 months, when most of the children in the study were being weaned to a cup, almost all who had begun pretend behavior used the bottle to feed the doll. The authors suggest that at 18 months the doll has been discovered as a representation of baby, and babies drink out of bottles. Self-feeding also increases, with the child exploring both being a feeder like mother and at the same time the linkage between self, doll, and baby. By 24 months, most children stop self-feeding with the play bottle. Concurrently, the doll is increasingly fed with cup and spoon. These findings indicate that at each age, the children selected a somewhat different aspect of the problem inherent in their daily life to attempt to explore and master. Noting that at 24 months the children began to move away from pretend behaviors that mimic conventional uses and also used familiar objects to represent other objects not immediately present, the authors suggest that problem solving takes two opposite forms of representation. One form is expansion and elaboration, which allows anything to be used to represent anything else (a bottle for a phone, a phone for a bottle). The opposite form is a stable, conventional symbol—the bottle goes with the doll as a collective symbol for infant nurturance. The findings of the authors suggest that the first form of representation moves toward solving problems by asserting novel, individual twists to whatever is being explored. The second moves toward solving problems by forming symbols that can be shared by others in a widespread social milieu or culture, thus contributing to affiliative motivations.

To return the discussion to the more familiar purview of psychoanalysis, let us consider an observation commonly cited as an exemplar of regression—the older toddler who starts to fingerpaint on an easel and then with increasing excitement shifts from an orderly approach to a wild, general smearing. The goal of the fingerpainting would be to explore the possibilities of color and line on paper, to create an idiosyncratic design expressive of the child's inner representational world, externalized within the set boundaries of the easel. But, the inner representational world of the older toddler is apt to be occupied with the need to learn bowel regulation, with inevitable struggles between orderliness and compliance-to-please on one hand and possessiveness of feces for its pleasure potential and aversion to interference with assertiveness on the other. The medium of fingerpaints strongly invites associative bridging from the exploratory motive in one system to expressive representation of the aversive system and problems in regulation in the physiological need system. Would it be correct to say that the source of the "regression," of the change to excited wild smearing, lies in exposing the child to the symbolic play opportunity provided by the easel? Because older toddlers can represent feces symbolically and link it with bodily sensual excitement states, are they made more vulnerable or prone to "regression" by their representational capacity? If not—and I believe the answer must be no—then what is an alter-

native explanation for the common finding that children engaging
in symbolic play often become overexcited and reckless?
Let us imagine two naturalistic scenarios. In one, an older toddler is before his easel with his finger paints. His mother has gone
out of the room to prepare dinner, or to make a telephone call, or to
go to the bathroom; or else she remains in the room engrossed in a
book or depressively abstracted in her somewhat angry, somewhat
withdrawn isolation. In the second scenario, the child at the easel
has his mother near at hand, working directly but not intrusively
with him and commenting encouragingly on his efforts. Intuitively,
she raises or lowers the tempo of her activity, her voice, her attentiveness to support his assertive efforts or calm his exuberance.
Clearly, in the second scene the toddler is more likely to maintain
as his principal motivation an assertive exploration of the fingerpaint medium and the easel. In the first situation, the mother failed
to provide the regulation a toddler needs to maintain his or her
exploratory-assertive motivation when the materials are so seductive to shifting the motive to obtaining sensual pleasure or expressing antagonism to toilet and orderliness training.

My point is this: symbolic play in each of these forms—assertive
exploration of color and line for the pleasure of efficacy and competence, smearing for sensual pleasure, disobedience and messing for
the excitement of power and rebelliousness—is an effort at problem
solving. The difference in outcome lies in the problem selected by
the self to be worked on. The question then shifts to what determines the problem the self will select? To answer "the mother's
presence" is correct but oversimplifies the issue. The mother depicted in the second scene is indeed a model of the parent likely to
be experienced by her child as a selfobject who meets his need for
precisely the regulation necessary to maintain the focus of his motivation on exploring the easel. But we presume more about her. We
presume that she has provided many similarly effective lived experiences in the past. Therefore, as her child has become capable of
giving full symbolic representation to her in primary and secondary
modes, she will be conceptualized intrapsychically as the one-to-
have-available to support a challenging and risky adventure into the
new world of symbolic play with fingerpaints.

In the examples mentioned earlier, it is likely that Anna's and
Andy's mothers would be represented as ones-to-have-available to
support and regulate risk taking in exploration and assertion.
Carey's mother and father would be represented as one-
to-have-available to encourage and support risk taking in exploration and assertion but not to regulate to ensuing excitement state

and its easy displacement into exploration of sensual and aversive motivations. Erik's mother would not be represented as one-who-would be available or one-who-even-could-be-available to support or regulate assertive and exploratory motives. Her unavailability left Erik alone to problem solve both in actuality and in his intrapsychic representation of her. Therefore, to explain a child's smearing his fingerpaints, Carey's becoming excited and frightened, or Erik's becoming isolated, it is unreasonable to implicate either the capacity for symbolic play or what is represented during the play. It does seem reasonable to give credit to the capacity for symbolic play for the developmental success of Anna's and Andy's assertion and exploration, and to give credit to the essential success of their prior and current lived experience for what they represent during their play.

The process as I understand it (see Lichtenberg, 1983b, chapters 10 and 11) is that lived experience prior to 18 months of age as it has been abstracted into episodic memory becomes recorded in the form of symbolic representation as soon as that capacity has matured. The result is that symbolic representation, a major developmental *transformation*, ensures a sense of experiential *continuity*. The relative sameness of affects makes the transition relatively seamless. Abstracted generalized episodic memories of the parent-infant relationship as it has been lived become encoded in the mobile, plastic form of representation that derives from the unique, dual modes of symbolic organization we call primary and secondary process. Let us return to Anna and offer another example of problem solving through the exploratory assertive potential of symbolic play.

Anna, at 20 months, was becoming increasingly comfortable in distancing herself from her mother when her mother began to bowel-train her. After an unproductive episode in the bathroom, including a mild expression of disappointment by her mother, Anna grabbed her doll and dragged it roughly across the floor. She vigorously dusted off the doll's soiled skirt, fussing angrily at the "bad dolly." She then threw the doll across the room and stood still, looking sad. After a bit, she retrieved the doll and, with a dreamy expression on her face, began rocking and soothing her.

This episode illustrates, first, how the primary and secondary affective-cognitive modes are employed together and, second, how by this symbolic play the child creates for herself a different lived experience and a different intrapsychic arrangement. The organizing of the entire play unit—its beginning, middle, and end has the sequencing of a tiny drama, that is, the ordering of secondary process. Many of the details of the play episode indicate the ordering of primary process. By displacement, soil stands for bowel. By condensation, the strength of the aversive attack on the doll combines the mother's mild expression of disappointment with Anna's own disappointment projected onto mother. By a reversal of roles, Anna becomes the irate mother and the doll the rejected, offending child. At first the scolded "child" is separate—a target of "mother's" feelings and actions and then cast away. While painful, symbolically representing the breach between mother and child in this exaggerated form does allow a living through of separateness and especially the learning of rules. Left at this point, the internal gain would be only the turning of passive into active and an identification with the "aggressor." But in the final action (the rocking and soothing and the dreamy look), a collapse in space and time, a reunion and restoration of pleasure in intimacy occurs between Anna-mother and her doll-baby. The shared cognitive-affective state becomes a gestalt of soothing, comforting and forgiveness. Anger has been expressed, but the final outcome is a self administered self-object experience and the restoration (even augmentation) of a mirroring maternal image and a loved and valued child.

To recapitulate: Anna's ability to respond to an aversive situation with this type of symbolic play derives from her recently acquired ability to organize her current experience in the modes of primary- and secondary-process representation. The representations themselves (of "mother" and "child") derive from Anna's current experience in the form in which she experienced it—an angry, rejecting critical mother and a "bad" child—and Anna's past experiences, largely of the presymbolic period recorded in symbolic, dual-process forms—a loving, soothing, forgiving mother and a responsive, restored infant. The problem to be solved by Anna centered on the attachment motivational system and the threat of aversive motives of antagonism and withdrawal to overwhelm intimacy pleasure. Through symbolic representation, the child could now explore the possibilities first for representing the problem as *she* experienced it, and second for asserting a different rendering of the outcome—a self-creation of a more affectively acceptable self and mother, and a re-creation of a more affectively acceptable past self and mother. By this self-created (autoplastic) change in self, the child propels herself a tiny step into the future, a future thereby partially of her own making. As Freud (1908) put it:

> Every playing child behaves like a poet, in that he creates a world of his own, or more accurately expressed, he transposes things into his world according to a new arrangement which is to his liking. It would

be unfair to believe that he does not take this world seriously; on the contrary, he takes his play very seriously, he spends large amounts of affect on it" [pp. 143–144].

Freud added that the opposite of play is actuality; it is the perceived actual that poet and playing child alter by means of symbolic representation.

Of course, the playing child is unaware of working on a problem, such as in the frustrating toilet training experience. The cognitive capacity to place a frame around the episode (largely secondary process) gives the game its special, make-believe quality. Bruner and Sherwood (1980) have noted that the capacity for make-believe derives from the intuitive inclination of mother and child together to invent games involving role playing, referring to nonpresent events, and combining elements to exploit the games' variability. Thus, symbolic play is essentially an attempt at problem solving. The problem to be solved may arise from tensions, conflicts, or incomplete regulatory attempts in any of the motivational systems. But the approach to solving the problem derives essentially from the exploratory-assertive motivational system. The approach is to explore adaptational possibilities and assert timid or bold attempts at change. The goal is to attain a feeling of efficacy and competence arising from the attempt to self-create a modification in self-experience. The two modes of symbolic representation provide the functional tools for the exploratory-assertive motivation.

We thus come full circle. We began with the presymbolic play of the infants who turned their heads to solve the problem of activating the light display and bubble with joy. We end with the spirited, imaginative play of Anna and Andy; the pressured, overexcited play of Carey; and the isolated, constrictedly concrete play of Erik. Each form of play is an attempt to explore the environment and to assert an idiosyncratic mark of self on the environment and thereby derive as much a sense of efficacy and competence as the empathic regulatory potential of the caregiver-child relationship, past and present, can facilitate.

The Aversive Motivational System

IS AN AGGRESSIVE DRIVE
A NECESSARY PRESUPPOSITION?

IN COUSINE BETTE, BALZAC WRITES, "The delights of gratified hatred are among the fiercest and most ardent that the heart can feel." Given the nature of man's cruelty to man, of warfare, terrorism and attempts at genocide, of rape, robbery, and mugging as ordinary daily events, of tribal wars and mayhem on the highways, it seemed self-evident to psychologists and common sense to both educated and uneducated men and women that there is, there must be, an aggressive drive or instinct. The law of the jungle is the law of man, since man is but an animal who takes and thereby cloaks his bestiality in rationalizations of needs, self-preservation, and patriotism. In other versions, all humanity struggles against original sin or a death instinct or is psychotic with a thin veneer of sanity and culture. Given these apocalyptic views of the adult, what of the child? For some, an age of innocence, the adorable cherub of Raphael. Shakespeare describes the "infant, mewling and puking in the nurse's arms, and then the whining school-boy, with his satchel, and shining morning face, creeping like snail unwillingly to school." Crying and vomiting, whining and unwillingness are all indications of aversive reactions, but are they manifestations of an aggressive drive? When infants and young children are observed directly, what evidence of aggressiveness is to be found?

The observational work of Parens (1979) is particularly instructive. Parens began with the intent to focus "on the emergence of aggression in the first three years of life" (p. 3). Parens started with the theoretical position that he was looking for evidences of discharge of a particular drive energy source and concluded that "aggression is an instinctual drive" that "inherently serves and motivates the ego's task to master and to adapt" (p. 124). Thus Parens began with a mind set and a theory base (primarily Mahlerian) and concluded with the same. It is all the more instructive, therefore, when we observe that in his observations Parens found nothing to substantiate that the infant has an inherent, primary destructive aim. To code his findings, Parens used four categories, each using terminology based on his preconception of a drive. Parens's first category is the unpleasure-related discharge of destructiveness, for example rage responses in infants who are hungry, frustrated, frightened, or in pain. Parens cites 12-week-old Rose, visually exploring

> a brightly colored, six-inch felt block for about one minute. She continues to look at it, seemingly becoming more and more activated: her arms move more and more, her legs kick rhythmically, her mouth opens now and then, her hands exhibit discharges of the grasp reflex. She seems to want to reach that block. Her affect appears pleasurable and she becomes more excited, her total motor activity increasing in energy and rate. . . .

> In spite of all her motoric activity, Rose cannot obtain the object upon which her attention cathexis is turned; for all her effort to grasp and mouth the block, she stays put and cannot achieve any tactile-mucosal exploration. At the peak of this activity, unpleasurable affect appears on her face, and she begins to cry. She is, in our judgment, frustrated and angry. Unpleasure seems to arise . . . when frustration seems to have mounted beyond a certain threshold, gratification having been held off too long [p. 19].

Rose's angry crying is, in my conception, an aversive response available from birth as an indicator of distress within the caregiver-infant unit; it signals the need for a response from the caregiver.

Parens's second category is the nonaffective discharge of destructiveness. Examples are sucking, chewing, scratching. Parens reported: " . . . 3 month olds pull their hair or mother's hair, or scratch their faces. But in our infants these seemed to be unsustained, discontinuous, *adventitious* movements, rather than movements motivated by some psychic, aim-directed energic source" (p. 107). Parens investigated the claim that humans retain their animal heritage as carnivores in aggressive-drive manifestions of chewing, sucking, and biting. Again he did not find the evidence. "We may postulate . . . that certain aspects of unaffective destructiveness (prey aggression) have become less explicit in humans than in other carnivores, due to the civilization and industrialization of food product" (pp. 105–106). In my view, chewing and sucking are primarily activities of the motivational system involved in the regulation of physiological requirements. Lions and tigers are not carnivorous destroyers of their mothers' nipples. Their fierceness with prey must be taught and practiced in play. It then becomes a motive of the exploratory-assertive system triggered by the need to regulate the physiological requirement of hunger.

The third category Parens describes is nondestructive aggression discharges. Examples taken from observations of Jane are: at two months, alert exploring; at three months, rolling over; at four months, crawling, reaching, and grasping; at five months, grabbing a toy from another child (the intention being to obtain the toy, not to deprive the other child); at six months, sitting; at seven months, pulling into the upright position; at eight months, taking a firm step alone; at ten months, increased busyness accompanied by preemptory demands on others; at one year, wanting what others have, tenaciously pursuing her goals, and persistently doing things herself; at 14 months, playing with a pull-toy as a pull-toy; at 16 months, patiently trying to put into a box blocks whose shapes fit only particular openings and putting donut-shaped blocks on a peg, carefully placing each in proper order of decreasing size; at 20 months, play-work with paper, crayons, clay, puzzles, glue; at 26 months, working to master the use of scissors, making things, and bringing them to mother for approval, washing and drying her hands attentively; at 31 months, insisting on taking her coat off herself, playing energetically despite a brief absence of mother.

Parens's examples from Jane are precisely those I have indicated as revealing the existence of an exploratory-assertive motivational system. They are often pursued energetically; they may involve the child in behavior that is aggressive; but they have little or nothing to do with destructiveness. This is what Parens came to while maintaining his own concepts of aggression and discharge:

> The qualitative aspect of the effort on fifteen-week old Jane's face, of the push of her entire musculature upon the rings for example, was of the type one empathically experiences as aggressive but not destructive, as one might experience pushing a wheelbarrow, or in the intellectual sphere, struggling with a theoretical problem. . . . Repeatedly I felt that at fifteen weeks . . . Jane was doing what at twelve, eighteen, twenty-four months of age and beyond would be considered good work. . . . This observed, clinical impression, repeated many times in all our children, was the foremost factor which for me jarred at their foundation the hypotheses that noninstinctual, innate neutral ego energy was at play, and that aggression was inherently only destructive [pp. 338–339].

When Parens writes that the observation "jarred at" the foundation of these hypotheses, he is expressing in a personal way the
problem his data pressed on him—to challenge two major theoreticians on key points. The first Parens discusses directly: Hartmann's
(1955) proposal of innate neutral ego energy does not do justice to
the compelling nature of the infant's functional activity. Everything
about the infant's energetic behavioral responses to stimuli, such as
to toys and the approach of a human face, belies the word neutral.
It implies a definitive motivational source coupled with the functional capacities that are active in its pursuit. Further it implies not
a "discharge of aggression" but seeking to create and re-create an
affective state of efficacy and competence. In many of his observations, Parens evidently is aware of the child's affective state but
does not carry it forward into his conception. The second hypothesis that his observations jars at its foundation is that aggression is
"inherently only destructive." Parens avoids a direct joust with the
many adherents of this hypothesis—Mahler, M. Klein, Kernberg,
and ego psychologists as well. He notes that, on clinical and theoretical grounds, Marcovitz (1973) argued against equating aggression with destructiveness. To me, this is an example in which
words, our great symbolic achievement, have trapped us—aggression connotes destructiveness, which we then have to negate.
Rather than categorizing the findings cited for Jane as nondestructive aggression discharges, it is, I believe, far preferable to catego-
rize them as exploration and assertion and as a part of the separate
motivational system described in chapter 6.

Parens's fourth category is the pleasure-related discharge of destructiveness, such as that of toddlers approaching their first birthday and beyond who act ragefully, push, kick, bite, and tease, with
intent to hurt and gain pleasure. For example, against her mother's
instructions, Mary goes into the hall. Her mother picks her up, and
Mary complains angrily, her face flushing, muscles tense and shaking. She yells. She does not hit her mother but strikes the couch
and the toy cart.

Or, take Jane. At 15 months,

Jane obtained a magazine her mother did not want her to have lest
she tear it. Mrs. K. took the magazine from Jane, and Jane grabbed it
back. After two such unexpected exchanges, Mrs. K lightly slapped
Jane's hand. Jane reacted reflexively and automatically by hitting her
mother back on the arm once [p. 238]

after which she turned to her mother for comfort.

I regard a major contribution of Parens to be that he did not take for granted that the upsurge of aggressive behavior and pleasure in hurting and thwarting that begins at the end of the first year was as spontaneous as it often appeared. By virtue of the observing team's knowledge of the children from birth, Parens was able to infer that each instance had been preceded by an "experience of psychic pain, of sufficient unpleasure" (p. 119). "Fourteen-month-old Candy seemed to just walk up to two-and-a-half-year old Donnie and strike him one rather solid blow on the arm. It appeared to be spontaneous. But it was not at all. Three days before, Donnie had struck her harshly" (pp. 118–119). At the time Candy had been aggressive with her twin and her toys. Now, three days later, Candy's attack on Donnie bore the earmarks of an intention related to "an intrapsychically registered antecedent" (p. 119).

In his first category—infants who react with crying and anger to frustration and pain—and his fourth category—toddlers who react to being thwarted and hurt—Parens describes what I think is better called the need to react aversively. let us review Parens's conclusions:

> In infants rage reactions did not occur spontaneously. . . . Rather, we found that *excessive unpleasure* seemed to be a precondition necessary for the emergence of our infant's rage reactions. . . . We found, furthermore, that this type of [reaction] could be prevented or stopped very early in life not by the child's destroying an object but rather by the mother's arresting the unpleasure which caused the infant's rage [p. 5].

And "hostile destructiveness, rather than being a constitutionally determined drive which obligatorily presses for discharge, is activated by specific experiences which have a common denominator, excessively-felt unpleasure" (p. 122). Parens concludes, *"The degree to which hostile destructiveness is mobilized and accumulates in the psyche [is related to] less than optimal life experiences"* (p. 122).

Stechler, in a series of papers (1982, 1985, 1987; Stechler and Kaplan, 1980; Stechler and Halton, 1987), that have been influential in my thinking, concludes that assertion and aggression have different origins in our biopsychosocial heritage, serve different functions in our lives, and are accompanied by different affective stages. According to Stechler, a central feature of the assertion system is that it is activated by an optimal level of variety in the environment. Its function is greatly enhanced when the actions of the infant are effective in producing an alteration. Its activation is associated with affects of interest, excitement, and joy. A central feature of the aggression system is that it is *reactive* to a perceived threat to the integrity of the individual. It operates through self-protective functions, such as an attack mode aimed at destroying or driving off the perceived source of the threat. It is associated with the dysphoric affects of fear, distress and anger. It also is sensitive to its own effectance.

Stechler (1987) notes further that, while derived from separate systems, assertion and aggression are commonly combined in fantasy and action. Because of the relative ease by which assertion may become contaminated with aggression, infants are heavily influenced by the handling they receive. If the handling is sensitive, the assertion system becomes organized independently. If the handling triggers frustration and anger, the assertive and aggressive systems lose their distinctive character.

> In those families in which the parents perceive the child's assertive moves around the pursuit of the child's own plan as an expression of aggressive challenge from the child, the parental pattern is likely to be one of thwarting, controlling, and perhaps punishing. This in turn does pose a true narcissistic threat to the child and mobilizes the child's self-protective reactions. Each partner in the interaction perceives him/herself to be threatened and a self-sustaining loop of aggression and counter-aggression becomes established. Under these conditions it is likely that the degree of contamination is high. Conversely, in families where the parents can discriminate appropriately between assertive and aggressive intents in their child, and in any event, limit the child's activities in ways that are respectful of the child's narcissistic sensitivities, the aggressive loops noted above will be much less prominent. The contamination will be much less pervasive [Stechler, 1987, p. 353].

I agree with Stechler that assertion and aggression derive from separate and distinct biopsychological origins and that these are best conceptualized within a systems theory context. I also agree that the assertion system activates spontaneously in response to exploratory opportunities in the environment, whereas the aggression system is reactive to stimuli perceived as threatening or distress inducing. It follows logically that when stimuli are frequently perceived as threatening or distress inducing, as they will be if parents misidentify assertion as aggression, the aggressive system will become dominant. These children come to expect that they will be frustrated, and they are ready to respond aggressively.

My view differs in that I believe, for two principal reasons, that aversion, not aggression, optimally designates the system. First, the innate response patterns that comprise the system are dual—antagonism being one and withdrawal being the other. This duality gives much greater adaptive flexibility to the system, as ethologists have recognized in the fight-flight reaction. Aggression as descriptor gives an inaccurately one-sided view skewed toward antagonism (or destructiveness). Because of this selective view, Stechler (1985) is forced to explain an individual's becoming "shy, retiring, disinterested, unimaginative, and severely blocked in action and in fantasy" (p. 540) as a profound inhibition of aggression. Inhibition of antagonism may indeed be the cause in some persons, but the exaggeration of a primary innate pattern of withdrawal and avoidance commonly plays a considerable part in this outcome.

The second reason I prefer aversion as designator for this system is that it places the motivations involved in a more accurate scale. In some instances the motive for the aversion system to function will be no more than that the baby is tired of sucking or the nipple is not optimally placed. Antagonism—actively pushing the nipple out—or withdrawal—turning away and closing the mouth—operate then as signals that when read and responded to appropriately by the feeder, contribute immeasurably to success in the operation of the motivational system for regulating physiological requirements. Aversion as a signal system is equally significant in the success of regulation in the attachment, exploratory-assertion, and sensual-sexual motivational systems. In other instances, the motives expressive of the aversion system are scaled at a much greater intensity and, rather than being signals in the other systems, involve a high level of organization of the aversion system itself. In these instances, the aversion system becomes the dominant system, the others subsets of it. Examples would be when one is engaged in an intense controversy in which anger is both an important component of the functioning and a self-vitalizing experience, or when one is fleeing from a dangerous situation, for example, escaping a fire or preparing for a storm at sea, in which fear is an important component of the functioning and is self-vitalizing as well.

Conceptualizing a continuum of aversion reactions of antagonism, withdrawal or both in this way portrays this system to be as broadly adaptive as each of the other systems. It lowers the apocalyptic tone of "aggression" in Stechler's definition of a system as reactive to threats to basic integrity and self-preservation through attack modes aimed at destroying the source of the threat. I do not question this battle-stations end of the spectrum of responses of an aversion motivational system. Occasional intense emergency responses of this sort can be substantiated through any observation of the functioning of infants. The more ordinary aversive responses include signals present in each of the systems and the more organized instances of antagonism and withdrawal need to deal with controversies and emergency danger situations. Such a range of responses portrays the aversive motivational system as having a full and varied line of adaptive developments, which, when facilitated by appropriate empathic responsiveness of caretakers, greatly enhances the capacity of the self.

Alternatively, as Stechler (1980) states, the activity of any motive, when blocked through excessive shaming and guilt inducement, may be contaminated by aggression and "may play itself out through violent behavior or undergo a further transformation under conditions of severe punishment, becoming profoundly inhibited" (pp. 539–540). Direct observations of infants and toddlers confirm analytic reconstructions of pathologic deformations of character that occur when caregivers block the developing child's attempts at exploration and assertion or physiological, attachment, or sensual needs.

My emphasis is to remove the system that both Stechler and I are delineating from the shadow of its potential for pathology and convey a clear appreciation of its normal vicissitudes before describing the results of serious failures in the empathic functioning of caregivers to infants and infants to their caregivers. Lest I leave a false impression from my stress on empathic attunement, I should say that I believe that for the child's (especially the older toddler's) normal development of the aversive motivational system to occur, the caregiver must be able empathically to suspend "empathy" (sympathetically sharing the child's point of view) and engage in meaningful controversy. Furthermore, the caregiver must empathically accept that it is to the child's advantage for the child to suspend the empathic linkage to the caregiver in order to formulate his or her own agenda and even at times to have a vigorously aversive reaction to interference with that agenda.

AVERSION REACTIONS IN YOUNG INFANTS

Probably the best known aversion reaction of infants is the lusty cry of newborns. Their vigorous protest against the impact of all the adjustments necessary in their suddenly changed environment assures those who hear it of the vitality of the newcomer. An experiment testing aversion to the noxious odor of ammonia revealed that two-hour-old neonates would energetically turn their heads away

(Bower, 1971). In another experiment, reported by Emde (1971), a light cloth was dropped over the face of three-week-old infants. Some used arm and head movements to rid themselves of the cloth, their faces registering distress. Others responded with closed eyes, withdrawing into sleep; some totally switched off into non-REM sleep. In an experiment cited by Beebe and Stern (1972), an infant, startled by a loud noise, cried, threw her head back into opisthotonus, her arms up and back, with her legs extended and then flailing. At an older age, she expressed her dislike of her mother's effort to put on her snow suit by arching her back and using total body stiffness to resist. Another child at the same age resisted by going limp as a sack of meal. Another infant was approached by an adult, who instead of holding her face in his midline gaze area, loomed her head right over his. The infant averted his eyes, turned head and body away, looking distressed and began to cry.

These examples—a misplaced nipple in feeding, an acrid odor, a cloth over the face of an awake child, a loud noise, being held with limbs bent and thrust uncomfortably into a garment, a looming head—are straight-forwardly noxious or frustrating. Accordingly, it is not surprising that infants would have innate patterns of aversive responses to them. Let us consider another group of observations, referred to in chapters 4 and 5, in which the infant's expectations were violated as the infant attempted to meet the needs of the attachment motivational system and experience the pleasure of intimacy. In an experimental situation, a 10-week-old infant girl was approached by her smiling mother. The baby immediately responded with interest, her full body eagerly moving forward. Instead of the mother's voice, however, the infant heard a recording of another woman speaking. The little girl's interest turned to startle, the look of joy on her face dissolved into distress, and she averted her eyes from her mother's face. In another experiment, the mother of a six-week-old boy was instructed to hold her face expressionless. The infant at first increased his effort to activate his mother. When she failed to respond, the infant's effort became more hectic and disorganized, until finally he lapsed into a pained immobility (Call, 1980). A similar example is an experiment in which mothers left four-month-old infants in three-second periods of darkness in a fashion unknown to the infants. After this was repeated several times, the infants turned away from their mothers and resisted their attempts to reestablish contact (Papousek and Papousek, 1975).

These experiments reveal aversion reactions of antagonism and withdrawal. What is the trigger? A woman's voice, an expressionless face, a few seconds in the dark, are hardly what we usually think of as noxious or frustrating. Yet we can easily sense empathically that for infants these experiences violate the pattern of recurrent, predictable exchanges between mother and infant from which infants derive both pleasure in intimacy and pleasure in competence.

When the aversive reactions to innately noxious or frustrating experiences or to violations of social expectancy are examined, the reactions themselves appear to be relatively ineffectual remedies. Crying, startle responses, becoming rigid or limp, flailing about, retreating into sleep, averting head or eyes, rejecting social overtures, do little in themselves either to put matters right or to protect against the offending source. Throughout the first six chapters I have emphasized that infants are remarkably well prepared innately and in learning capacity to participate in regulating their physiological needs, their needs for attachment, and their needs for exploration and assertion. I have argued along with Stern (1985) that the infant's adaptive potential has been underestimated in analytic concepts of oral dependence, narcissistic or autistic stages, undifferentiated boundarilessness, and symbiotic helplessness and merger, as well as in Piaget's concept of the need for step-by-step learning to integrate modes of perception. In contrast to their underappreciated adaptiveness, infants are relatively helpless to develop effective aversive motives. With the exception of some reduction in overall tension through crying, infantile fussiness, rocking, and head banging, the antagonism and withdrawal patterns that infants begin life with are relatively ineffectual to put an end to or repair aversive situations. If aversive reactions are not too intense, fretting or crying infants can self-soothe by finger sucking (activating the sensual system) and by shifting attentional focus to exploring a visual or auditory stimulus (activating the exploratory-assertive system). Notwithstanding these capacities to self-regulate aversive experience, *the primary constructive force of the innate patterns of the aversive motivational system in early infancy is restricted to their success as signals that evoke remedial responses from caregivers.*

An observation of Osofsky (1982) illustrates the general success and a single failure of communication of aversive signals by a very competent baby and her responsive mother. L. at 13 days of age awoke and looked at her mother, who was holding her cuddled in her arms.

[L.'s] expression changed and she began to fuss and cry. Her mother smiled, cuddled her, talked to her, and said that L. was fussing because she was dirty; she began to change L., who indeed had soiled her diaper. The mother said she could tell the difference between L.'s crying when she was hungry, dirty, or just fussy. After L. was changed, she was again easily consolable, responding to her mother's voice by quieting. . . . She then indicated hunger by rooting, not crying. The mother understood L.'s behavior and nursed her. . . . During this observation, I noted one minor area of dyssynchrony. As opposed to feeding, the burping was not quite a smooth a process. L. cried and seemed to want to resume nursing when her mother tried to have her burp [pp. 629–630].

At 24 days of age, L. fussed or moved her hands until her mother stopped looking at or talking to Dr. Osofsky and paid attention to her instead. Again the mother failed to attend L.'s signals that she was unprepared for and distressed during the burping.

The observations of L. address predominately successful signals of aversion and maternal responses to motives involving regulation of physiological requirements and attachment. Another example illustrates successful signaling of aversion involving exploratory and assertive motives. Johnny, age seven months, was playing intently with a brightly colored ball when it rolled away. He eagerly crawled after it, only to push it under the sofa. As his efforts to retrieve it failed, he began to cry and angrily hit at the sofa. His mother came to the rescue. She retrieved the ball and placed it where he could see it. She soothed him in her arms until his crying abated. She followed his eyes to the ball and, placing him on the floor, handed it to him. Johnny happily resumed playing with it.

Sroufe (1982), commenting on the meaning of security of the infant's attachment, notes that it reflects the sensitivity and responsiveness of the care the infant receives. Sroufe adds that the frequency of aversive signaling in itself cannot be taken as an indicator of secure attachment or its failure.

Recall that securely attached children may cry a lot or a little, cuddle and cling or use distance interaction to establish contact. . . . It is not that they cry more or less than others (or are slow or fast to warm up) but that the caregiver is an effective source of comforting and security for them. Similarly securely attached toddlers may be quite negativistic, for example when asked to put away attractive toys, but they do not tend to be noncompliant when seeking help in solving a problem [pp. 592–595].

In these statements about infants and toddlers, Sroufe makes reference to what I believe to be essential differences in the functioning of the aversive motivational system. In infancy, affective behavioral signs of an aversive experience ideally serve as signals calling for action by the caregivers. As I stated in discussing the sources of attachment, the caregiver's ability to respond more often than not to signs of distress, fear, or frustration and anger—through removal of the source where possible and through calming, soothing, and restoring—may be the single greatest factor in assuring the vigor of attachment. Mother and father are "to have," both as sources for direct intimacy pleasure in sociability and as sources of relief from aversive experiences. After early infancy, the signal function of affective expressions of aversive experience continues, but the functioning of the aversive system becomes more complexly related to problem solving.

AVERSIVE REACTIONS IN OLDER INFANTS AND TODDLERS

An important change comes with the subjective awareness of intentionality. Ten-month-old Jeremy, an active, energetic crawler, was pushing a toy wagon across the wooden floor until it was stopped by a shallow rug. Continuing to hum, he gave the wagon a push without effect. Jeremy looked over to his father, who was engrossed at his desk. Jeremy stopped humming and with a look of mild anger gave the wagon a more vigorous hit and push, sending it flying over the impediment. His expression turned to joy, and with mounting excitement he began to hit-push the wagon back and forth over the carpet. This observation demonstrates what Stechler called the common "contamination" of assertion by aggression or what I call the common augmentation of the motivation of the exploratory-assertive system. Stated more simply, when an older infant becomes aware of an intention to explore and be assertive and that intention meets with frustration, the antagonism to the dystonic state and the accompanying angry feeling often heightens vigor in overcoming the blockage. The infant learns that in circumstances such as these his anger becomes instrumental. Assertion augmented by anger is a source of power and can, as with Jeremy, have an intoxicating effect. When this happens, whether assertive motivation or aversive motivation is dominant is difficult to determine. Beginning in the second half of the first year, along with the sense of power that comes with freer physical motion, infants learn as part of their awareness of their own subjectivity that anger can add a vitalizing ingredient to exploratory-assertive efforts to overcome obstacles.

With freer movement, increased exploration and assertiveness, and a sense of anger further vitalizing their intentions, infants and toddlers encounter dangers without innate patterns of response that would protect them. Fire, knives, and electric sockets attract. Chasing the ball may capture full attention, the danger of the street none. Colored pills or a poisonous but colorless fluid may be ingested. Chairs become ladders, unstable coffee tables seem like handles to pull oneself up on. A staircase may be simply a passage to get to mother, who has entered on the floor below. Thus, around the same time that older infants and toddlers are gaining necessary awareness of the power that comes with exploratory-assertive motives augmented by aversive responses to frustration, it becomes necessary to make modifications in the aversive motivational system that provide protection and safety. In these instances, the indicator to the caregivers is the child's eagerness to enter a dangerous situation rather than a signal of aversiveness by fear or distress. The caregiver must recognize dangers in the situation that the child is unprepared for and oblivious of. The parents' activities provide not only security but a learning experience that the child uses for self-regulation.

Two experiments reveal the manner of parent-infant exchange that brings about this learning experience. In the Sorce et al. (1985) experiment referred to in chapter 5, one-year-old infants were placed on a table with an attractive toy and their mother at the far end. As they crawled toward the toy and mother, they came to a point at which there was the illusion of a drop in the level of the table. The infants stopped, registered uncertainty, distress, or fear, and then looked to mother's face for guidance. The mothers have been instructed to give, through facial expression alone, a look of smiling encouragement or a look of fear as a discouragement. Infants who received encouragement proceeded across the illusionary visual cliff, sometimes warily. Those whose mothers registered fear stopped, with increasing distress.

In the visual cliff experiment, the warning signal from the mother was aligned with the infant's own aversive response to crossing the "danger" zone. What about a situation of maternal signaling in which the stimulus provided the infant is attractive, neutral, or aversive? Three groups of 12-month-old children were tested with toys when their mothers displayed, by face, voice, and gestures, positive affect, negative disgust, or neutrality and silence (Hornik, et al, 1987). One toy used was a musical ferris wheel that attracts children. A second toy was stationary robot that recited facts about outer space in a machinelike voice and elicited neither strong approach nor avoidance. The third toy was a mechanical, cymbal-clanging monkey that children tend to avoid. The mothers, trained to convey negative affect, were told to imagine that all the toys were crawling with horrid bugs and to talk about how "yucky" they were. The researchers found that, regardless of the infant's inclination toward the toy itself, if the mother signaled negative disgust, the child treated the toy as aversive.

The researchers asked three questions: Did the child recognize the message as specific to the toy? Are the children more sensitive to negative or positive communications? Did the effect carry over time? Since the infants, given an opportunity for free play, were normally playful and exploratory with other toys and had no general alteration in mood, the researchers reasoned that the children regarded their mothers as delivering *specific* messages about particular objects in their environment. Second, since the infants were more influenced by mother's registering disgust about otherwise attractive toys than by mother's registering positive affect (go ahead, it's fun) about the ambiguous robot or the unappealing clanging monkey, they concluded that, in the test situation, infants responded more immediately to being warned off than to being encouraged. Third, the infants were retested with the same toys after a three-minute break. The mothers were now instructed to be silent and neutral. The infants maintained their aversion to the toys that had been singled out by the mothers as "yucky."

In the visual cliff experiment, mother confirmed danger; in the experiment with the toys with varied intrinsic appeal, the mother's designation of undesirable (Don't get near it) overrode the infant's spontaneous reaction, whether favorable, neutral or aversive. In this way, infants learn where mothers place emphasis for the child's protection and welfare. What about situations in which the infant's intrinsic motivations are more intense, especially those that occur naturalistically? Stechler and Kaplan (1980) provide a detailed record of observations of Nancy and her mother and father. The observations they recorded illustrate Nancy's clashes with Mrs. D and Mr. D and Nancy's learning about what needs to become aversive to her for her protection against bodily harm to herself, against inflicting harm on others, and against the loss of intimacy pleasure by transgressing against the rules of acceptable behavior of those to whom she is attached.

. . . When Nancy was 8 months old, her mother reported that she was "grinding her teeth!" Mrs. D was obviously distressed by Nancy's behavior and felt impelled to make her stop. Her initial, explicit, verbal prohibition, "Don't grind your teeth," merely elicited a happy grin from the baby. Within the next two weeks, Mrs. D reported that Nancy had begun to bite her mother's shoulder, to which the mother objected strenuously with a firm "uh uh!" Nancy would then persist, elicit a more forceful prohibition, and eventually cease. On another occasion, the baby picked up a piece of candy. The mother said, sharply, "Nancy, uh uh!" The baby looked at her, leisurely put the candy down, and went on to some other activity. A bit later, she picked up the candy again, elicited a sharp "uh uh" from her mother, and immediately dropped the candy. These were the first occasions on which the baby responded to a verbal prohibition with compliant behavior.

The father was reported to have been more impatient and more vigorous. When Nancy refused to take a nap, he gave her a spanking. Her angry response resulted in a second slap, a command that she put her head down, and compliance. . . . [pp. 95–96].

At nine months, Nancy recognized the difference between her father's play spanking her with a smile on his face and an angry spanking. If her father smiled, Nancy would enter the game with smiles and sounds of delight. When her father frowned, Nancy became upset and then actively engaged him to get him to smile.

[When Nancy was 11 months old] the mother reported: "We were down to this friend's house and Nancy was going after the radio knobs and I kept smacking her hand. She still kept going back. I slapped her hand so many times that it got red. Finally she walked away and didn't go back to it. I said, Well you're gonna learn one way or another not to touch things in other people's homes. She understands now" [p. 98].

During one developmental test, Nancy deliberately began to throw the cubes down on the floor, looking after them as they hit the floor. Mother expressed annoyance, then started a series of prohibiting "uh uhs," calling out her name with increasing loudness. Nancy restrained herself and looked searchingly at mother. She raised a cube to drop, again looked at mother, and finally let the cube just slip out of her hand.

When Nancy was a year old, during home visit to take video tapes,

Nancy greeted us at the door rather stolidly. She then became intrigued by all the equipment. She looked from one thing to another, gazing at each object with great interest. As she would reach out for some of the cords, mother would say no, and then move things out of her way quite matter-of-factly. Nancy would turn her attention to something else. But sooner or later she would go back to her original interest. Mother continued telling her not to touch whenever she reached out for the equipment. Nancy sometimes would stop her activity and look up at her mother as though questioning. She very clearly restrained herself from full activity and from reaching out and touching the camera under the impact of her mother's forbidding words. She would start to reach out; then, as her mother admonished her, she would somehow finish the movements so that it was not an abrupt cutoff of the activity, but she was very evidently holding herself back. At one point when both the mother and the cameraman left the room and I was sitting on a chair in the corner, the baby began to reach up and manipulate the knobs, which she hadn't been able to do before, with a very serious purposeful exploring. She seemed to be completely unaware of my presence, and it seemed to me that her expression had a quality of a great deal of satisfaction as, at last, she had an opportunity to really go at this camera the way she had been wanting to for some time. She continued this activity with great absorption for several minutes, but then as her eyes lifted for a moment and she caught sight of me, she became more tentative at manipulating and looked at me as though gauging my reaction. As I spoke to her and smiled, she suddenly broke forth into a most enchanting smile, as though sharing with me what fun this was. At this point her mother returned to the room and Nancy immediately discontinued her activity with the camera and moved toward something else quickly [pp. 98–99].

Stechler and Kaplan portray the subtle mixture of Nancy's learning that some of her intentions are to be treated as absolute aversions and abandoned (biting her mother), some as cause for pause and then attempts to get around (father's frown), and some as aversive as long as the enforcer is there but doable in tentative fashion if she is "alone" (touching the knobs on the equipment). The authors explain:

. . . Nancy's parents combined a clearly expressed definiteness about limits and prohibitions with a reasonable degree of flexibility. In general, they displayed a very nice balance in responding to Nancy, permitting her wide latitude and freedom within a framework of clearly defined, consistent, yet not always inexorable limits. Nancy adapted to this surround, accepted restraints, and gradually developed the capacity to impose limits on herself. On any number of occasions, her behavior increasingly reflected a choice: when, in an empathic climate, she was presented with the necessity to choose between behavior that reflected the pursuit of the desire versus that which constituted an alliance with the parent, she chose the latter [p. 100].

LEARNING TO REGULATE CONTROVERSY

I have described the functioning of the aversive system as involving signals that indicate to the caregiver the young infant's state of distress and need for removal of its cause if possible and/or calming and soothing. In the older infant and toddler, as subjective awareness of the affective experience of self and of others occurs, I have noted first the vitalizing effect of aversion in the form of anger to overcome obstacles. Second, I have described the need for caregivers to induce or support aversive responses in situations of physical and emotional danger through restraint and affect-laden sign-signal communication. Now I shall complete this survey of normal functioning of the aversive system in toddlers by discussing a crucial adaptive capacity that begins to develop in the presymbolic period—learning to engage in and regulate controversy. All these functions and the motives to which they are instrumental are further developed and often transformed through symbolic representation.

Parens's (1979) description of Jane at 13 months provides an example of the inevitability of controversy and of opportunities to learn to handle it:

> She is constantly exploring and 'playing' with things. This constantly leads her to want what others have—including my coffee. When I did not let her have my coffee cup, she turned to her mother and got juice. But, it is not so easy with her peers. She becomes more demanding and angry, pulling and holding onto things. She screamed twice and shouted in anger at Temmy and Vicki. But while she is more aggressive she is also more cautious, more *aware* of the conflict situation this creates. . . . She was tenaciously pursuing the purse that Temmy held. Temmy held on for about a minute, but Jane pressed her demand, kept pulling and verbalized angrily until Temmy let go of her end and cried standing in place. Jane's mother intervened [p. 33].

Parens described two controversies of Jane's, one with him over the coffee and one with Temmy over the purse. In each, Parens's account leaves off right where our interest in learning is aroused. What knowledge about handling controversy did Jane learn from each, and how did she learn it? From the first we can infer that Jane learned that when she was contending with a much more powerful person who was definite and firm in protecting his possessions, the struggle was too uneven to persist in. She may have learned that her vigor in pursuit of her goal was accepted without shaming or blame, but that her aversive reaction, whether anger, antagonism, hurt withdrawal, sulking, or crying, did not move a determined adult. Further, Jane undoubtedly did learn that when she was involved in a controversy and her mother was present, her mother would recognize the problem and intervene to offer an acceptable substitute. Whether Jane's mother also indicated her approval or disapproval of Jane's "stand" against Parens we do not know.

The encounter with Temmy over the purse is particularly intriguing in its potential for learning. Undoubtedly, Jane leaned that she could be an energetically vigorous pursuer of her side of a controversy when she picked the right opponent. Outtugging and outlasting the other gets the purse—a valuable lesson in itself. But it also has an effect on the other. Temmy cried. Then, as Parens tells us, "Jane's mother intervened." But how? What message did Jane get about how to handle a controversy? Did mother make her give the purse back to Temmy so that she would learn that when you win by besting your opponent in angry combat you must return the spoils? Did her mother let her keep the purse but make Jane aware of Temmy's crying? Did she then get Jane or both little girls involved in a search for another purse or a suitable alternative for Temmy, or a game the two girls could play together? If in her intervention the mother called Jane's attention to Temmy's distress, Jane would learn that in a controversy the other person has an emotional response. Since children at this age have a demonstrable inclination toward empathic awareness of another person's distress state and a tendency to respond with altruistic gestures, Jane's mother might activate this trend in Jane. Jane's mother could be seen as saying: Yes, you won and you can keep the purse; but the controversy can be brought to a more satisfying conclusion if we add another good feeling to the pleasure you already have from the triumph of assertion plus angry contesting. We can add the good feeling of empathic awareness, possibly an altruistic gesture, and some restoration of intimacy pleasure with your friend-rival Temmy.

This approach to learning to deal with controversy is optimal in my opinion. It consists first of the child's assertion of a goal valued by the self. Then, as opposition is encountered, the self is able to persist with the assertive thrust now augmented by anger and antagonism. At the same time, the child maintains a potential awareness of the impact on the opponent of the contesting child's anger and antagonism. At some point during or after the controversy, the child can feel empathic attunement to levels of distress in the opponent and to the potential for altruistic gestures or intimacy restorative activities. The interplay between Jane and the response I hypothesized for her mother enable this positive pattern of resolution of controversy. This favorable outcome of learning to handle controversy will not occur if the child's own distress is responded to by abuse and pain or if the child suffers a "narcissistic" injury, that is, if the child experiences a threat to the cohesion of the self.

Let us picture an intervention by Jane's mother that if recurrent could serve as a pattern or model scene that Jane might reenact unconsciously or struggle unconsciously against reenacting in later years. Suppose Jane's mother is directly angry and provocative. The controversy shifts from that between Jane and Temmy to one between Jane and her mother. The mother shouts at Jane, waving her finger in her face. Jane stamps her foot and turns away. The mother grabs Jane, screaming, "Don't you turn away from me." Jane tries to evade her mother's grasp, hitting her in the process. The mother reacts to being hit by a smack on Jane's bottom that evokes a hurt cry from Jane, who crumples in a heap on the floor. What would Jane learn from this experience? She would get a rather bewildering message. Her mother is attempting to make engaging in ordinary assertive-angry controversies with her peers aversive to Jane while provoking Jane into a controversy with her in which Jane has no self-aim. Jane learns further that controversies are resolvable by the stronger, more powerful contestor physically hurting the weaker, who is reduced to total defeat. This is the lesson that, learned and reversed, was called identification with the aggressor by Anna Freud (1936).

Suppose the interplay between Jane and her mother takes another form. In this imaginary scene, Jane looks to her mother to support her or at worse intervene sympathetically. Instead, Jane's mother snatches the purse out of Jane's hand and then, with a gesture of pseudomagnanimity, hands it to Temmy, saying to all who would hear what a nasty, grabby, greedy little girl Jane is. Jane's reaction might be to feel stunned by the failure of an expected and badly needed empathic support. Deeply hurt, she might withdraw from play and contact, suck her fingers or cling to her blanket. Especially if this were a recurrent interplay, Jane might try to act as though nothing had happened while freezing out both Temmy and her mother. What would Jane learn if her mother had handled the controversy in this way? She would learn that, as a patient put it, her mother knew how to go for her jugular and pull the rug out from under any expectation she might build of being supported and from any sense of accomplishment she might experience. Jane would know that in a controversy she might end up feeling unsupported, isolated, humiliated, hurt, and shattered, or for a time an empty, frozen shell of self. She would have to resort to her only recourse to attempt to restore her equanimanity, self-soothing and protecting her "dignity" through blocking external evidence of her distress. As a consequence of controversies that arose from her exploratory and assertive motivations, she would be plagued with a build-up of hatred like that described in *Cousine Bette* to the degree where it might become impossible to restore intimacy pleasure.

THE DESIRABILITY OF DELAY IN THE
ORGANIZATION OF THE AVERSIVE SYSTEM

Looking back at what I have discussed about the aversive motivational system permits us to integrate the central features of its organization. Aversive responses are important and necessary features of life from earliest infancy (and can be demonstrated in the fetus). Aversive responses fall into two general groupings, which I have called antagonism and withdrawal, others have called fight-flight. The affects in the infant that accompany aversive responses of antagonism are distress (crying), anger, and disgust. The affects in the infant that accompany aversive responses of withdrawal are distress (crying), fear, shame, and low-keyedness. In the choice of response an aversive situation elicits, certain situations, such as a noxious odor or a looming head, are apt to activate avoidance, while being poked at or restrained is apt to activate antagonistic responses. A general proclivity toward antagonism or withdrawal may involve factors often regarded as temperament, the specifics of which are as yet little known, although Kestenberg (1965a, b) connects them to innate patterns of movement.

Each of the other systems begins with an inherently triggered affect response of a pleasurable nature, which then serves as a goal to be reexperienced when the caregiver-infant pair creates and recreates the situation in which the affect can recur. We easily recognize the motivation to repeat the pleasurable experience that accompanies the meeting of physiological requirements (hunger satiety, ease of breathing, the restorative quality of sleep, tension reduction in elimination); all the multiple gross and subtle pleasures of intimacy (of being approved of, being smiled at and smiling back, feeling secure in the strong arms of the caregiver); the pleasure of exploring and asserting, with the sense of expansiveness that accompanies efficacy and competence; and the special, sensation-rich experience of sensuality, its soothing or its excitement potential. An adaptive gain is served by the *early* organization of, for example, seeking intimacy pleasure as a foundation of an attachment motivational system. Similar adaptive gains accrue from the early organization of the motivational systems for the regulation of physiological requirements, exploration and assertion, and sensual seeking in response to experiences of positive affects.

The timing of the organization of the aversive motivational system represents a special case. Whereas in each of the other systems, the *positive* affects inherently triggered during the successful functioning of the system provide a target motivating a search for re-creating the experience, in early infancy, the affects triggered by the functioning of the aversive system do not ideally become organized goals for re-creating in their own right. The infant does not ideally seek situations in which to reexperience crying, anger, disgust, fear, shame or low-keyedness. The part played by these dystonic affects is no less important in defining motivational goals to be sought; but it lies in the relief from distress signaled by these affects as the distress arises in each of the other systems. Thus, initially, aversive responses provide signals to the caregivers to relieve causes of distress, offer consolation, or both. The experience, beginning in early infancy, that significant others respond to one's distress effectively and sympathetically provides throughout life a particular form of valued attachment. Older children and adults have many resources for conveying distress and many resources for actively providing relief and restoration for themselves. The young infant can only use innately present behavioral-affective signals. Helplessness or symbiotic dependent needs as Mahler has construed them would apply then to the aversive motivational system in the period of the emergent self and the formation of the core self. Ideally the core self has a central pillar that develops from lived experiences in which aversive signals of distress are followed in not too long an interval by relief and calming due to appropriate caregiver responses. In that case, aversive responses of antagonism and withdrawal are largely restricted to their signal functions and do not yet become self-organized.

During the period of the subjective self, older infants become aware of their own emotions and those of their caregivers. They use this awareness of affect communication for signs that signal guidance. As I illustrated in the previous sections, at this stage of development, self-organization and self-stabilization of the aversive motivational system develops in response to three specific problems: learning the instrumental power of anger, learning aversive responses to danger, and learning to engage in and resolve controversy. Older infants form definable plans and intentions and encounter frustration of exploratory-assertive motivations. They then learn that anger provides a vitalizing force for overcoming obstacles to their exploratory and assertive intentions. Anger, as an experience to be sought to re-create the pleasure of its instrumental force in overcoming frustrations, becomes added to the sought-for motivational affects of pleasures that furnish goals in the other motivational systems. But anger, and the sought after pleasure of power that infants experience in carrying forth their intentions, places them in specific situations of physical danger and in conflicts with the intentions of others. Precisely in those situations in which infants lack aversive inclinations, caregivers must intervene not only protectively but didactically to build up a stable system of learned aversive responses to dangers. Thus, an aversive system needs to provide moments of motivational dominance self-organized around two affects. The first affect is anger, which augments the quest for efficacy and competence in exploration and assertion, enabling frustration and obstacles to be overcome, leading to a sense of power. The second affect is fear (plus disgust and shame), which provides a strong trigger activating withdrawal from situations perceived as dangerous.

In addition to signaling aversion for the caregiver to relieve, learning to augment assertion with anger when frustrated, and learning to be aversive in response to the caregiver's appraisal of danger, young toddlers learn to negotiate controversy. The key element in making this learning possible is the toddlers' subjective awareness of their affective states and the affective states of others. By recognizing pain and distress in others and experiencing an altruistic reaction to the person in distress, infants can learn to ameliorate the antagonism they use to achieve assertiveness and a sense of power in response to frustration. I say ameliorate because ideally toddlers confronted with opposition or obstacles should be able vigorously to stand their ground in putting forward their plans and preferences where danger or required prohibitions are not at issue. But at some point, the contending will end, and if intimacy pleasure is to be restored, toddlers must learn to utilize their sense of empathy and altruism. It is apparent that if the aversive system becomes organized and stabilized when toddlers can experience controversy in the effective manner I have described, they will be prepared to retain self-cohesion in the face of contradictory agendas from caregivers and from their peers. They will be less vulnerable to suffering or inflicting narcissistic injury in their relations with others.

If, however, the aversive motivational system becomes self-organized and assumes dominance earlier in infancy, infants will be prone to states of prolonged antagonism, withdrawal, or both. Antagonism states and withdrawal states will be what these infants experience as familiar and hence will seek for the self-cohesive effect of having expectancies met. Rather than seeking the positive affects of relief of distress that come after distress signals have been successfully responded to, these unfortunate infants are apt to gain a sense of security from the familiarity of anger, distress, pain, disgust, or shame. As they develop intentions, they may experience as pleasurable the power of opposing or of frustrating by withdrawal. I say they may experience this as pleasurable because I can offer no proof of this conjecture except that some infants do seem to behave as though they were seeking power in antagonism or withdrawal, and certainly toddlers, older children, adolescents, and adults often do seek power in these ways.

FACTORS THAT CONTRIBUTE TO EARLY AND POTENTIALLY PATHOLOGICAL ORGANIZATION OF THE AVERSIVE MOTIVATIONAL SYSTEM

Aggressive responses have long been associated with hormonal activity. In one study, Reinisch (1981) compared 17 females and 8 males whose mothers had been treated with synthetic progestin, an androgen-based compound, for complications with pregnancies, with at least one sibling of the same sex who had not been exposed. The mean age of the progestin-exposed females and their unexposed sisters was 11 years, 6 months (range, 6–17 years); that of the exposed males and their brothers was 11 years, 4 months (range, 6–18 years). The age-appropriate forms of the Leifer-Roberts Response Hierarchy and the Wechsler intelligence scales were administered individually to each subject. The Response Hierarchy includes six fairly common situations involving interpersonal conflict. Four choices of behavioral responses are provided as possible solutions to each situation: physical aggression, verbal aggression, withdrawal, and nonaggressive coping with the frustrator. Because males ordinarily obtain demonstrably higher physical aggression scores than do females, it was hypothesized that androgenizing a fetus of either sex would lead to an increase in tendencies for physical-aggressive responses. This hypothesis was confirmed. The physical aggression score for androgenized males was about double that of their nonandrogenized siblings, and the score for androgenized females was considerably higher than that of their normal siblings and very similar to that of normal males. Verbal aggression, withdrawal, and intelligence were not affected. Reinisch notes that although some studies have revealed not only verbal indications of preferences for physical aggression but increased aggressive *behavior*, confirmation is lacking that those children who chose that response in the hypothetical test situation would act accordingly in real life situations.

That genetic predispositions can contribute to aggressive tendencies is strongly suggested by research findings. Ginsburg (1982) states "Laboratory selection for aggressive behavior in a number of mammals demonstrates that this behavioral capacity has a genetic basis" (p. 70). Ginsburg describes two evocative experimental findings. In one experiment mice selected for aggressive behavior were compared with mice with other genotypes. The male mice selected for aggression would fight if they could not avoid each other, and females would cannibalize their young if crowded together. Mice selected for a nonaggressive genotype were more pacific and tolerated crowding, and the females cooperated in group rearing litters. When these two sets of mice were released from the laboratory into natural habitats, in times of crowding, the aggressive animals would disperse and colonize new areas, whereas the others adapted to the existing situation.

In the other experiment, Ginsburg found that a strain of mice that he found to be very aggressive were being reported to be pacific by another experimenter who was testing under similar conditions. The two experimenters worked together and recognized that two factors determined the outcome. First, the genotype of the mice used was labile to early handling variables. Depending on the regime of rearing during the preweaning period, a mouse could become highly aggressive or quite unaggressive. Ginsburg noted that other mice, without labile genotypes, would not respond variably to differences in preweaning rearing. "Given a vulnerable, labile genotype, the environmental conditions during a sensitive period of rearing are determining. Given a nonlabile genotype, the same range of conditions will not affect the behavioral outcome, which then appears to be genetic" (p. 58). The human population would comprise genotypes of mixed lability. Thus, the extent of vulnerability to a variety of interactive effects becomes very difficult to tease out.

We could reason that since hormonal and genetic predispositions can produce demonstrable tilts toward aggressive behavior, variants within the normal range of hormonal influence and genetic code may affect temperament. Although little has been demonstrated about it, a potential for fearfulness or anxiety proneness may also have an innate origin and contribute to an inclination to withdrawal. In a study that I describe in greater detail in chapter 10, Kagan, Resnick, and Snidman (1987) reported on 60 children who, at 21 and 30 months, were shy, cautious, and inhibited. The researchers found signs of activation of physiological brain and body circuits that respond to unfamiliarity and challenge. Moreover, 13 of the 60 inhibited children had high and stable heart rates in response to an unfamiliar event. At 5 1/2 years, they stayed close to mother and avoided contact with other children and with unfamiliar toys. During their first year, they suffered from a wide variety of physiological dysregulation. The rapid, consistently activated neurophysiological response pattern of these 13 children strongly suggests an innate, probably genetic source for a behavioral pattern of withdrawal. While it is conjectural that genetic and hormonal factors contribute to antagonism or withdrawal, the outcome of aversive experiences need not depend solely or even primarily on their effect. The outcome of aversive experience is also influenced by the infant's ability to recover from states of distress. Soothability, measured in the Brazelton Neonatal Assessment Scale, may be an independent, innate variable, or it may be related to irritability.

In a study of predictors of anger and punitive control of toddlers by adolescent mothers, Crockenberg (1987) argues that infant temperament, as measured by the time it took a baby to calm after intervention, is relatively independent of early maternal behavior. Crockenberg defines time to calm as the average amount of time that elapsed between the mother's first response to the baby's crying and the time the baby ceased crying. Time to calm in the three-month-old babies tested was significantly predicted by neonatal irritability (and neonatal irritability could be a factor pointing to heightening of aversive responses). Time to calm was unrelated to either a prenatal attitudinal measure of maternal responsiveness or any other measure of maternal behavior. Time to calm was not related to the amount of time it took the mother to respond to the baby's cries. Further, in the three-month-old babies studied, time to calm did not correlate with maternal attitude or behavior but remained a measure of the fussy-difficult versus calm-dimension of the baby's characteristics.

Crockenberg's research tested the intrinsic factor of the baby's soothability against factors the teenaged mothers carried into the relationship—their own early experience with their caregivers and the support they received after the baby's birth. Testing when the toddlers in 40 mother-child pairs were two years old disclosed that mothers who had been rejected in their own childhood and had received little support treated their toddlers angrily and punitively. Infant time to calm did not in itself predict maternal behavior. More easily calmed, less irritable babies were as likely to be mistreated as were more irritable ones. However, those toddlers who had been more irritable at three months and whose mothers had themselves been rejected and poorly supported were more likely to be angry and uncompliant and to exhibit less confidence than were easier-to-calm infants who experienced the same pattern of parenting.

What does Crockenberg's research tell us about the organization of the aversive motivational system? First, irritability in itself represents a proneness to aversive responses and as well a diminished capacity for soothability and calming. Second, maternal responses, if badly skewed by encoded memories (procedural and symbolic) of rejection and by current lack of support, can be an overriding factor leading to early and pathological organization of antagonistic motivation. When the two trends coincide, when the baby enters the world highly inclined to aversive states and the mother is ill prepared to meet any baby's needs, then the infant, by the toddler stage, has little confidence in exploratory-assertive and attachment motives and has aversive motivation that becomes a dominant system.

In a pioneering study with remarkable results, Broussard (1970, 1976) had mothers assess their first-born babies as "better than average" or "not better than average" at the end of the babies' first month. Eighty-five of the children in the original sample were examined in a blind study at the age of 4 1/2 and at 10 or 11. At 4 1/2 years, 66% of those babies who had been rated as not better than average by their mothers had a degree of psychopathology warranting therapeutic intervention, as compared to 20.4% of those rated better than average. Broussard added earlier maternal judgment, one made at one or two days after delivery, to reveal better the mother's *initial* fantasy about her baby. Eighty-two percent of babies viewed as above average in *both* assessments were diagnosed as emotionally healthy at 4 1/2, as compared to only 32% of those judged below average in both assessments. The predictive power of the mothers' initial fantasy of the worth of their infants continued when the children reached 10 or 11. Seventy-eight percent of the negatively viewed infants had diagnosable mental disorders in comparison to 49% of the others (astonishingly high figures in both instances!). Females were less vulnerable to their mothers' perception than were males. Broussard concluded that any male baby seen negatively by his mother in her initial fantasy, or as a result of her experience with him during the first month, is at high risk for future emotional difficulty. However, Broussard found, as have others (Appelbaum, 1982), that working with these mothers can affect their attitudes and facilitate significant changes from negative to positive assessments.

The studies I have referred to thus far document that babies' proclivities toward forming and persisting in aversive reactions and mothers' aversive attitudes toward their babies are two independent or interactive factors that tilt toward early and pathological organization of the aversive motivational system. Statistics of the type Broussard reports tell us of predictors and predispositions, but not how a pathological effect on the child's self comes about. One generalization that seems well founded from clinical experience is that mothers who are antagonistic to their infants lack empathy for them. Kropp and Haynes (1987) reasoned that the empathic failure of abusive mothers may result from their inability to recognize and identify aversive emotional signals from their babies. Kropp and Haynes tested 20 abusive mothers and 20 matched nonabusive mothers with slides of prototypic baby faces representing distress/pain, surprise, sadness, joy, interest, fear, and anger. Both groups had some difficulty discriminating between fear and sadness and between distress/pain and anger. Most significant, however, is that the abusive mothers were both less likely to identify the emotions and more likely to misidentify negative emotions as positive.

The finding of Kropp and Haynes that the abusive mothers misread their infants' signals explains their failure to respond adequately to their children's aversive calls for relief, but not why they misperceived or why they abused. Bertram Cramer and Daniel Stern (personal communication, 1985) have attempted to study how mothers' fantasies about their babies become actualized through interactions. On videotape they documented one of the mothers telling Cramer in an interview that her baby was antagonistic to her. As she spoke, she ignored her baby's signals for attachment responses. As the baby's appeals intensified, she behaved rejectingly and thus stimulated aversive signals. In addition, she poked at the baby when the baby was in her lap. When the baby reacted with an antagonistic gesture and some mounting anger, she exclaimed with a kind of triumph of confirmation, "See he doesn't like me. Look what he does." This remarkable study adds an essential ingredient to the work of Broussard (1970) on the negative effect of mother's initial fantasy, and the work of Kropp and Haynes (1987) on mother's misidentifying of signals. Cramer and Stern's videotapes demonstrate how a negative fantasy can lead a mother to misrecognize distress-aversive signals and how the mother's actual behavior can provide the aversive stimulus to bring about in the emergent and core self an early pathological organization of the aversive motivational system that accords with the negative fantasy.

Other studies deal with the emotionally or physically unavailable mother. A study of maternal propensity for postpartum depression (Cutrona and Troutman, 1987) indicated that temperamental difficulties of the neonate increased the mother's problem because of her lack of efficacy and competence pleasure. The interactive circle of a depression-prone mother, an aversion-prone baby, less availability of the mother for the baby, more disappointment and unhappiness for the mother as she experienced failure, created a high risk situation for both.

The effect of mothers' return to full-time work when their infants were four months or younger was studied by Barglow, Vaughn, and Molitor (1987). To evaluate the effect of mothers' absence, they limited their sample to low-risk infants from middle-class families. All the infants were looked after in their own homes by substitute caregivers who were not family members. At 12–13 months of age, the infants were tested using the Ainsworth Strange Situation to evaluate the types of attachment they had formed. On the one hand, 50% of the infants tested had formed secure attachments to their working mothers. On the other hand, the number of infants who had formed insecure-avoidant attachments was significantly higher than for a control group of similar infants whose mothers had remained in the home. This study too presents the problem of statistical trends—we know their direction but too little about their cause. What were the 50% of mother-infant pairs doing to bring about a secure attachment? What were other mother-infant pairs doing that eventuated in the infants' accentuated insecurity and aversive withdrawal motivation? How many of the insecure-avoidant pairs included mothers who never formed an initial maternal preoccupation with their infants? How many of the mothers suffered so much guilt about leaving their infants that the infants became aversive to the mothers as a reminder of their "failing"? Drawing on the theories of Main and Weston (1982), the authors suggest that ignoring the mother on her return, actively turning away from her, and refusing to communicate with her is a behavioral adjustment that permits infants to maintain control over a potentially disorganizing experience. The potential for disorganization arises "because the infant is simultaneously motivated to seek and to withdraw from contact with the attachment figures" (p. 952). They assumed that these babies experienced the daily separation from the mother as rejections and developed aversive responses to the disappointments in attachment that resulted.

Another factor that might contribute to accentuated dominance of the aversive motivational system is a child's being raised in a setting with a high incidence of anger. Commonly the anger arises from marital discord but might involve anyone in the living situation. Cummings (1987) set up an experimental situation to test the impact of being a witness to the anger of others. Cummings observed 85 four-and-five year-olds playing in pairs of same-sex friends in the presence of their mothers. While the children played, in an adjacent room models went through a planned conversational sequence in which they expressed a sequence of no emotion, positive responses, and no emotion, verbalized anger, no emotion, positive responses, and no emotion. The children were also interviewed concerning their feelings. Forty-six percent of the preschoolers were regarded as concerned emotional responders. They behaved as if they understood the seriousness of the situation, empathized with it, and wanted to ameliorate it. They later reported they had felt sad during the fight and wanted to intervene empathically. Fifteen percent were unresponsive behaviorally. Later they reported that their anger had been aroused but that they had controlled and suppressed the feeling and inhibited any response to the situation. Thirty-five percent of the children were classified as ambivalent. Some reported feeling happy during the anger exposure. Cummings explains that this unexpected finding reflected a generalized excitation that all the children experienced. The ambivalent children were more likely to become physically and verbally aggressive in their play with their friends. In comparison with the concerned and unresponsive children, they seemed more aroused; but their behavior lacked focus, and they experienced a loss of regulation.

In my view, Cummings identified a group of normal children for whom aversive motivation was tempered by empathic attunement to the affective state of others and an arousal of altruistic concern. Cummings also identified a group of unresponsive children whose aversive motivation had become dominant in the form of withdrawal and a group of ambivalent children whose aversive motivation, despite defensive efforts, had become dominant in the form of antagonism. These findings with four-and-five year olds were compared by Cummings with those obtained with toddlers exposed to the same conversational sequence. The toddlers had a more limited repertoire for coping with background anger. They evidenced more frequent distress and less social sharing. As we would expect, the older children whose perceptual-cognitive-affective functioning utilized symbolic representation, were able to substitute a "happy" response for anger or defend against anger with suppression or repression, whereas toddlers in the presymbolic period were not. Cummings notes that "ambivalent responders were already more susceptible to aggressive disregulation after exposure to background anger, suggesting that characteristic patterns of coping with anger may have early origins" (p. 984).

Cummings's suggestion that patterns of coping with anger may have early origins is supported by a study of seven male children with a parent diagnosed as manic-depressive (see chapter 6). With these children, fear entered in as well. At 12 months, these children were fearful during free play and evidenced prolonged fear after reunion following a separation. At 15 months, when most children are strongly fearful at times of separation, these children were relatively unresponsive. This finding is typical for children severely abused or neglected (Gaensbauer, 1982a). At 18 months, the sons of manic-depressive parents showed more anger in a low-stress free play situation with their mother and significantly more anger during a testing situation. In these families, the mother, although not necessarily the parent with the manic-depressive illness, was less attentive to her child's health needs, more negative in her feelings, and more unhappy, tense, and ineffective. She was often disorganized and inactive with the child. The authors (Davenport et al., 1984) state that because of the manic-depressive parent's inconsistent behavior

the infant never knows what will happen or whether his needs will be met and may come to believe he is always in a dangerous situation. Inconsistency may be evident, with moods shifting from affectionate, caring parent to one who is helpless, unavailable, irritable, and abjectly dependent, or, at the far end of the spectrum, to one transformed into a veritable monster who is abusive and psychotic [pp. 233–234].

As noted in chapter 6, it is characteristic of these families to regard the expression of affect as unsafe and to press for denial of feelings to maintain the status quo. The denial and repression create a pool of rage and fear that never quite disappears.

Given the pressure on the children to deny and repress emotion, it is not surprising that at two years of age their responses to a test situation involving a background climate of hostility, anger, and rejection was quite different from those of a control group. In the test (see Zahn-Wexler et al., 1984) the children played in a new room. Two female adults displayed affection and sharing. Then, after a neutral interval, the two women had a verbal argument over washing the dishes. Each accused the other of not doing her share of the work. After another neutral interval, the two adults reconciled with apologies. The mother of the child's friend left the room, followed by the child's mother. The test ended after a reunion period in which both mothers returned. It is noteworthy that after exposure to the women's fight, normal children became highly aggressive for a brief time and then quickly became modulated during the remainder of the session. In contrast, the children with a manic-depressive parent evidenced distress during the fight but did not display any antagonistic behavioral arousal immediately after the exposure. But "the cumulative stress of others' conflict and separation from their mothers led them eventually to express aggression with considerable intensity and to displace it onto their peers" p. 239). The strongest contrast occurred after reunion. The normal children become involved in play involving sharing and very little antagonism; the children with a manic-depressive parent had a breakdown of the prior denial of their anger. They showed no inclination to share but instead demonstrated a marked heightening of antagonism. The authors suggest that, while their anger was probably felt toward their mothers, these two-years-olds had channeled their aversive reactions to their peers.

These two-year-olds, like the preschoolers observed by Cummings (1987), were able to encode their experience in symbolic representations. This mode of representation entails complex cognitive processing; we can therefore assume that inclination toward direct antagonism and anger are subject to denial and that other affects, such as distress, may be experienced instead of anger. For a time the aversive responses were avoidance and ignoring. Then, with the added stress of the separation, antagonism overwhelmed the defense of denial. The children could still displace their aggression from their mother to their peers. Despite these more subtle and flexible attempts at adaptation, the children with a manic-depressive parent had a self-organized, self-stabilized aversive motivational system that, when dominant, lacked the ameliorating empathy and altruism available to the normal two-year-old. My point is that, with the advent of symbolic representation, children have available complex cognitive functions that psychoanalysis calls "defense mechanisms," and these add enormously to the flexibility of the aversive motivational system (Lichtenberg and Slap, 1971; 1972).

CLINICAL ILLUSTRATIONS OF THE PATHOLOGICAL ORGANIZATION OF THE AVERSIVE MOTIVATIONAL SYSTEM IN CHILDREN

In a seminal study of examples of withdrawal and antagonism in early infancy, Fraiberg (1982) reports on twelve children from birth to the age of eighteen months. They were referred because of neglect or suspected or actual abuse. All the mothers were severely depressed, and one was schizophrenic. All the mothers were considered to be psychologically absent for a large part of the infant's day. Occasionally, the mother's rage would unpredictably break through her depression, and the infant would register fear. All the babies evidenced severe avoidance of mother. They would neither look at her, smile at her, vocalize to her, reach or crawl to her, or signal her for comforting. They would make eye contact with father or with strangers. Fraiberg notes that the organization of a full pattern of avoidance of mother began as early as three months of age with Greg, whom I described in chapter 1.

> What we see is this. The baby is scanning the room, his eyes resting briefly on the stranger, the cameraman, or an object in the room, and in the scanning he passes over his mother's face without a sign of registration or recognition. There is not a pause in scanning or a flicker on his face that speaks for registration. In situations where gaze exchange or a gesture is nearly unavoidable because of the line of vision or the proximity of baby and mother, we see the patterns again and again [p. 619]. . . . [Alternatively,] hunger, solitude, state transitions, a sudden noise, or a stimulus that cannot even be identified can trigger states of helplessness and disorganization . . . together with screaming and falling about—a frenzy that gathers momentum to a climax which ends in exhaustion [p. 620].

Fraiberg regards the infant as "experiencing distress of such magnitude that pain reaches intolerable limits" (p. 621) when a cutoff mechanism obliterates the experience. Fraiberg describes these patterns as a fight-flight response followed by conservation-withdrawal in the emergencies of distress while the selective avoidance of his mother "sustains him in the face of objective danger for most of his waking hours" (p. 621).

Another extreme aversive withdrawal response Fraiberg describes is "freezing," a total immobilization that was noticed in babies of five months of age under circumstances that seem benign to an observer. During Mary's first visit to Fraiberg's office, Mary's mother propped her on the couch, and Mary sat glassy-eyed and frozen for twenty minutes or more. She did not look to her mother for reassurance. Her mother offered none, and when Fraiberg made tactful overtures to Mary she did not respond. Later, a tester introduced toys to her. Mary made a faint-hearted effort to touch the toys and suddenly began to cry. Her rigidity gave way to disorganized movements. Her cry became a scream, and the scream escalated into a mournful howl that lasted five minutes. During the scream, Mary seemed to be unaware of her surroundings, her personality fragmented, and all motivation and functioning other than this display of aversiveness disintegrated. Fraiberg suggests that the cost of maintaining immobility for a period of time is physiological pain. The added aversiveness of the pain forces a mixture of extremely primitive functioning of the aversive system, with admixtures of withdrawal and antagonism and loss of all possible links to attachment and intimacy.

Clearly on the antagonism side of aversive responses is Fraiberg's report of Joshua's fighting. Joshua at 13 months

> is obstinate, negative, and provocative with his mother, and he fights her with all his strength when she provokes him through her demands. Then when the fight fails before a stronger opponent, Joshua has a monumental tantrum. He throws himself to the floor; he screams, flails about. The screams become sobs, and tears stream down his face. He cannot be reached by his mother or his therapist. He is completely out of touch. On a few occasions . . . it took nearly ten minutes to bring Joshua out of this state. Afterward he was exhausted, shaky, and wet with perspiration [pp. 625–626].

Fraiberg believes that fear triggered Joshua's antagonistic outburst, which then propelled him into a disintegrative state. She bases this opinion on Joshua's awakening crying or in terror and remaining up for hours at night. She states that "there is a moment before each of the fighting episodes with his mother in which fear registers on Joshua's face. Just for a moment. Then all trace of fear vanishes from his face, and he begins to fight" (p. 626).

On the basis of these observations, fear can be assumed to be the trigger for Joshua's aversive motivational system to organize early as a dominant system with antagonism as the principal response. Gaensbauer (1982b) describes a girl who was physically abused by her father when she was two months old. She was removed from her parents' custody, and two months later, in a clinic, she displayed a fear-avoidance reaction to the approach of unfamiliar males but not to unfamiliar females. Her aversive response to males was trigged by fear and organized around withdrawal, unlike the response of Joshua, whose fear-triggered aversive response was to his mother and organized around antagonism. Like Joshua, this little girl expressed anger toward her mother during reunions that occurred at prescribed intervals. After removal from her nurturant mother, she had become depressed in unresponsive foster care. Thus, in the little girl, abuse triggered fear and the aversive response of withdrawal, while loss triggered anger and the aversive response of antagonism.

The child observations I have cited depict the early pathological organization of the aversive motivational system in situations that cause the infant to be powerless to restrict withdrawal and antagonism to signal responses that lead caregivers to relieve the infant's distress. The state that the emergent self, core self, and subjective self would experience as familiar is fear, distress, or anger, or, as in the case of Anne Adams, (chapter 3) hunger as well. For the developing self, stability and familiarity produce not relief of distress but fear, anger, or sadness. Similarly, in the psychoanalytic treatment of severe character disturbances, the self is often motivated to seek stability through the re-creation of aversive transference situations marked by fear, anger, and depression.

Lest we lose sight of the normal organization of the aversive system, I shall review a case example in which a little girl's withdrawal and antagonistic responses were confined for the most part to signals correctly perceived and adequately responded to by her parents. Nonetheless she developed an aversive response in the form of an infantile fear state of night terror. Often these phobia symptom experiences involve fears whose origin or triggering experience is never identified. Frequently the child's capacity for self-righting and spontaneous symbolic reorganization is, with the emphatic responsiveness of the parents, sufficient to restore the child to a state of cohesion. The fear often disappears or remains attenuated to a negative preference or, of course, at times consolidates into a specific phobic reaction. In the case of Jane, the triggering source was discovered years later by a remarkable bit of psychoanalytic detective work performed by Margaret Temeles (1987). Temeles tape recorded sessions during weekly home visits to Jane's family from the time of Jane's birth. At the time of Temeles's report, Jane was 12 ½ years old.

Jane's family consisted of her mother, who stopped working to be home during Jane's preschool years; her father, who worked two jobs, thus limiting his time at home; and Butch, a large, almost totally black cat who had the peculiarity of never making any sound. Both parents were actively involved in Jane's care and provided a nurturant environment for her. During her pregnancy and against her husband's wish, mother had acquired Butch as a compromise for her desire to have a dog. Butch was mother's companion during the father's absence. When Jane was born mother was estatic, and Jane came first thereafter. Father and Butch had relatively little to do with each other but occasionally locked gazes.

A few days after mother and Jane came home from the hospital, Butch leaped up on the bed to inspect Jane. Jane extended her arm, hitting Butch in the face. The cat fled; mother later stated Butch was jealous of Jane.

Temeles describes Jane's normal attachment responses and normal exploration and assertion with aversive responses confined to signals in each. When Jane was eight months old, Temeles observed the first of a series of specific aversive responses that seemed without explanation. Temeles presented herself wearing unmenacing, clownlike masks, and Jane reacted with soberness rather than the delight to novelty she had previously shown. Jane's mother spontaneously decided to enter the game and appeared wearing dark-rimmed glasses with an attached big nose and black moustache. Jane screamed, and mother removed the mask. At this point, we could conclude that Temeles and mother had violated both Jane's preference and expectancy, leading to a mild and then more intense aversive response. At 12 and 14 months, Jane vigorously rejected two quite attractive toys—a telephone with a face in which the eyes moved and a doll with beautiful eyes that opened and shut. At 29 months, Jane admitted being afraid of the dark and insisted on having the nightlight on all night. Even so, she would awaken crying in fear. After two months, mother realized that Jane was terrified of the pictures in her room that were faced with glass, but not the other art works. Once the glass-fronted pictures were removed, Jane's sleep disturbances promptly subsided.

Jane and Butch each behaved as if aversive of the other. Both avoided contact and acted as if the other did not exist. Jane evidenced no fear of Butch but refused to allow him to be in her room. Jane's sister, Winnie, born when Jane was three, liked Butch and capitalized on this shared affection to win affection from mother.

When Jane was almost six, Butch died. Mother mourned his loss, Winnie talked about him, and Jane felt uncomfortable at not feeling touched. Jane, who had never evidenced jealousy of Butch, was clearly jealous of Winnie. By now, Temeles had become alerted by research on infants' gaze-aversion responses to unexpressive or strange faces. Using this information, she concluded that Jane's dislike and avoidance of Butch had something to do with his face, specifically his gaze. Temeles related the aversion to Butch's face and gaze to Jane's other aversions: to the telephone with the face on it, to the doll with the rolling eyes, and to the glass-faced pictures. Two years later, when Jane was eight, she presented an "association" that confirmed Temeles's hypothesis. Jane and Winnie were talking about the death of a dog. Butch's death came up, and Jane insisted on telling a joke to Dr. Temeles. The joke was about a man who bought a presumably haunted mansion. He awoke at night and looked down at the foot of his bed. "There were two big eyes staring at him. He was *so* scared. He grabbed his gun and shot at them. And you know what (gleefully)? He shot one of his own toes! Get it? . . . the moonlight made his toes shine like eyes . . . Like me and Butch's face. It was his eyes!" (p. 373).

Temeles concluded that the aversion had been stimulated by the unpleasurable impact of the cat's unresponsive gaze and the curious quality of a cat's wide irises in the dark. For Jane this produced an "uncanny" experience, one for which she could not generate a hypothesis. Nor could Jane's concerned and empathic parents label or explain the problem and its source, because they did not recognize it. Temeles notes that initially gaze aversion dealt with the negative preference that Butch elicited. At some point, the consistent pattern of visual and general avoidance shifted into disavowal and denial of his existence. While gaze aversion and avoidance allowed Jane never to experience fear of Butch directly, objects and situations that confronted her with a similar fear-triggering stimulus activated her apprehension and distress. Evidence that the earlier lived experience was organized by symbolic representation can be found in Jane's night terror, in which the triggering stimulus became displaced to the reflecting glass on the pictures. Closing her eyes, a parallel to gaze aversion, no longer worked because the internal representation remained an active stimulus for the aversive experience. Parenthetically, the night terror occurred at a time when Jane was spending more time separated from her mother, who was now pregnant with Winnie, probably straining Jane's attachment and exploratory resources. Temeles does not believe that Jane's aversive responses developed into a phobic neurotic symptom or were likely to in the future. She makes an important distinction between situations in which the fear-inducing perceptual trigger is not primary to the caregiver-child relationship and situations in which it is, or comes to be represented as, failure of the caregiver. When the fear-inducing trigger is the caregiver, persistent symptomatic organization is more likely.

I began this chapter on the aversive motivational system with a quote from Balzac about hatred. Did Jane hate Butch as Cousine Bette hated her more favored cousin? Jane was implacable in her avoidance. She shut Butch out of her room and once cruelly asked that the cellar door be shut so he would be trapped there. She felt no loss or sadness at his death. We do not know that she derived pleasure from his victimization, as did Cousine Bette at her cousins's, but she evidenced all the other indicators of hatred. Was it because of his eyes alone? I do not think so. I suggest that Jane demonstrated a series of aversive reactions. The first was to Butch's expressionless, silent face, a negative preference. But Butch's face was not the only violation of her expectance. Jane experienced rich intimacy pleasure with her parents. In contrast, the cat's aloof, avoidant response constituted a source of aversive response. A "pet" who will have nothing to do with a baby, will not let the baby explore or be assertive with him, invites aversive responses and rejection. Jane could have no control over Butch or of her mother's liking of him. At the time when her mother became pregnant, and distancing from her mother and rivalrous feelings may have become ascendant, her fear was displaced from the cat's face to the glass-faced pictures. This is when we could speak of a smoldering resentment toward Butch. Being 29 months of age, Jane was able to give representation to Butch in both secondary and primary process. Thus she could feel toward him the resentment his indifference invited and also could displace to him resentments from other sources.

Can we speak of a narcissistic injury from a cat? I believe so. A child like Jane could reasonable expect a selfobject experience from every member of her household. But she may have partially protected herself from an injury that would be more painful by never opening herself to attempt closeness with Butch. By maintaining a shell of gaze aversion, avoidance, disavowal, and denial, she would never feel the disappointment of rejection. But Butch was there, and her accumulated resentment, even narcissistic rage, broke through from time to time. The final episode, years after his unmourned death, had her shooting him in the eyes in her good-humored joke about the man's toes, a joke that extended to her equally good-natured game of withholding and then giving satisfaction to Dr. Temeles's curiosity. It can be said that Jane had an adaptively developing aversive motivational system. She could be individualistic in her antagonism and withdrawal in accordance with her preferences without endangering her enjoyment of attachments and exploration and assertion.

CLINICAL ILLUSTRATION OF THE PATHOLOGICAL ORGANIZATION OF THE AVERSIVE MOTIVATIONAL SYSTEM IN AN ADULT

Mr. R, a dour-looking structural engineer specializing in the construction of tunnels, began his seven-year analysis when he was in his early thirties. Mr. R stated in the initial interview that he was coming because of irritability and depression. He was concerned that his wife was troubled by his moods. I inquired about his own reaction, and he answered that he knew his mood was altered only when his wife told him so. In telling about his childhood he gave a relatively clear picture of a household with a frequently depressed mother and a controlling, obsessional, but phobic father. The grandmother, a silent woman, dominated. A girl cousin a few years older lived nearby and was a frequent overnight guest. When I asked about his feelings about his mother's being depressed, he answered that he had no memory of it. He had spoken with his cousin and was simply repeating what she had told him. In fact, he added, he did not remember anything about his past. His statements about not recognizing his feelings and about having no memory of his childhood were both made in a matter-of-fact manner. He showed no reaction to the unusualness of these statements nor to my surprise.

In his first hours, Mr. R reported that he had had a dream in which he felt the need to yell and scream out but could not. He was frustrated and awoke making a sound that awakened his wife. He added that he had not awakened in terror; he had only wanted to get someone's attention.

During the course of the analysis, Mr. R never yelled or screamed. His motto was, "Don't get mad, get even." He sulked, he pouted, he missed hours—generally one for one that I missed. He never experienced terror except in dreams. He signaled distress mainly by yawning. After yawning, he would generally fall silent and remain so for an extended period. When I inquired about his experience during his silence, he would report in an affectless tone that he was reviewing his day schedule and planning the work he had to do. What we were talking about when he turned off was entirely obliterated from his memory. When I reminded him of the issue from which he withdrew, he would acknowledge the content, speculate on the emotion it might have triggered such as anxiety, anger, or sexual arousal, all equally unwelcome. And then he would yawn again. He began many hours by acknowledging he had not thought of what we had talked about, or that he had had a dream but did not remember it. Whether the subject was the content of the previous hour or an unremembered dream, he expected *me* to know what it was and to tell him.

Lest I convey a too one-sided picture of Mr. R's "pecularities," I should mention that he lived a quite ordinary married life, had attended prestigious schools from one of which he had received his doctorate, and was highly skilled and valued in his field.

Analytic material from the last weeks of the analysis conveys a picture of what Mr. R and I learned in the seven years about the way he organized his motivation.

Excerpt A—two weeks before end

Mr. R I have a disinclination to do anything for myself. I was reading about what gives a child confidence. My natural way is to do the opposite. To say to my children, "I told you not to do that." Being told not to has made me scared to do for myself. I wait to be shown. Even academically, where I am at my best, I'm insecure.

Dr. L If you try on your own, you could wind up with a chorus saying "I told you not to do that."

Mr. R I took the chorus in and now I tell myself not to.

Dr. L Ah yes.

Mr. R And I play out with you because I've learned to do it so well! Because I see you the same as my family. You're like them telling me what to do and what not to do. I don't like that. I'll show you—the back-door way to get power. Out of *spite*. If I were confident, I'd stand up for myself more. I'd say, Screw you. I'll do what I want. My way costs me more than if I took the risk, said No! and made you mad. But I don't change.

Dr. L With your sense of accumulated hurts from me, is it hard for you to want to do business with me outside of spite?

Mr. R   With Alice [his wife] too. I don't say let's talk it over and settle
it. Why don't I say, This is driving me crazy. I have to change.
I do try with Jane [his daughter], but it's so hard. I wanted to
take her to the pool. She said no, I want Mommy. I felt hurt. I
tried to joke. Jane was saying, Nobody will play with me. I
said, What am I, chopped liver? It's foolish that I should be
hurt over a kid wanting her mommy. But she's not reaching
out to me. I say, OK fine. You want her, you stay by yourself
until she's free. Spiteful.

Dr. L   When we consider that Jane is one of the few people you look
to to stir your joy and who sometimes reaches to you for her
joy we can understand your hurt when she doesn't reach out.

Mr. R   Yeah. It gets back to my parents. The pleasure I get out of
being spiteful is a poor attempt to replace the pleasure I'm
missing. Being deprived. If they won't reach out to me the
only pleasure left is being spiteful and that's better than nothing. But I end up skeptical and suspicious. The next person
comes along. I wait until I can see if I can count on you. I'm
expecting it so with the first disappointment, I react—see I
told you so. (PAUSE)

Dr. L   And you fall silent.

Mr. R   That's being spiteful. (PAUSE)

Dr. L   Then you wait to see if I will come after you?

Mr. R   Yeah.

Dr. L   And if I don't, you say that's what you expected.

Mr. R   You met my expectation. You failed my test. And I lapse into
I'll get back at you.

Excerpt B—two weeks before end

Mr. R   It occurs to me that what we talked about, the analysis, in retrospect has had a pessimistic tone. What might have been.
Wistful. When I wanted to stop last year, I was upbeat. I can
do this on my own. Unrealistic possibly, euphoric. Or I'm being unduly critical now. I realize that because analysis ends
doesn't mean the process for me ends. If I'm going to continue, the value is knowing when I've had trouble before. I see
the value in going over things. I still have a sense of regret. If
I knew then what I know now . . . I'll use it as a stimulus or
sink back into a negative defeatist attitude.

Dr. L   You're wondering, What will you choose when you get to that
fork?

Mr. R   I usually chose the pessimism of my parents. No good will come of it. Now maybe I'm more likely to resist it.

Dr. L   Were you asking me implicitly why I didn't let you leave when you were in an optimistic state? Why I didn't match your optimism with mine?

Mr. R   I hadn't thought it. But yes. Wouldn't I have been better off?

Dr. L   You could look at me as a pessimist. I'm saying I don't believe your optimism?

Mr. R   I know you were saying, Stay. Be optimistic. We can get something more done. But you were also saying, Don't go! Doubting. An echo of my parents. Be careful crossing the street. Even when I knew how and could.

Dr. L   Your parents would say inhibit long before you got to the edge of your potential.

Mr. R   (Excitedly) That's what I do here!

Dr. L   Yes

Mr. R   I could go on but I stop. The quicker we get moving, the quicker I am to turn it off. The net effect is I'm not capable. Don't build self-esteem. I can't go on my own. You encourage me. Say go on. But that kind of encouragement isn't strong enough. I need to be shown, not told. A kid wants to go beyond the end of the block with his bike. I got the feeling of being beaten down. Told "don't" so many times. Don't, it's dangerous. A kid loses interest in going further. I became convinced they were right. I lost my curiosity to go beyond. (Yawn) I need you not only to undo my parents' command, but to reinstate my curiosity. (Yawn)

Dr. L   Do you sense yourself waiting now for me to stimulate your interest, reinstate your curiosity?

Mr. R   And my enthusiasm. I know what you do and I know the successes I've had—like this year I went to Europe to learn the developments in a new field. But I used to go in believing I'd fail and at the first hint of failure, it's I told you so. Go back to never initiate.

Dr. L   Then you set up a test that is stacked against you.

Mr. R   Bound to fail. People are unlikely to express interest in me if I don't offer something first.

Dr. L   A very ebullient person like your cousin might ride right past that subtle testing and get you going?

Mr. R   Yeah. When Jane is enthusiastic, she overwhelms that. Gets to me before I have time to consider.

Dr. L   And that feels good and makes you want it again.

Mr. R   Yeah. But let down if I don't get it.

Dr. L   And helpless. Your approach left you feeling you had no resources of your own.

Mr. R   I hadn't the spark to be able to generate it myself.

Dr. L   And that's what you have to do now, to do what you can to do that.

Mr. R   It's easier because you haven't been as ebullient as my cousin and Jane. I've *had* to do more for myself.

Excerpt C—one week before end

Mr. R   Yesterday I was despairing. Never be able to change.

Dr. L   We don't know how locked in you may feel to unrealized expectations with me or how free you may feel when you are no longer fighting that battle with me.

Mr. R   That makes sense, but it's something I don't want to see. Spiting you is difficult to accept. That I am fighting.

Dr. L   At the end of yesterday's hour, you said you know how to initiate. You did it with your course. I agreed and you countered, But it wasn't fun.

Mr. R   Fun is not sanctioned.

Dr. L   You know it is by me. You are aware obliquely of my swimming pool, and my interest in sailing and art. Still you are fighting the old battles.

Mr. R   I assiduously avoided using you. I don't allow myself. Your way is not sanctioned. You couldn't be a good parent.

Dr. L   You feel you gave me an opening, and I didn't follow an exact channel.

Mr. R   I can't accept anything that deviates from the script. Get it and I go on. If I don't, the whole thing falls apart. I can't adapt to a different response. (Yawn)

Dr. L   Or it's hard for you to. It makes you anxious?

Mr. R   Yeah. My father's inflexibility. Avoiding anything that's new. The model for the script here is that it's open ended. Each statement opens the potential for going off in all directions. That makes me anxious. Like you going off in all directions. I want you right here! Not going off sailing or playing tennis.

Excerpt D—last hour

Mr. R   I kept feeling that I should quit. Get out of the trap. Is the hour up?

Dr. L   You devoted a lot of feeling to the idea that you could escape your trapped feeling by escaping from analysis.

Mr. R   Or I could escape my trapped feeling by escaping from feelings. Which obviously didn't—doesn't— work. I'm anxious about ending. Will I be able to put into practice what I've learned? Do more for myself and enjoy the positive reinforcement. I'm reminded at the end of *Portnoy's Complaint*, the last line: "Now we can begin."

What I have presented indicates, I believe, that Mr. R's personality, or "self," was organized pathologically around aversive motivation and that his adaptational strength centered on his exploratory-assertive motivation in his professional life. Regrettably, outside of his professional endeavors, his exploratory-assertive motivation was blunted. This was demonstrated by his restriction of memory and openendedness of associations during his analysis.

Material from other periods in his analysis revealed that each of the other motivational systems was affected by his aversiveness. At those times when each of these systems was dominant in childhood, his signals of aversion were often poorly recognized and responded to. In addition, his own tendency to respond to ordinary stimuli aversively complicated his adaptive efforts.

The Motivational System Involving the Need for Regulation of Physiological Requirements

Evidence emerged that his mother had failed to read his signals of satiety in feeding and overstuffed him into a borderline obese child. His mother, herself overweight, organized her own martyred, slavish existence around feeding her family and cleaning up. His sluggishness and passivity were encouraged by his being overweight and having had his signals of satiety overridden, Mr. R struggled against succumbing to passivity and associated his lack of friends in his preteen years with his weight. He then rebelled against his family's feeding pattern and instituted an iron-willed restrictiveness. As an adult when he found himself eating compulsively and having insomnia, he knew that his equanimity was shaken and that he must be depressed and irritable.

The Attachment Motivational System

When he was an infant, Mr. R's aversive responses to the violation of positive expectancies of reciprocal social smiling and playful exchanges more often than not went unanswered because of his mother's depression. He knew what a smile was and retained some capacity for intimacy pleasure. However, he was so entrenched in expecting a flat, expressionless response that he gave the signals for it, and eliciting nothing more fed his defeatism. With me he established a pattern of two greetings: a flat, perfunctory nod in the waiting room, and eye contact, with a faint smile, as he entered the consulting room. While the depth of his mother's depression does not seem to have been serious, the impact of her lack of delight in her baby was intensified by the dreary ambiance of the home. Mr. R's father mixed occasionally frightening outbursts of temper and argumentativeness with a general withdrawal into obsessive activities. When his father came home from work, Mr. R was never allowed to engage him until his father did his daily accounts and read the paper. Mr. R's grandmother was like a silent, gray eminence. His grandfather was subdued until her death when, as if liberated, he became a lively social being interested in his grandson's progress. It was the dour ambiance of the home that Mr. R hung, like a dark cloud, over the analysis, his employees, and at times his wife.

The Exploratory-Assertive Motivational System

In contrast to her discouragement of his interest in social relatedness and exuberant affects of any sort, his burdened mother was delighted to have him disengaged from her and involved in play with toys. In the analysis, after failures in communication and intimacy with me, he would disengage from contact with me. In the solitude of his mind he would explore his day calendar and assert his intelligence and mastery at a task from which he could derive competence satisfaction if not pleasure. What he could not do was "play" with me in our mutual task or share with me much about his personal task. As we understood it, his burdened mother had little or no play in her, and father was too worried and fastidious to play. But everyone in the family appreciated indications of his intelligence and the A grades he was to achieve. Consequently, the analysis was a double disappointment. He could not do it well because of his restrictive use of secondary process and his fear of primary process. Thus, he did not earn As, and his engineering skills could not bring him applause from me. Play was the crucial developmental step he had missed, although not entirely. Play had come to him special delivery in the form of his effervescent cousin, but it might disappear just as quickly, leaving him with a taste for exuberant pleasure and no confidence he could self-create it. He had never successfully taken the steps that lead from an infant's social and toy play to an older toddler's symbolic play and later to play as hobby and recreation, as well as to study and work, each being a source of efficacy and competence pleasure. He had learned to accept a life burdened with chores and obligations that he performed at the A level, and he hoped with pessimistic defeatism that exuberance in play some day again would be delivered to him.

The Sensual-Sexual Motivational System

Play moves into sensuality and sexuality. The ordinary activities of feeding, cuddling, changing, bathing, powdering, and eliminating stimulate sensation-rich mucous membranes, skin, and genitals. Soothing is itself sensual with great rhythmic overlap. Excitement of any sort easily spreads to the genitals, witness how often aroused, joyous toddlers will reach for their genitals. In Mr. R's situation, where intimacy pleasure was subdued and colorless, sensual-sexual motivation may be equally lacking in self-sustaining vigor and easily subdued by shaming and disapproval. With the asensual tone in the home in general, the overnight visits of his cousin, when they shared the same room, were excitement states both welcome and bewildering to the little boy. Puzzlement and embarrassment recurred in the analysis when he remembered and talked about occasional highly erotic dreams in which a lively woman fondled his penis. Their exciting play did not serve him as a bridge to masculine sexual seeking although he remembered wanting to play a game with her in which he was active. She insisted that they play "house" and that he be a doll she cared for, a game that further encouraged his passivity.

His sensual-sexual motivation organized around two core relational approaches. In one, he eschewed sensuality and developed into something of an effete person actively aversive to sexuality. He remembered with disgust his mother's body and genital smell. He remembered putting a pillow over his head to silence the sounds from his parent's bedroom. In the other approach, he hoped to be discovered by an ebullient woman who would seek him out and stir him up to sexual excitement and potency. When he met his wife, Alice, she was a vivacious redhead eager for exploration. Rather than lose this dream come true, a revenant of his cousin, he vigorously fought his family's disapproval, standing firm against his father for the first and possibly only time in his life. What he did not know consciously was that Alice had her own potential for depression. Burdened by his sulking and draining expectations of cheer from her, and by raising Jane at the expense of her career hopes, Alice no longer was able to "create" a sexual life for the two of them. He felt powerless to cheer her, and her appeals to him to be more romantic only exposed him to the humiliation that he could not be.

Now we are ready to return to delineating the pathological orientation of Mr. R's aversive motivational system. The scenario or "model scene" I envisioned from his associations, and especially from the transference and my responses, is of a mother-infant pair in which an ordinarily robust infant was dealt with relatively consistently by a conscientious mother. The problem was that Mr. R's mother responded to his aversive signals of distress in a ritualistic and desultory manner, leaving him chronically frustrated. He was tended to but with no room for the pleasure of intimacy to develop. A later memory conveyed the feeling of the early scene. Mother would prepare dinner slavishly, serve it perfunctorily, and before anyone could relax after eating, she would start clearing the table. Of the two forms of aversive responses (antagonism and withdrawal), withdrawal was implicitly encouraged by a burdened woman probably pleased to be left alone. Antagonism in all its forms was explicitly discouraged. Mr. R was reported to have had tantrums but, according to family lore, by the time he was a preschooler, superficially he had become the compliant good boy he was to remain. Thus, as in his initial dream, he could not yell or scream or even be fearful. What was sanctioned was his passive acceptance and his withdrawal. During latency, when frustrated he would retreat to his room, where he sulked, and waited for someone to come to him and redress his hurt feelings. More often than not, no one came, his silence and absence being misread as being without meaning. Assertive intentionality and anger as instruments for pressing on with curiosity were largely lost to him.

In contrast, learning the caregivers' assessments of danger was all too well absorbed. Not only were playful exploration and assertion regarded as dangerous by each family member, but also sexuality and all expressions of feeling. He was tamped down as if he had to maintain decorum appropriate in a mausoleum: grandmother's silent controlling providing a model both of manners and of secret power. In his initial dream, he not only could not yell or scream, but he had to deny his terror. Fear itself was treated as dangerous. He often complained of a trapped feeling which he tried ineffectually to escape. The trapped feeling referred primarily to his affectless rut, but it was also symbolized in a dream as a pit of depression. He craved joy, but it had to be brought to him, energetically sparked in him. With exploration and assertiveness restricted to work, he built a rut of seeking A grades. Without anger as an instrumental power, he would not initiate forceful opposition to his rut. One solution he dreamed of was to mercifully kill a wounded soldier who kept slogging along. By killing him he could put the other—whether the complainer himself, his mother, his father or me—out of his or her misery. With danger omnipresent, he was frightened of initiating, of disturbing the status quo with the slightest *open* expression of aversion to it. Here the collusion of male and female adults in two generations, all sending the same signal, "Don't," was almost overpowering to the developing self.

Left without an experience of the instrumentality of direct anger and an appropriately selective sense of danger, Mr. R was handicapped in handling controversy. Throughout his life, he attempted to avoid controversy by restricting his exploratory and assertive motives to intellectual and mechanical endeavors. In the toddler period, he learned to blunt the vigorous expressions of "I want" and "I don't want" that characterize a child's contributions to most controversies. Probably, "I don't want" was more present, if diffuse, except in the reported, never remembered, tantrums. The effect, as we could observe it, was a smoldering, persistent resentment rather than a clear assertion augmented by anger. Normally children are encouraged both to express and to constrain their intentions and anger during controversies. Adaptive constraint of antagonism during controversy is facilitated by the awareness of the child's potentially hurtful impact on others, combined with the toddler's innate altruistic tendencies (see chapter 5). Altruism has a double appeal: first, it is accompanied by a sense of the power to effect positive change in another person; and, second, after the aggressiveness inherent in controversy has been expressed, it allows the child to restore the pleasure of intimacy. But Mr. R's experience with his depressed mother had already failed to assure an awareness that he was able to exert a positive influence.

This important forerunner of altruism arises during social exchanges when a child is able to elicit smiles and to restore a momentarily distracted mother's interest in the fun of playful conversational runs. For an infant, older child, or adult not to have the sense of being able to positively influence those whom he or she cares about is a depressing experience indeed, one all therapists often have to live with. For Mr. R as an infant it probably contributed appreciably to his finding contact with his mother desulatory and unrewarding—the reward being sought, as Kohut put it, is the glint in the mirroring mother's eye. As a toddler, Mr. R could not engage in controversies in a lively manner because of the blunting of his positive assertion and reinforcing anger. Neither could controversies be ended by empathic sensitivity to the other's feelings and altruistic gestures restoring intimacy pleasure. Empathic sensitivity neither forms nor maintains well in states of chronic depressive sameness. To become encouraged and valued, altruism must be responded to positively.

In later life, controversies for Mr. R had no beginnings or endings he could recognize. He lived in a state of chronic, low-keyed resentment, punctuated by spiteful actions. During his parents' illnesses and ultimate deaths, he performed perfunctorily but felt no real sense of loss. In comparison, during the illness of his cousin's mother, who was a cheerful, venturesome person, he was emotionally moved and mourned her loss. We learned in the analysis that the significant factor was not only that she could make him smile, but that he could bring cheer to her. The reciprocity of joy in intimacy that had begun so well with Alice was lost when his excessive need for her to take the initiative and focus her attention on him overwhelmed her. He was able to rekindle the joy of reciprocal intimacy with Jane. When Jane wanted her Mommy, not him, to cheer her, he was hurt. The analysis itself constituted a rekindling of Mr. R's major narcissistic injury in the requirement that he be an initiator. He responded to the hurt he experienced with his version of narcissistic rage—spite. "Don't get mad, get even." He would not use the cheer or model of me that was available to him, except to get a second greeting from me, a smile close at hand.

Although Mr. R did not end his analysis with each of us convinced that he had become a man fully prepared to live a life of vigorous emotional fullness, he did end feeling and recognizing a lot more than when he started. He knew a great deal more about who he was. He knew he was a person who could feel. He also knew how he had gotten to be him. His memory and "narrative history" had largely been restored. My understanding of early development helped me to weather the draining effect of the slow, slow progress and to make sense of it, bit by bit, as we went along.

With my help, he understood what he had to do if he chose to do it. He was, I think, ready to begin.[1] While the verbal and affective exchanges reported here are fresh in the reader's mind, it may be useful to reflect on the analytic technique that was employed. Shane (1988), in a discussion of this case, stated:

In his responses, Lichtenberg models his own interchanges with the patient after model exchanges between infant and parent. For example, Mr. R mentions that he can now resist the pessimism of his parents, and Lichtenberg responds, "Were you saying to me implicitly, 'why didn't I let you leave the analysis when you were in an optimistic state? Why didn't I match your optimism with mine?' ", and the patient replies, "I hadn't thought of it, but yes." Lichtenberg's statement is reminiscent of infant research related to affect attunement and misattunement. At another point, Mr. R complains about his loss of curiosity to explore. "I need you not only to undo my parents' command, but to reinstate my curiosity," he says. By this time, after seven years, he begins to sound like Lichtenberg, and Lichtenberg replies, "Do you sense yourself waiting now for me to stimulate your interest, reinstate your curiosity?" Again, Lichtenberg probably is seeing the patient as attempting to use him as the interested other who offers the active self opportunities for appropriate interesting stimulation, an affect-intensity-regulating other. One other exchange is reminiscent of affect tuning. When the patient complains that he hasn't ever internalized the spark of his cousin's enthusiasm in order to generate enthusiasm by himself, Lichtenberg says, "That's what you have to do now." Mr. R then responds in a way which indicates that he has experienced an affect-attuning other, saying, "It's easier because you have not been as ebullient as my cousin. I HAD to do it more for myself." Here is a model scene of infant/other interaction transposed to the adult level and within the transference, or, more specifically, a new object experience in the analytic relationship. I am left with the impression that Lichtenberg has himself been inspired by the new view of human interaction that modern infant research has brought us. The whole ambiance of the analytic situation seems altered in Lichtenberg's hands, characterized by active, to and fro exchanges, the kind of intersubjective activity reminiscent of the infant/ mother dyad.

---

[1] I was encouraged about his progress when, eight months after ending, we had a chance encounter in a public place. Mr. R took the initiative to speak to me and introduce his wife, all in a friendly, forthright manner.

CHAPTER 8

The Sensual–Sexual Motivational System

MAIN PREMISE

M Y MAIN PREMISE IS THAT the sensual-sexual motivational system is built around needs and desires to achieve two separate but related affect states. I designate one of these affect states sensual enjoyment, the other sexual excitement. By sensual enjoyment, I refer to a particular feeling of pleasure that is triggered by many of the activities caregivers employ to soothe and express affection to infants and that infants employ to soothe themselves. When the affect state of sensual enjoyment dominates experience, it may serve as a "switch"—the outcome may be a diminution of tension leading to relaxation or a heightening of sensation leading to sexual excitement. By sexual excitement, I refer to a particular feeling of heightened stimulation that progresses upward to orgastic levels. Sexual excitement, like sensual enjoyment, is triggered by many of the same activities that caregivers employ to soothe and express affection and that children employ to soothe themselves.

Sensual enjoyment is, I believe, the outcome of an innate program of neonates and becomes a regular occurrence of normal daily lived experience. Sexual excitement, while also an innate response pattern, does not appear to be triggered as a part of normal daily lived experience until somewhat later in infancy. Five brief examples may help to convey the relationship between sensuality and sexuality.

1. A two-week-old infant is placed in her crib after having been fed, diapered, and given a brief period of social exchange. She evidences a brief aversive response by whimpering and then places her fore-

finger and middle finger in her mouth. She begins rhythmical sucking. The tension in her body diminishes somewhat, and the rhythm of her sucking stabilizes. On some occasions, she then can be observed fixing her eyes on a mobile attached to the crib. She will have switched from a dominance by aversive motivation (whimpering) to a brief dominance by sensual-seeking motivation (sucking) to dominance by exploratory-assertive motivation (scanning the mobile). On other occasions, she can be observed sucking and lolling into drowsiness and then sleep. She will have switched from a dominance by aversive motivation to a more prolonged dominance by sensual-seeking motivation to dominance by regulation of the physiological requirement for sleep.

2. Genital play of children of two and three will vary in form. At times of fear or loneliness, children often will reach for and gently stroke their genitals. Enjoyment may not be as pronounced as is the relief of distress. At other times, sometimes in states of joy, sometimes in distress, children will stroke their genitals more vigorously, with clear intent to experience excitement.

3. In adulthood back rubs or massages sometimes increase relaxation, and at other times they stimulate a tingling excitement and become precoital foreplay.

4. The clinical experience of an analyst's speaking in a soothing, sympathetic voice most commonly is that the patient is less likely to plunge into a distress state and the capacity for exploration will more easily be restored. Alternatively, the same tone may be experienced as seductive and as a stimulus to a sexualized excitement-seeking transference.

The view I am expressing is concordant in many aspects with that presented by Escalona (1963):

> One of the interesting things about bodily self-stimulation is that the very same behavior sometimes has a soothing effect, whereas at other times it is excitatory. As early as age four months babies are seen not only to comfort themselves by sucking (as even newborns do) but also to suck or chomp so vigorously as to create increasingly high states of excitation. From about age five months onward, some babies "cradle rock" in rhythmic fashion when distressed or tired, and this may lead to a reduction in bodily tension and to a more contented state of mind. Yet they may also start to rock while alert and unoccupied (one is tempted to say bored) and work themselves up to high peaks of excitation. In young infants tactile self-stimulation is very common, but it is difficult to say whether it tends to be excitatory or soothing.

Most often it appears along with other signs of increasing tension as, for instance, in the universal and more lasting pattern of rubbing the eyes when tired. Yet some infants can be seen to "entertain themselves" by stroking, scratching, or pinching portions of their skin with every appearance of mild pleasure, but no distinct signs of heightened tension [pp. 226–227].

By distinguishing between sensual enjoyment-seeking and sexual excitement-seeking, we are able to regard more accurately many manifestations at every stage of development than if we presume a unitary goal of seeking "discharge" analogous to orgastic states. The evidence suggests that sensual enjoyment is a more powerful motive force throughout the life cycle than has been previously recognized, whereas sexual excitement seeking is more periodic and episodic. This view allows us to appreciate the power of the sensual-sexual motivational system but shifts the relative significance of goals within the system.

INTRODUCTION

In planning to describe a motivational system that forms in response to the need for sensual enjoyment and sexual excitement, I assumed my task would be relatively easy. As a psychoanalytic clinician for over 30 years, I had been trained to think about sexuality as a powerful motivational source, the most powerful, or at least coequal to aggression. My experience with patients confirmed repeatedly the significance of defended-against sexual wishes in the formation of most psychoneurotic symptoms and in unraveling the meaning of many dreams. That the human being is interested in, captivated by, and often pathologically conflicted about the sexual aspects of life is confirmed by the movies we go to, the myths we have formed and subscribed to throughout the ages, and the sexual taboos that our, and every other society, professes, enforces, and regularly violates.

In chapters 3 to 8, I attempted to establish the distinctiveness of the motivational system under consideration as it originated in the neonate and as it organized and stabilized in the older infant and toddler. For each system I could find an impressive array of data derived from experiments and observations. My task was to select from and explicate this abundant information. When I turned to the literature on sexual development, however, I found to my surprise, that experimental studies of infants are virtually nonexistent, and systematic observations, other than those of a small group of psychoanalysts (Spitz, 1962; Escalona, 1963; Kleeman, 1965, 1974; Roiphe and Galenson, 1987; Parens, 1979, 1987; Kestenberg, 1965a, b), are rare. Cognitive and affect theorists appear to be uninterested in hypotheses about the infant's sexual development and have not applied the same ingenuity to studying sensual experience that they have to attachment or to exploration and assertion. Nor have many analysts challenged existing theory by systematically derived observations. With a few noteworthy exceptions, the trend within the analytic literature is toward reconstructions from later life, based on existing theory about infancy, or toward correcting many of Freud's hypotheses, especially his many misconceptions about female development.

Inevitably my effort to delineate the sensual-sexual motivational system will be more sketchy, less based on solid experimental and systematic observational evidence, than I would desire. I am forced therefore often to offer opinions derived intuitively and impressionistically. For example, I can understand and sympathize with the early analytic discoverers who enthusiastically recognized that once you look for it, you can find evidence of "sex" everywhere: embedded in the metaphoric use of language, myths, dreams, slips, symptomatic acts, and numerous transference manifestations. The quest for sensual enjoyment is so widespread in our daily life that analogies to it are ubiquitous (and are exploited daily in advertisement). This quest is drawn principally from the sensual enjoyment aim of the sensual-sexual motivational system. A sensual aspect that draws on both sensual and sexual seeking can be found in most experiences that trigger a "high"—from roller coasters to tickling, to alcohol, nicotine, caffeine, and stimulant drugs, to fast driving, skiing, prolonged exercise, to gambling and other risk taking. Likewise a sexual aspect can be found in many experiences that trigger a soothing "low"—hot tubs, lolling in a swing, eating, calming and sedating substances, soft fabrics, pleasant color combinations, soft music, candlelight.

Finally, the universality of sensual-sexual motivations can be seen in the plasticity of the capacity for bimodal symbolic representation that begins in the second half of the second year. All that the infant had previously made an object of contemplation (Werner and Kaplan, 1963) can now be recoded, and every subsequent meaningful lived experience will be coded, organized, and altered by symbolic representation. This uniquely human form of mentation is a rich endowment for providing seemingly limitless analogies and metaphors for the puzzles associated with sensual enjoyment and sexual excitement. Sexuality is a topic that we can never put aside because of the profound mystification of it that remains embedded in our psyches as a result of experiences with it in infancy and later. Where do babies come from? What was it like in my mother's womb? Where is her (my) penis? What is inside her (me)? What are they doing in that bed? Does having sex hurt you? Does it tear you apart? Does having a baby hurt you and tear you up? Why can't I marry my mother (father)? These are but some of the questions that later answers can coincide with but never fully satisfy. Conception and birth, phallus and hole, life's purpose and death, are interrelated puzzlements that never relinquish their hold on our capacity for symbolization.

I must add that I understand and sympathize with the objections to the centrality given to Eros in traditional analytic theory. Self psychologists note that many disturbances of cohesion do not involve sexuality and most problems that do involve conflicts over sexuality are strongly influenced by the broader relational context during the phase in which a disturbance developed. The self psychology view holds that in most instances in which problems of a sexual nature dominate the patient's pathology or when sexual origins can be deduced as latently involved, the essential problem is that of a threat to self-cohesion. Clinical experience indicates that the sexual activity or fantasy, rather than being the source of the threat to cohesion, is used to restore cohesion through either the soothing effect of sensual enjoyment or the vitalizing effect of sexual excitement. A clinical finding that offers further support to this view is that once the basic empathic failures that underlie the disturbance in cohesion are analyzed and worked through, much of the pathological sexual activity and fantasizing disappears and the remainder yields relatively easily to direct analysis. Self psychology is very sensitive to the sense of incompleteness of self that is involved in many problems of gender role and selection of sexual partner and regards these as stemming from empathic failures in parents who use their children to complete a missing sense of self.

In my presentation of the development of the sensual-sexual motivational system, I will present current data bearing on these differences between the views of traditional analytic theory and the theory of self psychology. My opinion is that only by examining each situation to determine whether sensuality and/or sexuality is an active or dominant aspect of experience can we accurately assess the significance of sex as a motivator and a trigger for disturbed cohesion or the source of a symptomatic compromise formation.

I shall describe the development of the sensual-sexual motivational system in connection with three issues: sensuality and sexuality as lived experiences, gender identity and gender role, and sensual and sexual object choice.

SENSUALITY AND SEXUALITY

No one before Freud, or since, has contested the observable fact that adults are motivated to seek sexual fulfillment and that adolescent males have erections and females excitement states. But what about babies? In the second of his three essays, Freud (1905) presented his evidence for infantile sexuality: rhythmical thumbsucking; rhythmical grasping or rubbing of body part such as the infant's own genitalia or someone else's ears or breast; the blissful smile and flushed cheeks of the baby falling asleep, satiated from the breast; holding back stool "till its accumulation brings about violent muscular contractions and, as it passes through the anus, is able to produce powerful" (p. 186) painful but pleasurable stimulation; finger masturbation of an "itching" anal zone in older children; arousal during urination; and masturbation by hand rubbing the genital and/or thigh pressure. For toddlers or posttoddlers, Freud cites the curiosity to see others urinate and defecate and to observe the genitals of others, as well as to exhibit their own. Cruelty and masochism are partially sexual, and intercourse when witnessed is perceived as sadistic. Curiosity about birth and sexual intercourse stimulates all manner of theories but ends in frustration and renunciation because the child cannot discover "the fertilizing role of semen and the existence of the female sexual orifice" (p. 197). Confusion about the female genitalia is responsible for the castration complex in boys and penis envy in girls, while actual seduction of children of both sexes leads to polymorphous perversity. Finally "sexual symbolism—the representation of what is sexual by non-sexual objects and relations—extends back into the first years of possession of the power of speech" (p. 194n).

From this brief summary it is clear that the core of psychoanalytic observations about sexuality in infancy and childhood were made by 1905. The analytic literature reveals two main trends since then. In one trend, through case material of children such as Little Hans and adult reconstructions such as the Wolf Man, Freud's theory of infantile sexuality and erotogenic zones has been elaborated and confirmed. In another trend, mainly during the last 20 years, one or another contention of the theory has been challenged. For example, Freud's (1938) conviction that in one way or another masturbation is implicated in a wide variety of disturbances ("The ultimate ground of all intellectual inhibitions and all inhibitions of work seems to be the inhibition of masturbation in childhood" p. 300) has been replaced by the belief that masturbation is a normal, ubiquitous outgrowth of genital play. Similarly, thoughtful arguments based on solid clinical grounds have been offered to contest the concepts of genital primacy as a signifier of mental health; of a clear sequence of oral, anal, and genital phases; of the significance attributed to penis envy; of female orgasm passing from clitoris to vagina; and of the inherent pathogenicity of fantasy distortion alone compared with lived experiences of seduction, abuse, and/or deprivation of affection.

The psychoanalytic literature confirming or disputing each of Freud's contentions about infant sexuality is voluminous. Outside of psychoanalysis much of the literature deals with gender differences in cognitive development. But a pivotal question is never asked: does an infant *experience* sexuality? In this regard, Freud's discoveries had the same shattering effect on the belief that had existed from time immemorial in the "innocence" of babies as had Columbus's proof that the earth was round. After a period of resistance, except among some laughable diehards, both new ideas were accepted, one confirmed by voyages across the oceans, the other by voyages into the unconscious.

For me, the question, does an infant experience sexuality, came to life as a result of exchanges I had with V. Demos. I had written in support of a revised erotogenic zone theory devoid of a concept of a special type of "libidinal" energy. Demos (1985) protested:

> Lichtenberg tries to retain the centrality of erogenous zones as developmental organizers while at the same time doing away with libido, and substituting Tomkins' idea of affects as amplifiers. But he cannot have it both ways! The central issues at stake here involve accounting both for the source of the urgency experienced as motivating and for the specific quality of the experience. In direct opposition to psychoanalytic theory, Tomkins argues that both the urgency and the specific quality are produced by the affect system. . . . Thus the organism not only cares because of the urgency of affective responses, but cares in a particular qualitative way, depending on which discrete affect has been evoked. It is this combination of a specific quality with urgency that places affect in the center as an organizer and motivator of behavior. Lichtenberg would like to use the affects for their amplifying power, but still hang onto the erogenous

zones as providing the organizing quality of experience. But libido
was more than simply energy. It was sexual energy, a particular qualitative kind of energy. And once he gets rid of libido, he also discards
all justification for assuming that the erogenous zones are of any psychic importance whatever, without affective amplification [pp. 564–5].

Two important questions arise from Demos's expostulation: First,
do the manifestations Freud (1905, 1908) cites as indicators of sexuality in infancy have a *qualitative* distinctness warranting the designation "sexual"? Second, what part do affects and/or zonal
stimulation play in organizing the experience? Let us examine these
questions as they apply to one of Freud's cardinal examples—the
baby's thumbsucking. Freud notes the baby's blissful smile. From
this observation we are entitled to infer that the baby is experiencing a discrete affect, that is, some gradient of enjoyment. The activity—rhythmical sucking of one body part by another body part—
triggers a discrete affective response that amplifies and gives
meaning to the perception of the action. So far Freud, Tomkins,
(1962, 1963, 1987), Demos, and I agree. Freud viewed thumbsucking
as a manifestation of an instinctual drive with a special kind of energy that gives the experience its special coloration and accounts for
its motivational (appetitive) significance. Tomkins also speaks of a
sexual drive, but one that derives its motivational power not from
any energy but from the affects it triggers. Demos implies that all
we should infer from the data is the affect of enjoyment, certainly a
powerful motivator. Demos does not tell us at what point in development we can infer a qualitative distinction in enjoyment that we
can call sexual or whether she believes that only the activity is sexual and the affect without special tone or coloration. The point I
wish to make is that the fabric of logic that Freud wove to connect
thumbsucking with kissing, and with other analogous rhythmic activities including coitus and fellatio, was plausible. As far as I know,
we have no solid data to confirm or disconfirm that a neonate or
young infant while sucking experiences enjoyment qualitatively the
same as or different from the pleasure of a social exchange or from
the pleasure enjoyed by a five-year-old masturbating.
    My claim that a motivational system built around the need for
sensual enjoyment and sexual excitement is present at birth rests
primarily on the same evidence cited by Freud. And despite Demos's protests, I still try to have it both ways. I do believe that
Tomkins's theory specifically allows for a conception of affect amplification and affect coloration as well and that the sensations of

the bodily parts noted by Freud contribute to the colorations I call sensual and sexual. Tomkins states, "My experiences of excitement at sexuality, poetry, mathematics, or at another's face can never be described as entirely identical 'feelings,' despite the identity of the triggering affects" (1987, p. 142). (See discussion in chapter 9.) As Tomkins puts it, a "feeling" of sexuality is different from a categoric affect of excitement. Thus we are forced back to the questions: What gives the feeling of sexuality its distinctive quality? Does the experience of the neonate have that distinguishing character? Or if not sexuality, does the experience have the distinguishing character of sensuality? I suggest that the source of the distinguishing coloration to the feeling of pleasure in thumbsucking lies in the special properties of its origins—the sensation-rich mucous membrane of the lips and mouth that Freud alerted us to. Similarly, the categoric affect distress "feels" different if the triggering source is hunger, a painful injury, or a violation of a social expectancy. The source can influence the affective state in either of two ways: by existing as a collateral source of stimulation that merges into the feeling state of the categorical affect or by directly altering the profile of the affective amplification. In the latter case the reasoning is: Tomkins states that affects simulate the profiles and levels of stimulation of their triggering sources, reproducing by means of facial, autonomic blood-flow, and vocal responses the *qualitative* characteristics of the eliciting stimuli. The eliciting stimuli of mouth, anal, and genital activity involve sensation-rich mucous membranes, highly vascular areas, and rhythmical muscular actions. I suggest that because in infancy the activities of the body parts designated erotogenic zones evoke high levels of stimulation, they will be strongly amplified by affects of interest and enjoyment. Moreover, these particular zones not only are intrinsically sensation rich but also involve activities in which frequent repetitive interactions with caregivers inevitably occur.

As I will demonstrate, observation suggests that the problem with existing psychoanalytic theory is not that erotogenic zones do not exist, but that their role as primary determinants has been overstated and the role of caregiver activity understated. As a result of feedback loops of body part and caregiver activities, the experience of sensuality and of sexuality occurs when the amplifying effects of enjoyment and of excitement respectively simulate profiles of the particular stimulation pattern of the rhythmic rise and fall of movement and flow of mouth, skin, urinary, intestinal, and genital activity.

To return to the second question: what part do affects and/or zonal stimulation play in organizing the experience? For Freud, (1905), the organizing factor is built into the instinct whose sexual aim

consists in obtaining satisfaction by means of an appropriate stimulation of the erotogenic zone . . . the state of being in need of a repetition of the satisfaction reveals itself in two ways: by a peculiar feeling of tension, possessing, rather, the character of unpleasure, and by a sensation of itching or stimulation which is centrally conditioned and projected on to the peripheral erotogenic zone [p. 184].

Freud added that the need can be evoked peripherally, but his instinct theory demands a central organizer projected to the zone "where some kind of manipulation that is analogous to the sucking" (p. 184) replaces the projected itch by producing a feeling of satisfaction. Freud added, "this strikes us as somewhat strange only because, in order to remove one stimulus, it seems necessary to adduce a second one at the same spot" (p. 185).

Freud's tortuous reasoning seems unnecessary. The organizing principle lies in a motivational system responsive to stimulation that aims to reproduce an experience of sensual enjoyment. Without the amplification of the affect of enjoyment, the peripheral "itch," as Tomkins and Demos note, would have little claim to forming a dominant motivation. But the way the motivational systems are organized, functioning may be initiated by any relevant cue—whether a peripheral sensation or a spur to memory to seek the repetition of the affective state. Most commonly, stimulation arises from a feedback cross-triggering of the amplifying affect by both endogenous and exogenous origins. Normally the stimulation of the sensual-sexual motivational system is assured by the receptivity of the innate program associated with the bodily zones that provide high-tension sensations and their stimulation in the ordinary caregiver-infant exchanges of feeding, eliminating, rubbing, fondling, and bathing.

What if the ordinary caregiver-infant exchanges do not occur? Babies who were not fed through their mouths because of congenital atresia of their esophagus never experienced pleasure in their mouth, nor did they regain the capacity for oral enjoyment after their esophagus was repaired and they could take food by mouth after they were a year old (Dowling, 1977). When mothers were encouraged, despite the mess, to sham-feed their babies, the combined general attention and specific stimulation of the mouth facilitated the normal development of pleasure in oral sensation.

From a study of 1,248 infants from birth to one year who were housed either in a penal nursery with their mothers, a foundling home, or their parents' home, Spitz (1962)

> found that (1) where the relation between mother and child was optimal, development in the first year of life surpassed the average in all respects, and genital play was present in all cases. (2) In the case of the infants where the relation between mother and child was a *problematic* one, genital play was much rarer and other autoerotic activities tended to replace it, while development, on the average, was rather erratic. (3) Where the relation between mother and child was absent, general development dropped below the average, and genital play was completely absent [p. 285].

Spitz's data revealed, unexpectedly, that during the first year autoerotic activities varied as a function of caregiver-infant relations.

The influence of normal variations in caregiver-infant interactions on the development of the sensual-sexual motivational system can be illustrated in four infant-mother pairs studied when these healthy babies were 28 weeks of age (Escalona, 1963). From a sample 128 healthy babies, Escalona selected Harry and Grace, the two most active; and Peter and Sybil, the two least active. All four infants had approximately the same IQ. Escalona began with the assumption that "in stimulating their own bodies infants provide for themselves sensations which previously they have experienced at the hands of their mothers" (p. 227). Her observations demonstrate that her assumption might stand true as a generality. However, when the mothers' preferred way to handle their babies is compared to the babies' preferred way to stimulate their own bodies, the outcome is quite complex. "Harry's mother was warm, attentive, and playfully stimulating. She touched him freely and seldom lost contact with him during his waking hours" (p. 201). However, Harry ignored touch or responded with displeasure. His mother was keenly aware of his irritability to touch; she even protectively warned others. Harry rocked and bounced gently when pleased, more intensely when distressed. During spontaneous play with toys, Harry's preferred mode of exploration and assertion was to gently mouth the object. However when, under the stress of being tested or when his mother actively played with him using objects, Harry would intensely suck, chomp, and chew.

Grace's mother was also warm and loving and inclined toward actively stimulating interactions. When Grace was tired and distressed, her mother rocked and swung her. Her mother sang to her, patted her, held her tight, all to no avail. Finally, she put the baby down and let her squeal, cry, cradle rock, and toss about. For Grace, rocking and bouncing was the preferred mode of responding both to pleasure and distress. Grace's skin was exceptionally reactive to touch. When her mother's handling was at all prolonged, or when she was irritable, touch evoked displeasure. Grace never tactilely stimulated herself when happy; only when distressed. Also when overstimulated in the testing situation, Grace, like Harry, engaged in "excitatory mouthing intense enough to be described as 'passionate and violent' " (p. 233).

Harry and Grace's intense mouthing response to the test could be viewed as primarily an expression of aversive motivation or of sexual excitatory motivation. Escalona's observations are interesting in this regard. Harry and Grace tended to fling themselves into any motivational state—explorations, social contacts, or aversions. When engaging in this excited mouthing activity, these babies were able to diminish their being drawn into strong responses to external stimuli—the person or toy with which they were engaged. Instead, for these few moments, Harry and Grace were oblivious to all else but their sucking, chomping, and chewing only to return to optimally mature functioning with the same objects used in the excitatory activity. Escalona concluded that "the more autoplastic mouthing during the test had adaptive virtues for the excitable Harry and Grace. It provided intervals of rest from external stimulation and apparently helped them to maintain tolerable levels of excitation" (p. 237).

Peter, the second most inactive infant, was played with by his mother incessantly but was rarely rocked or swung, and he was never observed to rock or bounce himself. When fed, Peter seemed blissfully oblivious of his very stimulating mother. While warm and caring, his mother enjoyed running her fingers along his body and tickling or stroking him so much that she ignored the absence of his pleasurable response. When left to himself he seldom touched himself. He seldom carried over socializing babbling and smiling, although he would experience full intimacy pleasure when his mother actively engaged him. His method of contact was through his mouth; he bit his mother's finger with her enthusiastic support and brought his mouth to her cheek and clothing. "It will not surprise the reader to learn that Peter's was the only mother who played oral games with him. She kissed him, blew at him, playfully pretended to bite him, and was once seen to run her tongue over his fingertips" (p. 235).

Sybil, the least active infant, was the most inclined toward tactile self-stimulation and the least prone to oral pleasure-seeking. "She often touched her thigh or belly in stroking or pinching motions, or rubbed her skin, or dug her fingers deeply into the soft portions of abdominal tissue" (p. 229). Sybil reserved her active touching to moments of pleasure and responded fully with intimacy pleasure in a social contact only if touch was added to the approach. When distressed she resorted to moderately vigorous rocking and bouncing. Sybil's mother "took excellent care of her baby, whom she valued highly, but did so in a remarkably impersonal manner. She touched Sybil seldom except during caretaking procedures, and even these were often carried out expertly but with an absolute minimum of social play. She left the baby to her own devices unless and until the baby needed something" (pp. 201–202). Because Sybil was not at all irritable, intense direct contacts were fewer than ordinary, and Sybil was seldom rocked or swung. However, it was a combination of being held firmly and rocked that fostered sleep. Her mother intuitively recognized that putting her in her jump swing or pushing her in her carriage would soothe her.

How well do the data substantiate Escalona's formulation that "babies in this age range select those patterns of bodily self-stimulation which generate sensations in the same modalities that have characterized intense contacts with the mother in the past, when it was she who provided the stimulation" (p. 229)? Sybil and Grace rocked themselves when in need of soothing, and their mothers used rocking and bouncing for the same purpose. Harry, who was only occasionally rocked, preferred the sensations of mouthing when in distress, and Peter, who was never rocked, never rocked himself. Sybil, who was played with and touched very sparingly, was a very active self-toucher, pulling people into her preferred mode if they wanted to get a full social response from her. Harry, whose mother was a frequent, active toucher, ignored touch, his mouth providing his preferred body mode. Grace was aversive to touch, turning to rocking and mouthing. Peter, whose mother was all over his body with her hands and mouth, seldom touched himself, but instead responded with his mouth. As Escalona (1963) states, "The relationship is not as simple" (p. 227) as assumed. It is true that "infants provide for themselves sensations which previously they had experienced at the hands of their mother" (p. 227) but this is less a causal statement than it sounds. Without the stimulation, infants will not provide it for themselves. This is proven by the deficiency studies of Dowling (1977) and Spitz

(1962). But when the stimulation is provided, as it almost invariably will be, infants are highly selective as to the mode of self-stimulation they prefer and choose. An infant may be actively aversive to touch, as was Grace, or indifferent, as were Harry and Peter, and the mother may override or respond accordingly. Or the infant (Sybil) may be very responsive to touch and be activated with only a modicum of encouragement, and the mother be the one who is relatively indifferent.

Escalona's initial assumption was in its implication too one-sided, too environmental. It portrayed infants merely as passive (symbiotic) partners in their preferences and choices. It did not give weight to the manner in which infants push or pull parents into interactions. And her assumption was too mother centered, leaving out the influence of modes of stimulation from fathers and others. Her contributions nonetheless are considerable. Far more sophisticatedly than erotogenic zone theory alone, her study places in perspective the manner in which infants experience pleasure. Her observations compel us to recognize that behaviors that trigger sensual enjoyment can be employed to activate or heighten pleasure or to relieve distress. One mode may be employed exclusively to activate or heighten pleasure or to relieve distress. One six-month-old infant may need only the sensual enjoyment of rocking and bouncing to be restored, while another may have to crescendo the affect (Harry and Grace in their "passionate" mouthing) to be able to switch from being distressed. It is difficult to tease out of Escalona's careful observations moments of unequivocal dominance by sexual excitement.

The experience of sexuality in infants seems at first glance to be confirmed by observation of genital arousal during REM sleep in adults and infants. Research on adults (Fisher, Gross, and Zuch, 1965; Fisher et al., 1983) indicates that in 95% of periods of REM sleep, men have erections and women have vaginal vascular engorgement. During an average night, erections and vaginal engorgement occur for 87 and 82 minutes respectively. Roffwarg, Dement, and Fisher (1964) and Wolff (1966) found that erections occurred in REM sleep periods of neonates, and Halverson (1940) found a high incidence of erections in 3–20 week old infants during both waking and sleeping states. There are no comparable studies of female infants.

Fisher et al. (1965) stated, "The phenomenology of erection, e.g., the subjective nature of the sensation associated with it, whether or not it is connected with sexual desire, etc., is in need of further investigation" (p. 41). The key words are the *subjective* nature of the sensation and whether or *not* it is connected with sexual desire. What led the authors to raise the possibility that it might *not* be? In the adult, for whom erections and vaginal engorgement during REM periods are often associated with overt or latent sexual content, the physiological response precedes the dreaming activity. It also occurs coincident with nonerotic dreaming. The existence of the pattern of nocturnal erections in neonates, in the elderly long after the loss of erectile potency, and even in decorticate infants, points to a physiological trigger unrelated to identifiable sexual contents.

Fisher et al. (1983) conclude:

> There is a reciprocal interaction between psychic content and the REM sexual excitation in both the male and the female. The physiological sexual arousal is ontogenetically primary, present at birth, and only later, when psychic structure matures, does the dream arise, interact with, and be acted upon by the somatic aspects of the sexual drive [p. 117].

Even after the connection is established between REM period genital arousal and dreams with sexual content, the nature of the sensation remains uncertain. Fisher et al. note that during sexual content dreams, genital arousal is not accompanied by cardiorespiratory increases. In contrast, when orgasmic states occur during sleep (nocturnal emission in men, orgasmic content and sensation in women), heart and breathing rates increase, as do sweating, flushing, and muscle contractions. Thus the dream state arousal parallels that of wakefulness in that "sexual arousal of considerable intensity in response to erotic stimulation from tape or film is not accompanied by cardiorespiratory increases" (p. 117) while with masturbation or intercourse the full physiological excitement state occurs.

These findings about REM sleep, dreaming, and genital arousal in infants and adults are compatible with my hypothesis of a duality of needs met by the sensual-sexual motivational system. As I view it, infants are born with an innate program for genital arousal. Initially, the arousal represents a physiological response pattern closely associated with the REM period sleep state but occurring at times during the waking state. The innate program is highly sensitive to triggering by sensations of sensual enjoyment that arise during ordinary caregiver-infant interactions—feeding, touching, stroking, bouncing, rocking; being cradled, sung to, and the like. For children raised without this kind of sensory enjoyment, such as those raised in foundling homes in "aseptic" conditions or whose bottles are propped routinely—like children with esophageal atresia or even like rats that are not licked by their mothers (Schanberg, Bartolome, and Kuhn, 1988) or monkeys that are neither touched nor groomed (Harlow, 1962)—the ordinary cross-connection between physiological genital responsiveness and sensual enjoyment is absent, weak, or delayed. Alternatively, in the presence of sensory turn-on, the elementary stage of the sensual-sexual motivational system becomes organized as infants seek repetitions of sensual enjoyment states. This motivated seeking is apparent in infants' responsiveness to caregivers' fondling and soothing as well as in their self-activated (autoerotic) actions.

Less apparent than the active/awake pursuit of sensual enjoyment, either during states where heightened pleasure is being sought or when distress is tempered by soothing, is the connection between sensual-sexual motivation and sleep and REM states. I offer the speculation that while the sleep requirement in the broadest sense is a component of the motivational system for the regulation of physiological requirements, REM sleep and the genital arousal that occurs during it become manifestations of the sensual-sexual motivational system. When the infant is awake, the enjoyment that is triggered by sensual sensation serves as a "switch," toning upward the level of vitality when the infant is "bored" or toning downward states of distress (soothing). I suggest that REM sleep periods in infants serve the same purpose of toning upward and downward through sensual enjoyment. This would help to explain three findings from adult life: First, that the preponderance of dreams have latent or manifest sexual contents or reference to the self state is explained by the intimate connection between sensuality and the regulation of the self toward greater vitality or relief of distress. This is supported by the finding of dream researchers (Fiss, 1987; Fosshage, 1988) that dreaming mentation functions as problem solving—sometimes in the formal sense of replaying and carrying forward problems of exploration and assertion, frequently problems of attachment and affiliation, and often struggling with aversive responses. The second finding from adult life is the general disturbance of self-cohesion that occurs as a result of deprivation of REM sleep. Subjects demonstrate irritability, anxiety, and a general lowering of regulatory controls. I suggest that one aspect of REM-sleep deprivation is the absence of the regular experiences of sensual enjoyment associated with genital arousal. Shakespeare, speaking from the standpoint of a man suffering painfully from deprivation, has MacBeth tell us how much he misses "sleep, that knits up the ravel'd sleeve of care, and death of each day's life, sore labor's bath, balm of hurt minds, great nature's second course, chief nourisher in life's feast" (Act 1, Scene 2). An inelegant scientific paraphrase is that sleep contributes the physiological restorative power of non-REM sleep and the soothing retoning effect of sensual enjoyment derived from REM sleep and genital arousal. The third finding is the absence of cardiorespiratory rate increases and other evidences of excitement unless orgasm occurs. By distinguishing between sensual enjoyment and sexual excitement, we are able to explain how genital arousal and frequent sexual dream content in REM periods can be without the kind of sexual excitement that is more likely to awaken the sleeper, risking the loss of sleep's problem-solving (REM) and its physiologically restorative function (non-REM).

The distinction between sensuality and sexuality helps to reconcile conflicting conceptions of traditional drive theory and self psychology. Traditional drive theory assigns considerable importance to sexuality as a motive force, as do I, but regards the aim to be discharge. Freud (1905), in formulating an instinctual drive that would guarantee the preservation of the species, took orgasm with full "release" or discharge as the model for sexual gratification. The human organism was seen as struggling with dammed-up libido. Pathology and discontents (Freud, 1930) inevitably resulted from the inhibitions to the discharge of libido demanded by civilization. Sensuality and the seeking of sensual enjoyment was "the best soporific" (Freud, 1905, pp. 180f), a link to the object, an experience contributing to foreplay after genital primacy had been achieved, and a stirrer-upper of excitement states that could not lead to discharge except through pathologic channels. A constant linking of sexuality to repression, conflict, and pathology does not permit full appreciation of the vital role of sensuality and the seeking of sensual enjoyment in heightening or creating pleasurable moments and relieving distress.

Starting with the premise that the goal of the self is to initiate, organize, and integrate experience in order to preserve cohesion, self psychology has given full appreciation to affect states that heighten vitality and reverse tendencies toward depletion and fragmentation. Self psychology has centered attention on the facilitation of self-cohesion through empathic responsiveness by caregivers and has deemphasized sexual needs and the "discharge" theory. Kohut (1977) was particularly concerned that psychoanalytic clinicians not be bound by preconceptions of conflicts about guilt over sexual urges but be free to be responsive to the disturbances of self-characteristic of "Tragic Man." The tendency of self psychology has been to use rather broad concepts, such as "empathic responsiveness leading to a selfobject experience." I believe that often embedded in the general terms that self psychology uses for normal development are references to the experiences I consider as triggering sensual enjoyment: touching, stroking, rocking, soothing, rhythmic vocalizing. Put another way, I suggest that often the affect state described as a selfobject experience includes sensual enjoyment and that the soothing aspect of sensual enjoyment is cohesion restoring. In summary, traditional drive theory has emphasized sexual experience but given undue weight to excitement as the goal; self psychology has emphasized selfobject experience but given insufficient weight to sensual enjoyment as instrumental in promoting and restoring self cohesion.

We are most familiar with children's use of objects of a sensually pleasing nature to convey a sense of security. The legendary transitional object (Winnicott, 1953) is most commonly a scent-impregnated blanket or cuddly toy. However, infants also may employ hard objects for a (nonsensual) tactile-proprioceptive sense of security, for instance, by nestling against the hard bars of the crib. Tustin (1988) reminds us that infants may employ any of their bodily fluids and substance for sensual self-soothing. Tustin notes that severely disturbed children who derive little or none of their security and soothing from humans carry hard objects around with them or try to stick themselves to hard objects. They soothe and calm themselves by making shapes with sticky or slippery substances, such as bubbles of spit around their mouths, or by smearing urine, feces, or vomit. They may use the whole body to make shapes by rocking or spinning or use their hands to make stereotypic rolling gestures in air.

I have presented the evidence that as caregivers interact with neonates, an innate program for sensual enjoyment is triggered and the elementary stage of the sensual-sexual motivational system becomes organized. Relatively rapidly, sensual motivation becomes stabilized as infants seek repetitions of sensual enjoyment from both caregivers and their own agency. What does infant research tell us about sexual excitement as a motive? Kleeman's studies (1965, 1974) are particularly valuable. William, a well-developed, healthy little boy, was carefully observed by his mother. At eight months, for the first time, his mother noticed him visually discover his penis both on direct viewing and in a mirror. At 10 months, he was observed to begin clutching his genitals directly and through his diaper and to have frequent erections, often when being bathed. The manner of his fingering his penis strongly resembled the sensual manner in which he stroked his mother's nipple. Sometimes he tugged at his penis vigorously; mostly his stroking and fondling was gentle. At 10 months, the emotional response he obtained from genital play was hard to distinguish from other exploratory and pleasurable activities. At 11 months

> William grabbed at his penis and held it with one hand. He released the penis shortly thereafter, and pressed his genitalia with a plastic bottle he was holding in the other hand. He rubbed the bottle against his penis. He again put his free hand back on his penis and pulled back and forth on the foreskin, in fine movements with his fingers. He squeezed the penis and testicles together and moved them around. The penis became erect [Kleeman, 1965, p. 244].

Kleeman states that in the 11th month there were clear-cut examples of active self-stimulation with intent to excite but "nothing one could characterize as an orgasm" (p. 244). In his 12th month, he touched his genitalia on 17 of 29 days and looked, without touching, on two additional days.

For William, the dominant modes of comforting self-stimulation were thumb sucking and a soft diaper pressed against the cheek. Kleeman believes that in the first year, "genital tactile self-stimulation and visual exploratory behavior had the *primary* aim of establishing a closer relationship with his body and the erotic aim was distinctly secondary, in the sense that intentional self-arousal and self-absorption qualities were not prominent" (p. 249). From 15 ½ months on, his genital self-stimulation had a masturbatory character of self-absorption, mounting excitement with a climactic type of rhythm rather than lulling.

The developmental timetable for seeking sensual enjoyment and sexual excitement from genital play observed with William was confirmed both in other boys and in a sample of five girls. Like the boys, the five girls showed varied interest in genital play toward the end of the first year and the beginning of the second. The genital play was exploratory and without marked absorption or excitement. Then, as with the boys, beginning at about 18 months, genital play changed to an excitatory masturbatory type.

GENDER IDENTITY, GENDER ROLE, AND CHOICE OF SEXUAL PARTNER

"It's a boy!" "It's a girl!" No other designation announces a birth with such evocativeness. Not birth weight, assurances of health, lusty cry, or even the state of the mother will satisfy the curiosity of parents and family members. Why does the sexual designation of the newborn have this hold on our imagination? I believe it has to do with each parent being poised between two fantasy elaborations—one for his or her "boy," and one for his or her "girl." The enactment of the dual expectation often can be recognized from interactions the parents go through over naming, a fact not lost on Laurence Sterne, who in Tristram Shandy had the father opine that "there was a strange kind of magic bias, which good or bad names . . . irresistibly impressed upon our characters and conduct" (p. 52), only to have the women in his family give his son the name he abhorred most. Stated differently, the sex of the newborn leads each important caregiver (parents, grandparents) to cycle-in their conscious and unconscious expectations of the boy or girl. When these expectations are incompatible, the child develops in a world of conflicting pulls that will affect his or her gender role and under very aberrant conditions his or her gender identity (Stoller, 1975, 1985).

Babies are not, however, passive, helpless victims, their genital anatomy alone determining their destiny. Each sex brings to bear biological givens that affect the unfolding of its gender identity and role. Furthermore, there are indications that each baby has patterns of activity and potentiality for sensual enjoyment and sexual excitement that will give an individual casting to the masculinity or femininity of his or her boyness or girlness.

Sensory responses are generally better organized in girl than in boy newborns. Girls have greater responsiveness to taste, greater mouth activity, and more tongue involvement during feeding, as well as greater overall tactile sensitivity (Korner, 1973, 1974). Thus, a mother may find that the optimal arousal for her girl baby comes with gentler handling and that the baby responds especially well to oral comforting. The boy neonate's optimal arousal state may require more active handling and jostling or rocking as the mode of comforting. In the fantasies of the parents, these differences easily translate into models of the delicate, sweet (sugar and spice and everything nice) little girl and the rugged, robust little boy. This inculcation of a feminine identity and role for the girl and a masculine identity and role for the boy continues throughout the first year. Female infants at 12 weeks of age are more sensitive to auditory signals than are boys. Moss (1967) found that girls are talked to more than boys. Females who were touched, vocalized with, smiled at, and played with scored higher on the Bayley MDT whereas boys with very actively interactional mothers scored more poorly.

Mothers have a greater tendency to maintain physical closeness with six-month-old girls than with same-age boys (Goldberg and Lewis, 1969). By the end of the first year, masculinity and femininity seem well established in the reciprocal social interplay of infant and family (Fast, 1979). Boys will range farther from the mother and spend less time in actual physical contact with her in free-play situations (Messer and Lewis, 1970). When separated from mother by an artificial barrier, boys are more apt to actively explore means to return to her (go around, climb over), whereas girls are more likely to signal distress and a need to be rescued (crying, arms up in a gesture of appeal) (Korner, 1974).

Goldberg and Lewis (1969) suggest:

> In the first year or two, the parents reinforce those behaviors they consider sex-role appropriate and the child learns these sex-role behaviors independent of any internal motive: that is, in the same way he learns any appropriate response rewarded by his parents. The young child has little idea as to the rules governing this reinforcement. . . . As the child becomes older (above age 3), the rules for this class of reinforced behavior become clearer, and he develops internal guides to follow these earlier reinforced rules [p. 30].

Parens (1979) reports that during the third year a number of observations relating to gender role can be found. Boys begin to be more consistently compelled to push and pull things with their whole bodies, and to crash toys together, than do girls. Both boys and girls of this age more consistently react anxiously to observations of the genitals of the other sex. Parens found that by three years of age boys are commonly ready to chase girls, who run away to their mothers, squealing and smiling. At this age girls, seeing a small baby, will ooh and ahh with delight and express the wish to hold, touch, and feed the infant, while boys will often react with indifference.

The studies I have reported distinguish masculinity and femininity along lines of sensory responsiveness and interactive behaviors. To what extent can we regard the infant as having a sense of self along gender lines? To have such a sense, the infant would need to know that a distinction of significance exists and be able to integrate his or her own genital as a crucial representation of the distinction. Persuasive evidence points to the neonate's entering a milieu in which male and female others, father and mother in particular, are distinguished very early. As noted in chapters 4 and 5, Brazelton and Als (1979) could tell from four-week-old infants' actions alone whether the babies were interacting with mother (smoother rhythm) or father (more jerky rhythm). What about the babies themselves? By the beginning of the second year, boys and girls will look longer at photographs of children of the same sex and more quickly put aside pictures of other-sex children (Brooks and Lewis, 1974).

The genital itself plays an increasingly important role in the core, and subjective self. The occurrence of erections and vaginal engorgement from infancy on during both REM sleep and awake states indicates that the lived experience contributing to the sense of self emerging includes genital sensation that triggers some level of sensual enjoyment. However, for most infants, sucking and mouthing, rocking and bouncing, and general tactile stimulation are more prominent contributors to emergent and core self. Kleeman's (1965, 1975) studies indicate that the genitals are not discovered and explored visually and tactilly in a clearly purposive way until the end of the first year and that full masturbatory sexual excitement is not consistent until the middle of the second year. Observers of infants tend to agree that between 18 and 24 months, both boys and girls experience an increase in genital and perineal awareness and sensation (Roiphe, 1968; Roiphe and Galenson, 1981; Kleeman, 1975; Amsterdam and Levitt, 1980). This period is a time of great developmental activity and challenge in each of the motivational systems. Greater sphincter control and heightened anal and urethral sensation invite regulatory interactions and struggles. The toddler is increasingly mobile and exploratory and often experiences attachment crises in moving away from caregivers (Mahler, Pine, and Bergman, 1975). Growing assertiveness about self-defined goals promotes conflicts over opposing agendas and more intense aversive responses. All of this is given representation by symbolic process augmented by a massive acquisition of vocabulary.

What is the impact of the developments of the 18–24 month period on the sensual-sexual system? Let us review the development of sensual-sexual motivation to this point. First, gender identity is firmly, probably immutably, fixed by this point. Boys are boys, girls are girls, both in the eyes of caregivers and in their own awareness. Second, many aspects of gender role are solidly in place. Masculinity and femininity of gesture, movement, and interactional behavior are well established. While subject to change at later stages (feminine two-year-old girls may become tomboys; risk-taking, aggressive boys may become subdued preteens), a pattern of lasting significance is probably established. For both boys and girls, sensual enjoyment associated with genital sensation exists from the beginning of life. Only gradually does the genital assume a prominent role in securing sensual enjoyment and still later sexual excitement. Genital touching, rubbing, and fondling trigger sensual enjoyment and play a prominent role in securing the integration of the genital into the body self-representation. I believe however, that the masturbatory activity triggering sexual excitement states of the 18–24 month period is responsible for consolidating both image and function of the genital of both sexes into gender identity and gender role.

This hypothesis that genital masturbation and sexual excitement contribute to integrating the genital into gender identity and gender role suggests two important consequences. First, the male genital may be more easily integrated into the boy's gender identity and role than the female's is into her gender identity; second, the response of caregivers to the masturbatory excitement states will affect the emotional coloration of sexual motivation. In Kleeman's (1975) observations, genital self-stimulation in infant boys "surpassed in intensity, frequency, self-absorption, activity, and precise focusing anything seen in the girls studied" (p. 93). Kleeman suggests that because of the accessibility of the penis and scrotum, the little boy can touch his genitals more readily,

and, equally important, can see what he is manipulating or can look without touching. For example, if you compare the boy's *fingering* with the use of *thigh pressure* in the girl, he is registering the sensation in his genitals, his fingers, and his eyes. The sensation in the thighs is less clear and more diffuse [p. 94].

The girl usually can only touch and see her vulva and clitoris. Efforts to explore deeper into her genital are apt to elicit pain. Furthermore, parents usually name the penis and even the testicles earlier and more accurately than vulva, clitoris, and vagina. In addition, it is easier for the boy to associate his penis with thrusting than for the little girl to associate her vulva slit and clitoris with reception, since she often has no early experience with her vagina or even of its opening (Kestenberg, 1956). Kestenberg's study of prepubertal girls revealed that they had limited awareness of the vagina as an organ. Balanced against this anatomical limitation in gender role is the little girl's awareness of the full potential of her genital area for engorgement, sensual enjoyment, and sexual excitement.

The second consequence of the aforementioned hypothesis is that the integration may be adversely affected by negative parental response to the toddler's budding sensual and sexual expressions. Sears, Maccoby, and Levin (1957) document children's frequent denial of genital play and masturbation. Moreover, none of the parents observed verbally identified the children's affective state. Both of these failures represent striking "statements" by the parents—they are sending powerful messages to their children. At a time when almost every other activity of the child draws attention, positive or negative, and labeling is a prominent mode of exchange, not to notice, to avert the eyes, or to see and then grow tense and ignore all—signals to the child that this activity is "special," in the sense of being beyond the pale. The toddler thus lacks the tools for an ordinary coding by secondary process (Dorpat, 1983) and can resort only to primary-process symbolism. Amsterdam and Levitt (1980) note the shyness and self-consciousness of some toddlers when viewing themselves in the mirror. The authors speculate that the exchange between the parent and child when the toddler was masturbating or when he or she was proudly exhibiting his or her genital was responsible for normal or pathological self-consciousness. Tomkins (1963) suggests that shame is innately triggered if a sudden decrement in mounting interest or excitement occurs when an ongoing activity is interrupted. Thus "shaming" combines both the parent's disapproval as he or she inhibits the child's mounting enjoyment or excitement during self-fondling or exhibiting, and the child's innate affective response.

Let us return to a general consideration of the challenges of this important time of developmental spurts in each of the motivational systems. One way to look at the second half of the second year is that each developmental gain is accompanied by the potential for loss. The broadening of eating habits may lead to a threatened loss of the bottle or of the comforts of being fed as the baby. The acquisition of sphincter control may increase awareness of the loss of a "possession" of the body, especially if toilet training is instituted. Movement away from parents, exciting in its freedom, means the sudden loss of a counted-on physical closeness. Exploring and assertive activities with toys may mean being left alone for longer stretches of time. And all these gains are apt to put the child in some form of conflict with the parents—about eating, toileting, running off, exploring dangerous objects, and the like. All this occurs at a time when the child experiences increasing determination to have his or her agenda. Confrontations and aversiveness frequently take the form of temper tantrums.

I believe this common upsurge of aversive antagonism often has an effect on developments in the sensual-sexual system. Let us return to the supposition that the infant relies on sensual enjoyment as an important mode of self-soothing and that, depending on many factors (including hormonal levels), sensual enjoyment triggers sexual excitement. A circular pattern may develop. The toddler, troubled by intense aversive responses, will turn to self-soothing activities such as finger or bottle sucking and especially genital play. The very activity children are drawn to in order to restore cohesion may bring them into increased conflict with parents. Struggles about compliance and rebellion against restraint in other motivational areas become combined with comparable struggles about compliance and rebellion against restraint of sensual and sexual pursuits. The outcome is the beginning of a process in which sensual enjoyment and aversive struggles are paired under the same system subset. Many specific analogous struggles involving fears of body injury or confusions about genital differences easily become associated with dangers that appear inherent in seeking sensual enjoyment and especially sexual excitement. The particular experiences of the next several years as the developing child tries to find a place in the affectionate and sensual patterns of the family, its inclusions, exclusions, and its rivalries, may either temper the coupling of aversive responses to sensual-sexual motives or intensify them.

Several axiomatic statements about sexuality may be considered in the light of these suggestions. First, self psychology: the Oedipus *complex* is the result of empathic failures during the oedipal *phase*, and sexual symptoms are fragmentation products of disturbed cohesion of the self in the face of empathic failure. Second, traditional analysis: sexual symptoms and disturbances are the result of intrapsychic distortions that produce inevitable conflicts. Third, Stoller (1975): hostility, mystery, risk, and revenge play a role in forming and maintaining all human sexual excitement. My view combines parts of all three. The coupling of aversive responses to sensual enjoyment and sexual excitement is not inevitable because of a fusion of drives; it is not instinctual at all. It is the result of empathic failures on the part of caregivers whose own experience (procedural memory) has them consciously and unconsciously anxiously responding to some expression of the child's seeking of sensual enjoyment and sexual excitement. What is *inevitable* in my view is that empathic failures will occur. An empathic ambience can mitigate, but not eliminate, the fear, distress, and anger triggered by the mysteries confronting the child. Here I place emphasis not only on sexual differences but on physical vulnerability, the universality of death (relatives, pets, the squashed animals that litter our streets), the puzzles of procreation, and bedroom activities. Thus sensual-sexual motivation is inevitably subject to the pull of aversive responses on the one side and the need for attachment and intimacy pleasure (love) on the other. I do not, however, hold the apocalyptic view that men and women are driven by instinct. Rather, the complex challenges in the lived experience of infancy guarantee the inevitability of relatively frequent empathic failures in the parent's dealing with sensual-sexual motivations. So to me the question is not, will the fantasy life of each adult include some degree of hostility, mystery, risk and revenge in the self hype of sexual arousal, but how much will it? Does it interfere with loving, with commitment, and with functioning?

Thus far I have considered the sensual-sexual motivational system (as well as the other systems) using traditional generalities about phases and timing of development. Now I should like to make an appeal for the premise that each child's innate program, plus his or her parents, living environment, and cultures, are so distinctive that *individualizing* the idiosyncratic preferences, restrictions, and aversions affecting sensual-sexual motivation is as powerful an organizing principle as the view of a sequence of successive oral, anal, and phallic-oedipal phases. Escalona's (1963, 1965) Harry and Grace, Peter and Sybil are clearly different one from another both in their innate programs and in how the mother of each reacted to the infant's rhythms and preferences for sensual enjoyment and needs for soothing. Likewise, Kleeman (1975) cites distinctive patterns in the girls he observed. See also Kestenberg's (1965a, b) descriptions in chapter 9.

A recent study (Piontelli, 1987) combining ultrasound examination of one girl and one boy in utero with postpartum observations of each mother and infant for a year illustrates the striking difference between infants in both the intrauterine and extrauterine environment. Giulia's mother, Mrs. A, was a large, overweight woman with a warm smile and a calm, rather detached manner. Giulia, observed in utero, most of the time floated in the amniotic fluid following the rhythm of her mother's breathing, as if lulled by it. Occasionally she rocked herself to sleep, but her most constant movement was playing with her tongue, moving it in and out of her lips. On two occasions she was observed wildly licking the placenta. Although her birth itself was an extremely traumatic experience for her mother, Giulia seemed unperturbed. The next day, when her mother tried to introduce the nipple, instead of sucking, Giulia licked vigorously. Thereafter, feedings were times of rapid, furious sucking for two minutes and then a return to playing with her tongue. With obvious sensual enjoyment, she licked any surface or textile that came in contact with her face. At four months, when solids were introduced, Giulia ate so voraciously that at 10 months she weighed as much as a child of two. Giulia derived great sensual pleasure from "feasting" with her eyes and from hearing voices. Mrs. A noted that Giulia went wild whenever she heard a man's voice. "She is really a little whore . . . she is mad about men . . . " (p. 459). Later, Giulia derived sensual pleasure from endlessly rocking herself, and her grandmother observed that Giulia loved to have someone's arm between her legs. At one year, Giulia joined in by gurgling as Mrs. A sat at a table eating biscuits and drinking coffee, and talked nonstop with her own mother. Giulia's father reacted to the "eminently feminine universe" (p. 459) of the family by cynical ridicule and keeping his distance.

Piontelli's second example is of Mrs. B and her son, Gianni. After one successful pregnancy, Mrs. B's second pregnancy had ended in a stillbirth due to abruptio placentae. Throughout her third pregnancy, with Gianni, Mrs. B's anxiety about losing the fetus and about its sex pervaded her life. No reassurance satisfied her obsessive, repeated anxious questioning. Unlike the active Giulia, Gianni "remained immobile, tightly crouched in a corner of the womb, with his hands and his arms screening his eyes and his face, and with his legs . . . tightly folded and crossed" (p. 460). Birth was by Caesarian section, and Gianni was so crumpled in a corner of the uterus that the obstetrician had trouble pulling him out. During the first two months after birth, Gianni continued to be practically immobile. At the breast he sucked slowly, frowning, with his eyes closed, but he clung to the breast for hours on end. Mrs. B never looked at Gianni but spoke to others. Her conversations were filled with her obsessive preoccupation with reproduction and sex. One night when he was three months old, Gianni awoke, whimpered continually, and stared fixedly into space. To comfort him, Mrs. B walked with him, resting his face against her chest while tapping his back mechanically. When put down in his push-chair, he relaxed and stopped his disconsolate whimpering. At a year, Gianni could crawl but preferred to sit in a corner always holding the same toy. His mother would hold him "between her legs while saying laughingly, 'But why can't you stand more erect' " (p. 461). Gianni seemed more able to relax when cared for by his babysitter and after a holiday during which his father spent a lot of time with him.

Piontelli concludes, "What one derives from this research is . . . an idea of the complexities and differences at play in shaping every human being. Each child seems different and many and varied factors intervene in its subsequent development" (p. 462). For Giulia, all the possibilities for sensual enjoyment and subsequent sexual excitement began in utero, were fostered after birth by her mother, and were encouraged by her entire cultural milieu during her first year. For poor, sad, frightened Gianni, both in the womb and out, aversive withdrawal seemed the fully dominant motivational system. Nothing in Piontelli's report suggests that any capacity Gianni had for sensual enjoyment was either a dominant motivation in itself or an effective means to reverse the dominance of his aversion to a frightening world.

Another example of the ideosyncratic nature of development lies in the varied timing and intensity of children's reactions to the anatomical difference between the sexes. Roiphe and Galenson (1987) present the case of Sarah, one of many examples they have noted to support their claim that castration anxiety occurs during an early genital phase, during the middle months of the second year. When Sarah was 14 months old, she saw her father urinate. The following morning she straddled a toy train after observing a little boy do so. She lifted the toy train cover and stuck her doll in the bin. Straddling the train again, she rolled it back and forth with a dreamy, inwardly directed gaze. The authors suggest, "May not the special appeal of Sarah's activity have been that she recognized that the male child had something between his legs?" (p. 423). At 18 months, after a week's separation, Sarah was taken abroad on a trip by her parents. She was unusually anxious and clinging. On the trip she verbally, and insistently, claimed her father's penis to be hers.

Roiphe and Galenson's evocative observation has all the ingredients of chance occurrences, problems of interpretation, and convincing behavioral indicators. In contrast, Kleeman's (1965) reports do not demonstrate the same degree of castration anxiety. Kleeman tends to regard the genital play and sexual activity of this period as being of less emotional intensity than do Roiphe and Galenson. Parens (1979) also failed to find evidence of castration concerns in children between 18 and 24 months. Rather, he reports curiosity and interest without undue concern or distress. Do these discrepant findings result from a different weighting of the same observations or a greater variance in timing and intensity than the "phase" concept permits?

Along with the variance in timing and intensity of body damage fears, the problem of explaining the individual's choice of who and what to love erotically impresses us more than any other with the remarkable individuality of motivation in the sensual-sexual system.

The foregoing examples, plus those of Kestenberg (1965a, b) noted in chapter 9, indicate that the infant begins life with innate preferences for bodily experiences that trigger sensual enjoyment. The caregivers may be resonant with the infant's preference, or they may go their separate ways. One infant may enjoy both his mother's gentler fondling and rocking and his father's more rough and tumble jostling. Another may be aversive to one or the other. For all of this, we have good documentation. For another variable, which I speculate is of major importance, we have very little data, probably because of the difficulty in making assessments. This is: what messages infants pick up about how their parents regards them, and how does each parent regard the other? Does the mother want her daughter to respond to the father in a feminine way? (Note the mixed message in Mrs. A's comment about Giulia's being a "little whore, mad about men.") Not long after the infant enters the world, gender identity becomes rather firmly established, but the role and object choice for sensual-sexual involvement is only to a degree set by innate proclivities. Especially during the last third of the first year, the growing infant becomes increasingly aware of the signals he or she is receiving about the emotional valences that determine the interrelationships in the intersubjective world of families. Not withstanding the dyadic tilt given to early development in our theory, contemporary observations document that infants perceive and respond to all the people and things in their environment. Mother, father, siblings, grandparents, visitors, pets, bottles, toys, blankets, pillows, all are potential sources of sensual enjoyment. The importance of mother is that she—or whoever, male or female, is the primary caregiver—is the one the infant looks to for guidance about the safety and desirability of his or her choices. Mother signals that the stranger is dangerous and gives father the same look; or she signals that the stranger is welcome and gives father a look that says he is especially, excitedly welcome. Gunsberg (1987b) calls attention to the empirical studies by developmental researchers (Parke, 1981) and longitudinal psychoanalytic studies (Gunsberg, 1983; Herzog, 1985) that document the early and continuing importance of the father.

Another variable that has been obscured by the significance placed on parents is the fact that often the infant and developing child's most intense moments of sensual enjoyment and sexual excitement may not occur with either mother or father. Often under poorly controlled conditions, the child's most intense moments of sensual-sexual experience may occur with a sibling (Parens, 1987; Graham, 1987) with whom the child shares a room or a bed, with a babysitter, or with a seductive adult. In a surprising number of my analytic patients some form of sexually exciting play, often with an admixture of pain, with a sibling proved to be the most intense childhood experience. These experiences with siblings then played a significant part either in the later choice of sexual partner or in the mode of relating to the partner. (In the case presented in chapter 10, the sexually arousing playmate was a cousin.) Striking in a number of instances was that parents who were themselves generally appropriate and protective in their handling of the young child would blindly ignore the often overtly sexual exciting seductions between sibling pairs.

Williams (1987) reports the analysis of Mr. B, a man in his 40s, who had been molested anally at the age of two by a "friendly" male servant. The child's parents had divorced some months before, and he was in the care of his grandparents during the period when the seduction occurred. A first analysis failed to relieve his symptoms of depression, insomnia, inability to form an intimate relationship, and self-images of being soiled. After breaking off the first analysis, he lost the capacity to experience orgasm with masturbation. Working against the patient's complete lack of emotional expression and his strong inclination to seal off the meaning of the trauma, Williams explained to him that his violent and endless repetitive "dreams had preserved experiences and impressions of an indelible nature" (p. 152). "Neither his parents' divorce nor his mother's absences alone could have produced such a profound and lasting effect, as had been assumed in his first analysis" (p. 158). Commenting on the positive result of the second analysis, Williams states, "The overriding insight into the many ramifications of his traumatic seduction had the effect of liberating him" (p. 163).

The examples I have chosen place heavy significance on the lived experience of the infant and toddler. Williams's case report presents both the "chance" experience, the background of empathic failure in which it occurred, and many indications in the dream material and transference responses of the permutations of symbolic representation the lived experience were subjected to. After Freud abandoned the traumatic theory of the neurosis, emphasis shifted strongly to the effect of distortion based on drive and immaturity. What I have presented represents a reverse swing of the pendulum. It is not a simple reverse to trauma but to the intersubjective nature of the lived experience and of the child and the child's caregivers. The studies of severe sexual deviation point in this direction. For example, in his study of 15 very feminine boys and their families, Stoller (1985) found that the mother had regarded her newborn son as very beautiful. She engaged in excessive skin-to-skin contact and soulful gazing in his eyes. The distant, passive father had raised no objection to his son's feminization. Stoller believes that the mother regarded the son as the longed-for phallus she had needed to please her own mother, who had wanted a boy. Stoller's findings were tested by Green (1987), who failed to verify that the mothers of the feminine boys he studied spent more time with them than did mothers of a control group of masculine boys. Green confirmed that the effeminate boys were regarded as beautiful, the mothers felt that they had had a distant relationship with their mothers, and the fathers spent less time with these sons than did fathers of masculine boys. Stoller (1985) found that very masculine transsexual females in infancy had suffered a severe disruption in their relationship with their mothers and had become excessively close with their fathers. Siegel (1988) found the conspicuous absence among a group of homosexual females of memories of playing with dolls. "Instead, there was a lot of running, shrieking, breathholding, and other means of possibly releasing inner tensions" (p. 3). Siegel cites Kestenberg's (1982) proposal of an inner-genital phase at approximately two to four years of age during which the little girl becomes aware of early vaginal sensations. At this time, her inner sensations create tensions, excitations, and urges that are only vaguely perceived. The child must deal with them in the external world—partially in her relations with her mother, partially in the exploration of body parts, functions, and internality of space through doll play. Siegel's cases illustrate the failure of this normal mode of development and a consequent failure to recognize and acknowledge gender distinctions.

Meyer and Dupkin (1985) studied ten boys and two girls between the ages of 5 and 13 who engaged in cross-gender behavior. Meyer (1982) had found earlier that theories accounting for cross-gender behaviors fell into three groups: "the biological/imprint hypothesis, the nonconflictual identity hypothesis, and the conflict/defense hypothesis" (p. 390). Meyer and Dupkin conclude that the onset of the gender disturbance in the 12 children were related to early traumatic experiences within disturbed family settings. They believe their study tends to confirm the conflict/defense hypothesis. In none of the male children was evidence found to confirm Stoller's (1985) finding of a blissful symbiosis. For each child, the family situation and specific trauma varied: multiple separations between parents, parental absence, withdrawal or abandonment, bisexuality, repeated primal scene experiences, sexual overstimulation, and a full range of parental psychopathology. Frank cross-gender behaviors were noticed at age two to four in nine of the children (around age two, in five). The authors suggest that it is logical to look to those studies of infancy which document the upsurge of genital excitement at 18 months for clues to the normal and disturbed development of gender image and behavior. I believe these findings suggest that, for some children, gender identity is a sensitive barometer of early disturbances in any of the motivational systems. The traditional view that the disturbances are principally reflective of oedipal phase failures must be reconsidered. The lived experiences that fill the need for consolidation of gender identity require further study.

If these severe disturbances in gender role and choice of sexual partner are the result of skewed lived experiences, what is the role of fantasy? Roiphe and Galenson (1987) believe that a number of pathological outcomes may emerge from a common matrix of early disturbances. They cite one group of infants who emerged from this common matrix unable to accept the anatomical difference between the sexes and still maintain satisfying sexual functioning. They note the difficulty in prospectively determining the outcome. I believe the unpredictability lies in the enormous plasticity of symbolic representation. Through the use of the secondary- and primary-process modes of symbolic representation, the child after 18 months constantly attempts to blend the prior and present motivational pressures from each of the systems to promote, retain, and restore cohesion of the self. In its focus on sexual fantasies alone, traditional analysis often has taken the schema of the positive and negative oedipal relationships too narrowly and programmatically. The facts as I comprehend them indicate that it is necessary to distinguish between goals of sensual enjoyment and of sexual excitement and to recognize that gender role and the choices of whom to love, to share sensual pleasure with, and to share sexual excitement with involve many complicated motivational shifts. These motivational shifts are, from the very beginning of gender identity assignment, never made intrapsychically alone but always as a consequence of an intersubjective exchange.

The emphasis I have placed on infant development necessarily provides only an incomplete and unsatisfying tracking of sensual and sexual motivation throughout life. The principal issue lies in how motivations arising in the attachment motivational system and those of the sensual-sexual system can be integrated into what we call mature sexual love. Schwartz (1987) suggests this dual motivational source when he writes

human sexual behavior derives its appetitive urgency from the synergistic influence and participation of at least two neurophysiologically distinct reward systems—one generating a "high" and triggered by afferent data conveying the interest and desire of an appealing mate, the other producing the separate but also intently pleasurable sensations of erotic arousal and orgasm.

It is not surprising that powerful motives will draw on affective amplification from two or more motivational systems.

CLINICAL EXAMPLE OF A DISTURBANCE IN THE ENJOYMENT OF SENSUAL TENDERNESS IN AN ADULT

Mrs. S, whose disturbed regulation of bowel elimination was described in chapter 3, talked a great deal in her analysis about her inclination toward situations that involved physical or psychic pain. This was particularly defined in a game she and a boy cousin had played, which they called the "pain game." The goal was to see who could stand pain the longest. As her analysis progressed, her inclination to pain diminished and, parallel with this change, her capacity to experience and enjoy sexual excitement increased. This clinical example helps to demonstrate the value of distinguishing between sensual enjoyment and sexual excitement in the organization of the sensual-sexual motivational system.

Mrs. S opened her Monday hour by describing a desire to withhold. She related a dream in which she entered Montaldo's Knick-Knack store. She was buying a vibrator for her mother. It was expensive, and she asked if anything was on sale. Yes, everything, the store was going out of business. On the shelf was a lovely china figurine she thought she would get for her daughter. There were also silly looking owls. She hated them but thought she would buy them, although even in the dream she wondered why. She associated Montaldo/vibrator to a dildo and made some intellectual-sounding associations about the store going out of business being the analysis. I noted her lack of feeling and asked her about the urge to withhold that she had mentioned earlier. She responded that she found it easier to talk about her dream intellectually than to tell me about a photograph she had taken that pleased her. It was of a magnolia bud. She described in detail how she had arranged to get the lighting from the back so the petal opening could be seen. Inside was the soft, sticky bud itself, with a thin film of moisture that picked up the light.

In the background of my thoughts as I listened was my impression that photography was for her both a sublimation of voyeuristic tendencies and an attempt to resolve her conflicts about her self-worth. Having identified with her father's superficiality and exhibitionism, she had in dilettante fashion dabbled at being a dancer, actress, pianist, and poet. Toward the end of the middle phase she had taken up photography, which she believed to be an interest of mine. She attempted to approach photography with a depth approximating her idealized estimate of my expertise. She was extremely reluctant to talk about her photographs, fearing competition or, worse, a superficial, patronizing, "That's nice."

As she spoke, I visualized her narrowing her lens focus to the curve of a single bud. I conjectured that her resistance to talking about her creative effort had relaxed and that this indicated that she was gaining in her struggle to establish a more stable sense of self-worth. My attention was caught by the music in her voice—the unusual softness and gentleness—a soothing quality as she described the ever-so-slight stickiness and the light and shadows. A whole new image came into my mind: Mrs. S as a little girl, gently stroking her moist clitoris with a mixture of self-soothing and erotic pleasure. With this visualization a thought that had troubled me crystallized: while she was now heterosexually orgastic after years of total frigidity, her orgasms as she had described them had always seemed strained and tense, and her fantasies had definite sadomasochistic trends.

During adolescence there had been a complete suppression of direct genital masturbation. When she attempted genital masturbation for the first time as an adult, she had forcefully inserted a candle. We had come to understand that the repression of her childhood masturbation had occurred under the pressure of harsh reactions from her mother, reinforced by religious training and fixated by a displacement to her anus.

I was jarred into awareness of the affective discrepancy between my image of the little girl tenderly stroking herself and Mrs. S's dominant state of mind when she made the slightly irritable comment that I would probably assume the bud was a penis. She spontaneously took up the issue of masturbation and mentioned that she was now conscious of the urge when she was alone. The urge was no longer shifted to her anal rubbing. But her fantasies during intercourse that weekend were of a cruel king and queen who forced themselves on her. In her fantasy she resisted, and only then could she feel sexually aroused. I felt that my line of thought about gentle masturbation was out of keeping with her current emotion, and I asked her more about her fantasy. She said there was a painful build up of tension and then an exciting release—as with the enemas. She associated to her dream, stating that she could see how in the dream she arranged to increase her tension to enable herself to have the accompanying sexual sensation, but why would she want to buy the owl when she hated it? I said, "Ow." She responded, "It hurts! Of course."

In the Tuesday hour, her associations to a dream about a see-through nighty went to her being excited, getting a man excited, followed by a strange feeling of drowsiness. I interpreted that she was building up a sequence in which she was excited, would get me excited, go to sleep, and—she filled in: I would attack her and she could do nothing about it. She recalled the excitement of baths with her cousin: It had been her mother's message to her that she could look at her cousin until her eyeballs popped out, but *don't touch*. Go to sleep and if her cousin touched her that was O.K., but don't touch herself and don't let it be known that her genital was excited.

In the Wednesday hour, she began by talking about giving up in a game of tennis with her husband. He was so good that she was comparatively nothing. She added that I had helped her to know that she compared herself with her cousin and her father and that when she admired their penises she could fall into a hole of withdrawal. Even now it was hard to climb out. Reflecting to myself on her portrayal of me as having helped, I thought she would be receptive to an interpretation reopening the issue of her body image and her self-depreciation. I noted her feeling that if she did not have a penis, she had nothing and reminded her of the photograph she had been reluctant to tell me about. As close to her words and her tone as I could get, I repeated what she had described. She said with some surprise that she had originally thought of the bud as a penis but as I redescribed it to her she thought of it as a clitoris— especially the softness. She added in a poignant tone that she didn't value what she had—she never thought of the nice sensations she could get from her own body.

The next hour she related going to the theatre and weeping through the last act, during which the hero showed that he was unable to accept aspects of himself. She thought of her father, and the feeling persisted. She could not stand herself for having these feelings. I suggested that she found it difficult to accept her soft, deep feeling toward her father. She agreed and, after a silence, thought of the photo of the bud (and the fuzzy, soft substance). At the same time, she felt a strong urge to wipe out these feelings. She said that it was easier to think of herself with a spotlight on her, becoming all excited—but when the light went off she felt flattened out. I suggested that since childhood her excitement had been for fantasied male qualities—her whole body as a penis, her athletic limbs—and that when she lost that feeling she felt flattened out, as though she had no feminine body parts of value. She said that when she was growing up she had liked playing with girls, but that when she came home she would be afraid that she was too soft for her father.

She then described how the day before she had been alone and felt tense and thought of masturbating. It was a mad kind of desire—angry and rough. I asked if the angry roughness might be to cover her desire to touch herself as if she were a little girl soothing herself very softly and gently. She nodded and fell silent and pensive. Then she said she didn't know why she was silent. She didn't feel at all sleepy or resistant. I wondered if she might be giving herself a moment of privacy. She agreed, adding poignantly that she had never been able to feel really private, even with the door locked.

The theme of tenderness and gentleness then became a central motif, blending in with Mrs. S's mourning reactions during the months and hours leading up to termination.

Model Scenes, Affects,
and the Unconscious

I N RESPONSE TO MY CONCEPTION OF "MODEL SCENES" in the Prologue
to the *Psychoanalytic Inquiry* issue on Application of Infant Research to Adult Psychoanalytic Treatment, Gunsberg (1987) wrote:

> "Psychoanalytic researchers have studied infants in their homes and
> in laboratory settings, usually within the context of the infant-mother
> relationship. The questions they ask have to do with what can be
> learned about the presymbolic era, when the infant has experiences
> which are not represented symbolically and which are not, therefore,
> likely to be available to the patient and analyst. If early experiences
> either are not coded or are coded in a form different from that of
> adult memory, perhaps research and longitudinal observation can
> help provide the pictures, images, or 'model scenes' that are either
> reorganized on a symbolic level, or are lost forever [p. 301].

While "model scene" is an unfamiliar designation, the use of prototypic episodes to describe experiences of major significance to
psychoanalysis began with Freud's recognition that psychological
events structuring the dynamics of children of four and five were
dramatized in the myth of King Oedipus. For other examples, picture a 30-month old, somewhat reluctant toddler being persuaded
to try once more to use the potty seat, or the 20-month old toddler
moving excitedly away from mother and then, realizing the distance, glancing back for reassurance. Each familiar model scene ori-
ents a therapist to recognize a problem that a patient may talk or
dream about or reenact with the therapist. Interpretation is the
means that the analyst uses to convey recognition of the unfolding

model scene, the patient's part in it, and the part assigned unconsciously to the analyst.

Needles (1965) provides an example of a model scene in a dream that epitomizes a mode of attachment relatedness in a patient:

> "I am riding a horse. I do something which causes him to rear and throw me. As I lie on the ground, the horse approaches and licks my cheek. I feel sensuously pleased and tell myself: 'It was worth it!'
>
> The dream is a faithful reproduction of a circumstance in his childhood. Morbidly sensitive to his mother's coldness, he had striven desperately to elicit some token of love from her. A device that had proven effective was to nag her to the point of exasperation. She would then become penitently indulgent [p. 68].

With remarkable parsimony, the patient's dream and Needles' interpretation of it conveys to the reader a theme with the possibility of infinite variations that, once understood, would give meaning to events unfolding in the patient's contemporary transferential and non-transferential experience.

Needles's example combines rich visual symbolic representation with verbal puns. We can uncode the dream's meaning confidently, using the roadmap of our knowledge of secondary and primary process in dream formation. What provides the evocative power is not the cognitive transliteration, but the affects induced as we follow the dreamer's experience. The horse rears and throws us; we feel the startle, disorientation, and thud as we hit. Then the surprise as our affective state is transformed from pain to sensually pleasurable. We know as analysts that we are hearing some story, some model scene, that marks, signifies, and symbolizes important lived experiences. Actions and gestures that evoke affects, and affect themselves and their transitions, are thus the golden thread we follow to be empathically attuned with our patients.

But what if some patients cannot dream or talk about such discrete visual images of experiences that influence their responses because the model scene has never been coded by symbolic representation? What if the motivational base of their emergent and core selves has been compromised? Then we need to sense the sources of an adverse developmental experience from personality traits, from the interactions and intersubjective ambiance that the patient pulls us into, from peculiar behaviors that defy ordinary dynamic formulations and especially from gestural and affective revenants of early lived experience.

MODEL SCENES

My hypothesis about model scenes is that: (1) when immersed in the intersubjective field of an analysis, psychoanalysts often perceive the essence of analysands' communication in the form of a "scene" or representation that epitomizes a significant past or present experience; (2) analysts are enabled to form model scenes by their knowledge of specific life experiences that are significant organizers of major fantasy and transference dispositions; (3) each of the five motivational systems provides model scenes that typify specific developments at every phase of life; (4) model scenes that represent each of the motivational systems during the period of early infancy add new conceptualizations of normal and abnormal developments and correct unsubstantiated and inaccurate models currently in use; (5) the model scene an analyst forms from the communications of his analysand and his responses to them stand somewhere between a theoretical model scene of normal or skewed development and an unconscious fantasy of the analysand; (6) through the work of interpretation by the analyst and confirming and disconfirming responses by the analysand, the disparity is reduced between the analyst's provisional model scene and the analysand's memories of lived experience in infancy and symbolic representations in later life; and (7) the model scene thus refers to three constructs—a conception an *analyst* forms that epitomizes a significant communication from the analysand about his life, a conception that analytic clinical *theoreticians and infant observers* form that epitomizes significant developmental experiences of self alone and with others, and a conception (unconscious fantasy) the *analysand* has that epitomizes significant past and present lived experiences. The earlier the lived experiences and the model scenes, the more important it is to understand the way in which they are recorded, represented, maintained, or transformed. (See Loewald, 1975, and McDougall, 1982, for related conceptions).

WHAT IS "MODEL" IN A MODEL SCENE?

Model has three meanings, each adding value to the concept of model scenes. The most direct clinical meaning is a scene that *epitomizes* significant experiences from the past. The significant experience could be a prototype of recurrent states of being, or, less frequently, a galvanizing traumatic moment. An example of a prototype of a recurrent lived experience is a patient's reconstructed "memory," frequently reexperienced with the analyst, of tugging at mother's leg or skirt and sensing the stiffening of her mother's body as she resists the child's importuning. An example of a galvanizing traumatic moment is a patient's reconstructed memory of being happily explorative on her grandparents' porch. She saw what appeared to be a bucket of cool water. She put her hand in the liquid and carried her hand to her mouth. She suddenly experienced the total shock of a burn from lye.

The second meaning of model deals not with epitomizing a scene that is experienced but with the *schema*, or organization, that underlies the scene. The most likely basic referent for schemas that underlie scenes is found in neurophysiological tracts and substances (Reiser, 1985; Schwartz, 1987). I shall leave a consideration of that basic level to chapter 11, written by Dr. Hadley. A diagrammatic psychological representation can be constructed for schemas of each of the five motivational systems. The diagram would begin with a basic need, in response to which the motivational system forms and once formed becomes activated. The schema would include the motivational need and an abstracted representation of the lived experience that followed. For example, let us take the schema for the little girl tugging at her mother's leg to be a need for an exchange of intimacy → an intention to pull mother into being playful (potential affect of pleasure in intimacy from some prior experiences) → a recognition of resistance (brief activation of affect of sadness) → an activation of the aversive motivational system with fully experienced hurt-anger. The patient's memory of tugging at her mother's leg and the stiffening response can, as she told it, be compared with the motivational model. The scene as the patient remembered it ended with her mother's stiffening. In the schema, the event continues with the aversive system becoming activated, as we would expect when failure of response to a need in the attachment motivation system has occurred. Confirmation of the version depicted in the schema occurred as I recognized that hurt and anger were the outcome in the analysis each time that she experienced herself pulling at me for intimacy and felt that I resisted her appeal. The schema helped me to anticipate the full experience, to integrate otherwise fragmentary experiences of alterations in self-experience from loving to angry, to form a model scene of it, and to be in a position to interpret it to her. Furthermore, the relationship between the schema and the memory and the model scene of the recurrent experience from her early (presymbolic) life helped to place into perspective a later memory from the patient's preteen years.

She recalled pleading with her mother to let her accompany her on a trip. When her mother refused, the girl became increasingly agitated and angry. To the surprise of both, she exclaimed to her mother that she hated her. In the course of her analysis, the patient had come to understand one source of her desperation to be a fear of being exposed to sexual temptation when left behind with her father and brother. However, the full source of her angry outburst to her mother, which was very uncharacteristic of her, was understood only when seen in the light of the earlier experiences of her mother's rejecting her need for intimacy and the unremembered (denied and repressed) antagonism aroused by it.

The schema for the 20-month-old toddler who suffered the lye burn would be drawn from the exploratory-assertive motivational system. Exploration and assertion → shocking pain and distress → activation of the aversive motivational system in the form of withdrawal. As an adult, this patient suffered from what was incorrectly diagnosed as narcolepsy. She would fall asleep at work and frequently had to pull off the road when driving. With little effect, she resorted to stimulants to fight her sleep symptom and other medications to calm her from the effect of the stimulants. Drowsiness as a symptom occurred regularly in her analysis. First it was triggered if I mentioned her burn. Her family maintained a collusive determination to place the incident under an impenetrable veil of denial. The schema for that was exploration → anxiety → an aversive response of denial. However when this denial of the fact of the disfiguring burn, which had the more workable aspects of symbolic representation, was worked through, we were able to begin to approach the more broadly based personality disturbance that it both paralleled and masked. Each effort to be explorative and assertive, no matter what the arena, might at any moment arouse anxiety and the sudden, often overwhelming need to click off consciousness. This generalized tendency might be reduced in some area as a result of successful analytic understanding in that sector but retained the constant potential to occur in any situation of remote threat, transition, or surprise. This could only be understood as an effect of a presymbolic response to a trauma that happened to a child who was just beginning to employ symbolic representation. This is a period in which the recent developmental advance is extremely vulnerable to functional loss (Dowling, 1982a, b).

As we have seen, the first and second meanings of model are prototype and schema. The third meaning is exemplar, ideal, or, in terms of motivation, "normal" or adaptive, or in Kohut's (1971) term, in keeping with its design. When looking at the foregoing schema or when forming a model scene from the transference experience during analysis, we explicitly or implicitly measure it against a concept of an adaptive schema and scene. In the schema of the infant tugging at her mother's legs, a need for an exchange of intimacy → an intention to pull mother into being playful → a recognition of mother's resistance → an activation of the aversive motivational system may be compared with a need for an exchange of intimacy → an intention to pull mother into being playful (anticipation of pleasure in intimacy from prior experiences) → responses of receptivity on mother's part with consummation of social communication and the joy of shared pleasure. Or a need for an exchange → an intention to pull mother into being playful → a momentary distraction on mother's part → the activation of an aversive response of more angry pulling or vocalized distress → the aversive response recognized as a signal and responded to by the initiation by mother of a social interchange, with anger and distress being replaced rapidly by pleasure in intimacy.

The schema for the little girl who sustained the lye burn would be a need for exploration and assertion → interest in a bucket of liquid with positive anticipation → pain, shock, and the activation of an aversive response of massive withdrawal. This may be compared with the normal schema: a need for exploration and assertion → interest and functional activity → a sense of pleasure from efficiency and competence.

Other examples of normal or ordinary schemas from infancy are:

○ a need for nutrient-intake → the sensation of hunger and the affect of distress → sucking and intake experience → a sense of enjoyment and a sensation of satiety.
○ a need for attachment → distress and pursuit behaviors → opportunities for mirroring, sharing, and idealization → a sense of intimacy, pleasure, and self-expansiveness.
○ a need to respond aversively → distress and anger → withdrawal and/or antagonistic behaviors → (1) self-soothing and/or instrumentally effective use of anger or (2) relief of the source of distress and frustration, restoration of self-expansiveness and intimacy pleasure.
○ a need for sensual enjoyment arising as general distress and irritability and/or a specific sensation in a sensual target zone → soothing, stroking, rhythmic rubbing by self or other → (1) relief of distress and irritability and specific sensations of pleasure with reduced general tension or (2) relief of distress and irritability

and specific sensations of pleasure with heightened focal and general sensations of sexual excitement.

Each schema bears a particular relationship to a clinically significant model scene. Each model scene construct—the one formed by the patient in the course of life and during the analysis, the one formed by the analyst immersed in empathic, introspective, and role responsiveness, and the one formed by theoreticians and infant observers—is an aestheticlike product formed by primary- and secondary-process modes of representation. With its visual, auditory, action, and especially affective aspects, the "scene" tilts toward primary-process modes of representation. The "schema," with its diagrammatic linear aspects, tilts toward secondary-process modes of representation. The model scene is clearly nonlinear. Rather, the scene reflects a special quality of the self to initiate, organize, and integrate experience in a manner that captures from an overload of internal and external signs and signals the essence of some situation that is unfolding. Affects are the primary markers enabling the reflective and experiencing self to bring the order of a model scene out of the seemingly chaotic overload of an intersubjective world.

AFFECTS

In the century-old history of psychoanalysis, the aspect of psychic functioning that has been considered of central importance has shifted from trauma to instinctual drive and fantasy to ego functions and the structural hypothesis to object relations and now to affects. Sandler (1987) states,

> The prime motivators, *from the point of view of the mental apparatus*, are changes in feeling states. While drives, needs, emotional forces, and other influences arising from within the body are highly important in determining behavior, from the point of view of psychological functioning, they exert their effect *through changes in feelings*. The same is true for stimuli arising from the external world. This approach removes feelings from their total conceptual tie to the instinctual drives alone, and gives them a central position in psychoanalytic psychology [p. 296].

The importance assigned to affect in so many recent studies (Wurmser, 1981; Emde, 1983, 1988; Nathanson, 1987; Pine, 1986;

Schwartz, 1987) has led Stern (1988) to sound a cautionary note—
reminding us that affect is but "one of the attributes of experience,
among many (cognition, perception, motive, action)" (p. 238).
Stern's caveat notwithstanding, the emphasis on affect coincides
with my view of how we are able to track developments in each
motivational system longitudinally and cross-sectionally. Longitudinally, affects provide the principal thread linking infants' early
presymbolic experiences, alone and with others, to later, more cog-
nitively organized experiences. As Emde (1988) states,

> because our affective core touches upon these aspects of experience
> which are most important to us as individuals, because it organizes
> both meaning and motivation, it also allows us to get in touch with
> the uniqueness of our own (and others) experience. . . . It is the emo-
> tional availability of the caregiver in intimacy which seems to be the
> most central growth-promoting feature of the early rearing experience
> [p. 32].

It is this affective relational aspect that we track in psychoanalysis
through transference reactions years later.

Cross-sectionally, affects provide the principal means of identifying moment-to-moment shifts in motivational dominance. Crucial
to the application of my theory to the clinical "how," as I will demonstrate in chapter 10, is the ability of the therapist to appreciate
transitions from motivational dominance by one system to another.
In appraising shifts, we track overt and implied verbal patterns as
important indicators, but, as every therapist who has ever shared
the notes made from associations with colleagues knows, the hermeneutic text is generally subject to a multitude of interpretations.
Affect expression cues our choices from one moment to another
among this multitude of "logical" possibilities.

The assumptions I make with respect to affects are: (1) both the
theory that affects are discharge products and/or drive derivatives
and the timetable that places their development late in infancy are
incorrect and must be replaced; (2) major contributions to a theory
verified by observations of infants and their later development have
been made by Tomkins (1962, 1963, 1987), Kestenberg (1965a), and
Stern (1985); (3) innate programs for the categorical affects of enjoyment, interest, surprise, distress, anger, fear, shame, and disgust
exist at birth. An event achieves significance when it is amplified by
an affective response. Psychological magnification occurs through
the coassembly of similarly affect-laden experiences into model
scenes; (4) the presence of individualistic innate programs for pat-

terns of physical movements and the ease or tension that characterizes their flow create affect-triggering situations between infant and
caregiver in which the fit between the infant's innate tendencies
and the response of the caregivers lays down patterns of match or
mismatch recorded in both procedural and episodic memory;
(5) vitality affects are based on the intensity, timing, and shape of
categoric affects and movements and flow as they are triggered,
rise, fall, and undergo transition; (6) in early infancy *interactions* involve the caregiver's responses to the baby's innate programs of
physical movements and flow and to categoric affects by successful
or unsuccessful attunement and regulation. In later infancy *intersubjective* exchanges occur as the older infant seeks, recognizes, and is
guided by the caregiver's affective signals. Later affects are coassembled with symbolic representations in complex signal, expressive,
and defensively altered forms; (7) model scenes tend to form
around affect-laden situations in which the state of self is enhanced
when needs in each of the motivational systems are met or in which
the state of self is depleted when these needs are left unresponded
to; (8) clues that help to reveal unconscious model scenes of self-
state failures or successes are obtained from verbal associations and
recognizable categorical affects, from transitions from self-states of
vitality and cohesion or depletion and fragmentation as attunement
waxes and wanes, and from correlates of affects conveyed by postures, body tensions, facial expressions, vocal tones, rates, and in-
flections, odors, modes of dressing, which silently but effectively
stimulate and invite role enactments.

I have formulated a theory of motivation based on systems that
develop in response to five basic needs. Model scenes reflect the
experiences that persons have as caregivers succeed in responding,
or fail to respond, to these needs and the wishes that derive from
them. These concepts may appear similar to drive theory, modifying its pressure-from-within concept only by expanding from a dual
drive theory to a multimotivational theory. Furthermore, a similarity to ego psychology can be claimed in that I believe a call or opportunity to function is as much a motivational factor in innate and
learned programs as is need. Unlike drive theory or ego psychology's focus on anxiety, my theory places the full range of affects as
central to the functioning of each system and as the determining
feature in constructing and detecting a model scene. In placing affects centrally, I follow Tomkins in believing that events gain their
significance through the amplification of affect, and I follow Sander's (1983a) view that feelings and affect states become the target for
matches for desired repetitions of prior experience.

Tomkins (1978) views affect as the primary basis of motivation since needs, perception, memory, cognition, action, and feeling itself are all amplified through positive or negative affects. Without the amplification of affect, "nothing else matters—and with its amplification, anything else *can* matter. It thus combines *urgency* and *generality*" (p. 202). Tomkins also speaks of scenes that begin as soon as a neonate can experience an event with a perceived beginning and end containing at least one affect and one object of that affect (hunger and crying, being fed and enjoyment, focusing on a face and interest). Later, scenes become organized wholes including people, place, time, actions, and feeling. Affect amplification accounts for only the short-term importance of an experience. Long-term importance depends on

> psychological magnification, the phenomenon of connecting one affect-laden scene with another affect-laden scene. Through memory, thought, and imagination, scenes experienced before can be coassembled with scenes presently experienced, together with scenes which are anticipated in the future. . . . In infancy . . . magnification begins with immediately sequential experience but is severely limited in magnification potential whenever experience is separated in time [p. 217].

Conversation games between mother and infant can receive psychological magnification because they are affect laden and repeated within the timespan of infantile memory. A conversational exchange with a visitor may be amplified by both the innate enjoyment it triggers and the arousal of novelty, but it will not become coassembled with another scene experienced with the same visitor if the time interval between is too long.

An important feature of Tomkins's theory is his concept of the script: the individual's rules for predicting, interpreting, responding to, and controlling a magnified set of scenes. Initially scenes determine scripts; over time, script formation so consolidates experience that scripts come to determine scenes. I understand Tomkins to mean that initially scenes, that is, lived experiences determine scripts, or rules of expectancy. A smiling, rhapsodically vocalizing caregiver approaching with a bottle means that there is a high likelihood that a physiological requirement for food will be met. A frowning, angry-voiced caregiver approaching means that there is a high likelihood of an aversive struggle over something. Forming a set of rules for predicting, interpreting, responding to, and controlling repetitive experiences provides the infant with a powerful tool for mastery of the many typical lived experiences that arise in each motivational system. Once the rules of expectancy from others and from self that constitute the script are formed, they influence the scenes that follow. In scanning, conceptualizing, and providing behavioral cues, the older infant tends to determine the "scene" according to his or her inner script or expectancy. Thus, even in infancy, human beings are not merely passive reactors to events but actively construct, influence, and even determine some aspect of their lived experience. This is a part of what we mean by temperament.

When the needs in each motivational system are met more often than not, the script or rules of prediction that form are expectancies of satisfactory physiological regulation, intimacy pleasure, efficacy and competence pleasure, effective aversive signaling and instrumental power through anger, and sensual enjoyment. The constructor of such an optimistic script will, where possible, construe scenes in line with this expectancy. And of course, if we take so simplistic a view, the opposite, or pessimistic, script colors and structures scenes differently. In actuality, the tasks in each motivational system are sufficiently varied and demanding—but so compelling to be solved—that neither extreme is likely to persist without complexity, as I will describe next in Tomkins's theory of variants and analogs. Nonetheless, to return to temperament, affects triggered by specific instances of good or bad fit between need and response are gradually supplemented by affects indicating a state of harmony or disharmony existing over the general lived experience, combining in a particular feeling of self.

Tomkins describes different principles that govern the magnification of experiences dominated by positive and negative affects. Positive scenes are generally magnified by the principle of variants. A variant is a way of detecting change in an experience that in its core remains the same. An infant who is enjoying face-to-face contact with her mother notices mother's earrings and begins to explore them. In a later scene, the variant may be the enjoyment of exploring different earrings or eye glasses, or the variant may be hairpulling. All these are scenes with a mixture of pleasure in intimacy and pleasure in exploration and assertion. When coassembled, these scenes build (magnify) experiences typical of the motivational systems involving attachment plus exploration and assertion with mother.

"In contrast, negative affect scenes are typically magnified by the formation of *analogs*, the detection of similarities in different experiences. Analog formation involves a vigilant stance in which new situations are scanned for old dangers and disappointments" (Carlson, 1981, p. 503). The patient who as a little girl had her effort at exploration end in the disaster with lye increasingly experienced ordinary situations that offered safe exploration as potential dangers from which she had to withdraw, and she never knew what led her to take such a stance.

I suggest that coassembly of scenes by variants bears considerable similarity to linking by secondary process, and coassembling of scenes by analogs is similar to linking by primary process. Secondary-process organization asks, how similar is the basic identify before a variant can be accepted? Alternatively, primary process more fluidly displaces from one element to another, condenses the nonessentially related, and gives double meanings in the form of symbols to the metaphorically relatable. But Tomkins's distinction is, I believe, extremely valuable because coassembly by variants and by analogs could magnify scenes earlier than development of symbolic representation at 18 months of age.

The principle of variants would operate as if a 10-month-old infant, seeing her mother with a new hat, were to think, "This visual stimulus at its core is familiar. I can easily link it to and generalize it with other experiences I have had." Recognizing it, and the pleasure of intimacy it triggers, adds to (magnifies) the significance of attachment experiences.

The principle of analogs would operate as if a traumatized infant were to scan each new stimulus, not for its core similarity alone, but for any potential that even one of its secondary elements might have for triggering a negative affect and an aversive response, adding to (magnifying) the significance of aversive situations. Examples are the case of Jane in chapter 7, and that of Jenny, described later in this chapter.

Tomkins recognizes one set of scripts and scenes as nuclear. The nuclear scripts and scenes capture the person's most urgent, unsolved and often unsolvable problems. While oft-repeated, habitual scripts and scenes may account for much of our behavior, their very familiarity will in time evoke less feeling and thought. Those scripts which are nuclear underlie both good scenes we are insatiably eager to repeat and improve and bad scenes we can never avoid and never renounce the attempt to master. "If they are conflicted scenes, we can renounce neither wish, nor integrate them. If they are ambiguous scenes, we cannot simplify nor clarify the many overlapping scenes which characteristically produce pluralistic confusion" (Tomkins, 1978, p. 229). Tomkins identifies mortality and death, birth of a sibling, and the oedipal rivalries as likely nuclear scripts and scenes. (See Edelheit's, 1968, suggestions about primal scene variants and analogs.) Their basic significance lies in their being experienced with the most intense and enduring affects, with the sharpest gradients of change of the affect, and the most frequently repeated sequences of dense affects and affect changes.

I suggest that what I have called a schema underlying the experience of each motivational system is similar to Tomkins's nuclear script, and the model scenes that flesh out the schemas are similar to Tomkins's habitual and nuclear scenes. Let us take examples from the attachment motivational system. The simplest schema or script is the innate program of the baby to turn his eyes to mother's face, her responsive eye contact, and the baby's heightened interest and pleasure. The social games that build from this innate program add density, gradient, and repetition to the affect state of pleasure in intimacy. Mother and infant individually and jointly constantly search for variants that give magnification to the scenes. Kohut (1971, 1984) has identified three model, or nuclear, scenes: In one an infant gets an experience of affirmation from caregivers who are responsive to a whole developmental cycle of primary needs for soothing, guidance, and confirmation. In another an infant gets an experience of vitalized belonging from the awareness of sharing an intersubjective state with his caregiver. A third model scene portrays the experience of security, potency, and worth an infant may derive from the reflected strength, competence, and wisdom that radiates to the child from a valued (idealized) parent. Unlike Kohut, I do not believe that the keys to the infant's experience lie in preserving either grandiosity, omnipotence, or idealization, since these self-states presume fantasies about the self that I believe are developments of a later time. The words I have used—affirmation from parental responsiveness (the mirroring transference), vitalized belonging from sharing intersubjective states (the alter ego transference), and security, potency, and worth (the idealizing transference), are likewise somewhat adultomorphizing. The experience of the baby is best conveyed by visualizing a scene in which a smiling infant's whole body becomes taut and vibrant as his mother smiles back and exclaims, "Oh, what a beautiful smile!" The sense of sharing an intersubjective state is conveyed by a 10-month-old baby and her mother who are being entertained by father making funny faces, looking at each other laughing, almost simultaneously pointing to the "clown," and looking again at each other. The security of a slightly frightened baby can be readily seen as he stops moving away from a stranger when his mother takes his hand, confidently introduces him; his posture moves from concave to erect, and his face brightens. Or the expansive joy of the child securely riding on father's back or shoulders or being tossed in the air.

I regard the mirror, alter ego, and idealizing transferences, and the experiences beginning in infancy and continuing throughout life from which they are transformed, to be nuclear model scenes of the attachment and affiliative motivational system. When the appropriate lived experiences are present in infancy, the self will throughout life be motivated to repeat them, improve on them, and adapt new versions to new challenges and opportunities. When these experiences are inadequate at any time of life, the self will want to seek or restore them.

Kestenberg (1965a, b) has proposed schema or scripts that underlie model scenes in the motivational system derived from the fulfillment of physiological requirements and from the exploratory-assertive motivational system. Kestenberg attempts to relate movement patterns, such as sucking and general motor activity, to erotogenic zone theory by viewing specific patterns as illustrative of oral, anal, and phallic modes of tension discharge. I do not find the correlation she presents between the observations and presumed specific patterns of drive discharge to be convincing. However, I value highly the observations themselves, especially those which illustrate so well the relationship of a schema or script innate to the child and the model scene that arises when the mother succeeds or fails in her regulatory efforts in response to the infant's patterns of movement.

Kestenberg (1965) presents schematic diagrams and descriptions of preferred rhythms of tension flow in three children. Glenda alternated between high intensity in free flow and low intensity in bound flow with steepness in ascent and descent of intensity.

> Glenda's mother was very sensitive to the child's needs . . . she picked Glenda up with gradually rising tension flow and held her frequent short periods with lightness of effort and evenness of moderately bound flow. . . . She did take Glenda's fingers out of her mouth but ceased interfering because it "made the baby angry" . . . [I]n her crib [Glenda] would periodically perform like an acrobat, using sudden increases of free flow to propel herself. . . . Glenda's mother could develop enough steepness in ascent of flow to cope with the baby's motor feat, which she greatly admired. . . . Her adjustment to the child's rhythms was most noticeable in the manner in which she presented spoonfuls of food. Each spoonful reached Glenda's mouth at the precise moment when her mouth opened to receive it [pp. 551–552].

Kestenberg continues her observations of Glenda and her mother, noting that at age 11 Glenda appeared to be developing normally. She retained her basic patterns of movement with modifications based on her motivation and on the influence of her mother's preferences.

Charlie's preferred rhythms were for gradual ascent to high intensity and prolonged evenness of flow. When he was stimulated, the ascent was steeper and fluctuations increased. When held, Charlie felt heavy, hardly adjusting his body to that of the carrier. He appeared disturbed by the vivacity of his mother and siblings but greatly enjoyed sucking. His mother, however,

> regularly pulled his hand out of his mouth, admonishing him playfully to be a good boy. Possibly because of her own discomfort in holding the baby to whose rhythm of flow she could not adjust, she resorted to prop feeding relatively early. . . . When he began to teethe, it became evident that an inhibition of hand-to-mouth movements had diminished his resources for soothing himself [pp. 535–536].

> Charlie was not only prevented from autoerotic sucking but also from playing with solids. Objects were presented to him to distract him from messing and interfering with the mother's spoon feeding. At first Charlie was spellbound by objects and kept still during feeding, but he became dazed when objects were removed and substituted by others before he could finish his thorough examination of each toy [p. 541].

Charlie had moments when he lapsed into a vacant stare, and the flow of his whole body adjusted to the far-away look in his face.

> In his crib he would come to life again. Undisturbed he would practice motor skills and evolve a great many modifications of rhythm. . . . [At eleven] he responded poorly to verbal instructions and acted dazed. Even then he could learn with eagerness when one took special care to approach him gradually and to let him use his own methods of problem solving [p. 542].

Nancy's difficult-to-define patterns were characterized by bound flow, sharp reversals, and frequent flow changes. Because of her excessive flow fluctuation and very limited resources for flow stabilization, Nancy

> tended to veer from extreme bound flow to limpness. . . . When sudden jerks of free flow or a sudden decrease of flow would disrupt the

continuity of sucking, she responded with excitement that would soon lead to stiffening of her whole body. She would suck vigorously and continuously when her mother held her for feeding in the hospital [p. 536].

As soon as she came home, she was

left in a darkened room with the bottle propped on her pillow. As her whole body became immobilized to support her hold on the nipple, her hands would hardly get into the line of her constricted vision. Long after her contemporaries began to reach, Nancy would look at a rattle, listen . . . open her mouth, but her "bound" hands would not move to reach it [p. 540].

In addition her formula had not been changed so Nancy had to consume great quantities before her hunger was satisfied. She seemed to suck forever on the propped bottle and would not release the nipple even after the bottle was empty. . . . Nancy could neither suck her hand nor use it for reaching. Her hand as well as her other limbs became instruments of holding. . . . As soon as she could stand she would remain in that position for very long periods of time, as her stiff spine, bound legs, and clutching hands prevented her from moving. . . . Nancy could be soothed when she was crying by . . . quick and irregular fluctuations of tension flow. . . . Her mother would rock her with great abruptness and with a manner . . . both absent-minded and impatient [p. 536–537].

At 11, a maturational spurt had enabled Nancy to be more productive and spontaneous. She still relied on bound immobility, inhibition, and restriction of function when in an aversive situation.

Kestenberg connects the innate patterns of movement both to affects and to methods of exploration and assertion.

Movements with free flow make one feel carefree, while movements with bound flow evoke that shade of anxiety that we call caution. Conversely, when we feel carefree we move freely, whereas caution makes us bound. Movements that maintain an even intensity in free flow convey steady confidence; in bound flow they give the impression of steady concern. Variations in levels of intensity may give a dreamy quality to our feelings. . . . Sudden eruptions of free flow are associated with surprise, of bound flow with fright [p. 522].

Babies may be predisposed to approach exploration and assertion by transitory spurts of activity if their preference is for movements of steep ascent of flow intensity quickly followed by sudden descent.

A sequence of steeply ascending and descending free flow, followed by a quick alternation of small quantities of free and bound flow, may predispose the child to biphasic functioning in which enthusiasm wanes quickly and is revived after a phase of repetitious laboring. A baby's preference for maintaining even levels of flow intensity . . . may predispose him to stability, placidity, or attentiveness [as well as to stubbornness and inflexibility] [p. 530].

Kestenberg thus relates the observable tension flow of sucking, swallowing, grasping, scanning, crawling, walking, and self-stroking movements with predispositions to such affects as feeling carefree or cautious, interest in exploration, waxing or waning of enthusiasm, placidity, and stubbornness. While many of Kestenberg's hypotheses are subject to experimental confirmation or refutation, her assumptions about the correlation between movement flow and affects rest on their intuitive appeal. We easily connect free flow with being carefree, "loose," and "free as a bird," and bound flow with being anxious, cautious, "tight as a drum," "tied in knots," and on guard. The link between movement flow and affect is not specified.

For Tomkins (1962, 1963) movement flow would also have affective significance, but the main physical feature of affects is facial display. Associated with specific facial displays are vocalizations, autonomic nervous system changes, and other movements and behavior. Interest-excitement is registered by eyebrows down and fixed stare or visual scanning and tracking. The smiling response is the display for enjoyment-joy, while eyebrows raised and blinking eyes are the display for surprise-startle. Distress-anguish are displayed by crying, fear-terror by eyes held open, frozen in a fixed stare, or averted. Frowning, clenched jaw, and a red face display anger-rage; eyes and head lowered are the display linked with shame-humiliation. Tomkins also regards as innate affects "dissmell"—the turning away from anxious odors—and disgust—the turning away from noxious tastes.

Tomkins regards each affect as an entity (a brain program) that can be triggered by any perception, action, or other affect—a completely flexible system. However, a link is soon forged between a recurrent triggering event and the affect it triggers, what Tomkins calls a coassembly. The point of juncture between the theory I have advanced of five motivational systems and Tomkins's theory of affects is this: Each motivational system refers to innate programs of perceptual-action responses built around basic needs. The needs are recurrent. Each innate program will trigger particular affective responses. The same affects—enjoyment, interest, anger, and fear—

may amplify responses of any of the motivational systems. Some of the affects, however, will be more characteristically triggered by the particular set of causes and consequences present in each motivational system. Moreover, once categorical affects are regularly and recurrently triggered by perceptions, memories, thoughts, and actions occurring when a particular motivational system is dominant, significant nuances of difference are experienced in what starts out as an innate affect program. Tomkins (1987) states this beautifully: "My experiences of excitement at sexuality, poetry, mathematics, or of another's face can never be described as entirely identical 'feelings,' despite the identity of the triggered affects" (p. 142).

Restating Tomkins's observation in terms of my suggestion of motivational systems, the excitement at *sexuality* that is triggered when the *sensual-sexual* motivational system is dominant takes on particular feeling qualities. The flow of tension in body movement has a characteristic sharp acceleration and deceleration and fluctuations between bound and free flow. The sensation-rich genitals, mucosa, and skin activate particular neurophysiological pathways (chapter 11). The potential in sexual experience for sharing intimacy and affective attunement further adds to the categorical affect of excitement the vitalizing affective augmentation Stern (1985) describes. All of this becomes built into people's particular memories and conscious and unconscious sexual fantasies by which they orient their search for repetitions and variations.

The excitement triggered by *mathematics* arise from responses of the *exploratory-assertive* motivational system. The arousal of interest in exploration would involve a sustained level of tension, largely bound flow, in Kestenberg's terms (1965, 1966), with occasional fluctuations in freer flow. The sitting position of Rodin's Thinker might be a physical example. On occasion, the pattern may change; the opportunity to assert one's intellect to solve the problem arises and with it the full excitement of discovery, the disappearance of puzzlement, the triumph of problem solving. A further vitalizing affective experience may be drawn from imagined or real applause and affirmation.

The excitement at seeing *mother's face* is an affect triggered by responses activated when the *attachment* motivational system is dominant. The experience of another's face as a trigger to excitement begins in the earliest eye contact between neonate and caregivers. It involves the sharing of facial displays of affect and the discriminatory recognition of family members in the earliest months. I have referred to the special feeling of this form of enjoyment as intimacy pleasure. The enjoyment of the attachment experience for the baby varies from the quietest being-with to the exuberance of laughing together in conversational games or being tossed in the air and caught. Coming-toward stimulates approach excitement and pattern recognition (oh, it's daddy coming home) provides an additional factor. The movements of the child—turning toward, reaching, opening the mouth in anticipation—all contribute to the special feeling of this type of excitement. Further vitalizing comes when the caregiver contributes significantly to the direction of flow of excitement needed or desired at the particular moment. If a child has the need or desire to turn an enjoyable sharing into a more exciting one and the caregiver intuitively senses this, the intimacy experience is further augmented. Alternatively, if a child has a need or desire for calming or resting and this is responded to, the deceleration into restfulness or sleep adds a special sensual quality to the richness of the intimacy.

Excitement in response to *poetry* constitutes a special case. The appreciation of creativity and of a creative product as distinguished from a preferred perceptual experience cannot occur until the full development of the two organizational modes of symbolic representation and the consolidation of the self as a whole. Excitement in response to poetry or art or music involves not one or another dominant motivational system. Rather, excitement triggered by creativity is based on the capacities of the fully developed self to initiate, organize, and integrate elements that might draw their appeal from any of the motivational systems. Statements such as these, which draw parallels between poetry and the synthetic capacities of the self, whether poet or appreciator, must of necessity be reductionistic. Creativity is a special case because it is not reflective of the hierarchical shifts of dominance of one or another system. Rather, artistic creativity and its appreciation reflect an ability of the human self to set aside momentarily the motivational pressures from any of the systems as such and instead to function as a central assembly, synthesizing the special quality of an aesthetic experience.

The quality of an affective experience and its relationship to the five motivational systems can be further investigated through Tomkins's (1987) discussion of shame. Tomkins regards shame as an innate program that is triggered when for some reason a rapid inhibition of excitement or interest occurs. Once triggered, the shame response includes looking down with lowered eyelids, decreased tone in the face, lowering or tilting the head. Designating shame as an innate affective program evokes the argument: how can babies feel shame—what have they to be ashamed of? Of course, babies do lower their eyelids and head and lose facial expressiveness when interest and excitement is suddenly interrupted. So what is under consideration is not the existence of an innate affect program but the appropriateness of the choice of the designation "shame." And Tomkins makes the provocative assertion that discouragement, shyness, shame, and guilt are identical affects in that they reflect an identical innate program. As the separate names indicate, these affects are experienced differently because of separate coassemblies of perceived causes and consequences, all reflective of situations in which an aroused state of interest or excitement is brought to a halt.

Discouragement is associated with temporary defeat; it could be a temporary failure in regulation of physiological requirements (going off one's diet), in attachment (a date fails to show up), in exploration and assertion (losing a queen in chess), or in seeking sensual and sexual satisfaction (an episode of premature ejaculation). Shyness is experienced when an expectation of familiarity is breached, that is, when the established norms and forms of attachment and affiliative experiences are replaced by "strangers." Shame as a quality of affect experience rather than a general designator of the innate program is associated with feelings of inferiority, of failures to meet standards of accomplishment set by others (become potty-trained) or by the self (successfully solve a puzzle problem). Guilt is the affect experience of having committed a moral transgression (hurting another or committing a "sin" by masturbating). Nathanson (1987) suggests that guilt is shame coassembled with fear of reprisal based on memories of prior punishment. Thus, this group of negative affects based on an identical core affect program may be associated with any of the motivational systems, but one shading or another often has a particular link to the dominance of one or another system.

I will conclude this discussion of affect with a reconsideration of the feeding experience. The infant's hunger produces sensations. At some point, possibly at birth, these sensations are localized in the stomach. In any case, the physiological state is registered as neural firing that as it accelerates may trigger the affect interest (arousal), as it persists at one density level triggers distress, and at a higher level, anger. The affect displays of distress and anger, manifest in crying, a beet-red face, clenched fist, and body thrashing, are unmodulated in infancy so that crying itself triggers further intensification of the negative affect state. When feeding is instituted, a rapid deceleration of neural firing occurs, triggering an affective switch to enjoyment. The infant institutes an innate program of sucking, which has an individualistic pattern of tension rises and falls and rates of flow. The mother's capacity to match this pattern of flow, making tiny variations in it, promotes the maintenance of an affect of interest and efficacy enjoyment to add to the enjoyment of the relief from distress. Sensual pleasure (mouth stimulation) and enjoyment of intimacy exchanges (shared smile displays) provide fuller vitalizing to the affect experience.

Tomkins (1987) describes "dissmell" and disgust, two negative affect experiences that are specific to feeding.

> If the food about to be ingested activates dissmell, the upper lip and nose are raised and the head is drawn away from the apparent source of the offending odor. If the food has been taken into the mouth it may, if disgusting, be spit out. If it has been swallowed and is toxic, it may produce nausea and be vomited out, either through the mouth or nostrils. The early warning response via the nose is dissmell; the next level of response, from mouth and stomach, is disgust. . . . Dissmell, disgust, and nausea also function as signals and motives to others, as well as to the self, of feelings of rejection. They readily accompany a wide spectrum of entities that need not be tasted, smelled, or ingested [pp. 142–143].

To complete this section: Each of the five motivational systems have model scenes that characterize the experience when that system is dominant. Each of the scenes gains its particular experiential power from affects that amplify functional activities. Any affect may amplify the activities and events of any system, but some are particularly related to one or another, especially in the early stages of development.

THE FUNDAMENTAL LEVEL
OF THE UNCONSCIOUS

My hypothesis bearing on the unconscious is that (1) motivation, organized as five motivational systems, forms the fundamental level of the unconscious; (2) the five motivational systems shape and are shaped by lived experience prior to the development of symbolic representation; (3) the record of the early lived experience persists, for the most part shaping and being shaped by symbolic representation, but nonetheless contributing its own forms and rules of representation throughout life; (4) to realize further the goal of making as full as possible an empathic entry into the state of mind of an analysand, the analyst attends not only to the words and categoric affects that are regarded as the ordinary components of free association, but also to behaviors, gestures, and affects that reveal links to the deeper layers of experience of the unconscious; (5) from resonating empathically with these behaviors, gestures, and especially categoric and vitalizing affects, analysts can form model scenes that provide important links to the period of formation of each motivational system and the stability or instability of the contribution of each system to the emergent and core self; and (6) often the ability to form model scenes indicative of the deeper layers of experience of the unconscious results from the analyst's perusal of his own and the analysand's affect-laden role responses and enactments in the intersubjective field of an ongoing analysis.

In a manner of speaking, the unconscious does not exist. It is a time-honored construct used to make sense of irrefutable observational data about psychic functioning and experience. These data press on the observer the conclusion that people at all ages are influenced by factors, forces, and informational sources of which they are unaware. It has proven convenient to use a spatial metaphor—a realm or domain—to describe the unconscious. In this way we can speak of the unconscious as layered, as containing influences that are close to consciousness and others that are remote (deepest). Another valuable distinction is that in the unconscious are factors that by their nature ordinarily do not become conscious, such as procedures and rules, as well as a potentially experienced realm of episodic memories and motivational inclinations. The concepts of five motivational systems, of model scenes, and of affects present a different view of the patterns in which conscious and unconscious motivations are organized and experienced.

Along with the convenience of employing the metaphor of levels and realms, there is a danger of reification. The psychoanalytic unconscious is a dynamic concept correctly identified by Stolorow, Brandchaft, and Atwood (1987) as "an unconscious organizing activity" by which experiences are "unconsciously and recurrently patterned . . . according to developmentally preformed themes" (p. 12).

To eliminate a possible misconception, let me say that I fully subscribe to retaining the conception of the powerful organizing potential of unconscious fantasies. The lived experiences of oedipal seeking and rivalry, primal scene puzzlement, preoccupations with bodily functioning, physical appearance, and gender differences, the pulls and tugs, for mirroring, sharing, opposing, and idealizing, all are encoded in patterns and themes that color each subsequent perceptual experience. The view I propose expands the traditional psychoanalytic one by redefining the fundamental level and extending the scope of the not ordinarily experiential realm.

The fundamental level of the unconscious contains a record of the lived experience of the neonate and young infant (an experiential realm) and the organizational rules and principles that account for the ways in which the experiences come about and are recorded (a usually nonexperiential realm). It is appropriate to conceptualize a fundamental level because the lived experiences of the neonate and young infant not only are earliest but are organized differently. While far more complex than has been recognized heretofore, the lived experience of the neonate and young infant does not have the remarkable plasticity of the dual organization into two modes of processing (primary and secondary) of symbolic representation. The dual modes of organization employing verbalization as a major tool tend to overshadow the earlier organization, leading many analytic theoreticians to treat the fundamental level as either fanciful or irrelevant.

I believe that the fundamental level of the unconscious consists, at its core, of schemas for the organization of the five motivational systems. As each system self-organizes and self-stabilizes, the needs that constitute the system's core are met or fail to be met. As a result of the experience of match or mismatch, fit or failure, affects are triggered. It is the affects that give the event its significance as a *lived* experience. Memory organizations give permanence to the record of the lived experience. Rules governing preferences constantly tilt the lived experience in one direction or another. An underlying potential for initiating, organizing, and integrating lived experience emerges, forms its fundamental core, and becomes subjectively "known" as a sense of self. The fundamental level of the unconscious consists of schemas and experiences of the unfolding of the five systems, categoric and vitalizing affects triggered during the unfolding, memories that record the experiences, rules that govern the direction and shape that the experiences take, and the individualized sense of self that arises with and coordinates the five systems.

MEMORY AND RULES

Since psychoanalysis has centered attention on model scenes involving interactions and intersubjective experience between people, episodic memory has received primary focus. As I have indicated (chapters 4 and 5), Stern (1985), in attempting to delineate the nature of an interpersonal world of the infant, presents a solid array of evidence to support the existence of memories that contain reference to the self as the agent or experiences of an event and the unique environmental and human context in which the event occurred. Episodic memory lies at the heart of model scenes in each of the motivational systems. Episodic memories are easily transformed and reorganized by the dual mode of symbolic representation into the memories (screen and otherwise) and unconscious fantasies that lie at the center of the discoveries of psychoanalysis. It is other prototypic activities of the neonate and young infant that I focus on here.

In addition to affect-laden scenes that characterize each system, there are prototypic procedural activities, such as sucking, swallowing, visual and auditory scanning, grasping, averting, pushing away, stroking, rocking, and rubbing. The storehouse of unconscious procedural knowledge contains not only the pattern of these and similar activities, but rules that govern perception, cognition, and affect.

Many procedural rules are innate. Examples are the rules that govern maintenance of interest. First is the inborn preference for perceptual stimuli such as sounds in a particular range, visual displays having particular patterns. Next is mode of presentation. If a preferred pattern is repeated at fixed intervals, interest wanes. If a new pattern is introduced, interest reawakens; but if infants have a choice between a familiar pattern and an unfamiliar pattern of equal stimulus potential, they will attend the familiar. Kihstrom (1987) reports that, for adults, repeated presentation of a previously unfamiliar stimulus tends to increase the attractiveness of the stimulus. This occurs whether the stimulus is presented in an ordinary fashion or by subliminal perception. If instead of the same stimulus' being repeated and producing habituation, the stimulus is varied just a bit, interest will persist, just as in situations in which infants can themselves introduce small variations. A stimulus too unfamiliar (strange), or introduced too fast, may lead to an aversive reaction. If infants can experience themselves as the activator of a stimulus display, interest is aroused and sustained; if the display response is made erratic and unpredictable, aversion will occur. To summarize: Rules, unconscious in their nature, about novelty and familiarity, passivity, and agency, influence experiential responses of interest. These rules govern levels of awareness and interest in each motivational system and are central to experiences of the exploratory-assertive motivational system.

Throughout life similar rules govern many cognitive, physical, and emotional activities and preferences. Once learned, these activities become routinized through practice and their operations are rendered unconscious. In conversational speech, the listener is aware of the meaning of words but not of the phonological and linguistic principles by which the meaning is decoded. Kihstrom also cites routinized activities such as typing, driving, tying knots, which, once learned, are easily combined with tasks requiring conscious attentiveness. Kihstrom notes that in choosing between phrases such as the big red barn and the red big barn, we choose the former but are unaware of the rules that govern the choice. This, he notes, extends to emotional choices such as liking one face but not another or finding positive or negative qualities in an event.

Thus, in both infant and adult, a realm of the unconscious consists of rules and procedures that influence behavior. These develop both as original contents of procedural memory and as aspects of episodic memories that have become routinized "automatisms" (Hartmann, 1964). In its epoch-making exploration of unconscious influences, psychoanalysis has concentrated on those motives and functions associated with the subjective world laid down in episodic memory and later symbolically represented as components of conflict. Much of what I treat here as influences arising from unconscious rules and procedures has been conceptualized under the "black box" term constitution and has led to unresolvable arguments about the relative importance of constitutional and environmental factors. Studies such as Kestenberg's (1965a, b) present us with an opportunity to bring into the concept of the unconscious this neglected domain.

Let us consider procedures and rules that govern rates of flow and movement in the three children described by Kestenberg (1965a, b). Glenda had a pronounced innate preference for steep ascending and descending tension flow. This gave movements such as opening her mouth, sucking, and propelling herself in her crib a dramatic and acrobatic quality. Glenda's mother enjoyed the baby's patterns and coordinated her feeding, picking up, and social exchanges with the accentuated rises and falls of Glenda's rhythms. The lived experience for Glenda would be one of a coordination with shared enjoyment, many opportunities for variations, and vitalizing experiences. Her procedural memory would record the experience of her own patterns and the coordination with them at the fundamental level of her unconscious. Further experiences of a similar nature would provide continuity. Particularly through the greater plasticity of episodic memory and later symbolic representations, the early patterns could be altered and expanded without a loss of connectedness to the fundamental level.

For the other two children, the procedural memory would record a lived experience that revealed their innate rhythm of flow pattern but the absence of an augmenting, matching responsiveness from their mother. For Charlie, the prop feeding meant the absence of intimacy pleasure whereas mother's presence meant opposition—pulling his fingers out of his mouth and dazing him with her vivacity and intrusions. Only when alone could he find his own route into exploration and assertion. The fundamental level of his unconscious would contain the record of procedures engaged in with others that would be disconcerting at best. While his own rhythms and procedures when alone might be effective, the remembered lived experience would be devoid of easy transition to attachment and intimacy.

Nancy's procedural memory would record a pattern of self-induced rigidities necessary to inhibit her own erratic fluctuations in flow. Her procedural and affective response would be largely devoid of any helpfulness from a caring caregiver's intervention. Though hard to prove, a reasonable proposition would be that Nancy has a "rule" that when another person appears she can expect nothing from him or her, her own rigidity being her main resource. This fits the behavior at age 11 that Kestenberg reports.

Since procedural memory is based on lived experience, it records the fusion of innate proclivities with coordinate, deficient, or oppositional environmental responses so that the procedure that evolves is a combination of both. This means that the same procedure could arise primarily from the dominance of an innate pattern or from the dominance of external shaping or any combination of both. Jacobvitz and Sroufe (1987) studied 34 children who in kindergarten were diagnosed as hyperactive (having an attention deficit disorder with hyperactivity). Patterns of early maternal care and of neonatal and infant behavior were evaluated to determine what factors were predictive of the later hyperactivity. Patterns of maternal intrusive care, seductive behavior, and overstimulation were assessed at 6 months, 2 years, and 3½ years. Maternal intrusive behavior and overstimulation proved to be significant predictors; seductive behavior did not. Of 38 variables used to test the neonates and infants, only one, immaturity, scored on the 7/10 day motor maturity Brazelton factor, differentiated the hyperactive children from controls and proved predictive. A finding of motor immaturity did not in itself predict maternal overstimulation or maternal intrusiveness. From this study it is reasonable to assume that procedural memories of lived experiences of hyperactivity and an attention deficit may be the result of an innate organic propensity in some children, an induced pattern in others, or a combination in still others. When the source is a combination, the triggering may be shared or not. The fundamental level of the unconscious will contain procedural memories of patterns of hyperactivity, that is, the experience as it is lived, regardless of the source.

Kagan, Resnick, and Snidman (1987) report observations on another dimension of behaviors that have their roots in flow of movements and leave a record in procedural memory: being inhibited or uninhibited in response to unfamiliar events. After screening over 400 children, the researchers selected 60 (30 boys, 30 girls) who, when faced with uncertainty, were shy and cautious and 60 who were outgoing and fearless. The criterion was consistency of inhibited or uninhibited response by the children at 21 or 30 months when exposed to unfamiliar rooms, people, or objects. The authors found that the behavioral qualities of caution and shyness or of being fearless and outgoing that were present in the second or third year persisted through the sixth year. Being inhibited was manifest in many behaviors, but one of the most sensitive indices at 5½ years was a reluctance to talk spontaneously to the female examiner during a 90-minute testing battery. This suggests that the full acquisition of symbolic representation and verbal capacities did not in itself propel the inhibited infants toward being more outgoing oedipal-aged children. However, about 40% of the inhibited infants became less inhibited at 5½ years. More boys than girls were in the group that changed. Only 10% of uninhibited children, typically girls from working-class families, changed to be more inhibited. In both groups, where changes occurred, interviews with the mothers indicated planned efforts either to overcome shyness and caution or to encourage caution. Kagan et al. report also that the inhibited children evidenced signs of activation of physiological brain and body circuits that respond to unfamiliarity and challenge. They postulate a different threshold of responsivity to uncertainty in limbic and hypothalamic structures that leads to withdrawal. The authors note a subgroup of 13 within the inhibited group who had high and stable heart rates in response to an unfamiliar event. At five and a half years, these children stared at an unfamiliar peer, stayed close to their mothers rather than playing with other children, and avoided contact with novel objects that suggested risk. During their first year of life, these children had suffered from chronic constipation, allergy, extreme irritability, sleeplessness, or a combination of these.

These studies suggest that lived experience in early life establishes patterns that tend to persist. When an infant develops an active interest in exploration and assertion, the patterns laid down in the fundamental level of the unconscious will facilitate treating new novelties as welcome challenges. On the other hand, aversive responses in the fundamental levels of the unconscious may establish patterns of withdrawal that only active and often coordinated efforts between older child and parent can reverse. When a fundamental response pattern is supported by physiological patterns that activate rapidly and consistently, as present in 13 of the inhibited children, the possibility of ameliorative efforts being successful diminishes.

UNCONSCIOUS PROCEDURES, UNCONSCIOUS FANTASY, AND ROLE ENACTMENTS

I have suggested that the fundamental level of the unconscious is based on lived experience and that lived experience is recorded in the form of procedural and episodic memory organizations. The fundamental level does not contain fantasies that are the product of symbolic representations in the dual coding modes of primary and secondary process, and it does not contain general or abstract knowledge stored without reference to the circumstance in which it was acquired (a much later development). Affects are the principal markers of the fundamental level. The affect triggered by the event recorded in episodic memory gives the activity, the sense of self, and the sense of "evoked companion" (Stern, 1985) its meaning and evocative power. Many procedures have inherent affective evocation power, as conveyed in free and easy flow of movements compared with tension, stiffness, or droopiness.

Which lived experiences receive a permanent record in the unconscious and which do not? Memory studies in infancy indicate that ordinary events repeated within intervals in time will receive encoding, while unrepeated, sporadic occurrences generally do not. The potential for efficacy pleasure can lead an infant to recall an opportunity for exploration and assertiveness such as kicking to make a mobile move and to repeat the procedure for eight days or longer if cued by the same setting (Rovee-Collier et al., 1980). Feeding, eliminating and diapering, social exchanges with familiar caregivers, repeated toy play, and repeated aversive experiences receive encoding in both procedural and episodic memories. Stern (1985) has indicated that repeated memories become encoded as events (episodic memory) in which the representations are generalized from the series as a whole. I have suggested (chapter 3) that such lived experiences as being fed and being talked to as an infant become permanent parts of the repertoire of the growing self (procedural memory) and are then repeated as feeder and high-pitched talker without conscious awareness of the procedures or the source of the "knowledge."

Traumatic episodes create special situations for memory. Gaensbauer (1982b) observed a girl who had been physically abused by her father. The father had been responsible for a fracture of Jenny's arm when she was two weeks old, and for a bruise on her back when she was seven and a half weeks. At counseling sessions, Jenny responded positively to her father as well as to her mother even after the second beating. Then at three months, Jenny was left with her father after her mother stormed out of the house during an argument. Jenny, who had been fed exclusively by breast, refused the bottle, and her father again attacked her. Jenny sustained a broken arm and a nondepressed fractured skull. In the hospital Jenny responded positively to her mother and to nurses, but her pediatrician noted that when approached by him or other males she was jittery, cried, and could not be soothed. At three months, 25 days, when examined by Gaensbauer, she again began to cry and withdraw but responded more positively to a female associate. During his approach to her, Gaensbauer noted expressions of fear and anger on Jenny's face. Jenny averted her gaze from him and turned to her mother with a sad and apathetic expression.

It is possible that in the first two instances of abuse, when she was two weeks old and later at seven and a half weeks, Jenny did not form a causal connection between her father and her painful condition. After the beating when she was three months old, she clearly recognized her father as the source of her distress and saw other males as posing an analogous threat. The response to the pediatrician was immediately after the assault, but the response to Dr. Gaensbauer was 25 days later, without any reinforcing incident or contact with her father. This suggests that even in early infancy, powerful affective experiences create special conditions in which memory encoding is more likely to occur. The specificity of Jenny's reaction toward men and not toward women tends to confirm that she had formed a memory of the content or scene of her trauma (episodic), a rule of prediction—men are dangerous—and a response (procedural) to avoid in fright.

Observations such as these tell us that specific incidents involving massive affective experience organize the emergent self toward an early dominance of the aversive motivational system. These observations, however, do not inform us how the impact will be played out in the fundamental level of the unconscious. I (Lichtenberg, 1983b) have suggested that the tendency to generalize and the tendency to particularize constitute two opposing pressures affecting the outcome of such moments of disruptive affective experiences. If abuse and the affects of pain, fear, and anger become generalized, the outcome may be a characterological disturbance with broadly experienced distrust, irritability, and skittishness. Or if the generalization is less extensive, an abused girl may be affected in her relations with males. I (Lichtenberg, 1983b) have reported a patient who, when anxious, would hold her mouth open as if to yawn but, unlike in a yawn, would not inspire air. Instead she would try to get her mouth to close. This peculiar symptom appeared to be the procedural particularizing of an experience of being bottle-fed in which the bottle was allowed to slip or was pressed into her mouth, shutting off her respiration. Other examples of similar specific experiences being encoded as procedural actions have been reported. Keiser (1977) describes a patient who held her hands in a particularly rigid manner that repeated procedurally her experience of having her hands tied. Anthi (1983), McLaughlin (1982, 1987) and many analysts in private communication report similar instances of early experiences persisting as closely related specific (particularized) actions or sensations.

Stern (1985) suggests another source of particularizing. A nine-month-old child described by Cramer manifested a full-blown aversive reaction to the bottle, but to nothing else. This occurred not only at times of feeding, but any time the bottle was in her sight. She would shrink back and throw the bottle away. The child manifested a subclinical failure-to-thrive low weight. Her parents functioned in states of emotional stress, but no specific traumatic event seemed to be the source of the focus on the bottle. Stern suggests that the bottle had come to be the most invariant attribute of a whole series of lived experiences that triggered negative affects: anger, depression, and tentativeness in mother, ambivalence to women in father, tension between the parents, intrusive overfeedings, and disruptions in caregiving. The reasoning here is that just as infants can abstract out of many experiences with their mother a face that is representative of her many changing facial expressions, hair-dos, and the like, the infant can particularize out of many experiences an invariant that best brings together and condenses her various sources and forms of agony. The bottle, like the "yawn" and the hands held together as if tied, is not a symbolic representation, an arbitrary signifier, like the word "bottle" or the dream image bottle in later life. The bottle in the nine-month-old's world is tied closely to the lived experience, the marker being the affects triggered in those experiences. The fundamental level of the unconscious when the lived experience is adverse may give representation to the negative affects through specific procedural and episodic memories, intimately related to a specific trauma or abstracted from many disruptive episodes. Alternatively, the adverse lived experience may be broadly generalized and may influence a wide range of the motivational systems. The rules that govern particularization and generalization are, I believe, little understood.

UNCONSCIOUS FANTASY AND ROLE ENACTMENTS

Two observations pose an intriguing challenge to our understanding of the unconscious. The first is the manner in which the unconscious fantasy of parents can influence and shape the conscious and unconscious experience of an infant. The second is the manner in which the unconscious fantasy of patients can influence and shape the conscious and unconscious experience of the therapist by drawing the therapist into unconscious subtle or gross role enactments. I believe that an understanding of role enactments in the clinical situation depends on an understanding of the means by which the unconscious fantasy of a parent is communicated to an infant. My reasoning is this: The communicative exchange in infancy involves one person, the parent, who possesses the capacity for symbolic representation, and another person, the infant, who possesses the capacity for modal and cross-modal perceptual-action patterns and affective amplification, but not for symbolic representation until the middle of the second year. The communicative exchange in the treatment situation involves two people, both able to give symbolic representation to whatever transpires between them. In fact, symbolic representations—largely in words, sometimes in constructed imagery with children in play therapy—are the principal means each employs to attempt to code the messages sent and decode the messages received. In infancy symbolic representation cannot be the means that the infant uses to code the messages sent or decode the messages received, yet infants are active senders and receivers. At first, infants can perceive their lived experience only on an interactional basis richly amplified with affect, and then toward the end of the first year as intersubjective, that is, as involving signs and signals experienced as affect-laden messages recognized as shared between self and others. The communicative potential from interactional and intersubjective exchanges persists along with communicative exchanges utilizing symbolic representation. My hypothesis is that the rules and procedures that permit interactional and intersubjective exchanges are important sources for the cueing that occurs in role enactments.

Let us consider a young mother-to-be who has a fantasy that her baby will be exceptional: if a boy, he will be handsome and bright; if a girl, she will be pretty and capable. When her daughter is born, she delights in outfitting her in pretty clothes and admiring the effect. The baby is handled gently, somewhat like a prized doll but with much more ado made over the indications of her animation. When the mother can elicit a smile, she reacts with enthusiasm, the baby's smile being "as pretty as can be." Without conscious awareness, the mother in her exchanges begins to model for the child her own winsome ways. Then, seeing imitative expressions and gestures, she proudly displays her pretty girl to her husband. At the same time as the mother uses her social exchanges to bring out the particular facial expressions and gestures that exemplify beauty to her, she uses other exchanges to encourage exploration and assertion. She gives the baby her fingers to grasp and then toys, expressing quiet pleasure in the accomplishments of toy play, crawling, pulling up and walking. She molds dough with her, has her around as she cooks or cleans, intuitively "explaining" long before the baby can understand the words. She gives the baby the opportunity to struggle briefly on her own and allows her to be frustrated, enjoying the augmentation of anger to give her efforts instrumental power. She starts teaching her letters as soon as she can, pleased with each evidence of the child's demonstrating to her how capable she is. In these exchanges the mother and child share a rich eye contact, when at times the child appears to be saying, "Am I on the right track?" and at other times, "See what I can do!"

In contrast to the actualizing of this positively toned fantasy between mother and daughter is the actualizing of the fantasy of the mother mentioned in chapter 3 that her adopted son was greedy and rejecting. The mother's own hunger contributed to her beating the child. The interactive pattern she followed was to override the infant's slower eating pace to the point where he would spit up. Overfeeding him this way pushed him to behavior that confirmed in her mind that he was greedy and created for him a procedural experience of rapid ingesting, regurgitation, and dissatisfaction. Further, his spitting up actualized for her his being a baby who rejected her. Furious at his "defects," she would batter him until she frightened herself into a terrified guilty state, adding conviction to her own sense of worthlessness.

At our present state of knowledge, we are not able clearly to depict a specific lasting effect of either infant's early experience. The capable, pretty little girl's experience is likely to flow rather seamlessly into her preschool years, facilitating her passage through an oedipal phase in which her mother can attenuate her own rivalry with pride in her replica of self and her father can respond with delight without lessening his appreciation of his wife. Clinical experience suggests that if her relationships with family members are marked by much general strain or traumatic events, model scenes will record and depict the particular nature of the empathic failure, absent selfobject experience, and associated conflicts. Nonetheless, we would expect that in some or many of her relationships with others, she would give gestural signals, eye contact displays, and emotional expressions that convey her sense of attractiveness and an invitation to confirm, share, and reciprocate. Activities of the exploratory and assertive motivational system would likewise build upon the procedural and episodic memories of efficacy and competence in the fundamental level of the unconscious.

The future impact of the abuse inflicted on my patient's son is even more difficult to envision, and unfortunately I do not have follow-up information. The question can be asked: was the abuse stopped in sufficient time for the generalizing of lived experiences to become more positive, given his mother's capacity for empathic concern when she had her conflicts under better control? Based on clinical experience with the effect of empathy (see chapter 10) in lessening the rigidity with which patterns are adhered to, I hypothesize that if his mother could begin meeting his empathic needs, especially in the regulation of his feeding and other physiological requirements, the selfobject experiences that would occur would tend to give him room for more flexible, less fixedly aversive responses in this system as well as in the attachment system. However, certain difficulties in reversing traumatic experiences must be considered. Repetitive prior mismatching between need and response in any system propels the infant toward developing frozen patterns of expectancies and responses. An infant's rigidity and stereotypy make it more difficult for caregivers to react empathically. Even when relative flexibility is present in another system, such as the ability to experience sensual enjoyment, the organization of any other system (physiological regulation, attachment, exploration and assertion) along rigidly aversive lines will tend to dominate experience. Aversive dominance predisposes infant and mother to a circularity of experience in which the infant cannot provide selfobject

experience for the mother, and the angry, guilty, disappointed caregiver cannot respond empathically.

Hence, it is unfortunately likely that the lived experience of the
abuse persisted as an active trauma even though the battering had
ended. What form or forms would the persistence of the adverse
effect take? Clinically we know of many different outcomes but cannot predict which will occur in any individual. In infancy, the child
might preserve an episodic memory and, like the child Gaensbauer
reported, be strongly avoidant of both his mother and other women.
This may then generalize later to distrust and general aversiveness
and be encoded in symbolic representations characteristic of borderline, paranoid, or psychopathic patients. The dominant themes may
not derive primarily from the physical abuse but from the general
instability in the family—the gross failures in empathy that characterized the parent's relationships with each other. In one study
(Gaensbauer, 1982), maltreated infants showed significant differences in their emotional reactiveness with fewer expressions of pleasure, greater sadness, and less sociability, suggesting motivational
disturbances of a depressive, devitalized nature. The abused child
may make developmental advances in physiological regulation and
attachment, but these advances may evidence a brittleness that
leaves self-cohesion vulnerable to depletion or fragmentation whenever these systems are under stress. Or the early experiences may
seemingly disappear, the boy proceeding apparently effectively
through the later stages of development. He might then function at
a relatively high level of social and professional capacity. He could
marry and, unexpectedly to himself and his wife, become explo-
sively abusive to wife and child, rekindling the procedural memory
and the affect state of his own infancy in response to some "trivial"
trigger.

The possible outcomes I have noted, as well as many others, cannot be predicted for any particular lived experience. Thus, in the
clinical situation with the older child or adult, we must be especially open to model scenes that convey a full range of the unconscious fantasy life of the individual. This statement says nothing
new or controversial. All analysts agree in principle to the precept
that analytic listening should be tuned to individual messages and
meanings conveyed through the patient's associations (Schwaber,
1981). What may be controversial, at least in the emphasis I give to
it, is the suggestion that only by being open to communications
conveyed not only in visual associations and categorical affects, but
also by signs that indicate general affect states and role responses in
both the analysand and the analyst, can the analyst be fully respon-

sive to the unfolding of transference experiences, especially those that derive from early life and those that appear as role enactments.

Other analysts have made related suggestions. Sandler (1976, 1981) has placed renewed emphasis on role enactments in all analyses. The gestural communications of analysands have been described by McLaughlin (1987), indicating both the parallels and the divergences of the messages encoded in the physical movements of which the patient is largely unaware and in the verbal and affective associative flow. Gardner (1983) has documented in depth parallel points of associative fantasy experienced by him and an analysand. (See also Simon, 1981, and Major and Miller, 1981.) Jacobs (1987) has described modifying his approach (role reciprocity) in accordance with the style and needs communicated to him by his patients and then using the information to further the analysis. I contend that these analysts have depicted a process that goes on in all analytic perception, only rarely documented as such. The flow of verbal association with its recordable text lends itself to more formal documentation and hermeneutic interpretation. Yet the verbal exchanges may give no more, and often less, information than the analysand's persistent eye aversion on entering and leaving, and the analyst's sensing a feeling of relief that he is not being scanned or that he is being pulled into a sense of hurt that his greetings are brusquely ignored. According to Schwartz (1987), a neuroscientific look at transmission of data about affects suggests that there are specific audible and visible correlates of feelings that aid in refining perceptivity.

The most extensive consideration of ideas similar to those that I am expressing can be found in Gedo's *Beyond Interpretation* (1979) and *The Mind in Disorder* (1988). Gedo cites the ubiquitous need for analysts to form judgments about adaptive or maladaptive behaviors that originate in the presymbolic realm of the unconscious. He describes the frequent necessity for analysts to help patients return to tolerable levels of stimulation and to integrate aims and goal so that patients can make choices among mutually exclusive alternatives. As Gedo (1985, 1986) has noted, our views overlap considerably. In three case examples of enactments that were "simultaneously symptom, defense, and communication" (1988, p. 104), Gedo shares my emphasis on role enactments involving the analyst as a source of information about early significant life experiences.

I shall conclude with three examples of role enactments in the clinical settings. In the first example, the information about my role "assignments" was conveyed largely verbally during the analytic hour; in the second, the information was conveyed largely nonverbally and during off-the-couch encounters; in the third, through nonverbal correlates of feeling over many, many hours on the couch.

The first example is taken from an analytic hour with the patient who remembered her mother's resisting her clinging to her leg. A number of years after college, the analysand had decided to return to a university to work on an advanced degree and despite success was vulnerable to drops in confidence about her intelligence. Well into her analysis with me she was experiencing considerable apprehension as she faced a series of interruptions for holidays. She reported a dream in which she was leaning against the leg of a girl from her school, straddling it in a strange way while she felt aroused. In the dream she experienced confusion about whether she was being sinful and whether what she was doing would be noticed. She admired and envied the attractiveness and intelligence of the girl in her dream, as she had her mother's. She asked herself why she had had the dream last night and thought it had to do with missing the next hour and the separations coming up. She then associated to her frustration over my "control" over her life. Her mother had had that kind of control, but she hadn't exercised it properly. She hadn't protected her from sexual play with her brother. I reflected that her complaint that her mother ignored or denied the sexual seductions of her brother was a familiar lament but in her dream she was portraying mother's "innocent" not-noticing of sexual activity in a new light—one in which mother herself was involved. I noted to her that in her dream she pictured the woman leaving her leg there for the sexual straddling and exciting rubbing that was going on right under her nose. I added that she seemed to be suggesting that she feels her mother and I were implicated in her confusion about sin and about whether notice was taken of the sexual sensations and contacts she sought in response to her loneliness.

After a pause, with a change in her manner and a slightly pained tone in her voice, she asked if what I suggested was patently obvious. After I had spoken, she had felt tight and tense. She had thought she was doing so well in associating to and understanding her dream. At that point I noted my own surprise and puzzlement. Before, she had been actively and comfortably confiding her sadness about missing me and her interest in sharing her dream. My response then had been to listen comfortably and sense her lonely feeling and her turning to sensual excitement as her mode of defending against the impending loss of intimacy. I was unprepared for her startle reaction as she shifted from dominance of wishes and feelings expressive of the attachment motivational system to motives related to exploration and assertion, that is, to concerns about her intellectual competence. As she talked on, I reoriented myself to the role in which she had cast me. Conceivably, I had spoken in a know-it-all tone, conveying a stance of "I see through the denial and disavowal deceptions you and her mother practiced." I could not be sure if I had done so or not; I rather thought I had not, but in any case that is what she experienced in the intersubjective field of our work. The dominance of one motivational system had shifted to another and with it my role as we were enacting it.

To move from enactment to conceptual sharing, I needed to inquire whether or not I understood it. I asked if she experienced me as criticizing her, as saying or implying that she should see what I see. She responded, "Not what you see, but *before* you see it in order to prevent your criticism. Otherwise I get whapped"—by which she meant suddenly transported from feeling close to me and doing OK to feeling dense and dumb. After more clarifying exposition of the view of me as critic and demanding parent, and of her anger toward me, she paused and returned to the original theme of loneliness and replacing her closeness with me by any means of soothing (cigarettes, food, sex) at her disposal.

In this example, the first cue that enabled me to identify the role enactment in which the patient had engaged me was the unexpected change in her self-state and the corresponding change in mine. We were both, so to speak, "whapped" by the other, but, by following her verbal associations, I was able to identify myself as the "whapper." I was experienced by her as exposing her naivete and supposed denseness. This scene condensed many painful episodes of empathic failures in response to her childhood attempts at exploration and assertion. For attunement to be restored during the hour, and for the principal theme of attachment to regain dominance, her shift in affective state and motivational dominance did not require an immediate exploration in depth, only a recognition and acknowledgment of her subjective experience. At other times, particularly when facing examinations, exploratory and assertive motives did require exploration in depth.

In the second example, the problem was not as easy to identify or the restoration of self so rapidly achieved. The patient in the second example is the analysand who, as a little girl of nearly two, had suffered the lye burn. During a period of many months, the hours were filled with attempts to understand her aversive responses. She avoided social contacts both at work and outside. She would retreat to her apartment over weekends and refuse to see anyone. It was clear that she wished me to intervene directly and especially to make weekend hours available to her as her friend's analyst did. At the same time she could not gain access to the anger and antagonism she felt toward me for disappointing her. She made excuses for me as she did for her family members who consistently neglected her. In all this we could recognize a major transference revealing the model scene of a little girl who felt burdened by the scars of her tragedy. Owing to the massive collusive denial by her family, she had had to bear alone the pain of her sense of being marred and inferior. In addition, in order not to risk the loss of love and not to incur her mother's sadistic bursts of wrath, she had had to accept her loneliness without complaint or anger. This model scene could be experienced and interpreted only in painfully slow increments to prevent her total withdrawal on the couch into chaotic confusion states or sleep. While this verbal associative interchange occupied our focus during the hours, another model scene was being enacted off the couch.

For years the patient had taken medicines of one sort or another, mostly stimulants to help control her lapses into sleep during the day and sedatives to help regulate her sleep at night. Feeling ashamed of her medicine use, she tended to be secretive about it. I asked about it from time to time and felt encouraged when she turned to a psychiatrist who was considered knowledgeable about drug regimens. On the occasions when she would mention during the hour her contacts with him and anything about drugs, I related this theme to other parts of her associative flow. At the same time, I was also aware of other perceptual input. I observed that as she walked in or out of the office, her gait would seem at times overly stiff, at other times slightly unsteady. In rare phone calls to cancel hours, her speech might be slightly slurred. All of this set off brief concerns in me about her use of medicines, drugs, and alcohol and about her physical state. I chose to work as actively as I could with any references within the analytic hours, but I reasoned (rationalized) that she was in the care of a psychiatrist who would be actively monitoring her medicine usage. Thus, although my anxiety mounted over time, I did not make her drug use a central preoccupation during the hours, nor did I otherwise intervene directly; and she maintained her level of relatively productive analytic work. Then one day the patient forced an immediate action response. She came to the office in so demonstrably toxic a state that I instructed her to leave her car, to take a taxi home, and not to return to work. It was necessary that her family and psychiatrist be contacted immediately and a program of detoxification arranged for. She accepted and carried out my instructions. After a period of time she resumed her analysis, and we were able to recognize and analyze the model scene we had enacted.

In her use of the drugs, she was reenacting her situation as a little girl naively assuming that the oral intake of the cool water would be pleasant and would constitute no danger. She approached the quantity and mix of the medicines as though these "benign" substances would be pleasant to ingest and interesting to explore. Her state of mind was that of the ingenuous child whose motivation was captured by a pleasant anticipation without regard for danger. This is the state of mind of the toddler until the aversive system has incorporated the adult's protective teachings about danger. In my patient's situation the adults had failed her, and this was the failure I was "induced" to reenact with her. The lye episode had occurred when she was at her grandparents' house. Many adults were present, each assuming that someone else was looking after the child, but no one was. She had as an adult unconsciously recreated this situation. The psychiatrist and I acted as the caregivers who failed her directly, while all other family members, coworkers, and friends were too preoccupied to respond until her "cry" galvanized everyone into action.

In the first example, the cues to constructing the model scene that was unfolding as a role enactment lay in the verbal flow and affect change during a single analytic hour. In the second example, the cues were present in postural and vocal changes indicating an altered state of self that occurred over a period of months, largely outside the analytic hours.

In the third example, taken from the analysis of a young man, the cues were provided over many months largely outside of the verbal text of the analysis but within the frame of the hours. The verbal content itself revealed an expression of problems appropriate to analytic interest. These centered on loss of motivation when his efforts at work were unappreciated and on his distress that love affairs, which began with pleasure and promise, slowly but persistently deteriorated into lack of interest and perfunctoriness. Despite the potential for joint analytic exploration in these themes, after the first ten or so minutes of the hour, my attention would drift off. I would struggle to refocus on the dreams or events he was reporting but consistently had to fight off a leaden sense of disconnectedness. At first I attempted to examine my responses for a possible countertransference reaction to him as a person or to the subject matter he was presenting. Other than acknowledging a mild frustration at the slow pace of the analytic work, my introspection failed to reveal the source of my hourly lapse of optimal attentiveness. In fact, it seemed to me that my principal frustration was with my failure to maintain empathic entry into his state of mind, and with it a loss of pleasure in my competence.

Shifting my attention back to the intersubjective field, I began to notice subtle shifts in the affective level of his communication as the hour progressed. His voice tone would become more monotonous, his words a bit more spaced, slightly slowing the pace. His hand gestures would become less active and general body movements more reduced until by the end of the hour he moved little. The change did not seem principally in his expression of categorical affects. If he spoke of fear or anger or sexual excitement or pleasure in a meal, the affective expression was appropriate. What occurred as the hour proceeded was an alteration in the prosodic rather than the phonetic elements of speech, and with this subtle decrescendo a draining off of all vitality affects. I was being drawn into this persistent, insidious state of joint deflation and devitalization.

An opening to construct the model scene that we were enacting occurred during an hour when I associated my attentional drift to how I reacted when I sat with my young children watching a child's TV show in which I had only a distant interest. I would attend to the content enough to talk about it with them, but otherwise I would think my own thoughts. Within a few minutes, the analysand mentioned (as he had in passing on previous occasions) that when he came home after work he turned the TV on. He and his girlfriend would make dinner and the evening would drift away without conversation and without his accomplishing many long-overdue tasks. Cued by the correspondence of my association to his (Gardner, 1983), I asked about his turning on the TV. He described beginning to listen to the news, but then the TV would become a general background blur, which he would tune out of his awareness. He would then enter a state of remoteness and drift in which he and his girlfriend shared a common space without making emotional contact. This state was both induced and made bearable for both by regular use of marijuana. The parallels to the experience occurring with me during the hour were easily recognized. We were thus provided with the formal elements of a model scene of two people who begin with an attachment that shows promise but then deteriorates into a parallel detached purposeless state of coexistence.

Stimulated by dream images of the placement of furniture in his childhood apartment, he began to recall a scene that provided a model for the experience he was reenacting with his girlfriend and with me. In this scene, he was sprawled on the floor with the TV on in front of him. His mother sat behind him, knitting or reading, a clear parallel to our physical positions. His father had gone off to work, leaving him, as he saw it, to keep his lonely, depressed mother company. In desultory fashion, he was watching the TV while playing with a rope imagined to be a cowboy's lariat. No conversation passed between him and his mother. The only sounds were the TV. His drifting attention was dominated by anger-filled fantasies of heroic battles. A mood of depressed remoteness, irritability, and mutual withholding characterized the exchange. In our exchanges his speaking was our TV, giving the news to which we both listened for a while. Then we drifted off as he unconsciously adjusted the sound and visual display to provide a background buzz while we attended to our mutual but detached inner states. The recognition and interpretative exchanges connected with the exploration of this model scene marked the end of this period of dominance by aversive responses of foreground withdrawal and hidden antagonism. Positive aspects of attachment, exploration, and sexual motivations came to the fore as the analysis moved into an active phase.

Empathy, Motivational Systems, and a Theory of Cure

EMPATHY AND LIVED EXPERIENCE

MANY DISCUSSIONS OF EMPATHY either claim that it is the quintessential approach to analytic understanding or insist that it is so universal an approach that it requires little further comment. Other discussions either emphasize the validity of empathy as a tool for acquiring information about an analysand's inner life or raise questions about subjectivity and bias.

My approach (Lichtenberg, 1981) has been to regard empathy as a particular mode of perception that characterizes the optimal state of listening by an analyst. In this optimal state of attentiveness, analysts center perceptual focus on the inner state of mind of their analysands. Analysts hone in on their analysands' feelings, thoughts, attitudes, and fantasies. Analysts use their trained perceptiveness to sense what is paramount in the foreground of the analysand's awareness as well as what is on the edge, in the background, and possibly about to emerge.

The analyst gains information from other sources within the analytic experience. For example, in making an appraisal of an analysand's receptivity for a particular intervention, analysts call upon comparative observations made during many prior exchanges (Gedo, 1984). In addition, analysts draw on their own experience, emotions, fantasies, and urges as they immerse themselves in the intersubjective field and interchanges of the analysis. Analysts also may draw on information not in the immediate intersubjective field (Atwood and Stolorow, 1984) or in the analysand's current state of mind "such as the particulars of the patient's developmental history, the elements of the physical appearance and demeanor of the patient, and even some extra-analytic information about the real-life situation of the patient" (Goldberg, 1988, p. xiii). Whatever the source, all of the information analysts acquire, all of the model scenes they form, "need to be recast in terms of what they mean to the patient, that is to the subjective state. Each observation and every association is perceived by the analyst in terms of what it does to the patient, what it means to the patient, what it feels like to the patient" (p. xiii). Making the state of mind of the analysand the central point of reference constitutes the principal orientation of prolonged empathic immersion.

Let us compare this way of viewing a central process of the analytic situation with the approach I have taken to giving meaning to the motivation of infants. At first glance the differences seem to overshadow similarities. The analysand wants to be understood and thus cooperates within the limits of his sense of security by communicating, in verbal associations, his state of mind. Access to the infant's state of mind is nothing the infant wishes to provide or cooperates in communicating. In fact most of the observations and many of the experiments I have reviewed are described by outside observers collating behavioral responses and interactions. Nonetheless, by referring each observation of response and interaction to a motivation amplified by an affect, I have maintained an important connection to the empathic vantage point. My main premise has been that whatever infants do repetitively with insistence and persistence is motivated. This premise bridges the gap between the perceptual-affective-action patterns of infants and the symbolic representations of adults. Largely through verbal communications, we empathically perceive older children and adults to be telling us the motives behind what they do repetitively with insistence and persistence. The observations I have reviewed in each chapter have been gathered from many perspectives—cognitive psychology, Piagetian theory, affect theory, ethology, neurophysiology, as well as psychoanalysis. Whatever their source, I have related the observations to five motivational systems, each expressive of needs basic to the survival and well-being of infant and adult.

Thus, conceptually I have followed a path that ultimately leads to and constructs an empathic mode of perception for the infant. The path starts with an observation—a mother and baby repetitively and persistently engage in an animated, joyful exchange of eye contact and vocalizations. The information from naturalistic observations of this interactional mode is supported further by experiments in which the infant evidences aversiveness to altering the conditions of expectancy by the mother. From this evidence I infer that a need for attachment is being responded to and that the infant experiences an affect state of pleasure in intimacy. Affective experiences in infants are whole body states involving facial expression, vocalizations, the autonomic nervous system, and generalized tactile and proprioceptive responses. They are best captured by videotape where, in slow motion and stop action, they can be held for observation (Demos, 1988) despite the rapidity of their build-up and collapse. Once a recognizable affective state is accepted as an invariant component of a particular perceptual-action pattern, the path to the empathic mode of perception is complete. Sensing the state of mind of babies engaged in a conversational game with their mothers, we empathically perceive that they are enjoying it, that they are motivated to pursue it, that they are distressed if their expectancies for it are not met, and that they are motivated to reexperience the same pleasure in intimacy with mother and others whenever the opportunity presents itself. An empathic entry into the state of mind of the infant has been established. Similarly, an empathic entry into the state of mind of the mother has equally been established, linking infant and adult.

A further analysis of this exemplar of the attachment motivational system in action focuses attention on what each of the participants is for the other. From the standpoint of the observer, each is a necessary partner in the interpersonal dance—it takes two to tango. From the standpoint of an empathic perceiver, the baby is experiencing a self expanded by virtue of the activities (smiling, reaching, tensing, jiggling, vocalizing) and the affect of enjoyment. For the baby to have this experience, the mother is a necessary contributor, an ingredient as implied in the term selfobject. The infant can build a representation in memory of this powerfully motivating experience through only one means—repeated lived experience. The infant can track contingency, abstract from each repetition, and generalize the oft-repeated lived experiences of attachment into strongly desired, expanding, and varied expectancies of intimacy pleasure. The availability and emotional responsiveness of mother, father, and others provide the sources for the selfobject experience of vitalization as the infant's need for attachment is met. Self psychology has recognized three forms of vitalization that accrue to the developing child from attachment responses: the sense of feeling mirrored (appreciated for being himself or herself by the glint in his mother's eye); the sense of having an alterego, a caregiver who can share the same perspective, intent, and affect; and the sense of radiating in the power, security, and liveliness of an idealized caregiver.

From the standpoint of an empathic perceiver, the mother is experiencing the conversational game in many ways similarly to her baby. She has a need for the expansion of self that comes with her smiling, vocalizing, reaching, holding, and jiggling as her baby responds to her. She gains pleasure in intimacy both as source and stimulus for the conversational game and as recipient of her baby's positive responses and active entreaties for more. The baby's responsiveness thus is a necessary contributor (selfobject) for her experience as mother-in-intimacy with her attaching baby. Unlike the baby, who is restricted to lived experience, the mother forms representations of her baby primarily through symbolic coding in primary- and secondary-process modes. When she and her baby are apart or not interacting, she can keep in mind and activate the representation of her baby placed in numerous contexts that alert her to the planning and timing she needs to fulfill the baby's needs in each of the motivational systems. She is guided and pressured by her unconscious procedural memory of her own infantile experience, while preconsciously and consciously attempting to follow a learned program of child care. Her current program and procedural memory may be compatible and differences easily reconciled, or, at too great a variance, may lead to inconsistency and inner turmoil. In the latter case, the mother, seen through the eyes of an empathic observer, may sense her baby at times as the source of a selfobject experience of great pleasure and at times as a source of internal conflict and depletion of her sense of self. Her lived experience and her capacity for symbolic representation combine to create a baby-in-mind and a baby-in-interaction whom she will tend to shape one way or the other. When the mother interacts with her baby in ways that do not fulfill the baby's needs, we generally refer to this as an empathic failure of the mother. At times this is inaccurate. The mother may indeed sense empathically the infant's need for an attachment experience but be aversive to providing it, often as a result of inner conflicts about closeness rationalized as not "spoiling."

Our references to empathy are, I believe, often oversimplified. First, empathy as a general characteristic may result in differing outcomes—sometimes caregivers and therapists sense correctly and follow with appropriate responses; sometimes caregivers and therapists sense correctly but react aversively and oppositionally; and sometimes caregivers and therapists are able empathically to perceive some needs correctly while being impervious or unreceptive to others. Second, the empathic mode of perception as a specific technique of optimal analytic listening has become defined specifically from studies of the analyst at work during the clinical situation. I have "borrowed" the central features of this approach to apply to the data of infancy and utilized them to construct a sense of the infant's inner experiential world.

Other attempts have been made by analysts well informed by the data of infant research to conceptualize the intrapsychic world of the infant: Spitz's (1959) genetic field theory of ego formation, Weill's (1970) basic core, Escalona's (1965) concrete experience, Sander's (1980, 1983a) organizing process, and Stern's (1985) stages of development of the self. My point of departure, which is closest to Sander and Stern, is that innate response patterns of the infant are triggered by intuitive active response patterns of caregivers. As the infant's response patterns become activated, the response automatically triggers affects that augment (give psychological meaning to) the patterns. The whole response pattern functions from the beginning of life as a component of a motivational system. By focusing on motives and affects activated in contexts of human interaction, I provide a rendering of infancy that invites empathic resonance into aspects of the infant's inner world. Empathic perception of an infant's multiple motives and affects can be made without making a *false* presumption of a symbolic representational world before 18 months—an error that mars the praiseworthy effort of Kleinian theorists to recognize the infant's psychological life (O'Shaugnessy, 1984). Stern's (1985) suggestion that memory encodes a record of lived experience abstracted and generalized as a result of the inevitable repetitiveness of these experiences provides a hypothesis compatible with the research data. The view that conceptualizes lived experience as motivated patterns affectively augmented portrays an intrapsychic world of infants as open to empathic resonance and the formation of model scenes as is that of the adult analysand. The differences between infants and adults as subjects of empathic perception lie not in the basic motivations or affects present in both, but in the differing modes of organization whereby the motivations are brought to fruition or are prevented from adaptive realization.

THE EMPATHIC MODE OF PERCEPTION AND THE FIVE MOTIVATIONAL SYSTEMS

Exponents of an empathic vantage point for analytic listening (Schwaber, 1981; Lichtenberg, 1981; Ornstein and Ornstein, 1985) have taken care to describe the difficulties entailed in carrying out the technical precept to immerse your attentiveness as much as possible in the state of mind of the analysand. Nonetheless, oversimplification remains. Empathic entry into an analysand's state of mind implies an agreed upon way to perceive one's way in. The complexity becomes apparent when we recognize that analysts who employ as their guide widely divergent theories all believe themselves to be empathically attuned to their patients. However much we attempt to listen "theory-free," there is broad agreement that theory shapes technique (see Pulver, 1987) and technique influences what and how associations are perceived and interpreted. An analyst informed by a drive-defense orientation may recognize resistance to sexual feelings as central to the analysand's state of mind, where an analyst informed by an object relations theory could infer evidence for entangling the analyst in an envy-driven devaluation, and an analyst informed by self psychology could sense the analysand's attempt to stave off a loss of self-cohesion by inviting a mirroring response. Analysts attempting to empathically sense the infant's state of mind have regarded the infant as autistic, preoccupied with coenaesthenic sensations, struggling to extrude death instinct-derived destructiveness; or born "strong," ready to merge into a protective mother-infant matrix.

In our desire to improve the accuracy of our hypotheses and test our theories, we have some advantage with infants. We can cite solid evidence to *disprove* the assumption of an autistic shell, coenaesthetic inner-centeredness, destructiveness, or fantasies of merger (Lichtenberg, 1983b). We can cast serious doubt on theories that posit intrapsychic conflict to the infant before 18 months and the advent of symbolic representation. In contrast, I have cited the evidence for the strength of ambitendant inclinations, of self-assertive agendas that contend with parental desires, and of the organization of patterns of cooperation, submission, or aversiveness in each of the motivational systems. These inclinations and their accompanying affects are encoded in both episodic and procedural memory and are constituents of the fundamental level of the unconscious (chapter 9).

Since I have approached the data of infant research and observation with a theoretical bias for a self-psychological theory, my claims of empathic entry are as subject to selective skewing as those of other theoreticians. Self theory tilts the observer's stance just as does drive theory or the hypotheses of ego psychology. And the presumption of self psychology that throughout life we experience a particular form of cohesive, enhancing experience, the selfobject experience, when a specific need of the individual is met, has led me to "attune my listening" to the basic needs of the infant and the affective experience that occurs when these needs are or are not met. Thus, I am sensitive to the potential both for circular thinking (finding what I am looking for no matter now weak the signals) and for the sometimes disconcerting but stimulating experience of going beyond what I was anticipating. From the standpoint of self psychology, both confirmation and extension occurred. Observations of cross-model attunement between mother and infant, of sharing of affect states as reference points for security and enhanced enjoyment, and of the delight of the child in the power and skills of parents amply confirms the significance of mirroring, alter ego, and idealizing experiences (chapters 4 and 5). But the immense body of data supporting motivational systems other than that concerned with attachment calls for an expansion of the types of lived experiences that affect the infant's cohesion and vitalization. Stolorow, Brandchaft, and Atwood (1987) state that the assumption of an inevitably tripolar structure for the self

> unnecessarily narrows the vast array of selfobject experiences that can shape and color the evolution of a person's self organization. We suspect that a great variety of selfobject functions and corresponding structural configurations of the self remain yet to be discovered by analysts whose empathic-introspective efforts are guided by differently situated points of view [p. 20].

Similarly, Goldberg (1988) writes: "[the] pressing need is to go beyond the commonplace and to struggle with advancing self psychology . . . Kohut . . . hoped for a multitude of investigative efforts to fill out his ideas, to push them further, to challenge and modify them" (p. xviii). A review of the development of all the motivational systems permits us to ask a number of challenging questions, the answers to which can come only from clinical investigation.

Regulation of physiological requirements: Self psychologists have demonstrated that disturbed regulation of physiological requirements in adult patients is a fairly frequent result of primary disturbances or deficiencies in mirroring, alterego, or idealizing experiences—what has been called fragmentation products. Other clinical experience points in a different direction. Many disturbances of eating, eliminating, sleep, breathing, and equilibrium appear to be *primary* defects in lived experience (either innate program dysregulation or failures in coordination between caregivers and child) (Krueger, 1988). Would not disturbances in the attachment transferences, then, be reflective of failed expectations of physiological regulation? If the lived experience had been a dysregulation of hunger and satiety, or of constipation and diarrhea, of a persistent sleep disruption, might not the affect states related to these disruptions and the current motives related to them require specific empathic focus for us to understand the particular failure of selfobject experiences that patient suffered?

Attachment and affiliation: In addition to affirming, twinship, and idealizing, attachment transferences include guide, advocate, mentor, sponsor, lover and rival. Affiliate transferences are to family, team, country, religion, and professional group—all with specific allegiances to values and ideologies.

Exploration and assertion: In formulating a tension arc of talents and skills and in frequently referring to normal assertiveness, self psychology has demonstrated considerable understanding of the development of exploratory and assertive motives. Is it better to think of talents and skills as vehicles for obtaining mirroring, experiencing twinship, or appreciating idealization; or is it closer to the inner state of mind to recognize a separate motivational system in which the pleasure of efficacy and competence is itself a self-enhancing aim? Certainly, analysts have always appreciated the hollowness of mirroring if the analysand lacks an inner sense of sustained task interest, accomplishment, and competence. However, the issue here is dominance of experience by one or another motivational need and desire. At a particular moment, is an analysand primarily concerned with exploring a problem she is having with maintaining interest or achieving competence in an endeavor of school, recreation, or work, and does the lack of selfobject-enhancing experience stem from that source; or is she concerned with the absence of a much hoped-for mirroring or twinship response for her exploratory and assertive efforts?

Aversive antagonism and/or withdrawal: Through its extensive study of narcissistic rage (Kohut, 1972; Wolf, 1988), self psychology has made a major contribution to one aspect of the development of the aversive motivational system. When an insult to the fabric of the self is experienced, the result is a sense of utter helplessness, with the implied impossibility of defending the self. Narcissistic rage is triggered in response to the need to eliminate the offending danger (person) from the face of the earth. For some time, the individual's experiential world is dominated by aversive motives. The wounded person cannot free himself from antagonistic, vengeful, or avoidant inclinations toward the offending source and anything even remotely connected with it. Might it be desirable to consider, in addition to disappointments in attachments, other sources of narcissistic rage? Might a rage reaction be triggered if a state of utter helplessness results from failed expectations in response to the other stabilized and organized motivations? Further, how do frustrations and disappointments in motives for affiliation with groups and causes fit in? While we are certain that one source of narcissistic rage lies in failures of an expected selfobject experience from people to whom the wounded person is attached, are not disappointments in affiliation an equally severe source of hurt? Many people who have suffered narcissistic injury in attachment and remain narcissistically vulnerable seek their pleasure in intimacy from affiliations in groups and causes, only to be disappointed again. Does not empathic observation supply evidence that they may be filled with rage and the desire to withdraw or seek revenge?

What about other response patterns and affects of the aversive motivational system: the sense of power deriving from anger that augments aims of assertion; the need for fear as a warning signal to respond to learned contexts of danger; and the complex mixture of affect responses of anger and tolerance, fear and confidence, insistence and patience, willfulness and altruism needed for effectiveness in controversy? Wolf's (1980) and Lachmann's (1986) excellent start in developing this area have been largely neglected. Wolf speaks of progressive moves to make the self stronger when the child confronts the control exerted by his caregivers. During the "period of negativism, when 'no, no, no' is asserted without apparent rhyme or reason" (p. 125), the child requires a parent empathically able to be both ally and antagonist. The mother is an ally confirming the child's strengthening of self through the exercise of verbal-gestural refusal as an aversive stand "while simultaneously . . . an antagonist against whom self-assertion mobilizes healthy aggression that promotes the cohesive strength of self" (p. 125–126). Although self psychology has had little to say formally about the developmental need for an empathic inculcation of an appropriate sense of danger, Kohut (1984) sensed this deficit when he told a patient who bragged about his persistent reckless driving, "You are a complete idiot" (p. 74).

Following the traditional lines of the loves and rivalries of the oedipal phase, Wolf and Kohut have identified the selfobject experiences that result when one parent confirms the maturing romantic desires of the child and is idealized, "while the other parent becomes the needed selfobject-antagonist against whom the aggression that strengthens the self can be mobilized" (Wolf, 1980, p. 126). A proposal of an adversarial transference has developed from these considerations. Would it not be in accordance with an empathic sensing of the almost endless variety of conflicts through which the developing child must negotiate his way, to give greater emphasis to the problem of managing controversies of all sorts? As self psychologists have affirmed, the oedipal child needs a rival who can stand firm and secure, against whom the child can butt his or her head without undue guilt or concern about hurting. But controversy between children and all their main figures of attachment and affiliation is ubiquitous, as are the conflicts children will have with their own contradictory motivations.

Sensual enjoyment and sexual excitement: In chapter 8, I suggested that embedded in the phrasing used by self psychology, such as "empathic responses that promote and restore self cohesion," are experiences that trigger sensual enjoyment: gentle, rhythmic vocal tones, stroking, rocking, soothing, being and feeling "touched." In my view, traditional drive theory, with its emphasis on sexuality, has given undue weight to excitement as the goal, seeing sensual enjoyment only as foreplay. Self psychology has emphasized the way in which sexual excitement may be activated to prevent devitalization of the self. Speaking of the child's attempting sphincter mastery, but whose unempathic mother has been neglectful or overstimulating, Wolf (1980) states:

> Such a fragmented child would be left with a disposition toward warding off feelings of emptiness or deadness by seeking the phase-appropriate erotic pleasures of the anal mucosa and by reconstructing a new but impoverished and distorted self around the pleasures of anal sexuality to make up for the lost joy of a whole self [p. 125n].

To appreciate the power of this formulation it is important to recognize the existence of sensual enjoyment and sexual excitement as independent dominant motives that contribute to selfobject experiences of the "whole self."

SHIFTING MOTIVATIONAL DOMINANCE AND THE CLINICAL CHALLENGE

Ten-day-old Harry is sleeping. Mrs. T, his mother, is napping too. As Harry begins to stir, Mrs. T awakens and goes to prepare his bottle. Harry begins to cry, and Mrs. T picks him up, cradles him in her arms, rocking him gently, and begins to feed him. Harry sucks lustily and then stops. Mrs. T looks down at him, and Harry rolls his eyes up to her. Mrs. T begins to talk to him in a rhythmic, high-pitched, rhapsodic voice. After a bit, Harry begins to fret and Mrs. T resumes feeding. Again Harry stops and frets again. This time

Mrs. T holds him up on her shoulder, firmly supporting his head as she pats his back to induce a burp. Harry, once supported, begins to scan with his eyes and stops fretting. After the feeding, Harry's face reddens, and his attention seems turned inward as he defecates and urinates. Mrs. T places Harry on the diapering table and changes him. All the while, she talks to him, getting her face in his midline about 10 inches away as he kicks and gurgles excitedly. After the diapering, she plays with him a bit more, making eye contact, and then places him in his crib. The crib mobile is stirred, and Harry, lying on his back, struggles to fix his eyes on it while moving shoulders, arms, and legs with active, jerky movements. Then he begins to fix his eyes on his arms as they cross before his midline. Finally, he begins to struggle to get his right thumb into his mouth. First he strikes his lips and starts sucking movements; then he succeeds in getting his thumb into his mouth. Now, as he begins rhythmic sucking, the rate of his arm and leg movements diminishes. After a period of quiescent awakeness, he becomes drowsy, loses his thumb, frets, cries, and falls asleep.

In an observational sequence such as this, it is relatively easy to follow shifts in motivational dominance. We can note how attuned Harry and Mrs. T are as she tracks Harry's needs as they change from regulation of physiological requirements for sleep, food, elimination, and tactile and proprioceptive stimulation to the need for attachment exchanges, to the need for disengagement and exploration and assertion, to the need all along to signal momentary aversiveness, to the need for sensual enjoyment for both pleasure and soothing. I have suggested (chapter 1) that conceptualizing motivational *systems* accords better with the constant change and plasticity we observe in these alterations of state. Furthermore, the properties of systems accord well with the manner in which motivations are constantly changing, organizing, integrating, transforming, and reorganizing at higher levels of complexity. In the observational sequence of Harry and his mother we can recognize needs, modes of functioning, and affective responses that form the central core of each system. As the innate and rapidly learned response patterns that are the core of each system are activated by the repetition of the infant's need and the readiness for empathic response by caregivers, each system becomes self-stabilized and self-organized. As the infant forms an emergent and core self, dominance shifts, establishing a hierarchy of motivations. Under particular circumstances, one system may be dominant; one or two others, subsets; the remainder, dormant. The subset-dominant relationship may be consistent as attachment and feeding, for example. Efficacy pleasure and aversive signals tend to be ubiquitous subsets. We can also construe a tension (a dialetic interchange) between systems as a small child is pulled between sleep and playing with a rattle presented to her or as an adult struggles with a conscious or unconscious conflict.

When we try to determine the cause of a change in motivational dominance, we are often reduced to generalities and stating the obvious. For example, when we consider the shift of the neonate from states of sleep, alert wakefulness, quiescent wakefulness, drowsiness, and crying, we give preeminence to regulation of physiological requirements. By emphasizing the development of subjectivity (Stern, 1985) at 9 to 15 months, we treat attachment motives as dominant, while an emphasis on a practicing subphase (Mahler, Pine, and Bergman, 1975) treats exploration and assertion as dominant. The wooing of the opposite gender parent by the oedipal child denotes dominance of the sensual-sexual motivational system, while school activities in latency evoke exploratory and assertive dominance. Since each motivational system is active during any life phase, these generalities about dominance are apt to be more a focus of the interest we place for research or theoretical reasons than a clear and accurate guide to the cause of a shift in dominance.

Those shifts in dominance in whose cause we have the most confidence traditionally are those which occur peremptorily at consistent ages. Considering Freud's biological orientation, it is not surprising that shifts in dominance toward sexual motives led him to conclude that their source lay in the unfolding of expressions of a preprogrammed, innate drive. Indeed many pubertal boys and girls feel driven from within by uncontrollable urges to masturbate and to engage in macho or seductive behaviors. This dramatic impact of sexual motivation on many young adolescents tends to blind us to the great variability of timing and intensity of sexual dominance on others (Offer and Offer, 1975; Berman, 1982).

Parens and his co-workers' (1976) study of the entry into the oedipal phase by three normal girls demonstrates the commonalities and variability of dominance as it affects developments in the attachment, regulation of physiological requirements, and sensual-sexual systems. All the changes reported as indicative of entry into the oedipal phase took place in the third year of life, primarily in the second half.

The first change noted in Candy was that her previously easily attained bladder control was lost, resulting in great embarrassment. This was quickly followed by anxious depression over a hole in her sock and broken objects. Within weeks, Candy experienced an upsurge in genital masturbation. She rubbed her perineum on her mother's thigh and touched her breasts. Candy tried to urinate like a boy, showed interest in boys' genitalia and anger at her father's attention to her sisters. She showed a new depth of warmth toward infants and expressed a desire to be a mother and have a baby. She was warmly and coyly responsive to males, giggling and squealing at her success at enticing a boy to chase her—all this between two years and five months and two years and seven months of age.

At two years and three months, Mary began three months of intense interest in and possessiveness toward babies. This interest triggered excitement, distress, and conflict for her. She began squirming excitedly when sitting on either her mother's or her father's knee. She expressed the wish both to have a baby and to have a penis. More overt masturbation followed, and, at age three, she doused herself with her mother's perfume and, in mother's absence, seductively, with fluttering eyelashes, asked her father to go dancing and to a movie.

Jane announced at two years and four months that she was going to marry daddy and have two babies. This began a period of months characterized by full-blown expressions of rivalry with her mother and seductive possessiveness of her father as well as genital masturbation. While she commented on the difference between boys and girls and expressed a wish to urinate like her brothers, this element lacked the intensity present in Mary and Candy.

What can we conclude from this study? During the third year of a little girl's life, she will experience dominance of sensual-sexual motivation and changes in the nature of her attachments. Issues of bodily concerns and the regulation of physiological requirements, especially of urination, may become dominant as well. But along with substantiating these generalizations, the studies of Parens and his colleagues (1976) establish beyond question the existence of pronounced individual variability. Yet they offer the explanation of only an innate, programmed domination "by a heterosexual genital drive pressure" (p. 105). This does little to help us understand the presence only in Candy of a loss of urinary regulation, the different strength of the sensual enjoyment and sexual excitement directed by each child toward her mother, and Jane's diminished concern about anatomical differences.

The most far-reaching attempt to relate shifts in life phase to shifts in motivational motifs was Erikson's (1959) *Identity and the Life Cycle*. Erikson defined a phase-specific developmental task that must be solved in each phase. Citing basic trust as the principal task of infancy, Erikson points to attachment motives when he describes a sense of trustfulness in others and trustworthiness in one-self. Alternatively, in his statement that the baby "lives through, and loves with, his mouth; and the mother lives through, and loves with, her breasts" (p. 57) Erikson points to the regulation of physiological requirements. The attachment motivation system seems to be predominant in his view that "the *amount of trust* derived from earliest infantile experience does not seem to depend on absolute *quantities of food or demonstrations of love* but rather on the *quality* of the maternal relationship" (p. 63).

For the toddler, Erikson believes, the main task is to develop a sense of autonomy, of self-control without loss of self-esteem. Central is the regulation of elimination, the resolution of tendencies toward retention with tendencies toward expulsion. In his descriptions, Erikson also brings out developments in the motivational areas of attachment: the ratio between love and hate, cooperation and willfulness; and of exploration and assertion: the ratio between the freedom of self-expression and its suppression.

Initiative, the main task described for the four- and five-year-old, involves a mixture of attachment through identification and the building of a conscience; of exploration and assertion through consuming curiosity and intrusion into space by vigorous locomotion, into other people's ears and minds by aggressive talking; of aversiveness by intrusion into other bodies by physical attack; and of sensual and sexual exploration and excitement seeking.

For the grammar school child, Erikson emphasizes a sense of industry: a sense of being useful, to make things and make them well. Dominance is given to developments of the exploratory and assertive motivational system, and the setting emphasizes affiliative motives: being busy with others in school "a world all by itself, with its own goals and limitations, its achievements and disappointments" (p. 83).

Erikson's major contribution is conceptualizing the strengthening of the sense of identity as the task of adolescence. Identity as Erikson defines it more closely approximates my concept of self as an independent center for initiating, organizing, and integrating experience than it approximates any of the motivational systems.

> The growing child must . . . derive a vitalizing sense of reality from the awareness that his individual way of mastering experience is a successful variant of the way other people around him master experience and recognize such mastery. . . . [identity] is the accrued confidence that one's ability to maintain inner sameness and continuity . . . is matched by the sameness and continuity of one's

meaning for others. Self esteem . . . grows to be a conviction that one
is learning effective steps toward a tangible future [p .89].

These formulations of identity bring up the significance of having
one's identity matched by one's meaning for others—suggesting the
dominance of the attachment and affiliative motive of being mirrored and confirmed.

Erikson describes three phases of adulthood, for which the tasks
are intimacy and distantiation, generativity, and integrity. Intimacy
involves both attachment and sexual motives whereas distantiation,
"the readiness to repudiate, to isolate, and, if necessary, to destroy
those forces and people whose essence seems dangerous to one's
own" (pp. 95–96) involves aversive motives of antagonism. Inciden-
tally, distantiation constitutes Erikson's only reference to the dominance of aversive motives as healthy. For each of the tasks, he lists a
dominant organization of the aversive system as representing an
unsuccessful or pathologic outcome: mistrust, shame and doubt,
guilt, inferiority, identity diffusion, isolation, stagnation, and despair. Generativity, like intimacy, involves attachment and sexual
motives—only directed toward procreation and child rearing or di-
verted to altruistic concerns and creativity. Integrity, like identity,
refers mainly to the overall sense of self: "the acceptance of one's
own and only life cycle and of the people who have become significant to it as something that had to be . . . and acceptance of the
fact that one's life is one's own responsibility" (p. 98).

Overall, Erikson's rendering of the dominant tasks of the life cycle provides, at best, a loose and inconclusive fit with the five motivational systems. This seems less surprising when we recognize
that Erikson's theoretical stance of combining a theory of drives,
organ modes, ego functions, and sociological milestones varies considerably from the motivational theory of self-development I have
followed. Life span models (Noam, 1985; Noam et al., 1988) can
shed light on many features that explain aspects of dominance. It is
reasonable to hope that life span studies based more closely on motivational systems will provide answers to what systems tend to be
dominant in what life phases and to the dynamics of their hierarchical arrangement.

Let us change our focus from generalized life cycle approaches to
the narrower challenge of the clinical situation. Within the clinical
encounter we can expect to be on more solid ground in recognizing
shifts in motivational dominance and the triggering source since we
are trained to follow dynamic shifts in themes and feeling states
from their antecedents, to their enlargement, to their conclusions.

Nonetheless, even within an analytic hour we often face uncertainty. A reconsideration of the first example of role enactment (chapter 9) is an example. In my view, the patient had shifted from dominance of attachment motivation to dominance by explorative-assertive motivation in response to a sudden aversive reaction to a "correct" interpretation by me. The "obviousness" of what I had pointed out to her triggered a feeling of being "whapped" and criticized, and of being intellectually dense and dumb. I am indebted to Lawrence Friedman (personal communication) for a plausible alternative assessment. Friedman suggests that the whole sequence can be seen as involving attachment motivation. The patient had begun to see the analytic relationship as between buddies, research partners, or father and favorite daughter and suddenly felt that she had been told to wake up and remember that she is a patient. This explanation, however, underplays the intensity of her feeling of not *knowing* the "obvious," of intellectual incompetence in this intellectually extremely ambitious young woman. Nevertheless, Friedman's depiction of the activation of a self humiliated by the analyst she wishes to mirror and to love her characterizes the subset position of the attachment transference after the breach in a positive state of intimacy. Thus, for this woman, intimacy pleasure, sensual enjoyment, and competence pleasure are generally intertwined, with shifting dominance. The interruption of any one leads her to an aversive reaction—in this instance abrupt and acute—and often a shift in dominance to repair the cohesive sense of self.

An hour taken from the psychotherapy of a young professional man by an attractive young female therapist provides an opportunity to examine permutations of the motivation systems in dynamic flux.

Mr. A arrives 20 minutes late. He apologizes for his lateness, explaining that his boss (a female) was crying from exhaustion. He felt he could not leave her like that. Then he apologizes for not sending his payment; he had the bill in an envelope but did not have a stamp. Would it be OK if he dropped it off tomorrow?
Therapist: Yes.

[Comment: Mr. A occupied himself primarily with issues centering on attachment with assertive motives as a subset. His success as his boss's comforter and his failure with lateness and payment were used to invite an acceptance that conveyed to him a sense of his specialness. The therapist chose neither to empathically state her understanding nor to challenge his portrayal.]

Mr. A states that he feels unhappy and was not sure why. It feels hard to talk about. (pause) He feels it's related to Jane (his wife). They are both under a lot of pressure at their jobs. Jane is angry about all the details she has to attend to with their new house and feels she's doing more than he. He thinks maybe she's right and doesn't like the distance between them. They haven't made love in a long time.

Therapist: How long?

Mr. A thinks it's been a month or a month and a half. They made love Sunday, but it was upsetting. He hadn't felt close and to do it that way leaves him feeling guilty. It also makes him angry with Jane for putting him in that position. He finds himself wondering if Jane is the kind of woman he *can* feel close to. If she is attractive enough.

[Comment: Mr. A began the "hour proper" by stating that the topic he was motivated to explore was his unhappy feeling, and the therapist positioned her questioning responses from the standpoint of an interested listener. Mr. A pinpointed his intimacy problems with Jane, describing her complaints, his guilt, their counterblaming, and the failure of sex to breach their attachment problems.]

After a brief pause, Mr. A says, on another point, that he feels good about therapy, and the therapist invites him to elaborate.

Mr. A describes having a meeting at work he was troubled about. He had a period alone and was aware of his anxiety. He realized that he didn't have either to deny his fears or to act on them. He could just feel his feelings, and he *did* and thought to himself that therapy really works. It felt good to feel that. After the meeting, in which he felt he had been very successful in getting his boss to come round to his plan, he felt great. He went home eager to tell Jane, but she took the position that it might be politically unwise for him to put himself so forward. He had to agree but felt very upset.

Therapist: You wanted to stay with the good feelings about yourself.

[Comment: Mr. A shifts the focus from his problematic attachment with Jane to his more rewarding attachment to the therapist. This shift occurred because of his concern that Jane was not attractive enough to stimulate him sexually. Here he was probably referring to an ill-disguised, ongoing eroticized transference that neither partner had found it easy to explore. Also the theme of being torn between one woman and another—

crying boss to therapist, boss to Jane, Jane to therapist—was not picked up. The therapist offered interest through a neutral question. Mr. A described his success in self-exploration and how pleased he was to recognize and feel his feelings. He used his awareness to help bring an exploratory-assertive problem to a successful conclusion and experience competence pleasure. He tried to explain to Jane, thereby affirming his sense of competence and promoting intimacy pleasure with her. Her criticism evoked an aversive reaction, which for him takes a momentary submissive form. The therapist accurately picked up his wish to retain his sense of competence pleasure.]

Mr. A responds to the therapist that he had felt angry or rather disappointed with Jane. His view was, "OK, maybe there are other things to consider, but let me ride this good feeling out for a while." He started to tell Jane and she did understand, but a friend visited. Jane ignored his being upset, and they never got back to it. The tension between them continued into their lovemaking. He felt bad and distant and has continued to feel unhappy. Jane feels he is not supportive of her, and he's not. It's hard for him to be.

Therapist: How did the good feelings you had about therapy affect how you felt on the weekend?

[Comment: Mr. A expanded on his anger and disappointment and placed the sequence of events more clearly in perspective. Rather than acknowledge her recognition of this sequence (competence pride at work, disappointment and anger at Jane's failure to mirror his feelings, frustration at the interruption of their discussion, all setting the stage for sex without closeness, triggering his guilt and depression), the therapist, possibly inviting further consideration of the transference, especially the underinterpreted comparison of Jane with her, referred him back to his good feelings about therapy.]

Mr. A responds that he did not have a shift from the positive feelings about therapy. He just got lost in his feelings about Jane. He speaks in an indirect, rambling manner about the meeting and Jane's reaction.

Therapist: So it seems Jane's failure to respond to your good feeling about the meeting was the significant event of your weekend.

[Comment: When the therapist attempted to redirect Mr. A from a focus on his intimacy problems with Jane to herself,

Mr. A was thrown off and repeated his previous comments with diminished vitality. This is the turning point in the hour for both therapist and patient. The therapist became alerted to a problem in Mr. A's associative flow. His motivation to explore diminished. Did he react aversively to her comment about the transference reference, shifting his motivation from exploring to avoidance (resistance?)? Or was his reaction one of feeling a loss of the intimacy pleasure of being engaged with an understanding therapist? In other words, did the therapist inadvertently repeat the missing mirroring of his unhappiness and its source, comparable to Jane's failure with his good feeling? Just as when he heard Jane saying he had erred in putting himself forward, was he now hearing the therapist saying that he chose the wrong theme? The therapist chose the latter to attempt to rectify rather than directly comment on.]

Mr. A responds that he didn't consider Jane's failure that significant, but maybe the therapist is right. Now that he thinks about it he was *very* disappointed. He describes in detail how Jane wants him to do more around the house. He agrees, but the tension he feels about the pressure of his work interferes.

Therapist: Are you disappointed that Jane didn't seem to understand the time constraints you felt under, as you yourself see them, giving you more a sense of freedom to choose what you feel is best to do?

Mr. A agrees enthusiastically that he does feel that way, that it would be wonderful if Jane could!

Therapist: Do you want more of a "building" experience with Jane, that you and I talked about in our previous hour, a feeling of sharing together, of openness to your feelings, that you have been experiencing with me?

Mr. A nods a vigorous affirmation and returns to talking about Jane. He describes the anger he feels toward her that makes him tense and guilty and how he tries to protect himself.

[Comment: Mr. A's vitality returned, and he enthusiastically endorsed the therapist's recognition of his affect state of disappointment. Having helped to correct a partial failure in their joint effort to explore, the therapist saw them in a state of shared observing and attempts to expand the range of meanings. She reintroduced the theme of comparing Jane with her. Again, Mr. A agreed and opened further his struggle with aversive motivation: anger leads to tenseness and guilt and efforts to avoid the whole sequence.]

Therapist: Were your apologies to me at the start of the session, for being late and failing to mail the payment efforts to protect yourself from an experience of confrontation and anger?

Mr. A (a bit thrown off, startled) is not sure what she means. Did he want to protect himself? He doesn't feel that he did.

Therapist: Did you hope that he could feel the freedom to decide yourself what you needed to do, such as remaining with your boss when she was so upset and have me be understanding?

Mr. A can see some relationship, in that he doesn't feel that way with Jane . . . (silence) . . . he feels himself pulling back . . . feeling angry . . . as if he were reacting as Jane does with him.

Therapist: Are you reacting to a feeling that I am off target to what you have been saying?

Mr. A agrees. He didn't feel she had been at all close to his wanting to talk about his unhappiness with Jane.

Therapist: You want so much to be with someone who can understand where your feelings are, and when this doesn't happen, you feel angry and withdraw. (The hour ends.)

[Comment: The therapist treats Mr. A's words "protect himself" as a switching point, preconsciously linking his aversive response to Jane with his aversive response to her at the beginning of the hour. This is clearly a logical supposition from the standpoint of an external observer, and only Mr. A's response would reveal if he could resonate with this suggestion. Mr. A reacts with startle, confusion, and denial. The therapist repeats her suggestion, framing it now in a more acceptable way for Mr. A. He reacts now with an open statement of the anger he feels, even adding recognition of his identification with the withdrawing, sulky Jane. The therapist attempts to capitalize on the exchange that has occurred between them by reviewing the pattern of a breach in empathic understanding leading to his confusion and anger. Why did the therapist's suggestion about the double meaning of "protecting himself" fail to be expressive of his state of mind as he experienced it? The answer can only be conjecture since the aversive trigger was never explored beyond its being experienced as an empathic failure. My supposition is that Mr. A had organized his attachment motivation along the lines of Jane's being an unempathic woman and the therapist's being a mirroring woman. The therapist did not notice that she had changed the setting from Jane at home to the clinical situation without bridging. Further, Mr. A probably treated their exchanges on his arrival about lateness and absent payment as framed "outside" the hour proper, which began for him with his "unhappy weekend."]

In this hour, three motivational trends are left unexplored. The first is the place of sensual-sexual motives in the scheme of his attachments. The therapist, now fully aware from supervision of Mr. A's and her joint avoidance, is gingerly attempting to open this area for exploration. The second is Mr. A's intense need for mirroring and his vulnerability to anger, withdrawal, and deflation in response to an empathic failure. This aversive response to an attachment failure was clearly demonstrated by his response to Jane and the therapist, but it is premature to place it in a larger historical context. The third lies in the organization of his aversive system. The therapist clearly demarcated the sequence of hurt, disappointment, anger, guilt, and withdrawal. However, Mr. A's employment of compliance, his apologizing, and his ready assumption of blame and agreement to criticism require further investigation.

A second clinical example is taken from the analysis of a young woman law student, Miss B, with a male candidate. Her Monday hour begins.

Miss B: I had to meet Helen, an instructor, to get help with my writing project, and I was so nervous. Helen said why don't we go out to lunch, and I want to, but I have so little time. I'm terrified of her. I was thinking, I bet she's a lesbian. The last time I became friends with a woman, Patsy turned out to be a lesbian.

Analyst: You have no female friends now?

Miss B: I do, but Helen is different. She knows a lot about this area of law and I don't. I'm embarrassed about it, embarrassed about the kind of law work I do. I thought she'd think I was a traitor, to not be working on women's issues. I felt so refreshed talking with her. There are kinds of law I like and can be good at and people are not smarter than me. Helen said that if I wrote a paper on this, I could get it published. First I thought, Don't do this to me. Then I liked it. I feel the same way about you. You have always thought I should be able to do everything—talk with you, go to school, work, study—and I can't do it all. I looked to you to tell me I can't do it all, so I can slow down. You don't. I'm looking for acknowledgment that I can't get everything done. And it can't be from *me* because I'll say, No, just let me do a little more. In the past Peter [her boss] would say, just a little more, and I'd do it like I don't have my own needs and wants. And I feel I'm valuable to him because I do that. If I don't, he won't offer me a job when I graduate. Something about Helen really scares me—she works hard, and weekends she helps her friend at the bookstore. She's everything I'd like to be. And I'm worried I'd be bumbling and she won't like me.

Analyst: How old is she?

Miss B: She's my age. I feel like I found a friend. To have lunch with her this weekend is too soon though. I'd feel like I was running after her. It's like I can't be an adult woman with her, but a child wanting to please her, have her proud of me. I want to be her friend, but I feel if I treated her like an equal, she won't like me. If I say something she doesn't agree with, she won't like me. So she won't know any part of me that won't be a reflection of her. But I don't want to do that. She could be a friend, but it makes me nervous.

Analyst: You feel she might be a lesbian?

Miss B: I don't know if it's my attraction to her that scares me. I never had a lesbian relationship like my sister did. With Patsy, when I got to know her I found I was a better negotiator than she. I didn't want to be better than she. I wanted her to keep me as a little kid. With Helen, maybe I could be good, publish an article. There's something dangerous about it.

Analyst: You seem afraid that if you're competitive with her, you'll lose her.

Miss B: It's true. I get so frightened. I want to write the article but she would publish it under her name, not mine. But I don't like that anymore.

[Comment: The analyst indicated that he believed the opening theme centered on Miss B's conflict about homosexuality, an issue he wanted very much to open to analytic inquiry. Thus his questions: "You have no female friends now?" "How old is she?" and "You feel she might be a lesbian?" were all conceptualized by him as "neutral" exploratory entries into her sensual-sexual motivation. In my view, the dominant motivational thrust Miss B is talking about lies in the area of her professional work—exploratory-assertive motives. She is desirous of mentoring and sponsorship but has a wide range of fears about contrary motives in the mentor she turns to. The mentor may want to turn the request into a seduction. Helen might be ethically outraged at Miss B's choice of subject, or expect too much of her, as she feels the analyst does. Helen, analyst, and Peter might exploit her ambition and her desire to please and to gain approval. The mentor might resent her dependency or appropriate her work. In other words, subset motives from the attachment, aversive and sensual-sexual systems all present problems to be explored.

How did the analyst's misassessment (in my view) of Miss B's dominant motivation affect the intersubjective field of the analytic session? Miss B brushed aside his first question-accusation with a simple negation and returned to Helen. She answered the second question factually without seeming to ponder what was behind it. The third explicit question, about lesbian fears, she answered directly with mixed acceptance-negation and moved rapidly back to the problem Patsy and Helen presented as mentors. She seemed then to hold her ground with minimal aversive response, a positive attachment-exploratory alliance seeming to dominate their work together. Finally, the analyst abandoned his agenda and tuned in accurately to one of her concerns about mentoring help for her exploratory-assertive ambition—her fear that if she was competitive she would lose her mentor.

Competitiveness became the dominant motive explored during the week's work. Miss B revealed a fantasy that as soon as she climbed a rung in a ladder, someone—mother, sister, analyst—would push her down. With respect to the analyst, Miss B indicated that a triggering event occurred when the analyst persistently interpreted her fear of losing her mentor if she became competitive as her defended-against murderous wish rather than her long experience of disastrous failure in handling controversies.]

For the reader to understand better the meaning of these clinical examples and the technical application of the motivational systems, I shall review my conception of the analytic process and its inevitable uncertainties.

THE ANALYTIC PROCESS

In *Psychoanalysis and Infant Research* (1983b), I presented a view of the analytic process that I believe to be compatible with the data of infancy. Here I shall reconsider that conception of analysis from the standpoint of the five motivational systems.

People undertake psychoanalysis for a variety of conscious and unconscious reasons. For a successful treatment to occur the goal for the partners in the analytic relationship is not to form a relationship; the goal must become to effect a positive change in the analysand through an in-depth understanding of the nature of a problem or problems. Analyst and analysand do not meet to form an intersubjective field in which a complex play of shifting dominance of motivation will occur, but this process inevitably occurs. However much at any particular moment analyst and analysand share a goal of exploring the nature of a problem, their differing perspectives will lead to the emergence over time of divergent motives. Each is under strains that, as they interact, provide the major dynamic leverage of the treatment (Friedman, 1982).

The *analysand* will be under all the strains and tensions brought to the analysis as a consequence of the accumulation of unresolved problems in any or all of the five motivational systems. In the analysis, the analysand will feel an internally obligatory (and analytically necessary) pull to seek full realization of his or her perceived needs and wishes, expressed—overtly or covertly—as an immediate "demand." At the same time, the analysand will be motivated to share with the analyst an attempt to confine action and interaction to exploring meanings. An inclination by the analysand either toward peremptoriness or toward an openness to an exploratory attitude may occur when any of the five motivational systems is dominant. A sense by the analysand of being responded to empathically tilts motivation in any system toward exploratory sharing and away from peremptoriness. A repeated challenge during analysis arises when an analysand who does not feel empathically responded to feels driven to obtain immediate response in order to restore self-cohesion. Peremptory motives derived from any system present the analyst with demands that are, in turn, often more difficult to respond to empathically.

The *analyst* too is under constant strains and tensions that threaten the flexibility necessary for optimal listening and responsiveness (Bacall, 1985). The analyst's motivation must be dominated by the goals of the exploratory-assertive system and combine functional elements derived from both play (London, 1981) and work (Olinick et al., 1973). At the same time, the analyst must be open to empathic resonance with themes, and particularly affects, derived from each of the motivational systems in complex combinations. The analyst struggles to maintain an exploratory dominance into, say, a physiological regulatory, or an attachment, or an aversive, or exploratory-assertive, or sensual-sexual motivation of the analysand. This struggle must be won much of the time but inevitably lost at other times. The pull of the analysand's peremptoriness, the nature of communication by role enactment (chapter 9), and the analyst's personal motivational propensities constantly act to induce momentary or more lasting dominance by attachment (a desire for closeness), sensual-sexual (a desire for an erotically tinged exchange), aversive (a desire to argue or withdraw), or physiological requirements (a desire for sleep, food, or relief of physical distress). Thus the analyst inevitably has three sites for focus—the analysand's state of mind (the primary focus), his or her own state of mind, and the interaction between them.

Besides the pull to maintain an open channel for exploratory dominance into both the analysand's and the analyst's own state of mind, the analyst has a degree of tension centering on how he or she attends to the information. In trying to explore the meaning of the information, the analyst is pulled toward an ideal of being free from preconceptions so as to be fully responsive to the individuality of the patient's experience. At the same time, known configurations (theories) are indispensable guides organizing the seemingly infinite variety of data. For example, Freud's recognition of the phenomenon of transference and Kohut's conceptions of transferences that sustain cohesion of the self alert the analyst to experiences that clarify the intersubjective world of the analysis. Without these guides to transference, the psychoanalytic experience, as we know it, could not exist. The five motivational systems and the model scenes that derive from each are meant as extensions, revisions, and clarifications of existing guides for the analyst. And so the analyst struggles to maintain an optimally flexible listening stance while oscillating between contradictory pulls of the overall dominance of exploratory-assertive motives versus temporary dominance by any motivational thrust; primary focus on the analysand's state of mind versus temporary dominance by focus on the analyst's own motivation; and the dominance of informational processing by maximal immersion in the particular analysand's immediate state of mind versus the more removed cognitive access to theoretical constructs, in order to achieve matching of patterns.

The analytic relationship, therefore, is characterized by varying degrees of strain at the junction of the activities of two people, each of whom is simultaneously under varying degrees of internal tension. As a result of the shifting strain, the analysand produces associations that provide the basic information of the analysis.

Through empathic immersion into that information, while sensitively responsive to an introspective understanding of his or her own tensions, the analyst learns about its meanings and conveys this to the analysand through interpretations and constructions. Achieving conscious awareness of unconscious configurations by means of pattern matching has therefore been the goal highlighted in traditional accounts of insight as the curative agent making the unconscious conscious. However, as most recent conceptions of the way analysis works (Kohut, 1984; Friedman, 1988) attest, achieving conscious awareness of unconscious configurations does not, in itself, constitute the most significant informational exchange. These patterns have meaning only as they apply to a context in a relationship (Stolorow, Brandchaft, and Atwood, 1987). A unique feature of analysis is that the shifting strains at the junction of the analysand's and analyst's activities create a relational exchange, one that calls for definition and a comprehensible set of emotion-laden meanings. Thus, the relationship between analyst and analysand provides more than the working basis for the analysis—its shifting strains provide crucial data, from which the most significant aspects of understanding are derived.

HOW IS UNCERTAINTY REDUCED?

Everything I have presented throughout this book can be seen as making the analytic enterprise appear more problematic. If lived experience governs the early formative and permanent foundation of the unconscious, how are we to recover these lived experiences or even know when we need to recover them? If the best lead-in to these early lived experiences lies in following the thread of affects into the maze of five motivational systems present at birth (or before), how well can one human being sense into the affect state of another adult, much less the infant the adult was? Given that almost all of early lived experience is subject to reorganization by symbolic process in two modes, is it not difficult enough to uncode meanings in these complex informational modes? If these modes tilt between priorities for veridical renderings and mythopoetic embellishments to portray and enrich human experience, and do so under the shifting dominance of diverse goals of five motivational systems, how do we recognize the impact of "truth" from "fiction," narration in one system from "historicising" in another? How does an analyst know when he or she is under the spell of affiliate alliances to supervisors and other ancestors, the ghosts in the analytic

session that theory inevitably brings in, rather than being in au-
thentic resonance with the analysand? How do analysand and analyst know not whether, but to what degree the analysand is
conveying a motivational state crafted to fit the intersubjective
world of the analyst as the analysand construes the *analyst* wants it
to be? No simple answers exist for these challenges, nor are answers likely to be found that clinch the case for scientific certainty
about meanings of experience arrived at during an analysis. I have
offered a greater certainty by providing what I hope is a more accurate reading of the internally recorded text of infancy through my
organization of the development of self and the five motivational
systems. I have demonstrated through clinical examples how the
five systems help to explain findings of children and adults. These
aid the hermeneutic endeavor to find keys to open the secrets of the
associational text.

An optimal outcome from my point of view would be that clinicians, having studied and mastered my proposals on motivation,
would find they have rich clinical utility. The analyst would be
more able to locate him or herself in the analysand's state of mind
by recognizing which system is dominant, which active as subset,
and what past and present aspect of the system helps to elucidate
the meaning of the analysand's associations. This would indeed
convey to the analyst (and analysand as they work together) a
greater conviction about the meaningfulness of their endeavor. It
will not, unfortunately, confirm the validity of my conception. As
we must recognize from the certainty of adherents of contradictory
theories in psychoanalysis, the circularity between preconception
and findings in the texture-rich domain of human experience makes
the clinical situation alone a suspect experimental field for "proof"
(Poland, 1988). I look to clinical fit for support of the theory and to
suggest areas of revision. I look to experimentation and careful observation for greater certainty.

The main approach I take to reducing uncertainty in the analytic
situation lies outside the traditional hermeneutic effort to read the
text of the unconscious through following the associational flow. In
this model, the goal of the analyst is to provide complete and accurate interpretations for which the analysand provides confirmation
through insight-enhancing memories. While this "idealized" version of events during an analysis does occur and we often proudly
display its occurrence in our written clinical vignettes, the principal
activities that indicate the play of strains at the working junction
between analyst and analysand are more mundane but no less valuable.

Let us imagine a set of hypothetical stage directions, or soliloquies about procedures, that analyst and analysand give the other to arrange their interchanges.

Analyst: Tell me by word, facial and bodily expression, and vocal tone what motivation dominates your state of mind. I will listen quietly and attentively until I can recognize and identify it.

Analysand: I *am* telling you something that matters to me (even were it protestations that nothing matters to me today) and I want, hope, expect, demand that you do something about it.

Analyst: I am having difficulty entering your state of mind. You haven't said enough yet, or I am getting too much static from my own motivational pressures, or this is too new and I haven't caught up with you. You need to continue.

Analysand: I am going along and will continue. I believe that you understand just fine; or I don't know if you understand or not and I want to know soon, or I will have trouble going on for much longer; or I believe that you don't know and my motivation is turning from whatever it is to my being aversive to *you.*

Analyst: I believe I am empathically in tune with your state of mind and here is how I perceive what you are saying.

Analysand: What you say strikes me as all well and good as far as it goes, but it doesn't respond gratifyingly to my wish—it only identifies the wish more or less well. I'll try again to get you to respond more directly.

Analyst: I pick up your frustration that I limited my response to a recognition of your wish, and I will recognize that and the frustration (aversiveness) that you feel as a result of it.

Analysand: OK, I sense your effort and I sense you to be close enough to me. I'll move a bit toward your exploratory goal, and we will try to look at what my motivation is. I'll state it with affective vigor and further associations.

Analyst: I sense our moving closer together, sharing an imaginary "observation platform" (Lichtenberg, 1981, 1983a, b) on which we both can stand and communicate together about what I understand, the model scene I am forming, and the introspective awareness you can form. Sensing this sharing, I will offer a preliminary suggestion about what I believe your motivation to be.

Analysand: What you said strikes me as almost right, just a little off. You don't understand how a subset motivation works.

Analyst: I will refine what I understand to be closer to your sensing and add a dimension that applies more directly to your experience of the context of our relationship here.

Analysand: Your revision is acceptable but *I* am not ready to shift *my* focus from where *I* have set it to the situation between us.

Analyst: I can see that what I said triggered an aversive response, but I don't understand why that should be, so I will acknowledge that we are off the observation platform and try to follow the associations to empathically tune into your view of me that led you to push us apart.

This view of the analytic dialogue pictures an ebb and flow of closeness between analyst and analysand with respect to sharing an exploratory motive. This view envisions a communicative exchange characterized by the analyst's offering interpretations that are partial successes and partial failures. The nature of such an ebb and flow and partial success and failure determines an experience in which, at times, each partner may be certain only that he is uncertain of the meaning of the other. Thus far I have considered mainly the dimension of communication in the analytic exchange. When we include the impact on cohesion of the self, we add a further source for evaluating the degree of certainty or uncertainty. The assumption we hold from infant observation is that empathic attunement enhances cohesion, while breaches in empathic resonance lead to depletion or fragmentation. Particularly with patients who are vulnerable to disturbed self-cohesion, we can follow the ups and downs of the self-state to indicate when analysands sense whether or not the analyst is empathically in touch with their state of mind. It is important to clarify that the certainty we are discussing is the certainty of understanding the analysand's inner world as he or she experiences it. Thus analysands who perceive the analyst to be perfectly in rapport with their inner state will experience cohesion whether or not the analyst is in that rapport. An analysand who experiences the analyst as lacking empathic connectedness will experience depletion or fragmentation regardless of the analyst's own self-appraisal. As the (verbal and nonverbal) dialogue passes between them, the analyst can reduce his uncertainty about his understanding of the analysand's inner experience as the analysand perceives it to be.

The analysand's affective state, plus the contents of associations within the dialogue, constantly provides orientation to the analyst about the impact of the analyst's interventions (verbal, silent, and nonverbal, such as movements, breathing rate, and the like) on the analysand. The analyst, as a result of training and experience, becomes able to identify the two extremes of impact—a gross failure of understanding and a deep state of attunement. Gross failures in understanding and interpretation alert the analyst to consider three possibilities: (1) the analysand's motivations are so unknown to the analysand (dynamically unconscious), and the analysand has so much habitual self-obscuring (unconscious defense) to work against, that the associative flow is obscure, strained, and repetitious; (2) inadequacies in the analyst's training, in his or her conceptual range of understanding alterations in self-cohesion and in shifts of motivational dominance, limit conceptual-affective bridging; (3) the analyst's own motivations are interfering—the analyst has formed an aversive response of antagonism or withdrawal to the analysand at their working juncture.

Alternatively, during an optimal state of responsiveness, analysts have a unique experience—one that I characterized in chapter 9 as often occurring when the analyst constructs a model scene. At these moments, analysts often experience rapid shifts in viewpoint. This shift is commonly facilitated by a state of bodily equilibrium, relaxed but alert. The analyst senses the analysand to be providing affect-rich associations from a perspective of working within a dialogue, with a shared motive of exploring a feeling state, symptom, dream, or puzzling interchange. The analyst may shift from attunement to the patient's inner state to envisioning the experience the analysand describes as though he were a witness, sensing the ambiance and the attitudes of the participants (Schlesinger, 1984). The analyst's attention may then fall on how the analysand is experiencing the analyst, even though the patient's focus is not manifestly on the transference. The analyst's quickly alternating attentiveness may again shift to his or her own response to the shared closeness. Does the analyst feel pulled to share intimacy pleasure, sensual enjoyment, the desire to solve a puzzling enigma, vengeful and antagonistic feelings toward an abuser, a state of hunger or pain?

At times the analyst may move away from the more emotional side of empathy or introspection and suddenly see, from the shared platform, a whole vista of the experience of the hour, as well as previous hours. From this sudden coming together, the analyst may construct a new set of integrations. The new formulation will seem to the analyst to subject the analysand's problem that is under their joint consideration to a deeper, more penetrating inquiry. At these moments, the analyst experiences a sense of "Aha," of fit, of excitement, and of competence pleasure—in a word, of certainty. In my view this sense of certainty is generally warranted insofar as the analyst has come to a creative solution to a problem he has set for himself, but with far less certainty can the claim be made that the "solution" fits a problem *as the analysand construes it*. Once again the process to reduce uncertainty is the same. The analyst must return to a focus on the analysand's state of mind and, with appropriate timing and tact, begin to convey the understanding reached. In the dialogue that ensues the understanding will be tested, tempered, and modified—its limits probed.

Another example from a difficult but successful analytic exchange may help to illustrate this way of conceptualizing the analytic dialogue. A depressed, irritable woman, conflicted about her profession and about having children, Mrs. R began analysis with an experienced female analyst. With the deepening of the transference, Mrs. R experienced a sense of being painfully exposed, as she felt an inner pressure to share her secret, shameful desires. She both craved and dreaded the analyst's responses. The tension that developed in response to her need to reveal and her need for and fear of response became the focus of an interpretation that Mrs. R experienced as the analyst's major intervention of the analysis.

While relating a potentially shame-arousing fantasy, Mrs. R stopped her narrative and said that she had the distinct feeling that the analyst did not care for her. Mrs. R wished she would die and be with her loving and understanding father. "I want to escape you—and I want to outrage you, shock you, or excite you. It is so humiliating to have to beg for your response. I'm not like this when I'm not around you. What is happening to me? I don't understand."

In many previous interchanges, Mrs. R had reacted aversively to the analyst's efforts to interpret her wish for the analyst to respond in a manner that meshed with Mrs. R's inner experience. Analyzing the basis for Mrs. R's continuing feeling of not being understood, the analyst concluded that, for her interpretation to be effective, she had to be comprehensive enough to encompass Mrs. R's bewildering affects—the urgent demands of the past now experienced in the present. The analyst said that the *urgency* with which Mrs. R had been sharing the most private and secret of her fantasies must have been experienced by her as if she were tearing off all her clothes, as if she were standing naked in front of the analyst, just as she felt when, as a little girl, her T-shirt had been ripped off in front of her family. The analyst continued: this evoked in Mrs. R a special kind of anxiety, as if she were saying, "I want you to look at me—to see me as I really am. But then I want to be able to look at you—to see what your eyes say. Do they say that my body is beautiful? What if they don't?" There was a long silence, and then Mrs. R said, "This is correct. How well will I be able to integrate it all? The little girl I never was. I always wanted a daughter. Did I tell you I had a name for her for a long time?"

Then, reflecting back on the analyst's interpretation, Mrs. R stated that it made her feel confident about the analysis and comfortably close to the analyst. "I felt that I had integrated something here with you. It was strange. Your interpretation brought a lot of associations, primarily to being a little girl. I felt sad. I was amazed by what you said in a lot of ways. That you knew the *intensity* of it. Just words about it could have destroyed it all. I feel very connected to you now. It feels as if you like me okay. You don't need to like me above everyone."

Mrs. R and the analyst continued to work effectively with the meaning to Mrs. R of telling her fantasies. They had to have shock value. They had to excite and involve the analyst. The closeness that accompanied her feeling understood worried her. Was she making the analyst into her father, so that they became two male buddies and she sacrificed her femininity? This period of positive feelings ended with Mrs. R's becoming enraged at a brief but unexpected vacation of the analyst.

It should be noted that Mrs. R and her analyst had struggled for some time to understand two themes that came together at this time. One theme was the meaning to Mrs. R of having secret fantasies, about which she felt ashamed. The second was the nature of the exchanges between analyst and patient. Both had learned through a series of partial failures that cognitive or hermeneutic accuracy about the nature of the message encoded in Mrs. R's associations produced little meaningful insight. In fact, Mrs. R reacted aversively, claiming that the analyst's "words" had destroyed her feelings of closeness. Only when the analyst succeeded in conveying an acceptably accurate appraisal not only of the formal elements of the model scene she had formed about a sense of shameful exposure, but also of the *affective intensity* of the experience, did Mrs. R feel empathic attunement. Then the two could share for a moment a sense of being together on an "observational platform" looking at the past and present wishes for a mirroring attachment. The same issues of revelation of secret shames came up in subsequent hours for further exploration. And now, with the changed transference relatedness, came an aversion to closeness because intimacy itself represented a threat of loss of femininity.

I should like to call attention particularly to Mrs. R's statements, "It feels as if you like me okay" and "You don't need to like me above everyone." In the first statement, Mrs. R is saying that for the moment an external condition of a "deficit" in feeling liked has been responded to. In the next section, describing how analytic cure occurs, I shall describe this as a microexample of self-righting. When a patient experiences this type of restoration of attachment intimacy and with it a vitalizing of self-cohesion, the stage is set for an advance in the analytic process—the reorganization of symbolic representations.

Let us now consider Mrs. R's second statement, "You don't need to like me above everyone." How can we conceptualize Mrs. R's representations of self and analyst before and after the interpretation she experienced as integrating? We might have assumed that in her regular rejections of her analyst's efforts to be understanding, to be helpful, and to provide her with insight Mrs. R had an insatiable craving for love, reassurance, and praise. We might have traced these desires to a regressive and dependent drive with, in my mind, questionable links to the way a small baby experiences mothering. In any case, Mrs. R's self was insecure and unhappy in the nature of her attachment. The analyst was experienced as incapable, unwilling, or inept in providing the responses Mrs. R felt she needed. The more she demanded and rejected, the more Mrs. R experienced herself as wanting total and exclusive intimacy and admiration. The *urgency* and *intensity* of her demands were a further source of shame. With the change in her feeling of being responded to, Mrs. R could rearrange the nature of her self-representation to one who, when liked convincingly, did not require total and exclusive responsiveness. The representation of the analyst then changed from one who could never give what was needed to one who could and did give and therefore could give *enough without giving all*. This self-representation of Mrs. R as being able to share intimacy pleasure and an exploratory-assertive motivation with the analyst continued until the disruption of the unexpected vacation.

SELF-RIGHTING AND SYMBOLIC REORGANIZATION

Uncertainty about the analytic endeavor is revealed in the many theories of how analysis works and what brings about change (Greenberg and Mitchell, 1983). Even when examining identical clinical material (Pulver, 1988), analysts disagree markedly about meanings and process. A possible reason for this lack of agreement lies in the psychoanalytic method's trial-and-error origins. Empiricism guided the changes in method from hypnosis, to suggestion enforced by brow pressure, to free association for periods of only a few months, to contemporary analysis lasting years. Freud sought a theory of cure that had a developmental basis as reflected in the cathartic method for the release of strangulated affects associated with childhood memories. Whether the source of their symptoms lay in trauma, as in the early theory, or in fantasy, as in the later theory, patients had to come to terms with happenings from early life. Theorists attempting to explain beneficial change have tended to emphasize the object relational aspect of the treatment or the understanding (insight) that is gained. Despite a continual emphasis on childhood, no information about early experience was available to conceptualize the developmental underpinnings for a theory of cure.

In *Psychoanalysis and Infant Research*, I (Lichtenberg, 1983b) stated that "the essential process by which cure occurs is in continuity with growth" (p. 238). Olinick (in press) refers to "a homeostatic psychobiologic principle by which the organism tends toward optimal functioning." Kohut (1984) states, "The patient protects the defective self so that it will be ready to grow again in the future, to continue to develop from the point in time at which its development had been interrupted" (p. 141). The goal of growth, to Kohut, is to be able to function according to an inherent design. Both Kohut's and my use of "growth" are suspect as implying "a teleological view that the self is moving toward preordained self-integrations, self-validations, and self-realizations of a higher order and inferred higher purpose" (Oremland, 1985, p. 102). In other words, without further specification, citing growth as a basis for cure may be little better than invoking God's will.

I suggest that pathological developments may be corrected or reversed by two processes—the tendency for self—righting and the capacity to reorganize symbolic representations.

Self-righting refers to an inherent tendency to rebound from a deficit with a developmental advance when a positive change in an inhibiting external condition occurs. In self-righting, a normal developmental step that has not been taken or a normal experience that is absent becomes possible. The term self-righting was originally coined by Waddington (1947, 1966), an embryologist who proposed a genetically programmed self-organizing and self-righting tendency (also called canalization) that is an inherent property of all developing organisms. The environment (of surrounding cells in an embryo) induces the genes to turn on or off. Thus, self-righting results from a combination of the organism's own contribution and that of the environment. Psychologists (Fajardo, 1988) have borrowed the term, recognizing many useful explanatory analogies that derive from it.

Sander (1975, 1980; Sander et al., 1976) studied two groups of newborns. For ten days one group was fed on a four-hour fixed schedule in a lying-in nursery; the other group was fed on an around-the-clock demand schedule in a rooming-in arrangement. The fixed schedule-fed newborns cried and were more active at night than during the day; the demand-fed babies established by ten days a pattern of longer day activity and longer night sleep. After ten days, the babies were transferred to a setting where they were all looked after by a single caretaker in a rooming-in arrangement. As soon as they were transferred to the surrogate mother, the fixed schedule-fed babies reversed the day-night activity pattern—even overcompensating by having greater time awake during the day hours and less sleeping. This is self-righting in the motivational system involving the regulation of physiological need.

Institutionalized infants who are never played with or cuddled develop limp hypotonia—stiff, wooden, unpliable body postures—pleasureless rocking, and excessive sleep. When approached by an interested, smiling adult, these infants cease rocking and are capable of responsive interest. With careful handling, molding responses occur, body tension can be restored to normal, and social seeking activated. Older children who have become extremely touch aversive because of tactile hypersensitivity can be desensitized by planned exposure techniques. Once this occurs, they may go through episodes of seeking out tactile experiences and human contacts with insatiability "as if they were making up for lost time" (A. Lichtenberg, 1982; Ayres, 1979). These are examples of self-righting in the motivational system involving the need for attachment and the regulation of physiological need.

Tolpin (1986) sees in self-righting not only the tendency to rebound from a deficit but the tendency to create in the environment the conditions required for the reversal of the deficient experience to take place. She sees a major component of self-righting to be insistent promptings to get "the selfobject to 'act right' " (p. 120). "The baby's tendency toward self-righting by looking at and reaching toward the selfobject is a primary given; it is designed into the baby's self, even as the ability to read the baby's motor, gestural, and vocal signals is designed into the self of the parent who functions as the baby's selfobject" (p. 121). In contrast to the gross deprivation of the institutionalized infants, Tolpin is describing self-righting on a micro scale in adequately cared-for infants. An example is a well cared-for infant's response to a distracted mother's hurried, tense handling during a particular feeding. The memory images of recurrent satisfying feedings will prevent adverse consequences from dissatisfaction in the actual experience, since memory tends to abstract and generalize each fresh occurrence (chapters 4 and 5). Another micro example is the activation of familiar attachment patterns by the child on reunion after an absence of tolerable length.

Macro self-righting is exemplified by infants raised in the Guatemalan highlands. These babies, while always close to their mothers, are restricted for over a year inside a windowless hut, often in a back sling with no toys and little human interaction. At one year they are quiet, unsmiling, minimally alert, and physically passive. They are far behind U.S. children in cognitive development. In the middle of the second year, however, when they become mobile and are allowed to leave the hut, their development leaps forward dramatically. When the children were tested at 10 to 11 years, their cognitive and perceptual abilities were at the same level as American, urban, middle-class children (Kagan, Kearsley, and Zelazu, 1978). This is an example of self-righting in the exploratory-assertive motivational system.

Skeels's (1966) study demonstrates self-righting that seems to affect the development of the self in all the motivational systems. During the depression of the early 30s, 25 deprived children in a foundling home were observed. When they were between seven and 36 months of age, 13 of the children were placed in the care of women who were living in a home for the mentally defective, and the other 12 remained in the foundling home. All the children placed with the mentally retarded surrogate mothers and most of those remaining in the foundling home were eventually adopted by families in the community. After 30 years, all were found and studied. All 13 who had received the surrogate mothering were relating to others and functioning at socioeconomic levels appropriate to their adoptive families. Some had attended college; most had graduated from high school. Eleven were married and had families. Of the 12 who had remained in the foundling home before adoption, only one had achieved economic independence. Eleven were drifters or engaged in menial tasks. Their median educational attainment was the third grade, and only one was married.

Commenting on Kagan's and Skeels's findings, Freedman (1975) states that the deficiencies that arise from protracted periods of environmental deprivation during the first three years of life can be compensated for by appropriate modifications in the environment. Responses such as those made by the infants in Skeels's study to the opportunity for adequate caregiving by the mentally defective surrogate mothers "make it necessary to assume a considerable degree of plasticity in the developing infant" (p. 69). Freedman adds that in his experience generalized deprivation syndromes are probably not reversible after age four. Freedman draws an important distinction between "a lack of experience and a distorted experience" (p. 78). Infants who have suffered one form or another of abuse (Steele and Pollock, 1968) will show lasting effects of their earliest experience.

Although examples of self-righting are most commonly selected from infant development, the self-righting tendency exists throughout life. For example, a person deprived of the five or six REM episodes that normally occur each night will have a compensatory rebound when permitted to sleep until the deficit is made up. Most important to my hypothesis is that self-righting is a regular occurrence in each motivational system and that it plays an important part in all analytic experience—invariably on a micro level, as I suggested in the case of Mrs. R, and occasionally on a macro level. To conclude: Self-righting is the innate growth factor that is available to the infant to correct a deficit. It continues to be available to the older child and to the adult who, in addition, have available the plasticity of symbolic representation to correct maladaptive patterns.

Symbolic representation is the result of information processing in the two cognitive-affective modes that develop simultaneously at about 18 months of age. Each cognitive affective mode has its own formal characteristics. When a toddler responds with comprehension to mother's statement, "Give me the spoon and I will feed you the custard," the toddler has coordinated a semantic sequence, an action sequence, and a pleasurable visual-gustatory sequence. The rules of logic apply to these sequences, and the rules of causal linkage to the relationship each has to the other. This is secondary process. Alternatively, if a toddler clangs a spoon on the table and mother holds up the custard jar and says, "Yummy! Yummy!" the whole percept coordinates sound, action, a nonsense word, and a gustatory stimulus into a holistic image of exuberant joy. The rules that govern the sequence are those of time collapsing toward synchrony rather than delaying into contingency, of rapid substitutions (displacement), of associational linkage rather than more discrete, stable referents. This is primary process. Play therapy utilizes the child's innate tendency toward symbolic reorganization largely through enactments. In adult analysis, symbolic reorganization occurs primarily through verbal communication.

Mr. Y, a businessman, began analysis because of multiple diffuse complaints. In his third year, he reported a dream in which he entered a large auditorium with a feeling that he did not know where to go. A decision was to be rendered by a government regulatory agency against Mr. Y and in favor of all the many others there. He felt all alone and paranoid. As the hour progressed, Mr. Y did seem greatly distressed. He noted that a decision similar to that in the dream was to be made, but he had no reason to believe it would go against his company. He and his wife had been arguing, and he was particularly upset by her bitterness in response to his father's request for help with his mother, who had to be hospitalized again. After this, he spoke in a listless, detached voice. I suggested that by the tone of his voice he might be telling me that he was feeling all alone, as he had in his dream. He agreed and with a touch more vitality complained about his parents' long-time helplessness and the burden on him since he was an only child. I suggested that in his dream he had a problem he was now attempting to solve but felt helpless to do so by himself. Gradually, with back and forth comments about his distressed emotional state, the trigger of his father's pleas for help, and his fear that rather than be helped he will be treated punitively, he spontaneously said he thought that *I* believed his distress was not about his business but about his guilt at not helping his parents—that he was not being a good son, but only thinking of himself. And that he felt that no matter what he did, somebody would be angry with him—his parents and me for not helping, his wife for helping. The next hour his affect changed dramatically as he reported that he had elicited the help of his comptroller, who made a plan for financing his mother's hospitalization, and that he had faced up to talking to his wife.

What is the process of this small change in affect and functional capacity? To answer, insight—meaning his recognition that the source of his guilt was his failure to act in his parent's behalf—is to give an incomplete explanation. In his dream, he depicted his struggle as problem solving at work, where he felt all alone while a decision (verdict) was going to be rendered against him. This accurately portrayed his inner self-state, and he did worry a lot about this decision; but it displaced the whole arena of his struggle. The reorganization of symbolic representations occurred as we slowly came closer to empathic entry into his immediate state of

mind. First, we shared recognition of his feeling alone in the intersubjective world of the analysis. Second, we recognized that the
principal source of his distress was not an exploratory-assertive
business problem but a complex attachment problem involving parents, wife, and me. During the course of these mutual efforts to
close the gap in understanding between us, my status in his symbolic world changed from one who was aligned with all the others
against him, to one who spoke empathically about his distress and
wanted to help search for its source, to one who, while siding with
the judges against him, also sided with his ethical and moral values.
Thus, my symbolic representation changed to someone whose presumed alignment with his ethical and moral standards buttressed
his resolve to be assertive with his wife. I say presumed because, as
he became more able to accept his discomfort as internal guilt
rather than external persecution, he made empathic entry into *me*,
the working analyst, and had me interpret his guilt about his parents. In this instance, he was actually a bit ahead of me in the particulars of his insight (an example of self-righting on a micro scale
contributing to symbolic reorganization). Certainly other interpretations I had made would permit his placing me in this ethical position. What mattered here was that Mr. Y used it as he did to
reorganize his representation of self from being all alone, helpless,
and guilty, and of me as aligned against him, to himself as having
principles on which, aided by me, he could act effectively. He was
thus enabled to make a small change in his psychic balance, to a
restored (micro-reorganized) sense of self able to initiate, organize,
and integrate experience when immersed in an empathically perceived attachment—permitting him greater flexibility of choice in
problem solving.

I suggest that the analytic method promotes both self-righting
and symbolic reorganization. This assertion helps to resolve the apparent disagreement between the self-psychological and the conflict
view of psychopathology. The self-psychological view states that all
psychopathology involves risk of failure to achieve a needed selfobject experience, with self-fragmentation as a consequence. The analyst's empathic recognition of the analysand's self-fragility "best
prepares the soil for the developmental move forward that the
stunted self of the analysand actively craves" (Kohut, 1984, p. 141).
Kohut's reference to interrupted development moving forward is
another way of saying self-righting, and the soil for the forward
move is empathic responsiveness. The intrapsychic conflict view
states that all psychopathology involves maladaptive psychic struc-

tures resulting from compromise formations based on perceived or misperceived infantile danger situations—loss of the object, loss of the love of the object, loss of bodily integrity (castration fears). The resolution of intrapsychic conflict, the creation of a new balance in the compromise formation, and the replacement of pathological psychic structures by more adaptive structures results from insight. Insight, defined as understanding that produces structural change, is, I believe, a synonym for symbolic reorganization. The background required for insight has been conceptualized as a working, or therapeutic, alliance, the foundations of which are, I believe, the same factors that contribute to self-righting.

Let us consider factors often cited as curative:

1. The experience of catharsis or abreaction: the traumatic experience is recreated under conditions in which the emotion, previously disavowed, repressed, or simply unexperiencable because of shock, can be felt and described in an empathic setting, facilitating basically a self-righting.

2. A linking of current unconscious wishes to their source in childhood, leading to a renunciation of the wish and a shift in goals. This works through a reorganization of symbolic representations.

3. The sense that disruptions of the analysand's self-cohesion and ruptures in the intersubjective mutuality of purpose between analysand and analyst are repaired when the analysand feels empathically understood: the conditions of lived experience have been altered to favor self-righting.

4. Gaps and fragmentation in the sense of narrative continuity of life experience are repaired: this works through a reorganization (re-synthesizing) of symbolic representations as repressed information becomes available.

5. The analyst's concern, reliability, consistency, patience, honesty, directness, and resilience in the face of antagonism and withdrawal disconfirm expectations patients have that the past inevitably will be repeated. To whatever extent these traits of the analyst constitute a new experience, they facilitate self-righting.

6. The gradual development of the sense that in every situation in which the analysand consciously or unconsciously experienced himself or herself as helpless, victimized, incapable of assuming responsibility, mystified, shame filled, humiliated, or guilty and evil, the analysand can experience a self having initiative, pride, respect, and understanding. This can come about only as a result of deepened awareness and the reorganization of symbolic representations.

What are the implications of this cataloguing of factors into self-righting and symbolic reorganization? I believe that we can no longer speak of nonspecific factors but now have a basis for relating such factors to a biologically grounded base in the biopsychological principle of self-righting. Further, we should move from the emphasis on one or another factor to a more comprehensive effort to understand how each works to facilitate the other.

Another implication is that self-righting and symbolic reorganization become terms too global for easy empirical study. I would suggest that whenever we believe self-righting is occurring, we ask, self-righting of functions in which motivational system? Is the self-righting tendency equally available in each system? If more than one system is adversely affected, does this limit reversibility?

The reorganization of symbolic representations is, I believe, the specific task that distinguishes psychoanalysis as a therapeutic technique. While it is proper to speak of a patient experiencing a deficit in empathic responsiveness and the self-righting that occurs as this deficit is repaired, it is necessary to recognize that the effect of the empathic failure is distortions and skewing in experience and representations of that experience. To resolve these distortions, understanding of their nature is required to facilitate their reorganization. My hope is that the conception I present of self-development, the five motivational systems, and the model scenes that typify them will orient analysts to appreciate deficits in empathy and distortions in experience. In this way we will be best equipped to make optimal use of basic properties that contribute to the adaptive plasticity of humans: self-righting, from which infant and adult gain resilience; and the capacity to reorganize symbolic representations, from which older infant and adult gain flexibility.

The reader will be aware of large gaps in my account of the development of symbolic representation, some of which are filled in *Psychoanalysis and Infant Research* (Lichtenberg, 1983b). I have made no effort to present a systematic account of developments in each system throughout later childhood, adolescence, or adulthood, although I have offered numerous hints and suggestions that would require much further study. Instead, I built my case for the development of self and the five motivational systems from the evidence from infant research and observation, particularly of the first years of life. In my own mind, I constantly integrated the knowledge I gained from clinical experience with patients of all ages and my understanding of the intersubjective matrix of the psychoanalytic situation with my growing conception of the lived experience of the infant in the interactive and intersubjective matrix of caregivers and baby. Chapters 9 and 10 illustrate this integration and support my claim that the five motivational systems can be observed and studied in the behavior and affects of the newborn *and* in the full range of communications of the adult in any therapeutic hour.

I therefore leave much to be done to confirm or disprove, validate or invalidate, my hypotheses as well as to fill in the large gaps between the infant studies and clinical accounts. For now, I have completed the presentation I hoped to make. My goal has been to offer psychoanalysts a way to conceptualize motivation that could replace the dual drive theory while accounting for all of the phenomena that theory helped to explain.

One question remains. If each motivational system is based on innate, preprogrammed patterns; if each system is immediately responsive to learning; if each system self-organizes, self-stabilizes, is subject to dialectic tendencies within itself and with each of the other systems; if each system adds complexity of function and capacity for dominance with maturation; then we would expect these *psychological* systems to have recognizable correlates in *neurophysiological* systems. Finding a strong correlation, while not offering proof, would render my hypothesis more plausible. This correlation is the subject of chapter 11, contributed by Dr. June Hadley. I believe that when we can claim for a psychological view of motivation a reasonable "fit" between the findings of infant research and observation, the clinical situation in children and adults, and the findings of neurophysiology, we must give serious consideration to that way of conceptualizing motivation.

The Neurobiology of Motivational Systems

June L. Hadley, M.D.

W HEN WE APPROACH the problem of defining the neurobiological substrate of any psychological function, we inevitably must conclude that virtually all functions are to a greater or lesser extent whole brain involvements. Nevertheless, given functions do involve certain areas more predominantly than do others. Therefore, we will first want to identify those areas most crucial to the systems Dr. Lichtenberg has outlined. It is noteworthy that his clinical approach so closely parallels clearly definable subsystems of the general "motivational" apparatus. It is gratifying when such correlations can be established, and that will be the purpose of this chapter.

There are two distinct organizing principles underlying motivational mechanisms. The first, and more compelling, (as well as the first to appear developmentally) is the maintenance of familiarity of neural firing patterns. This process depends on familiarity of stimuli (both internal and external) and is measured by comparator mechanisms in the limbic system, notably the hippocampal comparator mechanism (Deadwyler, 1987). It is the neurobiological substrate for the repetition compulsion.

The second process supporting motivation is the pleasure-punishment principle, which supplies both positive and negative motivations depending on the outcomes of the matching process and the addition of affect. This process is the basis for the pleasure principle.

These two processes are mediated through the basic information processing equipment of the limbic system and subserve all motivational subsystems (Fig. 1).

The execution of appropriate behavioral responses indicated by the results of information comparison is mediated through hypothalmic and basal gangliar activation, which have been preprogrammed either innately or by learning.

It is immediately apparent that Dr. Lichtenberg's exploratory assertive and aversive systems can be superimposed on this framework with only the modification that both the assertive and the aversive systems bifurcate from a common exploratory system (Fig. 2). Besides subserving the motivations of curiosity, exploration, benign assertion, aversion by fight or flight, it is clear that all other motivational systems rely on this basic equipment for response selection and implementation.

The motivational system based on regulation of physiological requirements is especially dependent on set-point systems important to homeostatic monitoring largely centered in the hypothalamus and brain stem with ancillary centers in the amygdala.

The attachment motivational system is independent of the physiological need system, although they frequently interact, and relies heavily on intact amygdalae.

The sexual motivational system is heavily dependent on hypothalmic-pituitary regulation as well as reflexive organizations of sexual behavior, which differ considerably with males and females.

Neurophysiologically, we must view the sensual motivational system as separate, although it is closely aligned functionally with both the attachment and the sexual systems particularly in the modality of touch. This sensual subsystem can be inherently quite pleasurable and is closely related to reward systems. It is essential to our higher aesthetic appreciations of music, art, literature, and the like.

Although these systems are functionally distinct, they also are capable of interaction by engagement and disengagement of various components. This flexibility allows for the enormous variety of human responses to stimuli. However, it also permits distortion of motivation and spillover from one system to the other. An example can be observed in eating disorders, where the physiological motivations are used in the service of control and effectance.

The mediation of pleasure and punishment is an important motivational issue. Extensive research, beginning with Olds (1977), on the subject of reward, clearly discloses that the mediation of pleasure depends on the intactness of the dopaminergic circuits of the ventral tegmental area and their target, the nucleus accumbens (Wise, 1983), and to a lesser extent the substantia nigra and its projections to the basal ganglia (Fig. 3).

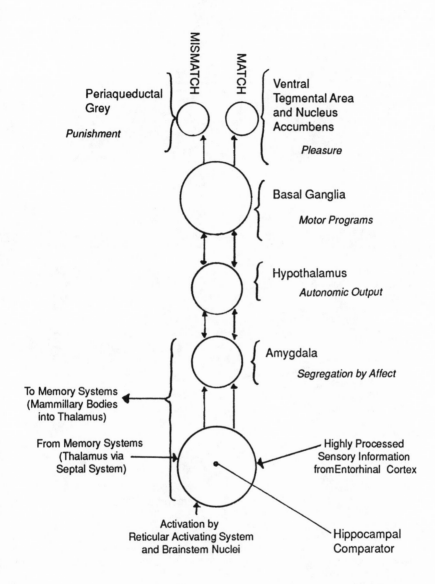

Fig. 1 Flow of Information Through the Limbic System

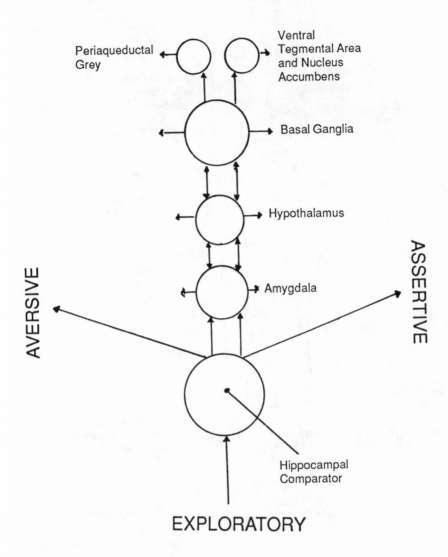

Fig. 2 Exploratory, Assertive and Aversive Mechanisms

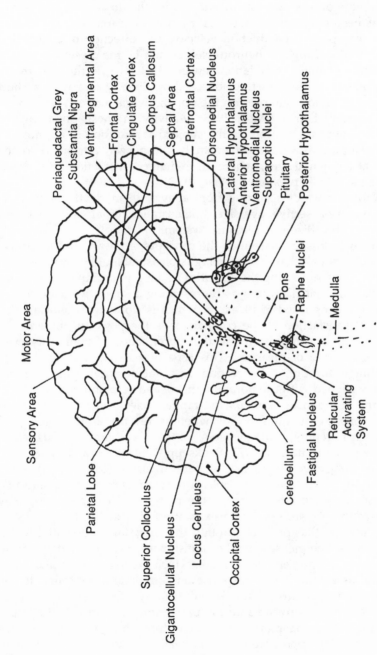

Motor Area

Sensory Area

Parietal Lobe

Superior Colloculus

Gigantocellular Nucleus

Locus Ceruleus

Occipital Cortex

Cerebellum

Fastigial Nucleus

Reticular
Activating
System

Periaquedactal Grey

Substantia Nigra

Ventral Tegmental Area

Frontal Cortex

Cingulate Cortex

Corpus Callosum

Septal Area

Prefrontal Cortex

Dorsomedial Nucleus

Lateral Hypothalamus

Anterior Hypothalamus

Ventromedial Nucleus

Supraoptic Nuclei

Pituitary

Posterior Hypothalamus

Pons

Raphe Nuclei

Medulla

Fig. 3 General Gross Anatomy, Brain Stem (dotted lines) and Hypothalamic Structures

Most other sites of reward on electrical stimulation, particularly the medial forebrain bundle as it passes through the hypothalamus, have more or less direct connections with the dopaminergic system. It has been determined, however, by studies of frequency response, refractory period, conduction velocity, and direction of conduction that the dopaminergic neuron itself cannot be the directly activated substrate of brain stimulation reward. Instead it is thought that a myelinated, fast-conducting, descending fiber system with a short refractory period synapses on the dopaminergic neurons of the ventral tegmental area (Wise, 1983). Activity in these dopaminergic neurons appears to produce the subjective sensation of euphoria.

The opiate reward mechanism has also been attributed to the ventral tegmental area, where an excitatory interaction with dopaminergic cells is presumed (Wise, 1983).

Natural rewards resulting from activity in motivational systems (exploratory-assertive, aversive, homeostatic, affiliative, sexual, and sensual) all utilize this pleasure system.

Much confusion surrounds the concepts of reward and reinforcement, for not all that is reinforcing is pleasurable. I believe that clarification lies in viewing the activities in the hippocampal comparator around the match process as representing a subjective state of satisfaction as opposed to pleasure (which is closer to euphoria). The state of satisfaction at the comparator is the powerful impetus for the repetition compulsion and the reproduction of familiarity even at the expense of pleasure. This type of activity, leading to reinforcement through collaboration with memory systems, is more closely aligned with the norepinephrine and serotonin systems originating in the locus ceruleus and raphe nuclei. This view also helps to reconcile the question of whether reward is mediated also through norepinephrine systems, as many authors have suggested (Crow and Arbuthnott, 1972; Panksepp, 1981; Ashton, 1987).

The subjective experience of pattern match (satisfaction) has a quality different from that of pleasure (with its euphoric quality) although in some circumstances the pattern matching process may engage the pleasure system also as affect is added to the process.

It appears that passage through the amygdala is essential to engage either the pleasure or the punishment systems (Hadley, 1985). The so-called punishment centers, which mediate escape and withdrawal as well as a rage response on stimulation, are found in the central gray area around the Aqueduct of Sylvius in the mesencephalon, extending upward into the periventricular zones of the hypothalamus and thalamus. Less potent punishment areas are also present in the hippocampus and amygdala (Guyton, 1987) (see Fig. 3).

The punishment centers appear to be rostral extensions of the pain transmission system, particularly the slow C-fiber system. The fibers in this system are thought to utilize both a conventional neurotransmitter (glutamate or aspartate) and a neuromodulator (probably substance P), which lowers the threshold for postsynaptic excitation (Terenius, 1987).

The pain/punishment system is antagonized by a serotonin-enkeplin system usually thought of as an endogenous analgesic system (distinct from the reward system). Seratonergic neurons with cell bodies in the raphe nuclei may directly interfere with transmission of the C-fiber neurons or may project to enkeplin interneurons, which act secondarily (Terenius, 1987).

With the reticular system and the brain stem nuclei (locus ceruleus, substantia nigra, raphe nuclei, and gigantocellular nucleus; (see Fig. 3) supplying the "power," as it were, for all the five motivational systems, we can now define a motivational functional system neurobiologically.

The five motivational systems are well-defined, interacting fiber systems in hierarchical arrangement up and down the neuraxis, each area providing more and more refinement as we progress from brain stem to cortex. Many of these systems or components overlap structurally, but it has been possible, through the use of electrical stimulation (in addition to simple anatomical connectivity), to designate certain areas of any given structure as parts of a functional system and affect-related systems above and below that are essential to the mediation of the specific function. Some of these systems depend more heavily on one structure than on others, and some are more dependent on one or more neurotransmitter systems than are others. These systems will be described in detail and will be illustrated in the structural drawings of the various motivational functional systems (Figs. 6–10). Before we can look at the components of the limbic system and basal ganglia that shape, coordinate, and in some cases inhibit the lower systems to produce true motivated behaviors, we must look at the components of the various systems in some detail. All systems have cerebral representations, but these will not be emphasized on the drawings. The components of each system will be approached according to the flow of information through the system.

THE HIPPOCAMPUS

The hippocampus is important to motivation as a gateway for stimuli to enter the processing assembly. It is the major site of processing of high-level, abstracted, multimodal information. It serves as both a comparator and as a mediator of the condition of familiarity.

The hippocampus is a sausage-shaped structure tucked into the inner wall of the temporal cortex (Fig. 4). Internally it is constructed of lamellae that are segmentally arranged along its longitudinal axis (Winson, 1985). Within the lamellae, the cell groups are arranged according to superior (CA1) and inferior (CA3–CA4) regions (Vinogradova, 1975). The CA3 area has inputs from the entorhinal cortex via the dentate gyrus, which delivers a summary of polymodal cortical activity, and also from the reticuloseptal system from below, which derives from the memory store. The efferents of CA3 relay on the lateral septal nucleus and through the fornix and medial forebrain bundle enter the hypothalamus and midbrain reticular formation. The function of this arrangement is to allow comparison of current input with stored information to determine the condition of novelty and to activate appropriate responses in the lower centers. The CA3 field is considered the location of the comparator mechanism (Vinogradova, 1975).

CA1 neurons, on the other hand, are unimodal and preserve some code of sensory quality. The main addressee of the CA1 field is the mammillary bodies. Vinogradova (1977) concludes that "CA3 works as a 'valve' or trigger which only in some definite state (novelty, mismatch) allows the passage of a signal containing specific information through the CA1 neurons" (p. 17). This passage through CA1 and then to the mammillary bodies is essential for registration in long-term memory. These coupled mechanisms evaluate ongoing stimulus conditions and route the flow of information to the amygdala and hypothalamus for addition of affect and to the mammillary bodies for encoding into memory.

Pribam (1977, 1980) has proposed an expanded role of the hippocampus in maintaining familiarity emphasizing its neurochemistry. He notes that the hippocampal-septal system is the brain site with most prominent uptake of adrenal cortical steroids. This substrate is acted on by ACTH and related peptides, the enkephlins. The hippocampal system is seen as regulating the coordination of arousal (amygdala/emotional) and activation (basal ganglia/motivational). This coordination involves "effort," which is the inverse of comfort, which he equates with familiarity. Pribam (1980) states, "Such a feeling implies equilibration, a feeling of a reasonable amount of stability and a smooth transition from one state to another" (p. 256). Whether we view familiarity simply as a "match" condition in the CA3 field or whether we expand it to include the neurochemical reactions secondary to that matching process, it is

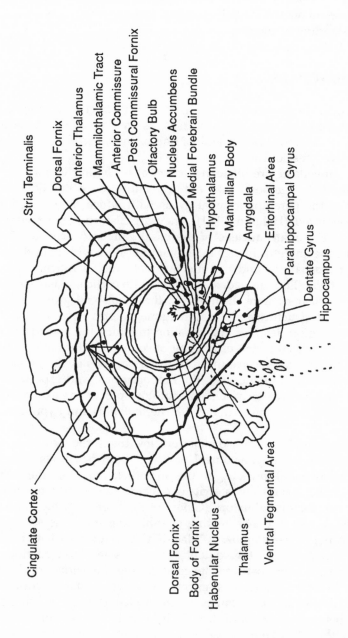

Cingulate Cortex

Stria Terminalis
Dorsal Fornix
Anterior Thalamus
Mammilothalamic Tract
Anterior Commissure
Post Commissural Fornix
Olfactory Bulb
Nucleus Accumbens
Medial Forebrain Bundle
Hypothalamus
Mammillary Body
Amygdala
Entorhinal Area
Parahippocampal Gyrus
Dentate Gyrus
Hippocampus

Dorsal Fornix
Body of Fornix
Habenular Nucleus
Thalamus
Ventral Tegmental Area

Fig. 4 The Limbic System (solid heavy lines)

helpful to understand the neurophysiological and neurochemical substrates of such a crucial concept. They serve as the basis for our understanding of mood.

THE AMYGDALA

The amygdala is important as a mediator of affect, attachment, and attentional and mnemonic processes, as well as lending a sense of reality to lived experience and as one of the structures essential to subjective consciousness.

The amygdalae are bilateral clusters of nuclei in the dorsomedial portion of the temporal lobe and are continuous caudally with the uncus of the parahippocampal gyrus with which they are densely interconnected (Halgren, 1981). They are also in contact with the tail of the caudate nucleus of the basal ganglia (Carpenter, 1976). This arrangement facilitates intercommunication with both the comparator mechanism and the affective/motivational functions of the basal ganglia. Each amygdala is divided into corticomedial and basolateral nuclear clusters. In humans, the basolateral group occupies most of the structure and has undergone extensive evolution during encephalization, leading to a situation in which the amygdala is increasingly crucial in the processing of cognitive information.

The amygdalae receive input from all portions of the limbic cortex, the orbital frontal cortex, the hippocampus, and especially the association cortices for visual and auditory processing as well as for heavily reciprocal connections with the thalamus and hypothalamus (Guyton, 1987).

The amygdalae have two major outflow tracts: the stria terminalis and the ventral amygdalofugal pathway. Both pathways influence the ventromedial nucleus of the hypothalamus, but the ventral amygdalofugal pathway is excitatory where as the influence via the stria terminalis is inhibitory (Gloor, 1978). Therefore, the amygdala has the option of either exciting or inhibiting the same set of neurons in the hypothalamus. A "decision" regarding excitation or inhibition depends on the content of the message received from the neocortex. It is my personal speculation that the *outcome* of the specific patterning of the match-mismatch process in the hippocampus/amygdala complex determines the precise constellation of signals to be either routed onward to the hypothalamus or aborted, and shapes the affective response or lack thereof to any stimulus event.

Mishkin and Aggleton (1981), offering much experimental evidence, conclude that "attachment of significance to a stimulus is critically dependent on the amygdala" (p. 412). They conclude that the site of the sensory-affective interaction is not the amygdala itself but that it serves as an essential waystation in the process. These conclusions further support the hypothesis that the amygdala compares the patternings received from the first match-mismatch comparisons and, combining these with stored representations (probably from *thalamic* stores), reads out patterns to be relayed to the hypothalamus, determining which affective display patterns will be activated. The amygdala does not *play* the pattern; it sends a condensed *score* to be played by the hypothalamus, basal ganglia, and brain stem structures.

The role of the amygdala in attachment will be dealt with more extensively in the section on the affiliative motivational system which is almost totally dependent on intact amygdalae. The role of the amygdala in the subjective consciousness is quite intriguing and has been studied in humans with implanted electrodes. Gloor (1986) was impressed with the findings that the "anatomical substrate for eliciting experiential phenomena is limbic and not neo-cortical" (p. 161). He was also surprised by the consistency with which he found "limbic structures, particularly the amygdala, rather than the temporal cortex to be involved in the evocation of all types of experiential phenomena be they perceptual, mnemonic, or affective" (p. 161). Furthermore, Gloor concludes, "involvement of affect is necessary to make a perception or memory emerge into consciousness, thus enabling it to be experienced as an event one is living or has lived through" (p. 166).

The amygdala uses a wide variety of neurotransmitters and neuromodulators (Price, 1987). Monoaminergic inputs from locus ceruleus, substantia nigra, and raphe nuclei converge particularly on the central nucleus. GABA is an intrinsic neurotransmitter and probably accounts for the predominantly inhibitory functions of the amygdala. The endorphins are plentiful in the amygdala, and the implications of this liberal endowment will be discussed in the section on affiliative motivational systems.

THE HYPOTHALAMUS

The hypothalamus is the hub of the motivational systems. Various areas of this structure are involved in all motivational subsystems. However, its components figure most prominently in physiological regulation. The organization of the hypothalamus may be viewed from several structural and functional viewpoints.

One of the most obvious delineations is the division into medial and lateral sectors. The lateral portion is 30–50% occupied by the tubular medial forebrain bundle, which contains ascending fibers from midbrain, pons, and medulla that originate in the locus ceruleus, raphe nuclei, and substantia nigra and pass to higher centers (amygdala, basal ganglia, cortex), and descending fibers from the basal telencephalon. This medial forebrain bundle is a major conduit in both directions for information pertinent to affect and motivation.

Beside and between the fiber pathways, the tube (medial forebrain bundle) is populated by cell bodies of the lateral hypothalamic nucleus. These have dendrites like the spokes of a wheel spread as if to monitor all the bundles of the tube. Another set of bundles forms a shell around these fibers. In this surrounding shell are intermingled fibers from all motor and sensory systems. This intermingling makes for ideal circumstances for integration and coordination of inputs and outputs (Olds, 1977). Therefore somatic motor and sensory information is added to physiological and affective information in a highly condensed and abstracted form.

The hippocampus and the amygdala also provide major sources of input to the hypothalamus via the fornix to the mammillary nuclei and the stria terminalis to the ventromedial hypothalamic nuclei respectively. This sort of architecture, coupled with the profound confluence of pathways, makes the hypothalamus clearly the integration center for ascending and descending information having to do with vital biological functions.

The delineation of this structure into lateral and medial segments holds functionally as well as structurally. The lateral sector is more involved with behavioral activation in general, with appetitive "go" systems in several modalities related to basal gangliar function versus a medial "stop" mechanism. This medial stop mechanism is related to affect and cortical arousal as well as to the arrest of behavior and amygdalar activation. These delineations are crucial to understanding motivational systems involving exploration, assertion, and withdrawal, as well as to an appreciation of the relationship between affect and motivation (interactions between medial and lateral sectors).

THE BASAL GANGLIA

The basal ganglia are particularly important to the concept of motivation as they provide both a background of motor readiness and the impetus to "go" and "keep on going" where motivated behaviors are concerned. Their inhibitory functions shape the tonic background supplied by lower centers and allow for automatic, nonconscious motoric behaviors to be performed according to a motor plan.

The term basal ganglia was originally used to describe all gray masses at the base of the brain including the thalami, but over time it became restricted to the corpus striatum (caudate nucleus and putamen) and the globus pallidus, which are located lateral and somewhat anterior to the thalami (Fig. 5).

A remarkable linkage has been documented between the basal ganglia and the limbic system via the ventral caudoputamen, the nucleus accumbens, and adjoining parts of the olfactory tubercle (Graybiel, 1984). We are struck by this anatomical connection, which suggests strong functional links between these structures, which had not been thought of as collaborative units.

The anterior half of the striatum is divided into a ventromedial limbic region and a dorsolateral nonlimbic section. The limbic region receives projections from the hippocampus, amygdala, ventral tegmental area, and frontal cortex, which then project to the nuclei accumbens and olfactory tubercle (Nauta and Domesick, 1984). The dorsolateral nonlimbic section is massively innervated by the sensorimotor cortex (Nauta, 1986). All regions of the neocortex project to the striatum in a well-defined topographical fashion that preserves the topology of the cortical mantle (Nauta and Domesick, 1984). Therefore, the striata are continuously apprised of conditions in the higher cortical areas that can affect basal gangliar output.

The other major afferent of the striatum is the nigrostriatal projection, a massive fiber system originating with the dopaminergic neurons of the substantia nigra (Nauta and Domesick, 1984). This system is essential for unlocking the system from tonic background contraction to produce smooth movement. It is particularly important to the motor components of basal gangliar activity.

There is also input to the basal ganglia from the intralaminar nuclei of the thalamus, which are closely affiliated with the reticular-activating system. This input is for the purpose of providing information about the overall state of arousal of the organism and of returning commands to that system.

The globus pallidus is also divided into dorsal and ventral segments. It receives essentially all its afferents from the striatum and serves as a motor relay by way of the thalamus to the cerebral cortex as well as downward to the spinal cord and the reticular activating system. The globus pallidus has another important related function: it provides background positioning of the body to stabilize trunk and limbs for the performance of discrete movements.

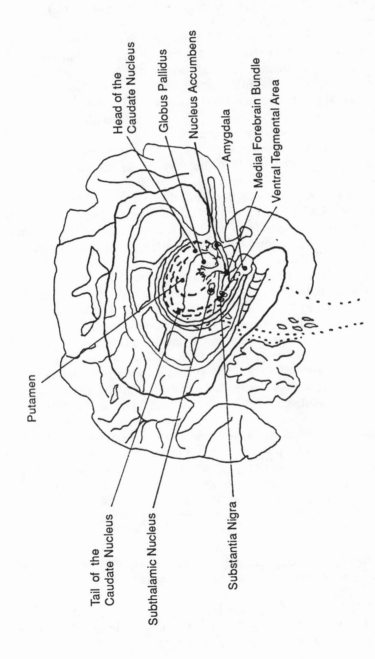

Head of the
Caudate Nucleus

Globus Pallidus

Nucleus Accumbens

Amygdala

Medial Forebrain Bundle

Ventral Tegmental Area

Putamen

Tail of the
Caudate Nucleus

Subthalamic Nucleus

Substantia Nigra

Fig. 5 The Basal Ganglia (broken lines)

The dorsal pallidum (nonlimbic) is afferentiated by the sensori-motor cortex (Heimer and Wilson, 1975). The recently identified ventral pallidum, formerly referred to as the substantia innominata, in addition to making the classical projections to substantia nigra and subthalamic nuclei, also sends efferents to the amygdala, the lateral habenular nucleus, the mediodorsal nucleus of the thalamus, the hypothalamus, and the ventral tegmental area, all of which are considered components of the limbic system.

Nauta (1986), taking this anatomical structure into account, proposes two major circuits of basal gangliar functioning. The classical extrapyramidal motor circuit consists of motor cortex → striatum (putamen) → pallidum → thalamic (ventral anterior and ventrolateral) nuclei → premotor cortex → motor cortex. The limbic motivational circuit consists of limbic system → striatum (caudate) → ventral pallidum → amygdala → thalamic (dorsomedial) nucleus → frontal and anterior limbic cortex. He concludes, "It seems plausible to suggest the limbic afferentiated striatal sector as an interface between the respective neural mechanisms underlying motivational and more strictly motor aspect of movement" (Nauta and Domesick, 1984 p. 20).

The neurochemical most commonly associated with the basal ganglia is dopamine, which is the transmitter of the striasomes (Islands in the striatum). Dopamine, along with norepinephrine, serotonin, and acetylcholine, is considered a slow neurotransmitter that provides the context in which glutamate and aspartate act as excitatory, and GABA as inhibitory, fast transmitters (Graybiel, 1984). GABA plays an essential role in the important inhibitory function of the basal ganglia.

Given these anatomical and chemical facts, what can we conclude about the functions of the basal ganglia as a whole? First, it appears that the strictly motor (nonlimbic) circuitry is largely inhibitory, controlling background muscle tone so that behaviors can be performed smoothly. The heavy intrinsic innervation of GABAergic neurons is compatible with this inhibitory function.

Second, the basal ganglia function to control gross intentional movements at a level of complexity we would consider behaviors that are normally performed without subjective awareness (Guyton, 1987). The decorticate animal in which basal ganglia are intact can walk, eat, fight, show rage, engage in sexual activity and have periods of waking and sleeping. However, these functions are all lost if there is severe damage to the basal ganglia.

Third, the basal ganglia have a crucial role in sensimotor orientation (Iverson, 1984; Pribam, 1977). Pribam concludes that the basal ganglia are capable of influencing visual processing through their connections with the lateral geniculate nuclei and the striate cortex.

Fourth, the ventral, or limbic, striatum is responsible for stimulating motivated behaviors (the "go" mechanisms referred to by Pribam, 1977, 1980), as a result of sensorimotor integration of interoceptive information, which is species specific and provided from limbic sources (particularly the amygdala). This mechanism is heavily dependent on DA transmission, and application of DA or its agonists to neurons in the ventral tegmental area stimulates motivated behaviors elicited by natural stimuli (Iverson, 1984).

Now that we have some understanding of the various components of motivational systems, we can look at how they link up to produce the five motivational systems.

THE MOTIVATIONAL FUNCTIONAL SYSTEM BASED ON THE REGULATION OF PHYSIOLOGICAL REQUIREMENTS

The several subsystems that constitute physiological homeostatic maintenance (hunger, thirst, elimination, sleep, respiration, and cardiovascular regulation) could be studied in detail, as each has representative components along the neuraxis. We will, however, following Dr. Lichtenberg's emphasis, deal primarily with food intake and elimination (Fig. 6).

Let us state at the outset that, although there is considerable overlap in the systems mediating feeding and attachment, they are indeed physiologically distinct, as we will see as we describe both systems. The fact of the overlap has probably led to confusion about their distinctness. However, in addition to Dr. Lichtenberg's observation that the attachment-affiliative system is far less urgent in quality, we also have evidence from anencephalic infants that feeding can be maintained without benefit of attachment per se. Such infants are born without brain structures above the mesencephalon, but in some cases have been kept alive for many months (Guyton, 1987). These infants are able to perform essentially all the functions of feeding, such as suckling, extrusion of unpleasant food from the mouth, and moving the hands to the mouth to suck the fingers. But normal social attachment cannot be formed or maintained in the absence of the amygdala, which does not mature until about two to three months, confirming our understanding that feeding and attachment are separate processes.

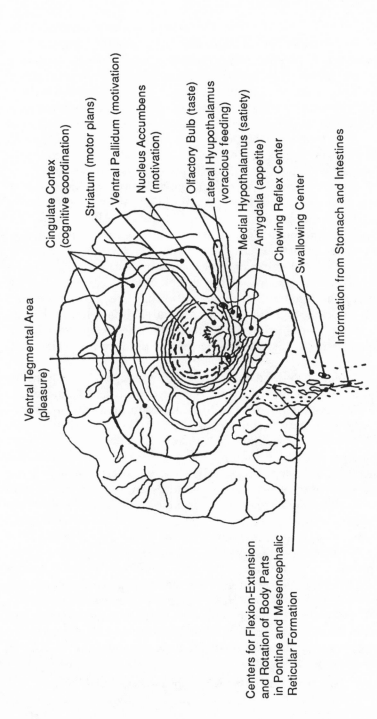

Ventral Tegmental Area
(pleasure)

Cingulate Cortex
(cognitive coordination)

Striatum (motor plans)

Ventral Pallidum (motivation)

Nucleus Accumbens
(motivation)

Olfactory Bulb (taste)

Lateral Hyupothalamus
(voracious feeding)

Medial Hypothalamus (satiety)

Amygdala (appetite)

Chewing Reflex Center

Swallowing Center

Information from Stomach and Intestines

Centers for Flexion-Extension
and Rotation of Body Parts
in Pontine and Mesencephalic
Reticular Formation

Fig. 6 Motivational System Based on the Regulation of Physiological Requirements—Feeding Mechanisms

The nutritive system consists of many components,[1] beginning at the brain-stem level to which we have already referred. This area provides stereotyped motor functions that can be stimulated by appropriate stimuli (touch to the cheek or lips) and have a reflexive quality. The precise location of "centers" for these functions has not been established in humans, but among those that are known to be organized according to flexion-extension, the center for rotation of body parts is located in the pontile and mesencephalic reticular formation. The chewing reflex is controlled by nuclei in the hindbrain. Swallowing centers are found in the medulla and lower pons.

Higher centers, however, are needed for the orchestration of when and how these mechanisms are to be utilized for the homeostatic maintenance of the organism. The hypothalamus is the primary site for the mediation of hunger and satiety. Stimulation of the lateral hypothalamus produces voracious appetite; stimulation of the ventromedial nuclei of the hypothalamus causes aphagia to a degree which can end in death if not alleviated. The lateral hypothalamus is designated the hunger or feeding area, while the ventromedial nucleus is designated a satiety area. It is believed that the satiety area operates primarily by inhibiting the feeding area.

But what stimulates the feeding area to produce a so-called oral drive?

The regulation of food intake can be divided into long-term, or nutritional, regulation, which is concerned primarily with maintenance of normal quantities of nutrient stores in the body; and short-term, or alimentary, regulation, which is concerned with the immediate effects of feeding on the alimentary tract.

Long-term regulation requires the action of several mechanisms in concert. A primary theory, called the glucostatic theory, holds that an increase in blood glucose produces an increase in electrical activity in the satiety area and a concomitant decrease in electrical activity in the feeding area. Observations support this theory. Furthermore, it has been observed that the satiety area and no other part of the hypothalamus concentrates glucose.

Increased amino acid concentrations also reduce feeding but not as strongly as the glucose effect. The overall degree of feeding normally varies inversely with the amount of adipose tissue in the body. The "lipostatic" theory proposes that since the average concentration of free fatty acids in blood is directly proportional to adipose tissue in the body, free fatty acids act in the same manner as

---

[1]Guyton (1987) provides much of the basic information contained in this discussion of the nutritive system.

glucose and amino acids to create a negative feedback regulatory effect on feeding. The mechanisms involved in nutrient intake appear to be different from those that regulate calorie intake (Wurtman, 1987). The proportion of protein to carbohydrate in daily intake seems to be genetically determined and the transmitter serotonin appears to be involved in regulating this proportion. Carbohydrate consumption produces an acceleration of serotonin synthesis and release, whereas protein consumption produces the opposite effect. Increasing brain serotonin decreases carbohydrate consumption. Consumption of carbohydrate-rich foods seems to lift mood by virtue of elevating serotonin in the brain, a fact that helps explain some of the abuses of the feeding mechanism in the service of modulation of mood.

Input from the gastrointestinal tract about its level of distention, as well as hormonal feedback via cholecystokinin, which is released in response to fat entering the duodenum, has a strong inhibitory effect on the feeding area. There is also a metering of food by "head receptors," which "measure" the amount of chewing, salivation, swallowing and tasting even if the food never reaches the stomach (as in esophageal fisula) and also produce satiety. The advantage of having both fast and slow control mechanisms is that the gastrointestinal tract can work at a steady pace rather than having to feed on energy demands.

The contribution of taste to appetite is a complex one. A positive response to sweet taste is innate and independent of caloric consideration. Smiling responses to sweetness can be elicited immediately after birth. Sour- and bitter-tasting substances elicit extrusion responses and grimacing (Steiner, 1977). A salty taste does not produce aversion at the mouth level, nor, apparently, do the osmolality monitors function very efficiently in newborns to prevent the ingestion of excess salt.

The condition of *alliesthesia* further complicates the evaluation of taste. Alliesthesia, as defined by Cabanac (1971, 1979), is the condition whereby the pleasantness of sensory stimuli is determined by the state of the internal environment. Stellar and Stellar (1985) have expanded this definition to include virtually all motivated behaviors, for which sensory responsiveness is determined by the state of the internal environment (beyond the neonatal period at least). This, of course, explains how sweetness (though innately pleasurable) can become aversive if blood glucose levels are already high (Cabanac, 1971).

At an even higher level of organization, we encounter the concept of appetite, which denotes hunger plus a desire for specific foods; quality appraisals are added to quantity considerations. The centers for appetite include especially the amygdala and the limbic cortical systems (infraorbital, hippocampal, and cingulate). The sense of smell is very prominent in the determination of appetite, and the amygdala is a major component of the olfactory system (Guyton, 1987). Pribam (1980) cites a case of a patient who had temporal lobectomy and amygdalectomy who ate voraciously on visual cuing from food while denying any subjective hunger. Moreover, inedibles are frequently mouthed in the Kluver-Bucy syndrome (amygdalectomy and temporal lobectomy). The amygdala, therefore, seems indispensable in the mediation of appetitive hunger.

When stimulated, some areas of the amygdala increase feeding while others decrease it. Stimulation of still other areas can trigger the mechanical acts of feeding, bypassing the control centers of the hypothalamus. The limbic cortical areas all have areas that, on stimulation, can produce increased or decreased feeding activities, but these areas also play a role in the exploratory search for food when hunger is present.

To summarize: The basic mechanics of feeding activities are organized in the brain stem. The hypothalamus operates as an integrator of multiple measures of blood glucose, amino acids, and fatty acids, as well as oral activity and gastrointestinal distention, to activate the feeding system or the satiety area, which in turn inhibits the feeding system.

The amygdala and limbic cortex contribute appetite, or the qualitative element, to feeding as well as working in concert with the hypothalamus to issue commands to the lower centers to initiate actual feeding activities. This system develops from below to above, with the brain stem and hypothalamus fully functional at birth and the limbic system maturing by three months of postnatal life.

The nutritive system is dominated by innately preprogrammed, set-point biochemical monitors and attains true motivational significance by aligning itself with the attachment and sensual systems. The idea of an oral drive has been much overrated, and the only case in which we see oral intake as usurping a prominent position among the motivational systems is in is misuse in the service of mood regulation or as a distortion of the effectance (power and control) system or assertion of "pseudoautonomy".

With this impressive array of capabilities for determining the internal needs of the organism and the ability to communicate need through crying, the neonate is prepared to interact with a caregiver in a most sophisticated way. If the caregiver is even moderately competent and not crippled by her own past experience with procedural memories of poor feeding experiences, which are not available for conscious revision, she will be able to compensate for the infant's motoric deficits and respond to its superior internal sensory monitoring.

The importance of regular internal signals creating discomfort and the assistance of the caregiver in helping the infant to restore comfort by reestablishing familiarity cannot be over emphasized as the substrate for the development of an emergent self (Stern, 1985). If, however, hunger experiences are chaotic and irregular, no strong baseline of familiarity can be laid down in procedural memory, and the development of coherent self-experience (so dependent on familiarity) is impeded. This is apparently independent of the attachment processes, which should be developing in parallel. The infant can, however, be simply hungry without craving human contacts and vice versa. Also the feeding mechanisms in the brain stem and hypothalamus are in place at birth, whereas the amygdalar contribution to appetite and active seeking for food cannot be present prior to amygdalar maturation at two to three months of age. We must conclude, then, that these systems are not inextricably linked.

The elimination systems are immature at birth, and wastes pass from the body in reflexively controlled processes until maturation of the external sphincter mechanism occurs. After the acquisition of voluntary muscle control (usually sometime in the latter half of the first year), relaxation of the internal sphincter and forward movement of feces toward the anus normally initiate an instantaneous contraction of the external sphincter, which temporarily prevents defecation. At this point, voluntary conscious control takes over to permit or deter defecation. If the external sphincter is kept contracted, the defecation reflexes die out in a few minutes and can remain quiescent for hours (Guyton, 1987). This process can be repeated to the point of producing a "voluntary" constipation, as is seen in children who get into conflict over bowel training or who use their bowel functioning to express other intercurrent conflicts particularly those involving autonomy and control. Such a state of affairs illustrates the way in which bowel function can gain true motivational "significance" by serving the attachment and assertive systems.

Here again, as well as with the feeding systems, we see that the child has sophisticated mechanisms to provide for excretion, and all that is required of the caregiver (whether the child is trained by "catching" or at a time when voluntary control over the external sphincter has been gained) is to facilitate and shape the child's use of his own capacities. The excretory functions are a veritable playground for power struggles, especially after the child acquires conscious control over this external sphincter!

As Dr. Lichtenberg has noted, "anal traumas" have been encountered less frequently in recent years. When present, they appear to involve a caretaker's attempts to violate the normal mechanisms of excretion by bypassing or overriding the external sphincter's voluntary control with enemas or laxatives. Our first reaction to this sort of situation is outrage at intrusion, but as Dr. Lichtenberg's case so clearly illustrates, other meanings can be attached to these events once secondary-process elaboration becomes available. Like "oral" mechanisms, the "anal" phase serves more as a marker for other more important intercurrent developmental issues having to do with social interactions. The motivational significance of both oral and anal issues has been considerably overrated.

Another source of complication lies in the close proximity of sexual and excretory orifices and their shared innervations through the pelvic nerves and pudendal nerve to the sacral segments of the spinal cord. This state of affairs leads to the propensity toward erotization of excretory functions; stimulation of the anus or the urinary tract as well as perineal areas can produce sexual sensations.

THE ATTACHMENT-AFFILIATION MOTIVATIONAL SYSTEM

Attachment is the internalized representation of repetitive interactions with caregivers, where expectancies are generated and usually met, resulting not only in a maintenance of proximity to the essential caregivers but also to an enhancement of the awareness of self as familiarity is established in this matrix (Fig. 7).

How is this internalized representation of familiar neuronal firing patterns built? Dr. Lichtenberg has supplied us with ample data about the contributions of audition to attachment. The visual system, though less mature at birth, is also crucial for an internal representation of attachment. The human infant is biased toward fixating visually on human faces and, as mentioned in the section on the amygdala, certain cells are able to respond differentially to facial features. A fairly good-sized area on the basal surface of the brain is specialized for facial recognition. The occipital portion is contiguous with the primary visual cortex, and the temporal portion is closely associated with the limbic system (Guyton, 1987). These areas interact to contribute to the visual portion of this system.

Somatic sensations, as well as auditory and visual inputs, are combined with vestibular sensations in the superior colliculus and

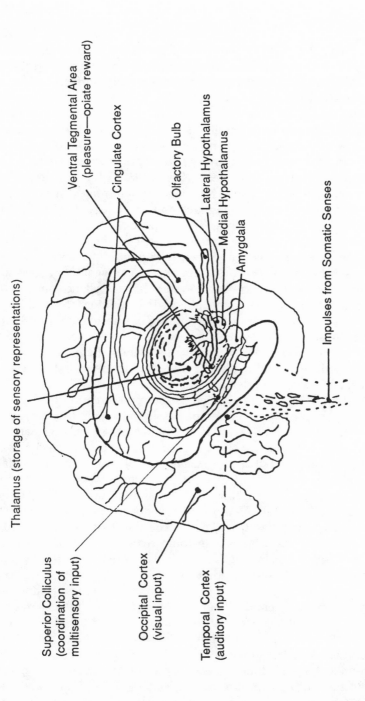

Thalamus (storage of sensory representations)

Superior Colliculus
(coordination of
multisensory input)

Occipital Cortex
(visual input)

Temporal Cortex
(auditory input)

Ventral Tegmental Area
(pleasure—opiate reward)

Cingulate Cortex

Olfactory Bulb

Lateral Hypothalamus

Medial Hypothalamus

Amygdala

Impulses from Somatic Senses

Fig. 7   Attachment-Affiliation Motivational System

are coordinated with movements of the body to fixate on stimuli. Kandel (1981) states that "in addition to the visual representation, the colliculus also contains maps of the body surface and of the cochlea" (p. 237).

This condensed and multimodal information is passed into the amygdala, which is absolutely essential to forming and maintaining attachment and affiliation. Amygdalectomized animals in free-ranging situations do not engage in appropriate social behaviors and become isolated from peers (Price, 1987). Humans after amygdalectomy show the usual Kluver-Bucy syndrome (inappropriate appetites: social, sexual and edible, and also a loss of the *significance* of what they are perceiving). The concept of attachment implies a significance or personal meaning as well as the perception alone that hippocampal processing yields. Hippocampal processing can be called the "knowledge" system and the amygdalar processing a "belief" system. Only the belief system has impellance and can activate behavioral systems and affect. The addition of the affective component is dependent on the routing of information into the hypothalamus, which activates the behavioral displays of affect and attachment (Hadley, 1985). The amygdala sends efferents to both the medial and the lateral hypothalamus, thus influencing both the assertive and aversive systems.

But how is significance added to the representation of the interaction with the caregiver by processing through the amygdala? Some dramatic findings by Panksepp et al. (1978) Herman and Panksepp, (1978) have shed new light on the possible mechanisms. Panksepp proposes that the social bond is sustained by opiate-sensitive systems of the brain, that normal social contacts may chronically activate the brain's opiate system, and that separation distress is the result of a relative endogenous endorphin withdrawal. He concludes that it is conceivable that maternal contact comfort stimulates a brain endorphin reward system in the infant that reinforces attachment formation. Panksepp and his coworkers speculate that this system operates throughout life to sustain social attachment and comment on its addictionlike qualities. Bridges and Grimm (1982) suggest that there is a complementary mechanism in normal maternal behavior that is opiate mediated.

But what of "bad" attachments? Because both "good" and "bad" encounters mobilize attention and affect, they mobilize the endorphin-enkephlin-attachment system and can account for the tenacity of attachment to an abusing parent (Hadley, 1985). It appears that a bad attachment is better than none at all, as we can see from the infants with marasmus and failure to thrive. Also the severe attachment disorders seen in some borderline person's preclude treatment because those persons are not able to mobilize social connection or a sense that anything matters enough to motivate the process.

At a more mature stage of development, affiliation becomes important, and the attachment system also serves an attachment to social groups, ideals, and symbols and is crucial to the development of conscience.

THE EXPLORATORY, ASSERTIVE, AND AVERSIVE MOTIVATIONAL SYSTEMS

These systems utilize the basic limbic information-processing assembly, including hippocampus, amygdala, hypothalamus, and basal ganglia, and are essential to all motivational systems. As Dr. Lichtenberg (this volume) puts it, "Exploration and assertion can be thought of as component properties of any motivational system that is dominant at a particular time." His assertion that these are motivational systems in their own right is also well-taken. (Fig. 8).

We must return to our concept of satisfaction in the pattern matching process for an understanding of the competence or effectance functions. The hippocampus is pivotal in the exploratory (attentive) process that actively seek linkages of stimuli and response in a system inherently activated by the reticular system (see section on The Hippocampus). It is clear from Dr. Lichtenberg's data that these exploratory and effectance functions predate the development of amygdalar (affective and attachment) functions and only later recruit the pleasure/reward system per se. The infant's smile of recognition appears to signal the functional competence of the amygdalar/affective system.

The exploratory and assertive motivations persist throughout life and are the mediators of curiosity and challenge. We climb mountains not "because they are there," but because our reticulo-septo-hippocampal exploratory system is active and we are receiving external stimuli that are sufficiently novel!

At the point of comparison, the results of match and mismatch have separate fates and branch into assertive and aversive behavior outputs. Both involve components of the amygdala, hypothalamus, and basal ganglia, which are all organized along activatory and inhibatory lines. Motor programs for outputs in both assertive and aversive modes are scattered throughout the neuraxis from the level of the brain-stem reflexive actions (sucking/assertive; extrusion/aversive) to high-level motor plans coordinated in the basal ganglia,

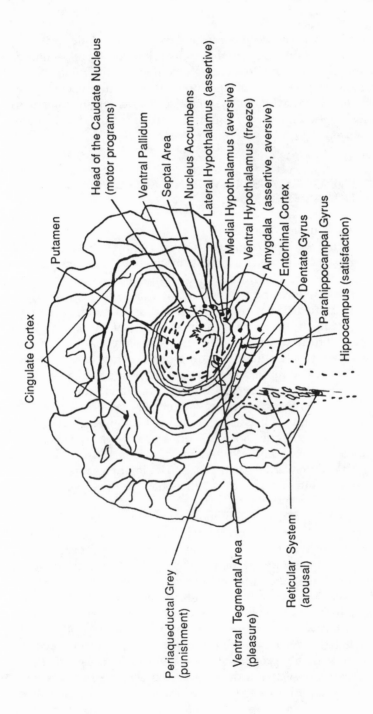

Cingulate Cortex

Putamen

Head of the Caudate Nucleus
(motor programs)

Ventral Pallidum

Septal Area

Nucleus Accumbens

Lateral Hypothalamus (assertive)

Medial Hypothalamus (aversive)

Ventral Hypothalamus (freeze)

Amygdala (assertive, aversive)

Entorhinal Cortex

Dentate Gyrus

Parahippocampal Gyrus

Hippocampus (satisfaction)

Periaqueductal Grey
(punishment)

Ventral Tegmental Area
(pleasure)

Reticular System
(arousal)

Fig. 8 The Exploratory-Assertive & Aversive Motivational Systems

which organize complex sequential actions and mediate the highest levels of creative functioning (painting a picture; playing a complex score on a flute). The fight or flight mechanisms are programmed similarly. Antagonism and withdrawal are augmented after the neonatal period by the affects of anger and fear, both of which have particularly energizing components and feed back into the reticular activating system to enhance arousal.

There is no evidence in the neurophysiological literature for an aggressive "drive," something that arises de novo somewhere in the system and requires discharge. Instead, all aversive responses are *reactions* to the condition of mismatch either in homeostatic mechanisms or the hippocampal comparator. This view coincides perfectly with that of Parens that "hostile destructiveness, rather than a constitutionally determined drive which obligatorily presses for discharge, is activated by specific experiences which have a common denominator, excessively-felt unpleasure" (quoted by Lichtenberg, this volume). A "freeze" mechanism, which can be elicited in several limbic structures on electrical stimulation and which are particularly prominent in the most ventral hypothalamus, appears to be the result of extreme cases of mismatch that are simply too intense to permit response selection. (Grossman, 1987).

The neurotransmitters involved in assertive and aversive systems are quite different. Dopamine and norepinephrine appear to be essential mediators of the assertive system, while serotonin and acetylcholine have been linked to the mediation of aversive states (Wise, 1983; Depue and Spoont, 1986; Ashton, 1987).

In the beginning, infants experience comfort or discomfort according to the outcomes of homeostatic processes but quickly expand their reportoire to exploration for the sake of matching patterns, with further stimulus feedback leading to "competency" and effectance satisfaction. This state of affairs is quickly supplemented by the maturation of affective systems, with their augmentation of affects lending pleasure and unpleasure to the processing of information (Panksepp, 1981).

THE SENSUAL MOTIVATIONAL SYSTEMS

In the light of their neurobiology, the sensual systems should be viewed as distinct from the sexual motivational system. It is true that both the attachment/affiliative and the sexual motivational systems, as well as the homeostatic system, rely heavily on sensual input particularly in the tactile and vestibular modalities. However, it is clear that sensual experience alone can be quite pleasurable and innately motivating. Let us turn to the tactile and vestibular systems to begin our exploration of sensual systems.

The cutaneous system is the first to mature, followed closely by the vestibular system. Both are functionally operative prenatally (Gottlieb, 1987). The skin is endowed with a multiplicity of touch, pressure, and vibratory receptors, including a newly identified tickle and itch receptor (Guyton, 1987). These receptors are specialized to discriminate not only the type of contact with the cutaneous surface, but also a broad range of intensities of such contact. These sensations travel via the spinal cord (medial lemniscus and anterolateral tracts) to the sensory thalamus and thence to the somatic sensory areas and the sensory association cortex (Fig. 9). The columnar arrangement of the cortex allows for return information (especially from cortical layers V and VI) to the thalamus and brain stem. It appears that sensations can directly access the hedonic centers in the ventral tegmentum and periaqueductal gray, and indirectly access them through descending fibers from layers V and VI in the association cortices, as well as producing pleasure or punishment through the amygdalar/affect system.

We know that certain levels and qualities of sensations appear innately pleasurable while others (such as itch or too intense pressure), which activate the pain system, are unpleasant even without affective information or contributions from memory. There also seem to be individual variations to stimulation tolerance, typified by Dr. Lichtenberg's example of Jimbo, who was supersensitive to all forms of light touch but apparently could tolerate pressure without overstimulation.

All sensual systems seem to have broad, innate generalities of pleasurable and unpleasant sensation. In general, very high levels of stimulation tend to elicit pain more or less directly. Very low levels of stimulation can lead to hallucinatory phenomena as a result of innate activity in the system without sufficient external input and are generally aversive. In the middle range the large majority of inputs from the sensors to the central nervous system are neither pleasurable nor displeasing, but indifferent (Cabanac, 1987). In this respect this system functions like the physiological homeostatic systems in that innately programmed patterns yield a measure of pleasure/pain without needing to be processed through the conparator assembly; that is, they are not learned. Cabanac (1987) concludes that "the most effective and probably only primary positive reinforcers are chemical, thermal and mechanical stimuli" (p. 956).

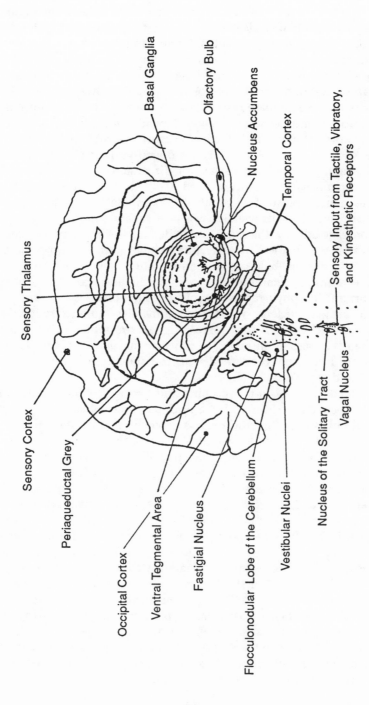

Sensory Cortex

Sensory Thalamus

Basal Ganglia

Olfactory Bulb

Nucleus Accumbens

Temporal Cortex

Periaqueductal Grey

Occipital Cortex

Ventral Tegmental Area

Fastigial Nucleus

Flocculonodular Lobe of the Cerebellum

Vestibular Nuclei

Nucleus of the Solitary Tract

Vagal Nucleus

Sensory Input from Tactile, Vibratory, and Kinesthetic Receptors

Fig. 9 The Sensual Motivational System

Of course we know that both learning and the state of the organism (sweet is no longer pleasurable in a state of satiety) can alter the hedonic response to any stimulus. Some stimuli, such as color, musical sounds, sweet taste, rocking, the human face, appear to be innately pleasing unless learning by aversive circumstances overrides the natural reaction. My reason for believing that these patterns are innate is that the neonate responds with apparent interest and positive hedonic tone to such stimuli and avoids others with a show of great discomfort *before* the affective/pleasure assembly is operative.

We know that the pain system is operative prenatally and that the anatomical connectivity exists for direct access to pleasure and pain mechanisms from birth onward (Gottlieb, 1987). It follows that sensual stimulation may be sought for its innately pleasurable sake alone or avoided for its aversiveness as a separate motivation.

In order to address the need for tactile and vestibular proprioceptive system stimulation in early infancy, we need to know something about the vestibulo-cerebellar apparatus. We will not dwell on the cerebellum in detail but will focus on the areas concerned with equilibrium, the phylogenetically old flocculonondular lobe and its related fastigial nucleus, which are intimately connected with the vestibular nuclei. From these areas, signals are sent up and down into the cord, passing through the reticular nuclei in the brain stem, which are intimately concerned with the state of activation of the system and sleep/waking (Guyton, 1987).

A related mechanism for soothing and toning vestibular function seems to be mediated through the nucleus of the solitary tract: electrical stimulation of this nucleus has a synchronizing effect on forebrain EEG activity that long outlasts the stimulation (Kandel and Schwartz, 1985). Stimulation of afferent fibers in the vagus nerve also produces EEG synchrony, as does mild, low-frequency (3–8 HZ) stimulation of certain cutaneous nerves. Kandel and Schwartz have suggested that, "perhaps this frequency-sensitive mechanism calms the gently rocked baby" (pg. 655).

As Dr. Lichtenberg has pointed out, however, pleasure from sensual systems can intrude on the normal functioning of other systems to exclude more normal motivations, as it does in the case of intense seeking of tactile stimulation in an infant deprived of such stimulation for a long time. On the other hand, we have to attribute our sense of esthetics to basic sensual pleasure plus a cognitive and affective component (Cabanac, 1987). I do not believe that we must view our esthetic enjoyment as a sublimation of sexual motivation but as a sensual motivation in its own right that has matured and gained cognitive and affective components.

THE SEXUAL MOTIVATIONAL SYSTEM

This system is extremely complex and is sexually dimorphic (i.e. males and females have differences in neural structure as well as function) (Fig. 10). It consists of many components from lower spinal reflexes to cerebral cortex with the hypothalamus serving as a critical way station for integrating many divergent components. This system, more than any other motivational system, is a neuroendocrine system, with hormonal influences on neural cell populations being very crucial to the overall function of the system.

Developmentally, the brain of a fetus is essentially undifferentiated and bipotential and will assume the female form and psychosocial orientation unless acted upon by male hormones (Kandel and Schwartz, 1985). The critical period for the actions of testosterone secreted by the testes of the male to operate on the reproductive tract and brain is 12 to 20 weeks of gestation in the human (McEwen, 1987).

In addition to masculinization by creating a permanent sensitization to androgens, the male brain is somewhat later "defeminized," rendering the estrogen receptor bearing cells resistant to behavioral effects of circulating estrogen (Kandel and Schwartz, 1985). Gonadal hormones, primarily testosterone, estrogen, and progesterone, exert their influences not only on peripheral organs but in hormone-sensitive sites in various regions of the brain. Estrogen is concentrated by cells in larger amounts than androgens, but both steroid hormones are found in approximately the same brain regions in both sexes. These steroid-concentrating cells are located primarily in the medio-basal (tuberal) region of the hypothalamus. These include the ventromedial, arcuate, and anterior nuclei; as well as the preoptic, cortical, and medial nuclei of the amygdala; the lateral septum; and to a lesser extent the ventral hippocampus. The mesencephalic central gray also contains estrogen receptor sites (Richmond and Clemens, 1987). Besides inducing selective responsiveness to hormones, events during the same critical period create in the brain a gender-specific, organizational blueprint that in adulthood will lead to the expression of appropriate sexual behaviors in response to hormonal stimulation (Kelly, 1985).

In response to neural activity in the hypothalamus, gonadotropic-releasing hormone (luteinizing hormone-releasing hormone LHRH) is produced. In the human the midbasal region of the hypothalamus is the area most importantly involved in influencing the rate of secretion of LHRH, which has a strong effect on inducing gonadotropin secretion from the anterior pituitary (Guyton, 1987). Both males

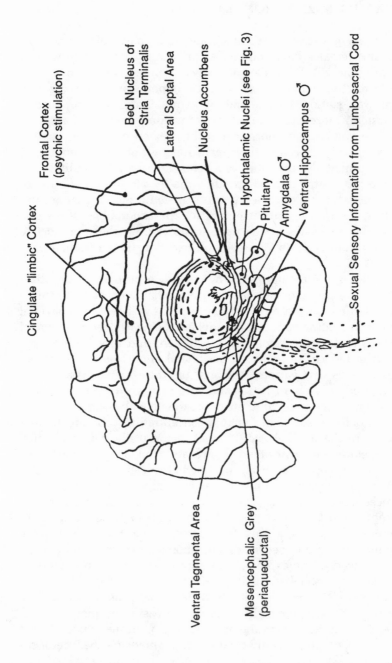

Cingulate "limbic" Cortex

Frontal Cortex
(psychic stimulation)

Bed Nucleus of
Stria Terminalis

Lateral Septal Area

Nucleus Accumbens

Hypothalamic Nuclei (see Fig. 3)

Pituitary

Amygdala ♂

Ventral Hippocampus ♂

Sexual Sensory Information from Lumbosacral Cord

Ventral Tegmental Area

Mesencephalic Grey
(periaqueductal)

Fig. 10 The Sexual Motivational System

and females secrete two gonadotropins (gonad-stimulating hormones) from the anterior pituitary: luteinizing hormone (LH) and follicle-stimulating hormone (FSH). In males these hormones are secreted at a steady rate, whereas in females a cyclic rather than tonic stimulation prevails (Kandel and Schwartz, 1985).

It is now certain that gonadotropin-releasing hormone is not secreted in childhood in males until some maturation process in the brain causes the hypothalamus to begin secreting LHRH at the time of puberty, although testes and anterior pituitary are all fully functional at birth if stimulated hormonally. It is currently believed that the maturational process necessary to trigger puberty occurs outside the hypothalamus, and the amygdala has been tagged as a possible locus of this function (Guyton, 1987).

At the onset of puberty, male and female hormonal events are quite divergent. In the male, the hypothalamus begins to secrete LHRH, which in turn stimulates the anterior pituitary to secrete luteinizing hormone, which then stimulates hyperplasia of testicular Leidig cells and the production of testosterone by these cells. Testosterone feeds back negatively to the hypothalamus to inhibit production of LHRH, thus keeping levels of both in equilibrium. Spermatogenesis is also a feedback relationship with FSH, and this mechanism is thought to be mediated by a product of the Sertoli cells (nutrients provide for developing spermatazoa) called inhibin.

In the female, puberty is produced by a gradual increase in gonadotropic hormone secretion by the pituitary, beginning in the eighth year of life and culminating in the onset of menstration between 11 and 16 years. The female menstrual cycle, with its characteristic variations in hormones, is generally familiar to us. We, therefore, will not dwell on this system but will go on to an exploration of the mechanisms of the sexual act itself.

In the male, the most important source of sensory impulses for initiating the male sexual act is the glans penis. The glans contains a highly organized sensory end-organ system that transmits into the central nervous system a special modality of sensation called *sexual sensation*, which appears to be different from ordinary cutaneous sensation. Impulses from this and adjacent areas of the anal epithelium, scrotum, and internal structures, such as the urethra, bladder, prostate, seminal vesticles, testes, and vas deferens, are transmitted via the pudendal nerve into the sacral portion of the spinal cord to areas of the brain stem, hypothalamus, and limbic and cortical structures. One stimulus to sexual arousal is proposed to be the overfilling of the sexual organs with secretions. Although psychic elements clearly greatly enhance the ability of a man to perform the sexual act, appropriate genital stimulation can cause ejaculation occasionally in humans even when the cord has been completely severed above the lumbar region. Clearly, then, the male sexual act results from inherent reflex mechanisms integrated in the sacral and lumbar spinal cord, and these mechanisms can be initiated by either psychic stimulation or actual sexual stimulation.

Erection and lubrication are parasympathetically controlled by impulses that pass from the sacral portion of the spinal cord through the nervi erigentes to the penis, causing dilation of the arteries to the corpus cavernosum. Emission and ejaculation are sympathetically controlled when sexual stimulation reaches a certain intensity, the reflex centers in the cord emit sympathetic impulses that leave the cord at L–1 and L–2, passing through the hypogastric plexus to initiate emission, the precursor of ejaculation. During emission, sperm, prostatic fluid and seminal fluid are expelled into the internal urethra and combine with mucus from the bulbo-urethral glands to produce semen. Filling of the internal urethra produces signals transmitted through the pudendal nerves to the sacral cord. These signals, in turn, produce rhythmic contractions of the ischio-cavernosus and bulbo-cavernosus muscles, the ejaculation proper. After ejaculation, male sexual excitement disappears almost entirely within one to two minutes, and the reflex system is refractory to further stimulation for varying lengths of time.

On the basis of studies using electrical stimulation, ablation, and implants, it has been concluded that the dorsomedial preoptic area is most important in maintaining male copulatory behavior and that the ventromedial nucleus is essential to sexually receptive behavior in the female. The amygdala, bed nucleus of the stria terminalis and rostral midbrain sites, seem to partially mediate functions of the sexual act and may be more involved in general arousal mechanisms accompanying the activity (Richmond and Clemens, 1987). In contrast to their roles in males, the amygdala, hippocampus, and septal areas do not play a very significant part in sexuality in the female.

There are many parallels but also some important discrepancies between male and female in the mediation of the sexual act. First of all, the buildup of sexual excitement and its waning after orgasm are far more gradual in the female than in the male. Sexual interest in the female is more dependent on high gonadotropin levels (estrogen in preovulatory phase) than males interest is on the vicissitudes of androgen. Also female receptivity seems less dependent on lumbo-sacral reflexes than is the male erection, but orgasm depends on them, with the implication that females require more psychic stimulation to attain orgastic capacity. Although not essential for conception, the orgasm does enhance the likelihood of impregnation by increasing uterine and fallopian tube motility and by dilating the cervical canal. Innervation of the sexual structures in general follows a course to the cord and back similar to that in the male. The genitalia are innervated with the same special sexual sensors as the penis.

What can we conclude about sexual motivation from these data? It seems clear that the sexual structures have a biphasic development and function. We may for convenience call the early phase nonreproductive and the mature phase reproductive. The sexual structures are functional at birth, as evidenced by erection in the male and engorgement in the female during REM sleep. Also the experience of pleasure from sexual organ stimulation is operative from very early on, and apparently this special category of sensation is inherently pleasurable (e.g., sweet taste). The capacity for masturbatory sexual activity, like nocturnal erection and engorgement, is present without the hypothalamic components, and masturbation continues in male primates even though copulatory ability is lost through destruction of the dorsomedial preoptic area (Richmond and Clemens, 1987).

Another aspect of nonreproductive sexuality is the form of juvenile play behavior. Rough-and-tumble play requires an *androgenized brain* even though androgens do not have to be present at the time of the behavior (McEwen, 1987).

Thus we can see that the sexual apparatus is a source of inherent pleasure and soothing (probably because of the rhythmicity of masturbatory activity) and only later acquires an object-oriented form when the hypothalamus, under the influence of maturation, begins to secrete gonadotrophic releasing hormone to stimulate the anterior pituitary to produce gonadatropins. Clinical experience with sexual abuse victims suggests that premature sexual stimulation by an outside agent can stimulate the hypothalamus to premature sexual maturation, producing precocious puberty particularly in females.

Masturbatory (nonreproductive) sexuality depends functionally on spinal reflexive organization in the beginning and only later recruits higher centers, for example, for the elaboration of fantasy (probably around age three). However, true object-related sexuality can occur only after hypothalamic maturation, when the sexual act acquires the enhancement of many sensory inputs and affect.

The sexual systems operate quite differently pre- and postpuberty. Indeed, we might say that this mechanism more fittingly belongs to the sensual system in the prepuberty and should be viewed as truly sexual only postpuberty.

Sexual sensation both before and after puberty, however, has a different quality from other sensual pleasures, which gives it its distinctive, compelling quality. This sort of stimulation is sought not only for its pleasurable quality, but also for soothing and as a mechanism for overall arousal and organization of neural firing patterns. As a matter of fact, the use of sexuality for purposes other than reproduction continually leads to *conflicts* in motivation (e.g., when a pregnancy results from a basically nonreproductive sexual activity). The preemptoriness of sexual sensation is probably the biological fact that lead Freud to assign this motivational system such a central position in his scheme of drives. However, as we have discovered by our explorations in this chapter, the sexual system does not deserve to be the centerpiece of motivation. Instead, a balance between systems appears to be the ideal situation.

OVERVIEW

With this complex arrangement of motivational systems, which are clearly distinct but operate in such proximity, the possibilities for one system to blend with another, or dominate overall motivation, or simply to get out of balance with another, are endless under the impact of lived experience. Indeed, the particular constellation of priorities of the various systems might be used to define individual personalities. Using the gastro-intestinal system to attain pleasure and to soothe anxiety in obesity and choosing inappropriate objects for sexual stimulation, in fetishism, are but two blatant examples of distortion in motivational systems. The use of several systems in the pursuit of a specific aim or goal is also universal. (It is assumed that each system has aims and goals that are developed and maintained by the memory system and mature epigenetically [Gedo, 1979].) Homeostatic mechanisms function to keep the organism in working order while it pursues effectance pleasure from the exploratory-assertive system, for example producing a work of art, which also stimulates the sensual motivational system. In the process, both satisfaction and pleasure are evoked and both deliver reward and provide reinforcement to repeat the rewarded activities.

The contributions that neuroscience can make to refining our theoretical concepts of mental functioning are immeasurable. How Freud would have loved to be alive in these times!

References

Ainsworth, M. D. (1967), *Infancy in Uganda: Infant Care and the Growth of Love*. Baltimore, MD: Johns Hopkins University Press.

——— (1979), Attachment as related to mother-infant interaction. In: *Advances in the Study of Behavior*, ed. J. B. Rosenblatt, R. A. Hinde, C. Beer & M. Bushel. New York: Academic Press, pp. 1–51.

——— & Bell, R. Q. (1969), Some contemporary patterns of mother-infant interaction in the feeding situation. In: *Stimulation in Early Infancy*, ed. A. Ambrose. London: Academic Press, pp. 133–170.

Amsterdam, B. & Levitt, M. (1980), Consciousness of self and painful self-consciousness. *The Psychoanalytic Study of the Child*, 35:67–84. New Haven, CT: Yale University Press.

Anthi, P. (1983), Reconstruction of preverbal experiences. *S. Amer. Psychoanal. Assn.*, 3:33–58.

Appelbaum, H. (1982), Using the administration of the Brazelton Neonatal Assessment Scale to encourage the bonding of parents to their newborn babies. *Psychoanal. Inq.*, 1:643–657.

Arlow, J. A. & Brenner, C. (1964), *Psychoanalytic Concepts and the Structural Theory*. New York: International Universities Press.

Ashton, H. (1987), *Brain Systems, Disorders, and Psychotropic Drugs*, New York: Oxford Medical.

Atkins, R. (1982), Discovering daddy: The mother's role. In: *Father and Child*, ed. S. Cath, A. Gurwitt & J. Ross. Boston: Little, Brown, pp. 139–150.

Atwood, G. & Stolorow, R. (1984), *Structures of Subjectivity*. Hillsdale, NJ: The Analytic Press.

Ayres, A. (1979), *Sensory Integration and the Child*. Los Angeles: Western Psychological Services.

Bacal, H. (1985), Optimal responsiveness and the therapeutic process. In: *Progress in Self Psychology*, Vol. 1, ed. A. Goldberg. New York: Guilford Press, pp. 202–227.

Balzac, H. (1846–47), *Cousine Bette*. New York: Penguin, 1983.

Barglow, P., Vaughn, B. & Molitor, N. (1987), Effects of maternal absence due to employment on the quality of infant-mother attachment in a low-risk sample. *Child Devel.*, 58:945–954.

Basch, M. (1977), Developmental psychology and explanatory theory in psychoanalysis. *The Annual of Psychoanalysis*, 5:229–266. New York: International Universities Press.

—— (1983), Empathic understanding: A review of the concept and some theoretical considerations. *J. Amer. Psychoanal. Assn.*, 31:101–126.

—— (1988), The selfobject experience of the newborn. In: *Learning from Kohut: Progress in Self Psychology, Vol. 4*, ed. A. Goldberg. Hillsdale, NJ: The Analytic Press, pp. 101–104.

Beebe, B. & Lachmann, F. (1988a), Mother-infant mutual influences and precursors of psychic structure. In: *Frontiers in Self Psychology: Progress in Self Psychology, Vol. 3*, ed. A. Goldberg. Hillsdale, NJ: The Analytic Press, pp. 3–26.

—— & —— (1988b), The contribution of mother-infant mutual influence to the origins of self- and object representations. *Psychoanal. Psychol.*, 5:305–357.

—— & Stern, O. (1977), Engagement, disengagement and early object experiences. In: *Communicative Structures and Psychic Structures*, ed. M. Freedman & S. Grand. New York: Plenum Press, pp. 35–55.

Bell, R. Q. (1975), A congenital contribution to emotional response in early infancy and the preschool period. In: *Parent-Infant Interaction* (CIBA Foundation Symposium 33). New York: Elsevier, pp. 201–212.

Berman, S. (1982), Psychic structure reorganization in drug-dependent adolescents. *Psychoanal. Inq.*, 2:507–578.

Blass, E. M. & Teicher, M. H. (1980), Suckling. *Science*, 210:15–22.

Bornstein, M. (1985), How infant and mother jointly contribute to developing cognitive competence in the child. *Proc. Natl. Acad. Sci.*, 82:7470–7473.

Bornstein, Me. & Silver, D. (1985), The mirror: Psychoanalytic perspectives. *Psychoanal. Inq.*, 5:195–337.

Bower, T. G. R., Broughton, J. M. & Moore, M. K. (1970), Demonstration of intention in the reaching behavior of neonate humans. *Nature*, 228:679–680.

—— (1971), The object in the world of the infant. *Sci. Amer.* 225:30–38.

—— (1976), Receptive process in child development. *Sci. Amer.* 235:38–47.

Bowlby, J. (1958), The nature of a child's tie to his mother. *Internat. J. Psycho-Anal.*, 39:350–373.

—— (1960), Grief and mourning in infancy and early childhood. *The Psychoanalytic Study of the Child*, 15:9–52. New York: International Universities Press.

Brazelton, T. B. (1980), New knowledge about the infant from current research: Implications for psychoanalysis. Presented at meeting of American Psychoanalytic Association, San Francisco, May 3.

———— & Als, H. (1979), Four early stages in the development of mother-infant interaction. *The Psychoanalytic Study of the Child*, 34:349–371. New Haven, CT: Yale University Press.

Bridges, R. & Grimm, C. (1982), Reversal of morphine distribution of maternal behavior by concurrent treatment with opiate antagonist naloxone. *Science*, 218:166–168.

Brody, S. (1982), Psychoanalytic theories of infant development and its disturbances: A critical evaluation. *Psychoanal. Quart.*, 51:526–597.

Bronson, G. (1963), A neurological perspective on ego development in infancy. *J. Amer. Psychoanal. Assn.*, 11:55–65.

Brooks, J. & Lewis, M. (1974), Infants' responses to pictures of self, mother and other. Princeton, NJ: Educational Testing Service, No. 100 (unpublished).

———— & ———— (1976), Visual self-recognition in infancy: Contingency and the self-other distinction. Presented at Southeastern Conference on Human Development, Nashville, TN, April.

Broucek, F. (1979), Efficacy in infancy: A review of some experimental studies and their possible implications for clinical theory. *Internat. J. Psycho-Anal.*, 60:311–316.

Broussard, E. (1970), Maternal perception of the neonate as related to development. *Child Psychiat. Human Develop.*, 1:16–25.

———— (1976), Neonatal prediction and outcome at 10/11 years. *Child Psychiat. Human Develop.*, 7:85–93.

Bruner, J., & Sherwood, V. (1980), Thought, language, and interaction in infancy., Presented at First World Congress on Infant Psychiatry, Portugal, March 30–April 3.

Butler, R. (1953), Discrimination learning by rhesus monkeys to visual-exploration motivation. *J. Comp. Physiol. Psychol.*, 46:95–98.

Cabanac, M. (1971), Physiological role of pleasure. *Science*, 173:1103–1107.

———— (1979), Sensory pleasure. *Quart. Rev. Biol.*, 54:1–29.

Call, J. (1968), Lap and finger play in infancy; Implications for ego development. *Internat. J. Psycho-Anal.*, 49:375–378.

———— (1980), Some prelinguistic aspects of language development. *J. Amer. Psychoanal. Assn.*, 28:259–290.

Carlson, R. (1981). Studies in script theory. *J. Personal. Soc. Psychol.*, 40:501–510.

Carpenter, M. B. (1976), *Core Test of Neuroanatomy*. Baltimore, MD: Williams & Wilkins.

Chugani, H. T. & Phelps, M. E. (1986), Maturational changes in cerebral function in infants determined by FDG positron emission tomography. *Science*, 231:840–843.

Cole, P. (1986), Children's spontaneous control of facial expression. *Child Devel.*, 57:1309–1321.

Crockenberg, S. (1987), Predictors and correlates of anger toward and punitive control of toddlers by adolescent mothers. *Child Devel.*, 58:964–975.

Crow, T. J. & Arbuthnott, G. W. (1972), Function of catecholamine-containing neurones in mammalian central nervous system. *Nature* (new Biol.), 238:245–246.

Cummings, M. (1987), Coping with background anger in early childhood. *Child Devel.*, 58:976–984.

Cutrona, C. & Troutman, B. (1987), Social support, infant temperament, and parenting self-efficacy: A mediational model of postpartum depression. *Child Devel.*, 58:1507–1518.

Davenport, Y., Zahn-Waxler, C., Adland, M. & Mayfield, M. (1984), Early child rearing practices in families with a manic-depressive parent. *Amer. J. Psychiat.*, 141:230–235.

Deadwyler, S. A. (1987), Evoked potentials in the hippocampus and learning. In: *Encyclopedia of Neuroscience*, Vol. 1, ed. G. Adelman. Boston, MA: Birkhauser, pp. 411–412.

Decarie, T. G. (1962), *Intelligence and Affectivity in Early Childhood*. New York: International Universities Press, 1965.

DeCasper, A. J. & Fifer, W. P. (1980), Of human bonding: Newborns prefer their mothers' voices. *Science*, 208:1174–76.

Demos, V. (1985), The elusive infant. *Psychoanal. Inq.*, 5:553–568.

——— (1988), Affect and the development of the self: A new frontier. In: *Frontiers in Self Psychology: Progress in Self Psychology, Vol. 3*, ed. A. Goldberg. Hillsdale, NJ: The Analytic Press, pp. 27–54.

Depue, R. A. & Spoont, M. R. (1986), Conceptualizing a serotonin trait. *Annals of the New York Academy of Sciences*, 487:47–62. New York: New York Acad. Sci.

Dickstein, S. & Parke, R. (1988), Social referencing in infancy: A glance at fathers and marriage. *Child Devel.*, 59:506–511.

Dorpat, T. (1983), Denial, defect, symptom formation and construction. *Psychoanal. Inq.*, 3:223–254.

Dowling, S. (1977), Seven infants with esophageal atresia: A developmental study. *The Psychoanalytical Study of the Child*, 32:245–256. New Haven, CT: Yale University Press.

——— (1982a), Mental organization in the phenomena of sleep. *The Psychoanalytic Study of the Child*. New Haven, CT: Yale University Press, 37:285–302.

——— (1982b), Dreams and dreaming in relation to trauma in childhood. *Internat. J. Psycho-Anal.*, 63:157–166.

——— (1985), A Piagetian critique. *Psychoanal. Inq.*, 5:569–587.

Edelheit, H. (1968), Mythopoiesis and the primal scene. *The Psychoanalytic Study of Society*, 5:212–233. New York: International Universities Press.

Eimas, P. (1985), The perception of speech in early infancy. *Scient. Amer.*, 252:46–52.

———, Siqueland, E. R., Judczyk, P. & Vigerito, J. (1971), Speech perception in infants. *Science*, 218:1138–1141.

Ekman, P., Levenson, R. W. & Friesen, W. V. (1983), Universals and cultural differences in facial expressions of emotion. In: *Nebraska Symposium on Motivation*, Vol. 19, ed. J. K. Cole. Lincoln: University of Nebraska Press.

Emde, R. (1981a), Changing models of infancy and the nature of early development: Remodeling the foundation. *J. Amer. Psychoanal. Assn.*, 29:179–219.

―――― (1981b), Recent research findings and methodology. Presented at Interdisciplinary Colloquium on Infant Research, American Psychoanalytic Assn., New York, December.

―――― (1983), The prerepresentational self and its affective core. *The Psychoanalytic Study of the Child*, 38:165–192. New Haven, CT: Yale University Press.

―――― (1988a), Development terminable and interminable: 1. Innate and motivational factors from infancy. *Internat. J. Psycho-Anal.*, 69:23–42.

―――― (1988b), Development terminable and interminable: 2. Recent psychoanalytic theory and therapeutic considerations. *Internat. J. Psycho-Anal.*, 69:283–296.

―――― Gaensbauer, T., Metcalf, D., Koenig, K. & Wagonfeld, S. (1971), Stress and neonatal sleep. *Psychosom. Med.*, 33:491–497.

―――― Klingman, D., Reich, J. & Wade, J. (1978), Emotional expression in infancy: Initial studies of social signaling and an emergent model. In: *The Development of Affect*, ed. M. Lewis & L. Rosenblum. New York: Plenum Press.

Engel, G. (1979), Monica: A 25-year longitudinal study of the consequences of trauma in infancy. Presented at meeting of the American Psychoanalytic Association.

―――― & Erikson, E. (1953), Growth and crises of the healthy personality. In: *Personality in Nature, Society, and Culture*, ed. C. Kluckhorn, H. Murray & D. Schneider. New York: Knopf, pp. 185–225.

―――― (1959), Identity and the life cycle. *Psychological Issues*, Monogr. 1. New York: International Universities Press.

Erikson, E. (1959), *Identity and the Life Cycle*. New York: Norton, 1980.

Escalona, S. (1963), Patterns of infantile experience and the developmental process. *The Psychoanalytic Study of the Child*, 18:197–244. New York: International Universities Press.

―――― (1965), Some determinants of the individual differences in early ego development. *Trans. N.Y. Acad. Sci.*, Series II, 27:802–817.

Fagan, J. F. (1976), Infants' recognition of invariant features of faces. *Child Devel.*, 47:627–38.

―――― (1977), Infants' recognition of invariant features of faces. *Child Devel.*, 48:68–78.

Fajardo, B. (1988), Approaches to the empirical study of resilience and self-righting (unpublished).

Fast, I. (1979), Developments in gender identity: Gender differentiation in girls. *Internat. J. Psycho-Anal.*, 60:443–453.

Fein, G. & Apfel, N. (1979), Some preliminary observations on knowing and pretending. In: *Symbolic Functioning in Childhood*, ed. N. Smith & M. Franklin. Hillsdale, NJ: Lawrence Erlbaum Associates, pp. 87–100.

Festinger, L. (1954), A theory of social comparison processes. *Human Relat.*, 7:117–140.

―――― Pepitone, A. & Newcomb, T. (1952), Some consequences of deindividuation in a group. *J. Abnorm. Soc. Psychol.*, 47:382–389.

Field, T. (1979), Games parents play with normal and high-risk infants. *Child Psychiat. Human Devel.*, 10:41–48.

—————— (1981), Fathers' interactions with their high-risk infants. *Infant Ment. Health J.*, 7:249–256.

Fisher, C., Cohen, H., Schiavi, R., Davis, D., Furman, B., Ward, K., Edwards, A. & Cunningham, J. (1983), Patterns of female sexual arousal during sleep and waking: Vaginal thermo-conductance studies. *Arch. Sex. Beh.*, 12:97–122.

Fiss, H. (1987), Experimental strategies for the study of the function of dreaming. Presented at 10th Annual Conf. on Self Psychology. Chicago, Oct. 1987.

Fisher, C., Gross, J. & Zuch, J. (1965), Cycle of penile erection synchronous with dreaming (REM) sleep. *Arch. Gen. Psychiat.*, 12:29–45.

Fosshage, J. (1988), Dream interpretation revisited. In: *Frontiers in Self Psychology*, ed. A. Goldberg. Hillsdale, NJ: The Analytic Press, pp. 161–176.

Fox, R. & McDaniel, C. (1982), The perception of biological motion by human infants. *Science*, 218:486–487.

Fraiberg, S. (1982), Pathological defenses in infancy. *Psychoanal. Quart.*, 51:612–635.

Freedman, D. (1975), Congenital and perinatal sensory deprivations: Their effect on the capacity to experience affect. *Psychoanal. Quart.*, 44:62–80.

Freud, A., (1936), *The Ego and the Mechanisms of Defense.* New York: International Universities Press, 1946.

—————— (1960), Discussion of Dr. John Bowlby's paper. *The Psychoanalytic Study of the Child*, 15:53–62. New York: International Universities Press.

—————— (1965), *Normality and Pathology in Childhood.* New York: International Universities Press.

Freud, S. (1900), The interpretation of dreams. *Standard Edition*, 4 & 5. London: Hogarth Press, 1953.

—————— (1905), Three essays on the theory of sexuality. *Standard Edition*, 7:135–243. London: Hogarth Press, 1953.

—————— (1908), On the sexual theories of children. *Standard Edition*, 9:209–226. London: Hogarth Press, 1959.

—————— (1913), The disposition to obsessional neurosis. *Standard Edition*, 12:317–326. London: Hogarth Press, 1958.

—————— (1915), Instincts and their vicissitudes. *Standard Edition*, 14:111–140. London: Hogarth Press, 1957.

—————— (1917), A childhood recollection from *Dichtung und Wahrheit*. *Standard Edition*, 17:145–156. London: Hogarth Press, 1955.

—————— (1918) The taboo of virginity. *Standard Edition*, 11:191–208. London: Hogarth Press, 1957.

—————— (1920), Beyond the pleasure principle. *Standard Edition*, 18:7–64. London: Hogarth Press, 1955.

—————— (1921), Group psychology and the analysis of the ego. *Standard Edition*, 18:67–144. London, Hogarth Press, 1955.

—————— (1930), Civilization and its discontents. *Standard Edition*, 21:64–48. London, Hogarth Press, 1961.

—————— (1938), Findings, ideas, problems. *Standard Edition*. 23:299–300. London: Hogarth Press, 1964.

Friedman, L. (1982), How does the analyst know what's what? Presented to the Balto-DC Society for Psychoanalysis, April 17.

—— (1988), *The Anatomy of Psychotherapy.* Hillsdale, NJ: The Analytic Press.

Gaensbauer, T. (1982a), Regulation of emotional expression in infants from two contrasting caretaker environments. *J. Amer. Acad. Child Psychiat.,* 21:163–171.

—— (1982b), The differentiation of discrete affects. *The Psychoanalytic of the Child,* 37:29–66. New Haven: Yale University Press.

—— T. J., Harmon, R. J., Cytryn, L. & McKnew, D. H. (1984), Social and affective development in infants with a manic-depressive parent. *Amer. J. Psychiat.,* 141:223–235.

Gardner, R. (1983), *Self Inquiry.* Boston: Little, Brown.

Gedo, J. E. (1979). *Beyond Interpretation.* New York: International Universities Press.

—— (1984), *Psychoanalysis and its Discontents.* New York: Guilford Press.

—— (1985), On the dawn of experience: the past recaptured. *Psychoanal. Inq.,* 5:601–620.

—— (1986), *Conceptual Issues in Psychoanalysis.* Hillsdale, NJ: The Analytic Press.

—— (1988). *The Mind in Disorder.* Hillsdale, NJ: The Analytic Press.

Ginsburg, B. (1982), Genetic factors in aggressive behavior. *Psychoanal. Inq.,* 2:53–76.

Gloor, P. (1978), Inputs and outputs of the amygdala: What the amygdala is trying to tell the rest of the brain. In: *Limbic Mechanisms,* ed. K. E. Livingston & O. Hornykiewics. New York: Plenum Press, pp. 189–209.

—— (1986), Role of the human limbic system in perception, memory and affect. In: *The Limbic System,* ed. B. K. Doane & K. F. Livingston. New York: Raven Press, pp. 159–169.

—— Oliver, A. & Quesney, L. (1981), The role of the amygdala in the expression of psychic phenomena in temporal lobe seizures. In: *The Amygdaloid Complex,* ed. Y. Ben-Ari. New York: Elsevier/North Holland, pp. 489–498.

Glover, E. (1943), The concept of dissociation. *Internat. J. Psycho-Anal.* 24:7–13.

Goldberg, A. (1988), *A Fresh Look at Psychoanalysis.* Hillsdale, NJ: The Analytic Press.

Goldberg, S. & Lewis, M. (1969), Play behavior in the year-old infant: Early sex differences. *Child Devel.,* 40:21–31.

Gottlieb, G. (1987), Behavioral Embryology: Prenatal Sensory and Motor Function. In: *Encyclopedia of Neuroscience,* Vol. 1, ed. G. Adelman. Boston, MA: Birkauser, pp. 119–121.

Graybiel, A. M. (1984), Neurochemically specified subsystems in the basal ganglia. Presented at Ciba Foundation symposium 107, London.

Graham, I. (1987), The sibling-object and its transferences: Alternate organizer of the middle field. *Psychoanal. Inq.,* 8:88–107.

Green, R. (1987), *The "Sissy Boy Syndrome" and the Development of Homosexuality.* New Haven, CT: Yale University Press.

Greenberg, J. & Mitchell, S. A. (1983), *Object Relations in Psychoanalytic Theory.* Cambridge, MA: Harvard University Press.

———— Morris, N. (1974), Engrossment: The newborn's impact upon the father. *Amer. J. Orthopsychiat.*, 44:520–531.

Greenspan, S. I. (1979), Intelligence and adaptation: An Integration of psychoanalytic and Piagetian developmental psychology. *Psychological Issues,* Monogr. 47/48. New York: International Universities Press.

———— (1981), *Psychopathology and Adaptation in Infancy and Early Childhood.* New York: International Universities Press.

Grossman, S. P. (1987), Motivation, adversive, biological bases. In: *Encyclopedia of Neuroscience,* Vol. 2, ed. G. Adelman. Boston, MA: Birkauser, pp. 685–688.

Gunsberg, L. (1983), Make no mistake about it: A child's father cannot be replaced. Paper presented at the Second World Congress of Infant Psychiatry, Cannes, France, April.

———— (1987a), Prologue to applications of infant research to adult psychoanalytic treatment. *Psychoanal. Inq.*, 7:301–306.

———— (1987b), Epilogue: Applications of infant research to adult psychoanalytic treatment. *Psychoanal. Inq.*, 7:453–456.

Gunther, M. (1961), Infant behavior at the breast. In: *Determinants of Infant Behavior,* Vol. 2, ed. B. M. Foss. London: Methuen.

Guntrip, J. S. (1971), *Psychoanalytic Theory, Therapy, and the Self.* New York: Basic Books.

Guyton, A. C. (1987), *Basic Neuroscience.* Philadelphia, PA: Saunders.

Hadley, J. L. (1985), Attention, affect and attachment. *Psychol. Contemp. Thought,* 8:529–550.

Haith, M., Hazan, C. & Goodman, G. (1988), Expectation and anticipation of dynamic visual events by 3.5-month-old babies. *Child Devel.*, 59:467–479.

Halgren, E. (1981), The amygdala contribution to emotion and memory: Current studies in humans. In: *The Amygdala Complex INTERM Symposium No. 20.* ed. Y. Ben-Ari. New York: Elsevier/North Holland Biomedical, pp. 395–408.

Halverson, H. (1940), Genital and sphincter behavior of male infant. *J. Genet. Psychol.*, 56:95–136.

Harley, M. (1971), The current status of transference neurosis in children. *J. Amer. Psychoanal. Assn.*, 19:26–40.

Harlow, H. (1962), The heterosexual affectional system in monkeys. *Amer. Psychol.*, 17:1–9.

———— (1960), Primary affectional patterns in Primates. *Amer. J. Orthopsychiat.*, 30.

Hartmann, H. (1933), An experimental contribution to the psychology of obsessive-compulsive neurosis: On remembering completed and uncompleted tasks. In: *Essays on Ego Psychology.* New York: International Universities Press, 1964, pp. 404–418.

———— (1955), Notes on the theory of sublimation. In: *Essays on Ego Psychology.* New York: International Universities Press, 1964, pp. 215–240

————— (1964), *Essays on Ego Psychology.* New York: International Universities Press.

—————, Kris, E. & Loewenstein, R. (1946), Comments on the formation of psychic structure. In: *Papers on Psychoanalytic Psychology.* New York: International Universities Press, 1964, pp. 27–55.

Heimer, L. & Wilson, R. D. (1975), The subcortical projections of the allocortex: Similarities in the neural associations of the hippocampus, the piriform cortex and the neocortex. In: *Golgi Centennial Symposium*, ed. M. Santini. New York: Raven Press, pp. 179–193.

Hendrick, I. (1942), Instinct and the ego during infancy. *Psychoanal. Quart.,* 11:33–58.

————— (1943), Work and the pleasure principle. *Psychoanal.,* 12:311–329.

Herman, B. & Panksepp, J. (1978), Effects of morphine and naloxone in separation distress and approach attachment. Evidence for opiate mediation of social affect. *Pharmacol., Biochem., Beh.,* 9:213–220.

Herzog, J. (1980), Sleep disturbance and father hunger in 18- to 20-month-old boys: The Erlkonig syndrome. *The Psychoanalytic Study of the Child,* 35:219–236. New Haven, CT: Yale University Press.

————— (1985), Fathers and young children. In: *Frontiers of Infant Psychiatry*, Vol. 2, ed. J. Call, E. Galenson & R. Tyson. New York: Basic Books, pp. 335–342.

Holt, R. (1967), The development of the primary process. *Psychological Issues*, Monog. 18/19. New York: International Universities Press, pp. 344–383.

Hornik, R., Risenhoover, M. & Gunnar, M. (1987), The effects of maternal positive, neutral, and negative affective communications on infant responses to new toys. *Child Devel.,* 58:937–944.

Iversen, S. D. (1984), Behavioral effects of manipulation of basal ganglia neurotransmitters. Presented at Ciba Foundation symposium 107, London.

Jacobs, T. (1987), How does therapy work? Notes on the treatment of the late adolescent-young adult. Presented at Workshop for Mental Health Professionals, March.

Jacobson, E. (1964), *The Self and the Object World.* New York: International Universities Press.

Jacobvitz, D. & Sroufe, L. A. (1987). The early caregiver-child relationships and attention-deficit disorder with hyperactivity in kindergarten. *Child Devel.,* 58:1496–1504.

Kagan, J. (1979), Structure and process in the human infant: The ontogeny of human representation. In: *Psychological Development in Infancy*, ed. M. Bornstein & W. Kessen. Hillsdale, NJ: Lawrence Erlbaum Associates.

—————, Kearsley, R. & Zelazu, P. (1978). *Infancy: Its Place in Human Development.* Cambridge, MA: Harvard University Press.

Kagan, S., Resnick, J. & Snidman, M. (1987). The physiology and psychology of behavioral inhibition in children. *Child Devel.,* 58:1459–1473.

Kandel, E. R. (1981), Physiology of the central visual pathways. In: *Principles of Neural Science*, ed. E. R. Kandel & J. H. Schwartz. New York: Elsevier/North Holland, pp. 236–248.

—— & Domesick, V. & Nauta, W. J. H. (1982), The amygdalostriatal projection in the rat: An anotomical study by anterograde and retrograde tracing methods. *Neuroscience,* 7:615–650.

—— & Schwartz, J. H. ed. (1985), *Principles of Neural Science,* 2nd ed. New York: Elsevier.

Kaufman, I. (1976), Developmental considerations of anxiety and depression: Psychobiological studies in monkeys. *Psychoanalysis and Contemporary Science,* Vol. 5, ed. T. Shapiro. New York: International Universities Press.

Keiser, S. (1977). Discussion group: Reconstruction and unconscious fantasy in psychoanalytic treatment. Meeting of American Psychoanalytic Association, New York.

Kelly, D. D. (1985), Sexual differentiation of the nervous system. In: *Principles of Neural Science,* 2nd ed., ed. E. R. Kandel & J. H. Schwartz. New York: Elsevier, pp. 771–783.

Kernberg, O. F. (1975), *Borderline Conditions and Pathological Narcissism.* New York: Aronson.

—— (1976), *Object Relations Theory and Clinical Psychoanalysis.* New York: Aronson.

Kestenberg, J. (1956), Vicissitudes of female sexuality. *J. Amer. Psychoanal. Assn.,* 4:453–476.

—— (1965a), The role of movement patterns in development. 1. Rhythms of movement. *Psychoanal. Quart.,* 34:1–36.

—— (1965b), The role of movement patterns in development. 2. Flow of tension and effort. *Psychoanal. Quart.,* 34:517–563.

—— (1982), The inner genital phase—prephallic and preoedipal. In: *Early Female Development,* ed. D. Mendell. New York: S. P. Med. & Scient. Books, pp. 81–125.

Kihlstrom, S. (1987), The cognitive unconscious. *Science,* 237:1445–1452.

Kleeman, J. (1965), A boy discovers his penis. *The Psychoanalytic Study of the Child,* 20:239–265. New York: International Universities Press.

—— (1975), Genital self-stimulation in infant and toddlers girls. In: *Masturbation,* ed. I. Marcus & J. Francis. New York: International Universities Press, pp. 77–106.

Klein, G. (1976), *Psychoanalytic Theory.* New York: International Universities Press.

Klinnert, M., Campos, J., Sorce, J., Emde, R. & Svejda, M. (1983), Social referencing. In: *Emotions in Early Development,* ed. R. Plutchik & H. Kellerman. New York: Academic Press, pp. 57–86.

Kohut, H. (1971), *The Analysis of the Self.* New York: International Universities Press.

—— (1972), Thoughts on narcissism and narcissistic rage. *The Psychoanalytic Study of the Child,* 27:360–400. New York: Quadrangle.

—— (1977), *The Restoration of the Self.* New York: International Universities Press.

—— (1984), *How Does Analysis Cure?* ed. A. Goldberg with P. Stepansky. Chicago: University of Chicago Press.

Korner, A. (1973), Sex differences in newborns with special reference to differences in the organization of oral behavior. *J. Child Psychol. Psychiat.*, 14:19–29.

——— (1974), The effect of the infant's state, level of arousal, sex, and autogenetic stage of the caregiver. In: *The Effect of the Infant on Its Caregiver*, ed. M. Lewis & L. Rosenblum. New York: Wiley, pp. 105–121.

Kotelchuck, M. (1975), Father caretaking characteristics and their influence on infant-father interaction. Presented at meeting of Amer. Psychological Assn., Chicago, September.

Kris, E. (1962), Decline and recovery in the life of a three-year-old. *The Psychoanalytic Study of the Child*, 17:175–215.

Kropp, J. & Haynes, O. (1987), Abusive and nonabusive mothers' ability to identify general and specific emotion signals of infants. *Child Devel.*, 58:187–190.

Krueger, D. (1988), *Body Self and Psychological Self*. New York: Brunner/Mazel.

Kuhl, P. & Meltzoff, A. (1982), The bimodal perception of speech in infancy. *Science*, 218:1138–1141.

Lachmann, F. (1986), Interpretation of psychic conflict and adversarial relationships: A self-psychological perspective. *Psychoanal. Psychol.*, 3:341–355.

Lamb, M. (1976), Interactions between eight-month-old children and their fathers and mothers. In: *The Role of the Father in Child Development*, ed. M. Lamb. New York: Wiley.

——— (1977), Father-infant and mother-infant interaction in the first year of life. *Child. Devel.*, 48:167–181.

——— & Oppenheim, D. (1989), Fatherhood and father-child relationships: Five years of research. In: *Fathers and Their Families*, ed. S. Cath, A. Gurwitt & L. Gunsberg. Hillsdale, NJ: The Analytic Press, pp. 11–25.

Lewin, B. (1950), *The Psychoanalysis of Elation*. New York: Norton.

Lewis, M. & Brooks-Gunn, J. (1979), *Social Cognition and the Acquisition of Self*. New York: Plenum Press.

Lichtenberg, A. (1982), "Hey, you're hurting me!": Observations on the world of the tactually defensive child. Paper presented for course in Advanced Educational Psychology, American University, Washington, DC.

Lichtenberg, J. (1978a), The testing of reality from the standpoint of the body self. *J. Amer. Psychoanal. Assn.*, 26:357–385.

——— (1978b), Freud's Leonardo: Psychobiography and autobiography of genius. *J. Amer. Psychoanal. Assn.*, 26:863–880.

——— (1979), Factors in the development of the sense of the object. *J. Amer. Psychoanal. Assn.*, 27:375–386.

——— (1981), The empathic mode of perception and alternative vantage points for psychoanalytic work. *Psychoanal. Inq.*, 1:329–356.

——— (1982), Continuities and transformations between infancy and adolescence. In: *Adolescent Psychiatry*, Vol. 10, ed. S. Feinstein, J. Looney, A. Schwartzberg & A. Sorosky. Chicago: University of Chicago Press, pp. 182–198.

—— (1983a), An application of the self-psychological viewpoint to psychoanalytic technique. In: *Reflections of Self Psychology*, ed. J. Lichtenberg & S. Kaplan. Hillsdale, NJ: The Analytic Press.

—— (1983b), *Psychoanalysis and Infant Research*. Hillsdale, NJ: The Analytic Press.

—— (1983c), A clinical illustration of construction and reconstruction in the analysis of an adult. *Psychoanal. Inq.*, 3:279–294.

—— (1987), Infant studies and clinical work with adults. *Psychoanal. Inq.*, 7:311–330.

—— & Slap, J. (1971), On the defensive organization. *Internat. J. Psycho-Anal.*, 52:451–457.

—— & —— (1972), On the defense mechanism: A survey and synthesis. *J. Amer. Psychoanal. Assn.*, 20:776–792.

—— & —— (1973), Notes on the concept of splitting and the defense mechanism of splitting of representations. *J. Amer. Psychoanal. Assn.*, 21:772–787.

London, N. (1981), The play element of regression in the psychoanalytic process. *Psychoanal. Inq.*, 7:7–28.

Loewald, H. (1975), Psychoanalysis as an art and the fantasy character of the psychoanalytic situation. *J. Amer. Psychoanal. Assn.*, 23:277–99.

MacFarlane, J. (1975a), Olfaction in the development of social preferences in the human neonate. In: *Parent-Infant Interaction*, ed. M. Hofer. Amsterdam: Elsevier.

Mahler, M. S. (1968), *On Human Symbiosis and the Vicissitudes of Individuation*. New York: International Universities Press.

—— Pine, F. & Bergman, A. (1975), *The Psychological Birth of the Human Infant*. New York: Basic Books.

Main, M. & Weston, D. (1982), Avoidance of the attachment figure in infancy: Descriptions and interpretations. In: *The Place of Attachment in Human Behavior*, ed. C. M. Parkes & J. Stevenson-Hinde. New York: Basic Books, pp. 31–59.

Major, R. & Miller, P. (1981), Empathy, antipathy, and telepathy in the analytic process. *Psychoanal. Inq.*, 1:449–470.

Markovitz, E. (1973), Aggression in human adaptation. *Psychoanal. Quart.*, 42:226–233.

McCarthy, M. (1963), *The Stones of Florence*. New York: Harcourt, Brace.

McDougall, J. (1982), *Theaters of the Mind*. New York: Basic Books, 1985.

McEwen, B. S. (1987), Sexual differentiation. In: *Encyclopedia of Neuroscience*, Vol. 2, ed. G. Adelman. Boston, MA: Birkhauser, pp. 1086–1088.

McKinnon, J. (1979), Two semantic forms: Neuropsychological and psychoanalytic descriptions. *Psychoanal. Contemp. Thought*, 2:25–76.

McLaughlin, J. (1982), Issues stimulated by the 32nd Congress. *Internat. J. Psycho-Anal.*, 63:229–240.

—— (1987), The play of transference: Some reflections on enactment in the psychoanalytic situation. *J. Amer. Psychoanal. Assn.*, 35:557–582.

Meissner, W. (1978), *The Paranoid Process*. New York: Aronson.

Meltzoff, A. & Moore, M. (1977), Imitation of facial and manual gestures by human neonates. *Science*, 198:75–78.

Messer, S. & Lewis, M. (1970), Social class and sex differences in the attachment and play behavior of the year-old infant. In: *The Female Orgasm*, ed. S. Fisher. London: Lane, 1973, pp. 71–72.

Meyer, S. (1982), The theory of gender identity disorders. *J. Amer. Psychoanal. Assn.* 30:381–418.

—— & Dupkin, C. (1985), Gender disturbance in children: An interim clinical report. *Bull. Menn. Clin.*, 49:236–269.

Mishkin, M. & Aggleton, J. (1981), Multiple functional contributions of the amygdala in the monkey. In: *The Amygdala Complex*, ed Y. Ben-Ari. New York: Elsevier/North Holland, pp. 409–420.

Mittelmann, B. (1954), Motility in infants, children, and adults. *The Psychoanalytic Study of the Child.*, 9:142–177. New York: International Universities Press.

—— (1960), Intrauterine and early infant motility. *The Psychoanalytic Study of the Child*, 15:104–127. New York: International Universities Press.

Modaressi, T. (1980), An experimental study of "double" (amphiscious) imagery during infancy and childhood. Presented at meeting of American Psychoanalytic Association, New York, December.

—— & Kenny, T. (1977), Children's response to their true and distorted mirror images. *Child. Psychiat. Human Devel.*, 8:97–101.

Moss, H. (1967), Sex, age and state as determinants of mother-infant interaction. *Merrill Palmer Quart.*, 13:19–36.

Murphy, C. & Messer, D. (1977), Mothers, infants, and pointing: A study of a gesture. In: *Studies in Mother-Infant Interaction*, ed. H. Schaffer. London: Academic Press.

Murphy, L. (1973), Some mutual contributions of psychoanalysis and child development. *Psychoanal. Contemp. Sci.* 2:99–123. New York: International Universities Press.

Nachman, P. & Stern, D. (1984), Affect retrieval: a form of recall memory in prelinguistic infants. In: *Frontiers of Infant Psychiatry*, Vol. 2, ed. J. Call, E. Galenson & R. Tyson. New York: Basic Books, pp. 95–100.

Nathanson, D. (1987), A timetable for shame. In: *The Many faces of Shame*, ed. D. Nathanson. New York: Guilford Press, pp. 1–63.

Nauta, H. J. W. (1986), A simplified perspective on the basal ganglia and their relation to the limbic system. In: *The Limbic System*, ed. B. K. Doane & K. E. Livingston. New York: Raven Press, pp. 67–77.

—— & Domesick, V. B. (1984), Afferent and efferent relationships of the basal ganglia. Presented at Ciba Foundation Symposium 107, London.

Needles, W. (1965), Exploitation of the sense of guilt. *Psychoanal. Quart.*, 34:66–78.

Nicolich, L. (1977), Beyond sensorimotor intelligence: Assessment of symbolic maturity through analysis of pretend play. *Merrill-Palmer Quart.*, 28:89–99.

Noam, G. (1985), Stage, phase, and style: The developmental dynamics of the self. In: *Moral Education*, ed. M. Berkowitz & F. Oser. Hillsdale, NJ: Lawrence Erlbaum Associates.

—— Powers, S., Kilkenny, R. & Beedy, S. (in press), The interpersonal self in lifespan perspective. In: *Lifespan Development and Behavior*, Vol. 10, ed. R. Lerner, P. Baltes & D. Featherman. Hillsdale, NJ: Lawrence Erlbaum Associates.

Noy, P. (1979), The psychoanalytic theory of cognitive development. *The Psychoanalytic Study of the Child*, 34:169–216. New Haven, CT: Yale University Press.

Offer, D. & Offer, J. (1971), *From Teenage to Young Manhood*. New York: Basic Books.

Olds, J. (1977), *Drives and Reinforcements*. New York: Raven Press.

Olinick, S. (in press), Changing psychic structure through treatment: Criteria for change. *J. Amer. Psychoanal. Assn.*

——, Poland, W., Gregg, K. & Granatir, W. (1973), The psychoanalytic work ego: Process and interpretation. *Internat. J. Psycho-Anal.*, 54:143–151.

Oremland, J. (1985), Kohut's reformulations of defense and resistance as applied in therapeutic psychoanalysis. In: *Progress in Self Psychology*, Vol. 1, ed. A. Goldberg. New York: Guilford Press, pp. 97–108.

Ornstein, P. & Ornstein, A. (1985), Clinical understanding and explaining: The empathic vantage point. In: *Progress in Self Psychology*, Vol. 1, ed. A. Goldberg. New York: Guilford Press, pp. 43–61.

O'Shaughnessy, E. (1984), Review of J. Lichtenberg *Psychoanalysis and Infant Research*. *Internat. J. Psycho-Anal.*, 65:492–495.

Osofsky, J. (1982), The development of the parent-infant relationship. *Psychoanal. Inq.*, 1:625–642.

Panksepp, J. (1981), Hypothalamic integration of behavior. In: *Behavioral Studies of the Hypothalamus*, Vol. 3-B, ed. P. J. Morgane & J. Panksepp. New York: Marcel Dekker, pp. 289–431.

——, Herman, B., Conner, R., Bishop, P. & Scott J. (1978), The biology of social attachments: Opiates alleviate separation distress. *Biol. Psychiat.*, 13:607–618.

Papousek, H. & Papousek, M. (1975), Cognitive aspects of preverbal social interaction between human infant and adults. In: *Parent-Infant Interaction* (Ciba Foundation Symposium). New York: Associated Scientific Publishers. \

—— & —— (1977), Biological aspects of early social and cognitive development in man. Presented at the 15th International Ethological Conference in Bielefeld, F. R. Germany, August 23–27.

—— & —— (1979), Early ontogeny of human social interaction: Its biological roots and social dimensions. In: *Human Ethology*, ed. M. von Cranach, K. Foppa, W. Lepenie & P. Ploog. Cambridge: Cambridge University Press.

—— (1986), Intuitive parenting: A didactic counterpart to the infant's precocity in integrative capacities. In: *Handbook of Infant Development*, 2d ed., ed. J. D. Osofsky. New York: Wiley, pp. 669–720.

——, —— & Bornstein, M. H. (1985), The naturalistic vocal environment of young infants: On the significance of homogeneity and variability in parental speech. In: *Social Perception in Infants*, ed. T. Field & W. Fox. Norwood, NJ: Ablex, pp. 269–297.

——— ——— Suomi, S. J. & Rahn, C. W. (1986), Preverbal communication and attachment: Comparative views. In: *Intersections with Attachment*, ed. J. L. Gewirtz & W. M. Curtines.

Parens, H. (1979), *The Development of Aggression in Early Childhood*. New York: Aronson.

——— (1987), Siblings in early childhood: Some direct observational findings. *Psychoanal. Inq.*, 8:31–50.

———, Pollock, L., Stern, J. & Kramer, S. (1976), On the girl's entry into the Oedipus complex. *J. Amer. Psychoanal. Assn.*, 24 (suppl.):79–107.

Parke, R. & Sawin, D. (1977), The family in early infancy: Social interactional and attitudinal analyses. Presented at meeting of Society for Research in Child Development. New Orleans, March.

——— (1979), Perspectives on father-infant interaction. In: *The Handbook of Infant Development*, ed. J. Osofsky. New York: Wiley.

——— (1981), *Fathers*. Cambridge: Harvard University Press.

Pavenstedt, E. (1956), The effect of extreme passivity imposed on a boy in early childhood. *The Psychoanalytic Study of the Child*, 11:396–409. New York: International Universities Press.

Pederson, F., Anderson, B. & Cain, R. (1977), An approach to understanding linkages between the parent-infant and spouse relationships. Presented at meeting of Society for Research in Child Development, New Orleans, March.

Peto, E. (1936), Contribution to the development of smell feeling. *Brit. J. Med. Psychol.*, 15:314–320.

Piaget, J. (1936), *The Origins of Intelligence*. New York: International Universities Press, 1952.

——— (1937), *The Construction of Reality in the Child*. New York: Basic Books, 1954.

——— (1954), *Play, Dreams and Imitation in Childhood*. New York: Norton, 1951.

——— (1952), *The Origins of Intelligence in Children*. New York: International Universities Press.

——— & Inhelder, B. (1960), *The Psychology of the Child*. New York: Basic Books, 1969.

Pinderhughes, C. (1986), Differential bonding from infancy to international conflict. *Psychoanal. Inq.*, 6:155–174.

Pine, F. (1981), In the beginning: Contributions to a psychoanalytic developmental psychology. *Internat. Rev. Psychoanal.*, 8:15–34.

——— (1985), *Developmental Theory and Clinical Practice*. New Haven, CT: Yale University Press.

——— (1986), The "symbiotic phase" in light of current infancy research. *Bull. Menn. Clin.*, 50:564–569.

Piontelli, A. (1987), Infant observation from before birth. *Internat. J. Psycho-Anal.*, 68:453–464.

Poland, W. (1988), Insight and the analytic dyad. *Psychoanal. Quart.*, 57:341–369.

Prechtl, H. F. (1963), The mother-child interaction in babies with minimal brain damage. In: *Determinants of Infant Behavior*, Vol. 2, ed. B. M. Foss. New York: Wiley, pp. 53–66.

Pribam, K. M. (1977), New dimensions in the functions of the basal ganglia. In: *Psychopathology and Brain Dysfunction*, ed. C. Schagnass, S. Gershon & A. J. Friedhoff. New York: Raven Press.

—— (1980), The biology of emotions and other feelings. In: *Emotion: Theory, Research and Experience*, Vol. 1, ed. R. Plutchik & H. Kellerman. New York: Academic Press, pp. 245–269.

Price, J. L. (1987), Amygdaloid complex. In: *Encyclopedia of Neuroscience*, Vol. 1, ed. G. Adelman. Boston, MA: Birkhauser, pp. 40–42.

Provence, S. (1983), Struggling against deprivation and trauma: A longitudinal case study. *The Psychoanalytic Study of the Child*, 38:233–256. New Haven, CT: Yale University Press.

—— & Lipton, R. (1962), *Infants in Institutions*. New York: International Universities Press.

Pruett, K. (1983), Infants of primary nurturing fathers. *The Psychoanalytic Study of the Child*, 38:257–280. New Haven: Yale University Press.

Pulver, S., issue ed. (1987), *Psychoanal. Inq.*, 7(2).

Rapaport, D. (1967), *The Collected Papers of David Rapaport*, ed. M. Gill. New York: Basic Books.

Reinisch, J. (1981), Prenatal exposure to synthetic progestins increases potential for aggression in humans. *Science*, 211:1171–1173.

Reiser, M. (1985), Converging sectors of psychoanalysis and neurobiology. *J. Amer. Psychoanal. Assn.*, 33:11–34.

Richmond, G. & Clemens, L. (1987), Sexual behavior, brain control. In: *Encyclopedia of Neuroscience*, Vol. 2, ed. G. Adelman. Boston, MA: Birkhauser, pp. 1085–1086.

Roffwarg, H. P., Dement, W. & Fisher, C. (1964), Observations in dream-sleep pattern in neonates, infants, children, and adults. *Child Psychiat. Monogr.* 2. New York: Pergamon Press, pp. 60–72.

Roiphe, H. (1968), On an early genital phase. *The Psychoanalytic Study of the Child*, 23:348–365. New York: International Universities Press.

—— & Galenson, E. (1981), *Infantile Origins of Sexual Identity*. New York: International Universities Press.

—— & —— (1987), Preoedipal roots of perversion. *Psychoanal. Inq.*, 7:415–430.

—— & Roiphe, A. (1985), *Your Child's Mind*. New York: St. Martin's.

Rovee-Collier, C., Sullivan, M., Enright, M., Lucas, D. & Fagen, J. (1980), Reactivation of infant memory. *Science*, 208:1159–1161.

Sameroff, A. (1983), Developmental systems: Context and evolution. In: *Mussen's Handbook of Child Psychology*, Vol. 1, ed. W. Kessen. New York: Wiley.

—— (1984), Comparative perspectives on early motivation. Presented at third triannual meeting of the Developmental Biology Research Group, Estes Park, CO, May.

Sander, L. (1975), Infant and caretaking environment: Investigation and conceptualization of adaptive behavior in a system of increasing complexity. In: *Explorations in Child Psychiatry*, ed. E. J. Anthony. New York: Plenum Press, pp. 129–166.

———— (1980), Investigation of the infant and its caregiving environment as a biological system. In: *The Course of Life*, Vol. 1, ed. S. I. Greenspan & G. Pollock. Rockville, MD: NIMH, pp. 177–202.

———— (1983a). To begin with—reflections on ontogeny. In: *Reflections on Self Psychology*. ed. J. Lichtenberg & S. Kaplan. Hillsdale, NJ: The Analytic Press, pp. 85–104.

———— (1983b), Polarity, paradox, and the organizing process in development. In: *Frontiers of Infant Psychiatry*, ed. J. D. Call, E. Galenson & R. Tyson. New York: Basic Books, pp. 315–327.

———— (1986), The inner experience of the infant: A framework for inference relevant to development of the sense of self. Presented to Mahler Symposium, Paris (unpublished).

———— Stechler, G., Julia, H. & Burns, P. (1976), Primary prevention and some aspects of temporal organization in early infant-caretaker interaction. In: *Infant Psychiatry*, ed. E. Rexford, L. Sander & T. Shapiro. New Haven, CT: Yale University Press, pp. 187–204.

Sandler, A. M. (1975), Comments on the significance of Piaget's work for psychoanalysis. *Internat. Psychoanal.* 2:365–377.

Sandler, J. (1960), The background of safety. *Internat. J. Psycho-Anal.*, 41:352–356.

———— (1976). Countertransference and role-responsiveness. *Internat. Rev. Psychoanal.*, 3:43–47.

———— (1981), Character traits and object relationships. *Psychoanal. Quart.*, 50:694–708.

———— (1987), *From Safety to Superego*. London: Karnac.

———— & Jaffe, W. (1969), Towards a basic psychoanalytic model. *Internat. J. Psycho-Anal.*, 50:79–90.

Sarlin, C. (1970), The current status of the concept of genital primacy. *J. Amer. Psychoanal. Assn.*, 18:285–299.

Schacter, S. (1959), *The Psychology of Affiliation*. Stanford, CA: Stanford University Press.

Schanberg, S., Bartolome, J. & Kuhn, C. (1988), Need for mother's touch is brain based. *Science*, 239–142.

Schlesinger, H. (1984), The process of empathic response. In: *Empathy II*, ed. J. Lichtenberg, M. Bornstein & D. Silver. Hillsdale, NJ: The Analytic Press, pp. 187–210.

Schur, M. (1960), Discussion of Dr. John Bowlby's paper. *The Psychoanalytic Study of the Child*, 15:63–84. New York: International Universities Press.

———— (1966), *The Id and the Regulatory Principles of Mental Functioning*. New York: International Universities Press.

Schwaber, E. (1981), Empathy: A mode of analytic listening. *Psychoanal. Inq.*, 1:357–392.

Schwartz, A. (1987a), Drives, affects, behavior—and learning. *J. Amer. Psychoanal. Assn.*, 35:467–506.

——— (1987b), On narcissism (unpublished manuscript).

Sears, R., Maccoby, E. & Levin, H. (1957), *Patterns of Child Rearing.* Evanston, IL: Row, Peterson.

Shakespeare, W. "As You Like It," *The Comedies of Shakespeare.* New York: Modern Library.

Shane, M. (1978), Discussion: Workshop for mental health professions—The significance of the data of infant research for clinical work with children, adolescents, and adults. Meeting of American Psychoanalytic Association, Seattle, WA, March.

Shevrin, H. & Tousseing, P. (1965), Vicissitudes of the need for tactile stimulation in instinctual development. *The Psychoanalytic Study of the Child,* 20:310–339. New York: International Universities Press.

Siegel, E. (1988), *Female Homosexuality.* Hillsdale, NJ: The Analytic Press.

Simon, B. (1981), Confluence of visual image between patient and analyst: communication of failed communication. *Psychoanal. Inq.*, 1:471–488.

Skeels, H. (1966), Adult status of children with contrasting early life experiences. *Monographs of the Society for Research in Child Development,* 31:1–65.

Slade, A. (1986), Symbolic play and separation-individuation: A naturalistic study. *Bull. Menn. Clin.*, 50:541–563.

Slap, J. & Levine, F. (1978), On hybrid concepts in psychoanalysis. *Psychoanal. Quart.*, 47:499–523.

Solnit, A. (1972), Aggression. *J. Amer. Psychoanal. Assn.*, 20:435–450.

Sorce, J. Emde, R. Campos, J. & Klinnert, M. (1985), Maternal emotional signaling: Its effect on the visual cliff behavior of 1-year olds. *Devel. Psychol.*, 21:195–200.

Spitz, R. (1957), *No and Yes.* New York: International Universities Press.

——— (1959), *A Genetic Field Theory of Ego Formation.* New York: International Universities Press.

——— (1960), Discussion of Dr. John Bowlby's paper. *The Psychoanalytic Study of the Child,* 15:63–84. New York: International Universities Press.

——— (1962), Autoerotism re-examined. *The Psychoanalytic Study of the Child,* 17:283–315. New York: International Universities Press.

Squire, L. (1986), Mechanisms of memory. *Science,* 232: 1612–1619.

Sroufe, L. A. (1979), The coherence of individual development: Early care, attachment, and subsequent developmental issues. *Amer. Psychol.*, 34:834–841.

——— (1982), The organization of emotional development. *Psychoanal. Inq.*, 1:575–600.

Starkey, P. & Cooper, R. (1980), Perception of numbers by human infants. *Science,* 210:1033–1035.

———, Spelke, E. & Gelman, R. (1983), Detection of intermodal numerical correspondences by human infants. *Science,* 222:179–181.

Stechler, G. (1982), The dawn of awareness. *Psychoanal. Inq.*, 1:503–532.

———— (1985), The study of infants engenders systemic thinking. *Psychoanal. Inq.*, 5:531–541.

———— (1987), Clinical applications of a psychoanalytic systems model of assertion and aggression. *Psychoanal. Inq.*, 1:348–363.

———— & Halton, A. (1987), The emergence of assertion and aggression during infancy: A psychoanalytic systems approach. *J. Amer. Psychoanal. Assn.*, 35:821–838.

———— & Kaplan, S. (1980), The development of the self: A psychoanalytic perspective. *The Psychoanalytic Study of the Child*, 35:85–106. New Haven, CT: Yale University Press.

Steele, B. & Pollock, C. (1968), A psychiatric study of parents who abuse infants and small children. In: *The Battered Child*, ed. R. Helfer & C. Kempe. Chicago: University of Chicago Press, 1974, pp. 89–133.

Steiner, J. E. (1977), Facial expressions of the neonate infant indicating the hedonics of food-related chemical stimuli. In: *Taste and Development*, ed. J. M. Weiffenbach. Bethesda, MD: DHEW Pub. No. (NIH), pp. 77–1068.

Stellar, J. R. & Stellar, E. (1985), *The Neurobiology of Motivation and Reward*. New York: Springer.

Stern, D. (1985), *The Interpersonal World of the Infant*. New York: Basic Books.

———— (1988), Affect in the context of the infant's lived experience. Some considerations. *Internat. J. Psycho-Anal.*, 69:233–238.

————, MacKain, K. & Spieker, S. (1982), Intonation contours as signals in material speech to prelinguistic infants. *Develop. Psychol.*, 18:727–735.

Sterne, L. (1759–1767), *Tristam Shandy*. New York: Random House, 1950.

Stoller, R., (1975), *Perversion*. New York: Pantheon.

———— (1985), *Presentation of Gender*. New Haven, CT: Yale University Press.

Stolorow, R., Brandchaft, B. & Atwood, G. (1987). *Psychoanalytic Treatment*. Hillsdale, NJ: The Analytic Press.

Strauss, M. (1979), Attraction of prototypical information by adults and ten-month-old infants. *J. Exper. Psychol.*, 5:618–632.

Streri, A. & Pecheaux, M. (1986), Tactual habituation and discrimination of form in infancy: A comparison with vision. *Child Devel.*, 57:100–104.

Temeles, M. (1987), Vicissitudes of an early infantile aversion. *Psychoanal. Inq.*, 7:364–380.

Terenius, L. (1987), Pain, chemical transmitter concepts. In: *Encyclopedia of Neuroscience*, Vol. 2, ed. G. Adelman. Boston, MA: Birkhauser, pp. 901–903.

Tolpin, M. (1971), On the beginnings of the cohesive self. *The Psychoanalytic Study of the Child*, 26:316–352. New York: Quadrangle.

———— (1986), The self and its selfobjects: A different baby. In: *Progress in Self Psychology*, Vol. 2, ed. A. Goldberg. New York: Guilford Press, pp. 115–128.

Tomkins, S. (1962), *Affect, Imagery, Consciousness*, Vol. 1. New York: Springer.

———— (1963), *Affect, Imagery, Consciousness*, Vol. 2. New York: Springer.

—— (1978), Script theory: Differential magnification of affects. *Nebraska Symposium on Motivation*, 26:201–236.

—— (1987), Shame. In: *The Many Faces of Shame*, ed. D. Nathanson. New York: Guilford Press, pp. 133–161.

Tuber, D., Berntson, G., Bachman, D. & Allen, J. (1980) Associative learning in premature hydranencephalic and normal twins. *Science*, 210:1035–1037.

Tustin, F. (1988), Psychotherapy with children who cannot play. *Internat. Rev. Psychoanal.*, 15:93–106.

Tyson, P. (1982), A developmental line of gender identity, gender role, and choice of love object. *J. Amer. Psychoanal. Assn.*, 30:61–68.

—— (1988), Historical review of the data. Presented at American Psychoanalytic Association Workshop for Mental Health Professionals, Seattle, March.

Vinogradova, O. S. (1975), Functional organization of the limbic system in the process of registration of information: Facts and hypotheses. In: *The Hippocampus*, Vol. 1, ed. R. L. Isaacson & K. H. Pribam. New York: Plenum.

Volkan, V. (1985a), The need to have enemies and allies; A developmental approach. *Pol. Psychol.*, 6:219–247.

—— (1985b), Suitable targets of externalization and schizophrenia. In: *Towards a Comprehensive Model for Schizophrenic Disorders*, ed. D. Feinsilver. Hillsdale, NJ: The Analytic Press, pp. 125–153.

—— (1986), The narcissism of minor differences in the psychological gap between opposing nations. *Psychoanal. Inq.*, 6:175–192.

Waddington, C. (1947), *Organizers and Genes*. Cambridge, Eng.: The University Press.

Walker-Andrews, A. & Lennon, E. (1984), Auditory-visual perception of changing distance. Presented at International Conference of Infancy Studies, New Haven, CT.

Watson, J. (1966), *Principles of Development and Differentiation*. New York: Macmillan.

—— (1972), Smiling, cooing, and "the game." *Merrill-Palmer Quart.*, 18:323–340.

—— (1979), Perception of contingency as a determinant of social responsiveness. In: *The Origins of Social Responsiveness*, ed. E. Thomas. Hillsdale, NJ: Lawrence Erlbaum Associates.

Weil, A. (1970), The basic core. *The Psychoanalytic Study of the Child*, 25:442–460. New York: International Universities Press.

Werner, H. & Kaplan, B. (1963), *Symbol Formation*. New York: Wiley.

White, R. (1959), Motivation reconsidered: the concept of competence. *Psychol. Rev.*, 66:297–333.

Williams, M. (1987), Reconstruction of an early seduction and its after effects. *J. Amer. Psychoanal. Assn.*, 35:145–164.

Winnicott, D. (1953), Transitional objects and transitional phenomena. In: *Collected Papers*. London: Tavistock, 1958, pp. 229–242.

—— (1956), Primary maternal preoccupation. In: *Collected Papers*. London: Tavistock, 1958, pp. 300–305.

—— (1958), The capacity to be alone. In: *The Maturational Processes and the Facilitating Environment*. New York: International Universities Press, 1965, pp. 29–36.

—— (1963), Communicating and not communicating leading to a study of certain opposites. In: *The Maturational Processes and the Facilitating Environment*. New York: International Universities Press, 1965, pp. 179–192.

—— (1960), Ego distortion in terms of the true and false self. In: *The Maturational Process and the Facilitating Environment*. New York: International Universities Press, 1965, pp. 140–152.

Winson, J. (1985), *Brain and Psyche*. Garden City, NY: Anchor Press/Doubleday.

Wise, R. A. (1983), Brain neuronal systems mediating reward processes. In: *The Neurobiology of Opiate Reward Processes*. ed. J. S. Smith & J. D. Lane. New York: Elsevier/North Holland, pp. 406–437.

Wolf, D. & Gardner, J. (1979), Style and sequence in early play. In: *Symbolic Functioning in Childhood*, ed. N. R. Smith & M. Franklin. Hillsdale, NJ: Lawrence Erlbaum Associates, pp. 117–138.

Wolf, E. (1980), On the developmental line of selfobject relations. In: *Advances in Self Psychology*, ed. A. Goldberg. New York: International Universities Press, pp. 117–132.

—— (1988), *Treating the Self*. New York: Guilford Press.

Wolff, P. (1960), The developmental psychologies of Jean Piaget and psychoanalysis. *Psychological Issues*, Monogr. 5. New York: International Universities Press.

—— (1966), The causes, controls, and organization of behavior in the neonate. *Psychological Issues*, Monogr. 17. New York: International Universities Press.

—— (1969), The natural history of crying and other vocalizations in infancy. In: *Determinants of Infant Behavior*, Vol. 4, ed. B. M. Foss. London: Methuen.

Woolf, V. (1927), *To the Lighthouse*. New York: Harcourt, Brace, 1955.

Wurmser, L. (1981), *The Mask of Shame*. Baltimore, MD: Johns Hopkins University Press.

Wurtman, J. J. (1987), Serotonin and the control of nutrient intake. In: *Encyclopedia of Neuroscience*, Vol. 2, ed. G. Adelman. Boston, MA: Birkhauser, p. 1083.

Yarrow, L. (1963), Research in dimensions of early maternal care. *Merrill-Palmer Quart.*, 9:101–114.

Yogman, M. (1982), Observations on the father-infant relationship. In: *Father and Child*, ed. S. Cath, A. Gurwitt & J. Ross. Boston: Little, Brown.

Zahn-Waxler, C., McKnew, D., Cummings, M., Davenport, Y. & Radke-Yarrow, M. (1984), Problem behaviors and peer interactions of young children with a manic-depressive parent. *Amer. J. Psychiat.*, 141:236–240.

—— & Radke-Yarrow, M. (1982), The development of prosocial behaviors: Alternative research strategies. In: *The Development of Prosocial Behavior*, ed. N. Eisenberg. New York: Academic Press, pp. 109–137.

——, —— & King, R. (1979), Child rearing and children's prosocial initiations toward victims of distress. *Child Devel.*, 50:319–330.

Author Index

Subject Index

A

Abreaction, experience of, 334
Abuse, 282
  future impact of, 285–286
Acoustic cues, 74
Act, sequence of initiation, 85
Activation, coordination of, 344
Adaptiveness, 187
  in young infant, 176
Adolescent, adolescence
  mother, anger and punitive
    control of toddlers, 191–192
  organization in, 10–11
  sense of identity in, 308–309
Adopted children, achievements
  of, 142
Adult
  aversive motivational system
    in, 204–215
  disturbance of enjoyment of
    sensual tenderness in,
    249–252
Affect, 259–273
  amplification, 162
  assumptions, 260–261
  change in, 332
  in departure-reunion
    situations, 99

displays, 26
  of distress, 34
  experience of, 26
  expression, 260
  importance assigned to,
    259–260
  mother's, 28
  positive and negative,
    experiences dominated by,
    263
  as primary basis of
    motivation, 261
  recalling of, 87
  role in sexual experience, 227
  triggering of, 270
Affect-laden scenes, 276
Affect memory, 26
Affect receptivity, 22
Affect scenes, 276
  negative, 263–264
Affect sharing, 25
Affect state, 22, 234
  analysand's, 323–324
  attachment-motivation and,
    100
  sharing of, 301
Affect-triggering situations,
  261

Psychoanalysis and Motivation

DATE DUE

AP 2 '92			
NOV 10 '94			
RT 2 '97			
ILL			
30HS79			

DEMCO 38-297